UNIVERSITY OF
WINCHESTER

Martial Rose Library
Tel: 01962 827306

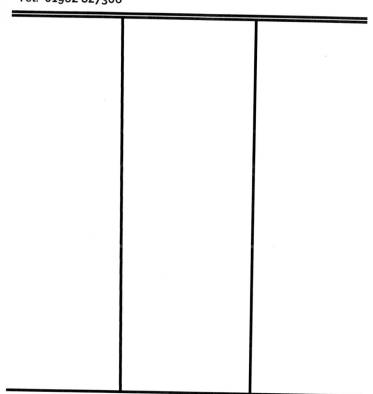

To be returned on or before the day marked above, subject to recall.

EDINBURGH READINGS ON THE ANCIENT WORLD

GENERAL EDITORS
Michele George, *McMaster University*
Thomas Harrison, *University of St Andrews*

ADVISORY EDITORS
Paul Cartledge, *University of Cambridge*
Richard Saller, *University of Chicago*

This series introduces English-speaking students to central themes in the history of the ancient world and to the range of scholarly approaches to those themes, within and across disciplines. Each volume, edited and introduced by a leading specialist, contains a selection of the most important work, including a significant proportion of translated material. The editor also provides a guide to the history of modern scholarship on the subject. Passages in ancient languages are translated; technical terms, ancient and modern, are explained.

PUBLISHED
Sparta
Edited by Michael Whitby

Sex and Difference in Ancient Greece and Rome
Edited by Mark Golden and Peter Toohey

Greeks and Barbarians
Edited by Thomas Harrison

The Ancient Economy
Edited by Walter Scheidel and Sitta von Reden

Roman Religion
Edited by Clifford Ando

Athenian Democracy
Edited by P. J. Rhodes

IN PREPARATION
Ancient Slavery
Edited by Keith Bradley

Ancient Myth
Edited by Richard Gordon

The 'Dark Ages' of Greece
Edited by Ian Morris

The Age of Augustus
Edited by Jonathan Edmonson

ATHENIAN DEMOCRACY

Edited by
P. J. Rhodes

EDINBURGH UNIVERSITY PRESS

© P. J. Rhodes editorial matter and organisation, 2004

Edinburgh University Press Ltd
22 George Square, Edinburgh

Typeset in Sabon
by Norman Tilley Graphics, Northampton
and printed and bound in Great Britain
by the Cromwell Press, Trowbridge, Wiltshire

A CIP record for this book is available from the British Library

ISBN 0 7486 1686 1 (hardback)
ISBN 0 7486 1687 X (paperback)

Contents

Preface

I am very grateful to Dr Harrison for inviting me to contribute this selection of articles on Athenian democracy to the Edinburgh Readings on the Ancient World, and for wise guidance and sympathetic encouragement while I was working on it; to the publishers' advisers, who made me think harder about what I wanted to include in this book and why; to the publishers' editor, Mr J. C. A. Davey; and to all who have been involved in the production of the book.

I am very grateful also to the authors and the original publishers of the articles included here, and to Dr R. Ireland for translating the article by Prof. C. Mossé for this book: full formal acknowledgment, with details of previous publications, is made at the beginning of each chapter.

P. J. R.

Note to the Reader

The articles included in this book were originally published in a range of different journals and books, and in various matters of presentation the authors and publishers had their own preferences. In this book a degree of uniformity has been imposed (for example, in the abbreviations used), but many of the conventions originally followed have been retained. This applies to spelling, both of Greek words and names and of English words, to punctuation, and to modes of citing modern works: chapters using the Harvard (i.e. name and date) system are followed by individual bibliographies; those using 'short titles' usually have footnotes and no bibliography, but some chapters list frequently cited works at the beginning. The bibliography on pp. 352–5 lists works cited by the editor.

In accordance with the policy of this series, translations of Greek and Latin texts and of phrases in modern European languages (apart from titles of ancient and modern works and of periodicals) have been supplied where they were not provided by the original authors. Editorial notes and translations are introduced either within square brackets [ ] or in asterisked footnotes *. Some Greek words and short phrases have been transliterated.

All abbreviated references to ancient texts, modern collections, books and periodicals, used either in the chapters or in the editorial material, are listed and explained on pp. x–xiv.

Other abbreviations have, in general, been avoided. The following abbreviations are contained within the republished articles: *ad loc.* ('at the place', used of a commentary on a particular text), *ap.* (quoted by), *c.* or *ca.* (about, used of approximate dates and figures), cf. (compare), ch/s. (chapter/s), dr. (drachma/s), ed./eds (editor/s), e.g. (for example), et al. (and other authors or editors), ibid. (the same work or text), id. (the same author), i.e. (that is), F/FF or fr./frs. (fragment/s), f./ff. (and following line/s or page/s), *loc. cit.* (passage cited above), *op. cit.* (work cited above), p./pp. (page/s), *pace* (in spite of), Ps.- (Pseudo-: used when a work is traditionally but wrongly attributed to an author; in some chapters this is indicated by enclosing the author's name in square brackets, e.g. [Xen.]), schol. (scholium, ancient comment, or scholiast, writer of an ancient comment), *s.v./s.vv.* (under the word/s, used of dictionaries), tav. (table), trs. (translated by); a superscript figure denotes the second or subsequent edition of a book, e.g. *Griechische Geschichte*^{2}, or the second or subsequent series of a periodical, e.g. CQ^2.

Abbreviations

1 ANCIENT AUTHORS AND THEIR WORKS

When an attribution of a work to an author is regarded as false, the author's name is placed in square brackets in the citation, e.g. [Xen.] *Ath. Pol.*

Aeschin[es]/Aischin[es]
Andoc[ides]/Andok[ides]
Anth. Pal.   *Palatine Anthology*
Ant[iphon]   *Tetr[alogies]*
Ar[istophanes]   *Ach[arnians], Av[es] = Birds,*
                              Eccl[esiazusae], Eq[uites] = Knights,
                              Lys[istrata], Nub[es] = Clouds, Pax =
                              Peace, Plut[us], Ran[ae] = Frogs,
                              Thesm[ophoriazusae], Vesp[ae] = Wasps
Arist[otle]   *E[thica] N[icomachea], Oec[onomica],*
                              Pol[itics], Probl[emata], Rhet[oric]
Athen[aeus]
Ath[enaion] Pol[iteia]   (when cited without author, the work
                              attributed to Aristotle – an attribution
                              which is accepted by the authors of some
                              but not all of the chapters in this book)
[Cassius] Dio
Cic[ero]   *Brut[us]*
Com[ica] Adesp[ota]   comic fragments not assigned to an author
Dem[osthenes]   *Mid[ias]*
Dinarch[us]
Diod[orus Siculus]
Diogenes Laertius
Dion[ysius] Hal[icarnassensis]   *Ant[iquitates] Rom[anae]*
Etym[ologicum] Magn[um]

Eur[ipides]   *H[eracles] F[urens], Herakl[eidai],*
Hik[etides] = Supp[lices], Ion

Eust[athius]

Harp[ocration]/Harp[okration]

Heliodorus   *Aethiop[ica]*

Her[odotus]

Hom[er]   *Il[iad], Od[yssey]*

Hyginus   *Fabulae, Poet[ica] Astr[onomica]*

Hyp[erides]   *Eux[enippus]*

Isae[us]/Isai[os]

Isoc[rates]/Isok[rates]   *Areop[agiticus]*

Just[in]

Lex[icon] Rhet[oricum] Cant[abriginese]

Livy

Lyc[urgus]   *Leocr[ates]*

Lys[ias]

Marcellinus   *Vit[a] Thuc[ydidis]*

Men[ander]   *Sam[ia]*

Nepos   *Milt[iades]*

Oros[ius]

Paus[anias]

Plat[o]   *Ap[ology], Clit[ophon], Ep[istles],*
Euthyd[emus], Gorg[ias], Hipp[archus],
Lach[es], Laws, Men[o], Phaed[o],
Prot[agoras], Rep[ublic], Soph[ist],
Symp[osium], Theaet[etus], Theag[es]

Pliny [the elder]   *H[istoria] N[aturalis]*

Plut[arch]   *Lives: Alc[ibiades], Arist[ides], Cim[on],*
Dem[osthenes], Nic[ias], Per[icles],
Phoc[ion], Sol[on], Them[istocles],
Thes[eus]
Mor[alia], including: *Amat[orius] =*
Dialogue on Love, An Seni [Respublica
Gerenda Sit] = Whether an Old Man
Should Engage in Public Affairs, De Sera
[Numinis Vindicta] = On the Delayed
Vengeance of the Divine Power, [De]
Her[odoti] Mal[ignitate] = On the Malice
of Herodotus, Praec[epta] Ger[endae]
Reip[ublicae] = Precepts of Statecraft,
Quaest[iones] Conv[iviales] = Table-Talk,
Reg[um et] Imp[eratorum]

	Ap[*ophthegmata*] = *Sayings of Kings and Commanders*, *X Orat*[*ores*] = *Lives of the Ten Orators*
Pol[ybius]	
Poll[ux]	
Quint[ilian]	
Sext[us] Emp[iricus]	[*Adversus*] *Math*[*ematicos*] = *Against the Professors*
Soph[ocles]	*Aj*[*ax*], *Ant*[*igone*], *O*[*edipus*] *T*[*yrannus*]
Steph[anus] Byz[antius]	
Strab[o]	
Suid[as]	also cited as *Suda* or *Souda*
Tac[itus]	*Germ*[*ania*]
Thuc[ydides]	
Xen[ophon]	*An*[*abasis*], *Ap*[*ology of Socrates*], *Ath*[*enaion*] *Pol*[*iteia*] (attributed to Xenophon but almost certainly not by him), *Hell*[*enica*], *Hipparch*[*icus*], *Lak*[*edaimonion*] *Pol*[*iteia*], *Mem*[*orabilia*]
Zen[obius]	

2 COLLECTIONS OF ANCIENT TEXTS

Bekker, *Anecdota*	I. Bekker, *Anecdota Graeca*
CEG	P. A. Hansen, *Carmina Epigraphica Graeca*
FGrH	F. Jacoby, *Die Fragmente der griechischen Historiker*
Fouilles de Delphes	
I. de Délos	*Inscriptions de Délos*
IG	*Inscriptiones Graecae*
Inscr. Brit. Mus.	*The Collection of Ancient Greek Inscriptions in the British Museum*
Kock, *CAF*	T. Kock, *Comicorum Atticorum Fragmenta*
LSCG	F. Sokolowski, *Lois sacrées des cités grecques*
Meiggs and Lewis	R. Meiggs and D. Lewis, *A Selection of Greek Historical Inscriptions to the End of the Fifth Century* B.C.
Michel	C. Michel, *Recueil d' inscriptions grecques*
OGIS	*Orientis Graeci Inscriptiones Selectae*

P. Hibeh	*The Hibeh Papyri*
PMG	D. L. Page, *Poetae Melici Graeci*
P. Oxy.	*The Oxyrhynchus Papyri*
SEG	*Supplementum Epigraphicum Graecum*
SIG³	*Sylloge Inscriptionum Graecarum,* ed. W. Dittenberger, 3rd edition
Tod *GHI*	M. N. Tod, *A Selection of Greek Historical Inscriptions*

3 PERIODICALS AND STANDARD WORKS

Abh. Berlin	*Abhandlungen* of the Academy in Berlin
AC	*L'Antiquité classique*
ΑΔ	Ἀρχαιολογικὸν Δελτίον
μελ.	μελεταί
AJA	*American Journal of Archaeology*
AJAH	*American Journal of Ancient History*
AM	*Athenische Mitteilungen (Mitteilungen des Deutschen Archäologischen Instituts, Athenische Abteilung)*
Archaeological Reports	*Archaeological Reports* (supplements to *BSA* and *JHS*)
BCH	*Bulletin de correspondance hellénique*
BSA	*Annual of the British School at Athens*
Bull. U. Texas	*Bulletin of the University of Texas*
CAH	*Cambridge Ancient History*
Chiron	*Chiron*
CJ	*Classical Journal*
ClMed	*Classica et Mediaevalia*
CP	*Classical Philology*
CQ	*Classical Quarterly*
CR	*Classical Review*
Econ. Hist. Rev.	*Economic History Review*
Gnomon	*Gnomon*
GRBS	*Greek, Roman and Byzantine Studies*
Hesperia	*Hesperia*
Supp.	Supplements
Historia	*Historia*
Einz.	Einzelschriften
HSCP	*Harvard Studies in Classical Philology*
JHS	*Journal of Hellenic Studies*
LCM	*Liverpool Classical Monthly*

LSJ	H. G. Liddell and R. Scott, *A Greek–English Lexicon*, 9th edition revised by H. Stuart Jones
Mnem.	*Mnemosyne*
Supp.	Supplements
PA	*Prosopographia Attica*, by J. Kirchner
RE	*Real-Encyclopädie der classischen Altertumswissenschaft*, ed. A. F. von Pauly, Neue Bearbeitung eds G. Wissowa and others
REG	*Revue des études grecques*
SbWien	*Sitzungsberichte* of the Austrian Academy, Vienna
TAPA	*Transactions of the American Philological Association*
U. Cal. Publ. Cl. Stud.	*University of California Publications in Classical Studies*
ZPE	*Zeitschrift für Papyrologie und Epigraphik*

MAP 1: Athens

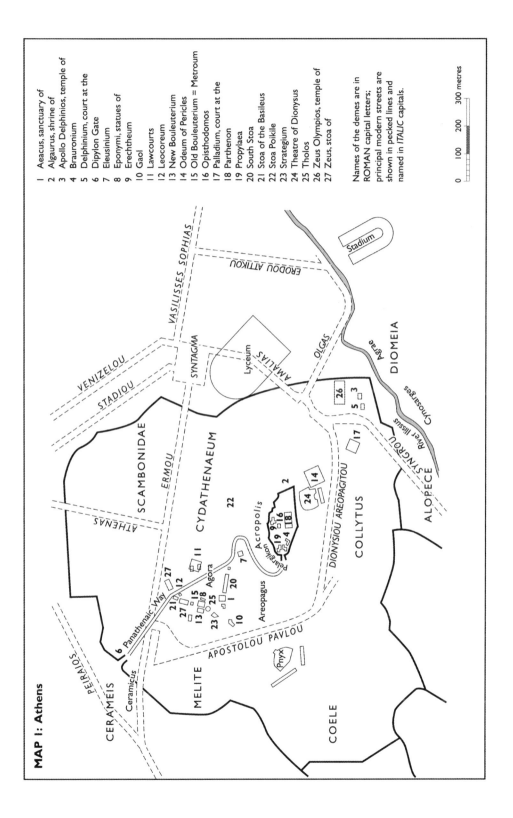

1 Aeacus, sanctuary of
2 Algaurus, shrine of
3 Apollo Delphinios, temple of
4 Brauronium
5 Delphinium, court at the
6 Dipylon Gate
7 Eleusinium
8 Eponymi, statues of
9 Erechtheum
10 Gaol
11 Lawcourts
12 Leocoreum
13 New Bouleuterium
14 Odeum of Pericles
15 Old Bouleuterium = Metroum
16 Opisthodomos
17 Palladium, court at the
18 Parthenon
19 Propylaea
20 South Stoa
21 Stoa of the Basileus
22 Stoa Poikile
23 Strategium
24 Theatre of Dionysus
25 Tholos
26 Zeus Olympios, temple of
27 Zeus, stoa of

Names of the demes are in
ROMAN capital letters;
principal modern streets are
shown in pecked lines and
named in ITALIC capitals.

0   100   200   300 metres

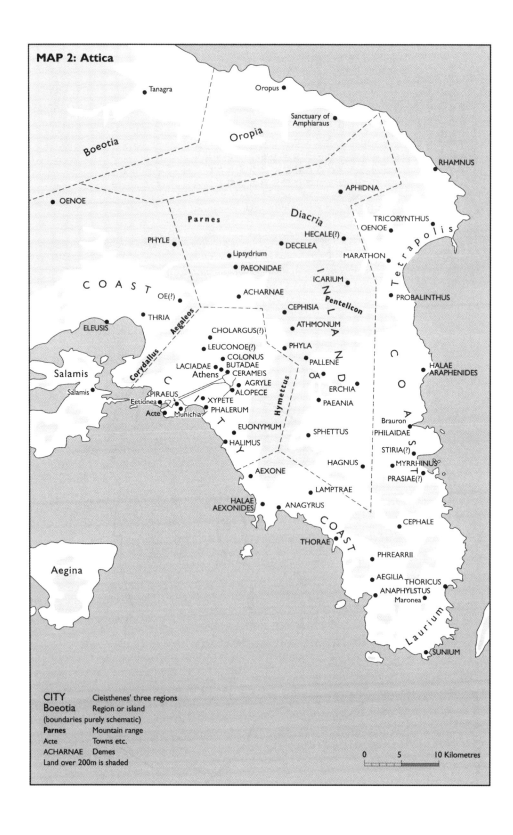

MAP 2: Attica

Tanagra

Oropus

Sanctuary of
Amphiaraus

Boeotia

Oropia

RHAMNUS

OENOE

APHIDNA

Parnes

Diacria

TRICORYNTHUS

OENOE

HECALE(?)

PHYLE

Lipsydrium

DECELEA

MARATHON

PAEONIDAE

ICARIUM

COAST

OE(?)

ACHARNAE

Pentelicon

PROBALINTHUS

CEPHISIA

THRIA

CHOLARGUS(?)

ATHMONUM

ELEUSIS

LEUCONOE(?)

PHYLA

Aegaleos

COLONUS
BUTADAE

PALLENE

HALAE
ARAPHENIDES

Salamis

LACIADAE
CERAMEIS

Athens

OA

Corydallus

AGRYLE
ALOPECE

ERCHIA

Salamis

PIRAEUS

XYPETE

PAEANIA

Eetionea

PHALERUM

Acte

Munichia

EUONYMUM

Brauron

PHILAIDAE

SPHETTUS

HALIMUS

STIRIA(?)

Hymettus

HAGNUS

MYRRHINUS

AEXONE

PRASIAE(?)

Aegina

LAMPTRAE

HALAE
AEXONIDES

ANAGYRUS

COAST

CEPHALE

THORAE

PHREARRII

AEGILIA

THORICUS

ANAPHLYSTUS

Maronea

Laurium

SUNIUM

CITY   Cleisthenes' three regions
Boeotia   Region or island
(boundaries purely schematic)
Parnes   Mountain range
Acte   Towns etc.
ACHARNAE   Demes
Land over 200m is shaded

0   5   10 Kilometres

MAP 3: Greece and the Aegean

THRACE

Byzantium
Calchedon

Amphipolis

Apollonia
Acanthus

THASOS

MACEDON

CHALCIDICE

Potidaea

Torone

IMBROS

Abydus

Troy

LEMNOS

EPIRUS

Dodona

CORCYRA

THESSALY

Pharsalus

AEGEAN

SCYROS

LESBOS

Mytilene

LYDIA

Heraclea

AETOLIA

Naupactus

Delphi

Oreus

EUBOEA

Chalcis

Eretria

Thebes

BOEOTIA

Delium

CHIOS

SEA

ACHAEA

ELIS

Olympia

Corinth

ARCADIA

Mantinea

Tegea

MESSENIA

Sparta

LACONIA

Megara

Athens

Marathon

Brauron

Thoricus

Cape
Sunium

DELOS

NAXOS

SAMOS

River Maeander

Miletus

CARIA

COS

CNIDUS

RHODES

MELOS

THERA

Cape
Taenarum

CRETE

Gortyn

0   50   100   150   200   250   300   350 Kilometres

General Introduction

HISTORICAL OUTLINE

While the Greek world of the bronze age (before 1000 B.C.) was a world of large kingdoms, the Greek world which emerged from the 'dark age' of *c*.1000–800 was a world of many small communities; and in the south and east of the Greek mainland, the islands of the Aegean and the west coast of Asia Minor those communities commonly took the form of *poleis* (singular *polis*), 'city states' based on a town and the land around it. By a process called synoecism, small *poleis* tended to coalesce and form larger *poleis*, but local loyalties and the desire for local autonomy remained strong. Athens was one of the few sites not abandoned at the end of the bronze age (but the rest of the surrounding region of Attica was not continuously occupied). It was one of the first places to recover from the depression of the dark age, but in the eighth and seventh centuries the lead in artistic and political development passed to communities in the Peloponnese (and, since the Athenians were able to expand into the rest of Attica, they had less need than some others to travel and to come into contact with other Greeks). The fact that a single *polis* controlled an area of about 1,000 square miles = 2,600 square kilometres made Athens very much larger than most Greek *poleis*; Sparta controlled a still larger area but had fewer citizens and a large subject population.

If the Greek *poleis* had at first been ruled by kings, those kings had not differed much from the other members of the families which emerged most successful from the uncertainties of the dark age, and rule by kings gave way to rule by officials appointed annually from the leading families. In several *poleis* an ambitious man on the fringe of the ruling aristocracy exploited a variety of discontents to seize power as a 'tyrant'; but within two or three generations the original discontents had been forgotten and the rule of the tyrant was itself a cause of discontent, so the tyrants were overthrown and what followed was commonly a regime in which all men rich enough to serve as 'hoplites' in the *polis*' army of heavy infantry enjoyed a measure of political power. It has thus become possible for one scholar to write of the development of a 'middling' as opposed to an aristocratic ethos in Greece, and for another to write of 'early popular government outside Athens'.[1]

In Athens the first attested historical event was the attempt in the 630s or 620s by Cylon to make himself tyrant – unsuccessfully, since the people supported the authorities against him. Perhaps in response to the killing of some of Cylon's supporters, in 621/0[2] Draco gave Athens its first written laws, including laws on homicide. In 594/3 Solon, who says in his poetry that he did not want to be tyrant, attempted a compromise between the advantaged and the disadvantaged: he liberated a class of dependent peasants, but did not go beyond that to confiscate land from the rich; to weaken the aristocracy he made wealth the sole qualification for office-holding, but he wrote that 'the people will best follow their leaders if they are neither unleashed nor restrained too much'.[3] That satisfied neither side, and Athens was ruled by the tyrants Pisistratus and his sons from 546 (after two short-lived earlier attempts) to 511/0: this had a centralising effect, establishing Athens more firmly as the political centre of Attica, and an equalising effect, since the leading citizens no less than the others were subject to the tyrants. After the overthrow of the tyranny Cleisthenes, attempting to gain more popularity than a rival, in 508/7 introduced a new articulation of the citizen body based on 139 demes (local units), combined to form ten tribes in such a way as to cut across old loyalties, with institutions providing for citizen participation at local level as well as *polis* level. Almost half a century later, in 462/1, Ephialtes transferred from the council of the Areopagus (a body comprising former holders of the office of archon, earlier the most important office in Athens but now being eclipsed by the office of *strategos*, general) to more representative bodies judicial powers of political significance.

The first signs of the concept of *demo-kratia*, people-power, appear about that time; shortly afterwards we find Athens imposing

---

[1] I. Morris, 'The Strong Principle of Equality and the Archaic Origins of Greek Democracy', in J. Ober and C. W. Hedrick (eds), *Demokratia*, 19–48; E. W. Robinson, *The First Democracies: Early Popular Government Outside Athens*.

[2] The Athenian year began in mid-summer: 621/0 is the year from summer 621 to summer 620.

[3] Not wanting to be tyrant, Solon fr. 33 West *ap.* Plut. *Sol.* 14. ix, fr. 34 *ap. Ath. Pol.* 12. iii; the people to follow their leaders, fr. 6 *ap. Ath. Pol.* 12. ii.

democratic constitutions on some members of its alliance, the Delian League, and we find Athens being regarded as a champion of democracy and its rival Sparta being regarded as a champion of oligarchy, the rule of the few. The year A.D. 1993/4, 2,500 years after Cleisthenes' reforms, was celebrated as the 2,500th anniversary of democracy; but in fact Ephialtes' reforms, though representing the culmination of a long development, which had been proceeding elsewhere in Greece as well as in Athens, are better regarded as constituting the defining moment in the creation of *demokratia*.

In the late fifth century Athens underwent two short periods of oligarchic government: in 411–410, when it was in difficulties in the Peloponnesian War against Sparta, and in 404–403, under pressure from Sparta, after the democracy had lost the war. Those regimes turned out to be so unpleasant that Athenians who remembered them did not want to repeat the experience. However, from the middle of the fourth century, fifth-century democratic principles did come to be modified in some respects, and the Macedonians were probably responding to their Athenian contacts when in 322/1, after defeating a Greek rising led by Athens, they imposed a regime based on a property qualification.[4] During the next half-century Athens had several changes of regime; after that it settled down again with a constitution which was democratic in principle, though perhaps more dominated in practice by an elite class of rich and ambitious citizens, and with a further move in the direction of oligarchy in the 80s.

The classical democracy of the fifth and fourth centuries was based as far as possible on active involvement of the citizens. (Citizenship was limited to adult males of Athenian ancestry, and therefore excluded not only children but also women, immigrants and slaves, but those exclusions were entirely normal: Rome was abnormal in repeatedly extending its citizenship and in making citizens of liberated slaves.) Making decisions was entrusted to the citizens directly, in an *ekklesia*, assembly, open to all citizens (some kinds of business required a quorum of 6,000, perhaps 10 per cent of the citizens before the Peloponnesian War of 431–404 and 20 per cent after), guided but not seriously limited by the *boule*, council, numbering 500, a representative body whose membership changed each year. Carrying out the decisions could not be entrusted to all the citizens together; but by dividing the work into a large number of small jobs, most done by committees of ten to which men were appointed by lot and on which they could serve only for one year, the Athenians involved over a number of years as many citizens as were willing to participate. The council oversaw the administrative process and saved it from excessive fragmentation; the generals and other military officials were elected and could be re-elected. Justice again was entrusted to the citizens rather than to experts: there was no separation of judiciary from executive, and the officials who had judicial powers were appointed in the same way as other officials; litigants had to plead their own cases (there were speech-writers whose services could be hired but not legal specialists); the juries which decided the major cases were picked at random from volunteers and were large (at least 200). To enable the poorer citizens to play an active part, small stipends were paid for performing various civilian duties (beginning with payment for jury service, probably in the 450s, and culminating in payment for attending the assembly, *c*.400). There were two principal respects in which democratic Athens differed from a non-democratic *polis*: there was no property qualification for the enjoyment of political rights (but even Athens had a qualification for office-holding, still enforced in the fifth century but not in the fourth, when the number of citizens was lower), and the stipends made it easier for the poorer citizens to exercise their rights; and the assembly was not dominated by the authorities but was a powerful body and one in which all the citizens could play an active part.

Explicit discussions of constitutional forms tend to be hostile to democracy. The 'Old Oligarch' ([Xenophon], *Athenian Constitution*, probably written in the 420s) regarded Athens' democracy as stable but bad, because it promoted the interests of bad people rather than good. Lysias XXV. *Overthrowing Democracy* 7–12, following the relativism encouraged by the sophists, the travelling teachers of the late fifth century, claims that nobody is an oligarch or a democrat by nature but each man will prefer the constitution which is to his own advantage. Of the fourth-century philosophers, Plato (in *Republic* and elsewhere) argued that states should be ruled by those qualified by superior knowledge; Aristotle (in *Politics*), acknowledging that lower-class citizens owned less of the *polis*' land individually but might own more together, and might be less good at deciding individually but better together,[5] was prepared where there was no supremely good individual to settle for a compromise between oligarchy and democracy. There are short defences of democracy in a debate ascribed implausibly by Herodotus to leading Persians in the

[5] Arist. *Pol.* III. 1281 A 39–1282 B 13.

sixth century, in Euripides' *Supplices*, and, in Thucydides' history, in Pericles' funeral speech and Athenagoras' speech at Syracuse.[6] While oligarchs tended to condemn democracy as rule by the *demos* = lower class, democrats tended to defend it as rule by the *demos* = whole citizen body, and to stress equality under the law and equality of political opportunity.

RESPONSES TO ATHENIAN DEMOCRACY[7]

The hellenistic kings from the third century to the first, and the Romans, whose empire eventually absorbed the whole of the Greek world, preferred oligarchies to democracies, though where they were not provoked they did not systematically intervene to do away with democracies. In medieval and early modern Europe monarchies became the norm, and while leading citizens often wanted to limit their powers they did not normally seek to abolish them. In the late eighteenth century the Americans demanding independence from Britain, and the French revolting against the *ancien régime*, preferred the Roman model of a republic in which the lower orders were kept in their place to the mob rule which they saw in Greek democracies. It was only in the nineteenth century that the concept of democracy began to gain respectability: Andrew Jackson in 1828 was the first American to be elected president under the label 'Democratic'; earlier Thomas Paine was one of the first men to use the word 'democracy' favourably, but was persuaded that the Americans' 'representation ingrafted upon democracy' was better.[8] In Britain George Grote wrote in support of democracy in a book review in 1826, and his *History of Greece* was the first history of Greece to portray democracy positively.[9] The nineteenth century saw the formal abolition of slavery and the extension of the franchise among men; the twentieth saw the enfranchisement of women and the freeing of the European states' colonial empires. In the nineteenth century Athens was criticised by those who still regarded it as too democratic; in the twentieth it was increasingly criticised as not democratic enough, by

[6] Her. III. 80–2 at 80; Eur. *Supp.* 399–456; Thuc. II. 35–46 at 37. i, VI. 36–40 at 39. Points made in defence of democracy are put together by K. A. Raaflaub, *ClMed* xl 1989, 33–70 = W. R. Connor et al., *Aspects of Athenian Democracy*, 33–70.

[7] For a longer survey of the development summarised here see P. J. Rhodes, *Ancient Democracy and Modern Ideology*.

[8] Thomas Paine, *The Rights of Man*, part ii ch. iii; quotation p. 233 in the World's Classics edition (1995).

[9] George Grote, 'Institutions of Ancient Greece', *Westminster Review* v (January–April 1826), 269–331; *History of Greece* (1st edition 1846–56).

those who focused on the inhabitants who were excluded from citizenship and on the empire which Athens made of its fifth-century alliance, the Delian League. But while Athens was criticised the concept of democracy gained almost universal acceptance: though in classical Greece it was a form of government of which some people approved and others disapproved, and for many centuries afterwards it was one of which most disapproved, in the twentieth century it became the one of which almost all claim to approve, though they adjust the definition to fit their own particular regime.

What we should regard as serious historical scholarship began in the nineteenth century. In 1817 A. Boeckh published *Die Staatshaushaltung der Athener* (the first book on Greek history which made serious use of the evidence of inscriptions),[10] and in 1819 G. F. Schoemann published *De Comitiis Atheniensium Libri Tres*.[11] In the late nineteenth and early twentieth centuries it was hoped that there could be an objective historical science, *Geschichtswissenschaft*, and a science of antiquity, *Altertumswissenschaft*, comparable to natural science, *Naturwissenschaft*; and the scientific approach to the study of the *polis* was thought to lie in *Staatsaltertümer*, the collection of factual 'constitutional antiquities'. Work of this kind was encouraged by the publication in 1891 of the Aristotelian *Athenian Constitution*, the one survivor from a set of 158 Constitutions, not preserved through the western manuscript tradition but found on papyrus in Egypt: while its first two thirds give a political history of Athens to the end of the fifth century, the last third gives an account, based on the laws, of the formal working of the Athenian constitution in the 330s–320s. The crowning glory of this kind of investigation was the still invaluable *Griechische Staatskunde* (study of the Greek states) of G. Busolt, the last edition of which appeared in the 1920s.[12] Work in this tradition has continued, for instance with many of the investigations of M. H. Hansen, who has concentrated particularly on the law-courts and the assembly (cf. below).

But in the twentieth century some scholars moved away from constitutional formalities. A. F. Bentley in 1908 suggested at a general level that a study of politicians and political groups could illuminate the working of a state.[13] This approach quickly found its

[10] A. Boeckh, *Die Staatshaushaltung der Athener*; trans. G. C. Lewis as *The Public Economy of Athens*.
[11] G. F. Schoemann, *De Comitiis Atheniensium Libri Tres*; trans. F. A. P[aley] as *A Dissertation on the Assemblies of the Athenians, in Three Books*.
[12] G. Busolt, *Griechische Staats-, Kriegs- und Privataltertümer*; 3rd edition entitled *Griechische Staatskunde* and partly ed. by H. Swoboda.
[13] A. F. Bentley, *The Process of Government*.

way into Roman history, in the work of M. Gelzer and F. Münzer in Germany, and of R. Syme in Britain;[14] but it did not have much impact on Greek history until the third quarter of the century, in (for instance) a series of studies by R. Sealey and P. J. Bicknell, W. R. Connor's *The New Politicians of Fifth-Century Athens*, and the collection and discussion of data in J. K. Davies' *Athenian Propertied Families, 600–300 B.C.*[15] Work on these lines banished – for ever, it is to be hoped – a tendency to write of Athenian politics as if Athens had political parties like those of modern Europe or North America (of which a striking but not atypical example was M. Croiset's *Aristophane et les partis à Athènes*[16]); but if taken to extremes it could suggest that politicians were concerned only with manoeuvring to strengthen their power base and were never committed to the rightness of particular policies.

In the second half of the twentieth century the idea that history could be an objective science came under attack. Historians in sympathy with Marxism, when accused of being ideologically driven, replied that all historians are ideologically driven, and that they were at least honest enough to admit to their ideology.[17] More recently 'postmodernists' have claimed that what originally happened in the past is irretrievable, that the texts which we use as sources were constructing history to suit their purposes, and when we work with the sources we are constructing history to suit our purposes – and when this is taken to extremes it should lead to the conclusion that any one person's construction has as much validity as any other's.[18] Thus in a review article on M. H. Hansen's *The Athenian Assembly in the Age of Demosthenes* J. Ober complains that 'in the absence of an explicit ideological point of view, his conclusions appear objective' but 'a monograph or article by Hansen, like any other text, is

---

[14] M. Gelzer, *Die Nobilität der römischen Republik*; 'Die Nobilität der Kaiserzeit', *Hermes* l 1915, 395–415; the two trans. R. Seager as *The Roman Nobility*. F. Münzer, *Römische Adelsparteien und Adelsfamilien*; trans. T. Ridley as *Roman Aristocratic Parties and Families*. R. Syme, *The Roman Revolution*.

[15] R. Sealey, e.g. the papers collected in his *Essays in Greek Politics*. P. J. Bicknell, e.g. his *Studies in Athenian Politics and Genealogy*. W. R. Connor, *The New Politicians of Fifth-Century Athens*. J. K. Davies, *Athenian Propertied Families, 600–300 B.C.*; and a discussion of the implications of the data in *Wealth and the Power of Wealth in Classical Athens*.

[16] M. Croiset, *Aristophane et les partis à Athènes*; trans. J. Loeb as *Aristophanes and the Political Parties at Athens*. Davies in *Athenian Propertied Families* was still willing to use such expressions as 'political shift to the Left' (p. 259).

[17] E.g. J. P. Sullivan in the Editorial of a collection of papers on 'Marxism and the Classics', *Arethusa* viii. 1 1975, 5–6.

[18] One writer among many who have taken a postmodernist view of history is H. V. White: e.g. the essays collected in *The Content of the Form*. For a recent study which attempts a fair appraisal of postmodernism but does not accept total relativism, see R. J. Evans, *In Defence of History*.

best understood as an ideological construct', and Ober regards
Hansen's constructs, which concentrate on Athens' formal institutions, as less satisfactory than his own, which focus on the successful efforts of the mass of the citizens to control the elite.[19] Ober is one
of those scholars, to be found particularly though not only in the
USA, who believe that study of the Athenian democracy can be of
direct relevance to the modern world, and he contrasts the active
citizen body of Athens favourably with the passive citizen bodies of
modern representative democracies.[20]

THE SCOPE OF THIS BOOK

It would be impossible to compile a definitive selection of a dozen
or so articles on Athenian democracy which every student ought to
read, but I have tried to put together a selection of studies from the
twentieth century (not all of them from the late twentieth century)
which are important in themselves and which illustrate the different
kinds of question which can be asked and the different kinds of
approach which can help us to answer them. I have not limited
myself to studies with whose conclusions I am in agreement: I indicate one or two disagreements, but I do not wish to use this book to
engage in quarrels with the authors whose work I have chosen, and
I have not thought it appropriate to parade all my agreements and
disagreements.

The chapters of this book are grouped according to the kind of
topic investigated, and a variety of approaches will be found in
each Part of the book. Part I is devoted to political institutions, with
chapters on Athenian citizenship (Chapter 1), voting in the assembly
(Chapter 2), the fourth-century mechanism for the allotment of
jurors to law-courts (Chapter 3), payment for service in assemblies
and juries and its effect on participation in those bodies (Chapter 4),
and the different forms of capital punishment and the rationale for
their use (Chapter 5). Institutions are an important aspect, but not
the only important aspect, of the Athenian democracy, and Part II
contains chapters on political activity: the demagogues as an essential

---

[19] J. Ober, 'The Nature of Athenian Democracy', *CP* lxxxiv 1989, 322–34 (quotations
p. 323), revised as *The Athenian Revolution* (107–)108–22 ch. viii (quotations pp. 109–10,
with 'a social' substituted for 'an ideological'). That was a response to M. H. Hansen, *The
Athenian Assembly in the Age of Demosthenes*; Hansen replied in 'Solonian Democracy in
Fourth-Century Athens', *ClMed* xl 1989, 107–13 = *The Athenian Ecclesia, II*, 263–9; for
Ober's view of Athenian democracy see *Mass and Elite in Democratic Athens*.

[20] See, for instance, the Introduction to J. P. Euben, J. R. Wallach and J. Ober (eds), *Athenian
Political Thought and the Reconstruction of American Democracy*, 1–26.

structural feature of the assembly-based democracy (Chapter 6), a study of the ways in which politicians manoeuvred within the framework of the democracy (Chapter 7), the function and the problems of competitive festivals in the *polis* (Chapter 8), and the unusual extent to which democratic Athens tried to separate public life from private life (Chapter 9). Whenever we believe that Athens first became democratic, the reforms of Solon (Chapter 10), Cleisthenes (Chapters 11, 12) and Ephialtes (Chapter 13) are commonly seen as milestones in Athens' political development, and studies of these form Part III. Finally, in Part IV, Chapter 14 is a general attempt to pick out what it was in Greek life that led to the development of democracy in Athens.

Several of the various lines of enquiry which can help us to understand the Athenian democracy are represented here. One is archaeology, and its uncovering of the buildings in which and the equipment with which various political procedures took place. Thus *Ath. Pol.* 68 describes the jurors' voting-tokens, hollow to vote for the plaintiff and solid to vote for the defendant, which could be held so that voters could feel but others could not see which was which, and many of these have been found: metal discs with a hollow or solid axle, some bearing the inscription *psephos demosia*, 'public ballot', so that there is no doubt about the identification.[21] More strikingly, there are references by Aristophanes and in *Ath. Pol.*'s account of the law-courts to *kleroteria*,[22] which for a long time were commonly thought to denote rooms in which allotments took place. The correct meaning was discovered by S. Dow, when he identified blocks of stone with slits in one face as allotment-machines in which the *pinakia* (tickets) of candidates for allotment will have been inserted (see Chapter 3). L. Gernet in Chapter 5 starts from the archaeological solution to another problem, the use of a set of buried skeletons to show what the procedure was in execution by *apotympanismos*.[23]

Comparison with other societies, whether in the Graeco-Roman world or more or less developed societies in subsequent history and in the modern world, can help us to make sense of Athens. In Chapter 5 Gernet reaffirms the use of throwing into a pit as an alternative to *apotympanismos*, against the attempt of A. D. Keramopoullos to reject it, by pointing to similar methods of

[21] Illustrated in many places, e.g. *The Athenian Agora: A Guide to the Excavation and Museum*[4], 245 fig. 149.
[22] Ar. *Eccl.* 681; *Ath. Pol.* 63. ii etc.
[23] E.g. Lys. XIII. *Agoratus* 65.

execution in other Greek states and in Rome, and contrasting *apotympanismos* as a secular method of killing common criminals caught in the act with the religious killing by throwing into a pit of those who had caused pollution by committing religious offences or major offences against the community. S. C. Humphreys has been one of the most anthropologically attuned of Greek historians writing in English. Chapter 9 is one of a number of papers in which she has been concerned with the division of social life into public and private spheres, arguing that awareness of modern attitudes in this area may help us to formulate questions about and to make sense of Athenian attitudes:[24] she begins it by contrasting the 'substantial disengagement' of public and private affairs in classical Athens with the greater interlocking in Homeric society, the hellenistic world and even the subordinate units of classical Athens; and, after investigating that disengagement, ends by remarking that she was led to this investigation partly from anthropological work on kinship and the difficulty of discovering what family life meant to an Athenian. J. K. Davies in Chapter 1, when asking why the Athenians held as they did to descent as the qualification for citizenship, notes not only that other criteria were considered but rejected in Athens *c.*400 but also that other Greek states, and in the hellenistic period even Athens, were prepared to replenish their treasuries by granting citizenship to foreigners willing to pay for it.[25] M. H. Hansen in studying the Athenian assembly has found a parallel in the *Landsgemeinde* of some Swiss cantons, and one of the purposes for which he uses this parallel is to support his argument, in Chapter 2, that when the assembly voted by show of hands the majority was adjudged without a precise count of votes.

It has always been known that fifth-century Athenian comedy abounds in allusions to current personalities and events, and that there are some reflections of current events in tragedy (e.g. Aeschylus' *Eumenides*, of 459/8, focuses on the council of the Areopagus shortly after the reduction of its powers by Ephialtes in 462/1). Recently, however, a new kind of historical approach to drama has found favour, linking both the issues explored in some of the plays and the institutional setting in which the plays were performed with the *polis* of Athens, and often specifically with the democracy.[26] R. Osborne is

---

[24] Cf. S. C. Humphreys, *The Family, Women and Death*, xi = [2]lv.

[25] Chs 1 and 9 both originated in papers read to a conference at Princeton University in 1977 on 'Kinship, Politics and Economy in Classical Greece'.

[26] I argue that the link should be with the *polis* in general rather than with the democracy in particular: P. J. Rhodes, 'Nothing to Do with Democracy: Athenian Drama and the *Polis*', *JHS* cxxiii 2003, 104–19.

a scholar who himself uses a wide range of approaches to Greek history and who insists on the importance of 'joined-up writing', of integrating the results of different kinds of enquiry to produce a multi-dimensional picture;[27] and in Chapter 8 he contributes to and broadens the new approach to drama, studying Athens' dramatic competitions within the full range of the city's competitive festivals.

The archaic period (*c.*800–500) is particularly vulnerable to the claim of the postmodernists that what originally happened is ir-retrievable (cf. above), since most of our written evidence for it is not contemporary but later, and in the case of Solon, while we have some passages from his own poetry, we know that in the fourth century the orators were prepared to attribute to him laws which were demon-strably much more recent. Doubts about Solon's reforms as presented in texts of the fourth century and later are not new, but in the late twentieth century they became fashionable: in Chapter 10 C. Mossé starts from the fourth-century view of Solon and treats it as a reconstruction, trying to work out what truth may lie behind it.

The two chapters on the reforms of Cleisthenes in 508/7 show how very different approaches can be used to illuminate the same episode. J. Ober in Chapter 11 focuses on the exile of Cleisthenes and his supporters and their subsequent return, and in accordance with his view that in the Athenian democracy the *demos* controlled the elite he argues that what led to their recall was not a process driven by political leaders but a spontaneous popular movement. D. M. Lewis in Chapter 12 looks at the end product, the registration of the Athenian citizens in a complicated new system of tribes, *trittyes* ('thirds') and demes, and he uses the detailed evidence for the location in Attica of Cleisthenes' units and the known associations of units which were joined together or kept apart in Cleisthenes' system to argue that Cleisthenes was engaging in clever electoral geography. R. Sealey in Chapter 13 argues that judicial procedures can come into existence and change without conscious acts of creation and reform, and gives a view of Ephialtes' reforms in 462/1 as based not on an ideological commitment to democracy but on the far less ambitious desire to end a particular abuse; C. Meier in Chapter 14 asks in a general way how and why politics and demo-cracy developed in archaic and classical Greece, and particularly in Athens, and gives an answer involving a more ideologically signi-ficant view of Ephialtes' reforms. Another chapter involving a broad-

[27] Cf. his inaugural lecture of 23. i. 2002, 'Changing Visions of Democracy', published in a forthcoming book.

brush approach is Chapter 6, the study of Athenian demagogues by
M. I. Finley, which argues that we should stand back from our late-
fifth-century sources' view of demagogues as upstart rabble-rousers
and see the political leaders as essential to the success of Athens'
assembly-based democracy; while I myself in Chapter 7 explore in
detail how Athens' politicians operated within the framework of
Athens' political institutions. In another detailed study, in Chapter 4
M. M. Markle reconsiders both the significance of the terms 'poor'
(*penes*) and 'without means' (*aporos*) in contrast to 'destitute'
(*ptochos*), and the comments made on their audiences by the
Athenian orators, in order to arrive at a more credible account of the
men who participated in the assembly and juries and of the effect of
the stipends paid to them.

Of Greek cities in the classical period Athens is the one for which
we have by far the greatest range and quantity of evidence; but I
believe firmly that not every phenomenon which is attested for democratic Athens in the classical period is specifically a product of or is
peculiar to the Athenian democracy,[28] and in putting together this
book I have borne in mind that it is a book about Athenian democracy, not a book (which would have to range much more widely)
about democratic Athens. I have omitted studies of subsequent
reactions to the Athenian democracy, outlined on pp. 5–8, above,
since that is a large subject which deserves a book in its own right.
And, since I doubt the value of publishing excerpts and abridgments,
I have limited my choice to items short enough to be reprinted in their
entirety.

---

[28] See, for instance, the article cited in n. 26, above.

PART I

Political Institutions

Introduction to Part I

This Part is devoted to articles which study the principal institutions of the Athenian democracy – citizenship, voting in the assembly, the allotment of jurors to law-courts, payment for attending the assembly and serving on juries, the execution of men condemned to death – and which approach those institutions in a variety of ways.

It is often stressed that the Greeks believed in citizen rights, not human rights, and that the *polis* was a community of *politai* (citizens). The doctoral thesis of J. K. Davies, who has recently retired as Professor of Ancient History and Classical Archaeology at Liverpool, was published in two books, *Athenian Propertied Families, 600–300 B.C.*, and *Wealth and the Power of Wealth in Classical Athens*; and classical Athens and its society has remained one of his academic interests. In 451/0 the Athenians decided, and after the Peloponnesian War they reaffirmed, that citizenship should be restricted to men who had both an Athenian father and an Athenian mother. Davies in Chapter 1 considers other criteria for citizenship which might have been used, and asks why, even after their losses in the Peloponnesian War, the Athenians held to citizenship by descent.

M. H. Hansen is a Danish scholar who is founder and Director of the Copenhagen Polis Centre (which has undertaken the neo-Aristotelian task of studying all the *poleis* of the classical Greek world in order to see more clearly what a *polis* was and what it was not), but who earlier worked specifically on Athens, concentrating particularly on the law-courts and assembly. In a series of studies and a consolidatory book[1] he has asked a range of practical questions about how the assembly actually worked. Chapter 2, on voting in the assembly, is typical of these studies, and is one of the papers in which

---

[1] Many of the individual studies are collected in M. H. Hansen, *The Athenian Ecclesia* and *The Athenian Ecclesia, II*. The consolidatory book is *The Athenian Assembly in the Age of Demosthenes*.

he has been able to use the Swiss *Landsgemeinden* to illuminate the Athenian assembly.

Allotment of candidates to offices and jurors to law-courts, as a means of distributing positions among men who were considered equally eligible, was a prominent feature of the Athenian democracy (though allotment was not limited to democracies). S. Dow (1903–95), who was both a student and a professor at Harvard University, was working in Athens for his doctorate in the early 1930s, when the American excavations in the Agora were beginning. It was in the course of this work, which resulted in *Prytaneis*,[2] that he solved the problem of the *kleroterion*: two of the inscriptions in his collection included the instruction that they were to be inscribed on a stone *kleroterion*, in one case the stone was well enough preserved to show rows of slots cut in one face, and he found other such stones. This led him to realise what a *kleroterion* was and how it was used in the allotment of jurors to courts and of candidates to offices, and Chapter 3 is one of his articles on the subject.

Another important feature of Athens' democracy was payment for the performance of civilian duties, to make it easier for the poorer citizens to play the part which they were legally entitled to play. M. M. Markle is an American who spent the later part of his career at the University of New England, in Australia. Earlier he studied in Oxford under G. E. M. de Ste Croix, one of whose academic passions was *The Class Struggle in the Ancient Greek World*, and for a volume in honour of de Ste Croix Markle wrote Chapter 4, which confronts the rival views that those who received the pay and participated in the assemblies and juries were the destitute, for whom a small payment was better than nothing, or that they were prosperous men who did not actually need the money – and argues against both that most participants were 'poor' men who needed to work and did work for their living, and that the payments fulfilled their intended function of enabling these men to devote some of their time to public service.

The French scholar L. Gernet (1892–1962) was a pupil of the sociologist E. Durkheim.[3] Gernet spent most of his career teaching Greek prose composition at the University of Algiers; but his research was inspired by Durkheim, and ranged over Greek law, religion and thought, setting all of these in the context of the city and its social

---

[2] S. Dow, *Prytaneis*: on the *kleroterion*, 198–215.
[3] See S. C. Humphreys, 'The Work of Louis Gernet', *History and Theory* x 1971, 172–96 = her *Anthropology and the Greeks*, 76–94.

structures. For many years he was isolated and unfashionable, but he returned to Paris in the late 1940s, and, particularly through his pupil J.-P. Vernant, he influenced a great deal of French work on Greek history in the second half of the twentieth century. Chapter 5 starts from an archaeologist's discovery of what was involved in execution by *apotympanismos*, reaffirms that that was one of two forms of execution used at Athens, and invokes religious considerations to show why different forms of execution were used for different kinds of offence.

1 *Athenian Citizenship: The Descent Group and the Alternatives**†*

JOHN K. DAVIES

I

Classical Athens defined the membership of its citizen body, and thereby its civic space, rigorously in terms of descent. Citizens were those who were male; were sons of a citizen father; were born from a woman who was the daughter of a citizen father; were born from a woman who was 'pledged' (*engyete*);[1] and had been accepted as members of their father's (phratry and) deme.[2] Concomitantly, only members of this body could own real property, assume the rights and

* Originally published in *Classical Journal* lxxiii 1977/8, 105–21; reprinted with the permission of the author and of the Classical Association of the Middle West and South.

† After its first presentation at Princeton on 2 April 1977, this paper was substantially rewritten before being read to the Oxford Philological Society on 29 April 1977: it is the second version which is published here. I am grateful to those who commented on each version, at the time or subsequently, at Princeton to Mrs. S. C. Humphreys, Dr. Cynthia Patterson, and Professors E. Badian, J. Hallett, A. Momigliano, H. North, and M. Ostwald, and at Oxford to Sir Kenneth Dover, Professor A. Andrewes, Mr. S. Hornblower, Dr. D. M. Lewis, and Mrs. B. M. Mitchell.

Abbreviations:

APF   J. K. Davies, *Athenian Propertied Families, 600–300 B.C.* (Oxford, 1971). References are to entries, not pages.

Harrison   A. R. W. Harrison, *The Law of Athens,* I: *The family and property* (Oxford, 1968).

Lewis   D. M. Lewis, *Hesperia* 28 (1959) 208–38, 'Attic Manumissions'.

MacDowell   D. M. MacDowell, *Athenian Homicide Law in the Age of the Orators* (Manchester, 1963).

ML   R. Meiggs and D. M. Lewis, *Greek Historical Inscriptions to the End of the Fifth Century B.C.* (Oxford, 1969).

Pečírka   J. Pečírka, *The Formula for the Grant of Enktesis in Attis Inscriptions* (Prague, 1966).

Pélékidis   Chr. Pélékidis, *Histoire de l'éphébie attique* (Paris, 1962).

Wyse   W. Wyse, *The Speeches of Isaeus* (Cambridge, 1904).

[1] Or, in the case of an *epikleros* ['heiress'], from a woman who has been allocated to a husband by the archon following an *epidikasia* ['adjudication'].

[2] I ignore here the question of how far phratry membership was in practice essential. See Harrison I 64 n. 1.

duties assigned to the four Solonian property-classes, and hold elective or allotted office. Apart form crises in 411, 403, and 322–306, the system remained stable through the fifth and fourth centuries B.C. and indeed well into the Hellenistic period, in spite of the violent fluctuations in Athens' circumstances. It is easy, therefore, to regard such a system as part of the background, against which more interesting events took place, and to suppose that it was largely uncontroversial. I do not think that either proposition is true. Of course, in any society such as Athens', which was reasonably stable demographically, we should expect the renewal of the community through time to proceed above all by the ordinary processes of family succession. What matters is how far those processes become a matter of political or legal interest, and to what extent they conspicuously are, or conspicuously are *not*, supplemented by other modes of entering the community. I shall argue that the subject did become, and remained, a matter of intense interest and preoccupation: that the questions 'Who is to be, and who is not to be, in the Athenian community, and why?' were continually being posed by pressures from within and without: that the process of finding answers, and of justifying them, was a very important component of Athenian public and intellectual life: and that the process yielded tensions, prejudices and insecurities which affected individuals deeply and inescapably. I shall argue, further, that the system which held in Classical Athens, stable though it was, cannot be understood if looked at synchronically alone, but that it needs to be juxtaposed with what preceded it and with what succeeded it. This involves covering a wide canvas very quickly and runs the risk of glib superficiality. I plead in mitigation that it is very much an interim report on work in progress, and that I should be grateful for criticisms and suggestions.

I begin synchronically, with the classical system – by which I understand the 'final version' of the rules as intensified by Perikles' citizenship law of 451/0 and by Aristophon's re-enactment of it in 403/2, re-enforced by the *diapsephisis* [vote on individuals in the demes] of 346/5. What is of interest for the moment is not so much the rules themselves, which are clear, as the degree of buttressing and re-inforcement which they receive throughout the classical period from institutions and from administrative or legal decisions. It amounts, I shall argue, to a substantial structure – indeed so substantial as to be unnatural. The reasons for it should become clearer when we look at the alternatives.

It is a statement of the obvious to say that throughout the classical period Athenian citizens were not merely a descent group but also

an interest group, disposing of privileges which were worth defend-
ing. I do not refer here to Athenians' privileges or power outside
Attika, but to their status within Attika vis-à-vis other inhabitants.
Citizens monopolized the economic privileges of owning landed
property and house-property in Attika, of inheriting property from
Athenians, of purchasing the leases of the silvermines,[3] of being
the recipients of regular or windfall distributions of money or corn
which came through the state, or of participating in tribal feasts
(*hestiaseis*) or in the maintenance associated with performing in some
public festivals.[4] Again, even more obviously, citizens monopolized
the political privileges of voting in lawcourts and Assembly, of
speaking in Assembly, of pleading in court (with a few exceptions),
of holding office, and of holding public priesthoods and other
honours.

A second mode of buttressing can be seen in the care which was
continuously taken to ensure that out-groups remained out-groups.
Proxenoi ['representatives', normally of Athens in their own state,
but the title tended to be awarded honorifically to foreigners in
Athens], for instance: key men though they were, foreigners given
status as proxenoi of Athens did not become citizens of Athens
even when they ended as refugees in Athens[5] or when (from the early
fourth century onwards) their grant of proxeny status usually
included the right to own real property in Athens.[6] Or *metroxenoi*: I
am persuaded by Mrs. Humphreys' recent argument[7] that those born
of citizen fathers and non-citizen mothers and not yet adult in 451/0
were excluded from citizenship, and were assimilated to the bastards
who were similarly to 'have no share in things sacred or secular',[8]
certainly from 403/2 onwards and almost certainly before then too.
Or the Plataians from 427 onwards: though Thucydides says they
were given citizenship by Athens, they remained a separate com-

---

[3] Exceptionally, *isoteleis* [non-citizens granted equality of obligations with the citizens] had
this privilege too, as the activity of Kallaischros of Siphnos and his family reveals (*APF* C 12)
[4] Thus, for instance, only citizens could sing in the choruses at the Dionysia and
Panathenaia.
[5] For example, no citizenship grant appears in the lengthy dossier of honours for
Potamodoros and Eurytion of Orchomenos (*IG* i² 68 = Pečírka 4 ff.; *IG* i² 69 + B. D. Meritt,
Hesperia 14 (1945) 110 f.; *SEG* X 84 lines 1–10; *SEG* X 84, lines 10 ff.; *SEG* X 84, lines 18–21;
SEG X 84 lines 21–40; *SEG* X 84, lines 40–8; *IG* i² 103 = *SEG* X 114).
[6] See Pečírka *passim*. Cf. also Pankalos Athenadou *proxenos*, who manumits two slaves in
the 320s (Lewis Face B, lines 17 and 21). He is presumably resident in Athens, and his status-
label '*proxenos*' is co-ordinate with the demotics of other owners. (For another instance *IG* ii²
1570, line 20.) Note also *IG* ii² 9304, the fourth-century gravestone of the wife and daughter
of Diogeitos Megareus *proxenos*.
[7] S. C. Humphreys, *JHS* 94 (1974) 88 ff.
[8] Dem. 43.51; Isaios 6.47.

munity, brigaded separately and resettled as such in Skione in 420,[9] while the use of the label 'Plataieus' in Aristophanes' *Frogs* 694 and in Lysias 23 seems to show that it came to denote some sort of favoured metic status.[10] So too with the members of other refugee communities such as Olynthians or Thebans, named as such in their capacities as slave-owners at Athens in manumission-documents of the 320s.[11] So too, most illuminatingly of all, with the limiting case of the *isoteleis*, those privileged metics who were assimilated fiscally and economically to citizen status but nonetheless remained politically outside, as *cives sine suffragio* ['citizens without the vote'].[12] Even in the case of the only other group enfranchisement we know of, the offer to the Samians in 405, the terms of the offer (the Samians to keep their own laws, running their affairs as they themselves wish) show that we have to do with *isopoliteia* ['equal citizenship rights'] rather than with true integration, a distinction confirmed by the fact that the provision about enrolling Samians in Athenian tribes concerns only the Samian envoys present in Athens.[13]

Conversely, and consistently, those inside the citizen body remain inside juridically even when they are remote geographically. The kleruchs on Salamis at the end of the sixth century are to ['Αθένε]σι τελὲν καὶ στρατ[εύεσθ]αι[14] ['pay (taxes) and perform military service for the Athenians']: the Athenians settled on Lemnos by the elder Miltiades at about the same time retain their membership of the Kleisthenic tribes:[15] and all that we know about the Athenian kleruchies of the fifth and fourth centuries shows consistently that the Athenians resident in them retained their citizenship and tribal affiliation, even though we know from Isaios and from Terence's *Phormio*, as well as other sources, that the geographical sundering caused difficulties and gave ample opportunity for chicanery and subterfuge.[16] In this sense the kleruchy is an institution unique to Athens, differing significantly from the relationships of dependence, subordination, and exploitation studied in F. Gschnitzer's *Abhängige Orte* on the one hand, and on the other from the relationships of

[9] Thuc. 3.55.3 (with Gomme's note) and 3.63.2: 5.32.1.
[10] This is also the implication of Hellanikos *FGrH* 4 F 171.
[11] Lewis, Face A line 242 (Olynthian): *IG* ii² 1569, lines 3 (Theban) and 62 (Troz[enian]).
[12] Gravestones *IG* ii² 7862–7881. As a separate status in the manumission documents: Lewis, Face A line 102, Face B line 99; *IG* ii² 1565, lines 5 and 20.
[13] ML 94, lines 12 ff. and 33 ff.
[14] ML 14, lines 2–3.
[15] *IG* XII Suppl. 337.
[16] See Wyse on Isaios 6.13.

independence, patronage, and *isopoliteia* which normally obtained elsewhere in Greece between colony and mother city: as such the creation, extension, and durability of the kleruchy, a new concept of the Kleisthenic period, well show the balance of values which came to be held in Athenian society.[17]

So too do certain old-established institutions. I pick out two, the *anchisteia* and the phratry. The *anchisteia* comprises those members of EGO's [a person's] bilateral kindred who are related to him as far as the degree of 'children of cousins' (μέχρι ἀνεψιῶν παίδων). There are difficulties in determining precisely whom this definition included, but they need not concern us here.[18] I merely note what is well known, that the group as thus defined had two functions. To quote Harrison, 'for the law of homicide it determined the body of relatives of a slain man on whom, in the absence of direct descendants, was laid the responsibility of avenging the dead man and whose unanimous consent was needed if the slayer was to be freed by an act of composition (*aidesis*) from banishment. For the law of succession it determined the limit of relatives of the deceased's father who were entitled <to inherit> before relatives of his mother could come in.'[19] It is hard to assess how actively the first function tended towards solidarity, but its effect cannot have been negligible. We can see that the role of the *anchisteia* was preserved in the 409/8 revision of the law on involuntary homicide,[20] that murder prosecutions remained *dikai* [private lawsuits], and that by converse the murderers of a person who lacked relatives or phratry membership were likely to escape with impunity.[21] However, the second function, that of regulating inheritance, can be seen from speech after speech to have been important. To speak of 'solidarity' here would perhaps be inappropriate, since the speeches which emerge from inheritance disputes reveal the usual compound of intrafamilial jealously, chicanery, injured innocence, and general breakdown of goodwill. Yet it remained true that the chance of an inheritance was a very strong reason for

[17] It was Professor Momigliano who brought the status of kleruchs into the discussion at the Princeton Colloquium. These few lines gratefully elaborate his idea.

[18] The phraseology of the law is preserved in Dem. 43.51 and Isaios 11.11. It is unclear whether the *anchisteia* ends with the children of EGO's cousins (as the wording of the law *prima facie* [at first sight] suggests) or with the children of EGO's parents' cousins, i.e. with EGO's second cousins (as is suggested by Theopompos' claim in Isaios 11 to the estate of his second cousin Hagnias). See Wyse 671 ff. and Harrison I 143 ff.

[19] Harrison I 143.

[20] ML 86, lines 15–16 and 21–2. See MacDowell 117 ff.

[21] Cf. the case of the murder of a family's freedwoman nurse, related in Dem. 47.68 ff., and discussed in detail by MacDowell 12 ff.

keeping contact with, and knowing the financial and personal
circumstances of, one's relatives (or at least, shall we say, one's *richer*
relatives): that several speeches[22] show us poor families of the *popu-
lus minutus* ['insignificant citizenry'] feeling (or at least expressing to
a citizen court) more in common with the values of rentier citizens
than with those of the poorer metics whose life-style they shared: and
that the (sometimes complicated) interactions between the inheritance law and the adoption law did keep the number of *oikoi* ['households'] more or less constant and prevented the emergence of a caste
of super-rich, marrying and inheriting exclusively among themselves.
Moreover, even if we may to tempted to regard financial interest as
a major vector, it would be fatuous to deny either that unforced affec-
tion and common action among *syngeneis, oikeioi,* and *prosekontes*
['kin', 'family', 'relatives'] will have been the norm, or that a very
high value was placed on family solidarity.[23]

Secondly, we note the role of phratries. I am not here concerned
with their growth and crystallization in the archaic period, with
the ways in which they came to be segmental divisions of Ionic tribes,
or with the relationship between *genos* ['clan': actual or imagined
kinship group] and phratry.[24] Whatever their earlier roles, the docu-
mentation of the classical period shows them as concerned partly
with revenues, in money and in kind, from property and sacrifices,
but mainly with the credentials of potential members and with the
cult ceremonies which symbolized the transitions to full membership.[25] Our picture of procedure is not entirely clear, but it is usually
agreed that there were two ceremonies, the *meion* and the *koureion,*
both occurring on the same day, the 3rd day (*koureiotis*) of the
Apatouria festival in Pyanopsion (*IV* = October). The *meion* is probably the presentation to the phratry of all (male) children born to
men of the phratry in the previous year: the *koureion* is probably a
rite de passage at puberty.[26] Isaios 8.19 gives us the form of words in
which the father has to swear that the child is legitimate. The speaker
says that 'our father introduced us into the phratries having sworn
in accordance with the existing laws that he was bringing in <chil-

[22] Cf. particularly Dem. 57 (with *APF* 3126) and Dem. 44 (with *APF* 5638). I take this
opportunity to correct a disastrous error in the stemma of *APF* 5638 (on p. 196): the lines of
adoption should descend from Archiades, not from Archippos.

[23] Isaios 1.5-6 (tr. Dover). Other references in K. J. Dover, *Greek Popular Morality in the
Time of Plato and Aristotle* (Oxford, 1974) 273 ff.

[24] See *imprimis* [primarily] A. Andrewes, *JHS* 81 (1961) 1 ff.

[25] For details see Davies, *Gnomon* 47 (1975) 376.

[26] For the complications and uncertainties see Wyse 357 ff. and Busolt–Swoboda,
Griechische Staatskunde (Munich, 1920–6) II 961 n. 1.

dren born> of a citizen and pledged woman.'[27] If the child's legitimacy was challenged, the offering of sheep or goat made by the father on the altar was taken away, and the phratry members voted on the matter, carrying their votes from the altar. Procedures, then, are elaborate, and become even more so in the only phratry that we know much about.[28] While there must have been an effective and informal side to phratry activity, it is not too much to say, on the evidence we have, that a classical phratry *is* first and foremost a mechanism for buttressing descent and legitimacy.

Comparable procedures took place at the levels of *oikos*, deme, and state. Within the *oikos* the ceremony of the *amphidromia* on the 5th, 7th, or 10th day after the birth of a child was partly indeed a purification ritual, but was also evidence that the father recognized the child as legitimately his and therefore admitted it to the *hiera* ['sacred rites'] of the *oikos*. Demosthenes leaves us in no doubt, and Isaios shows that holding the ceremony was reckoned to be good evidence of legitimacy in court proceedings.[29] Within the deme *Ath. Pol.* is explicit about procedure.[30] Plainly, public preoccupations are partly with age, but mainly with parentage and status within the descent group. Even more pronounced are these values at the *anakrisis* ['interrogation' at their *dokimasia* ('validation') before entering office] of the Archons.[31] Here we can see well enough how subordinate other considerations were to the primary questions of proper status within the descent group.

One further mode of buttressing descent-group thinking needs to be noticed: its formalization in official political myth.[32] For Apollo the tradition is explicit. Harpokration's entry s.v. reads in part: 'The Athenians publicly (κοινῶς) honour Apollo Patroos ever since Ion: for when Ion had synoikized [combined in a single state] the Athenians, as Aristotle says,[33] the Athenians were called Ionians and

---

[27] The phraseology is identical elsewhere (see Wyse 501, and add Andoc. 1.127), and clearly reflects a public law of the State imposed upon phratries, very likely Perikles' citizenship law of 451/0.

[28] Cf. Nikodemos' amendments to the procedures for the Oikos of the Dekeleieis, *IG* ii² 1237, lines 68 ff.

[29] Dem. 29.22: Isaios 3.30.

[30] *Ath. Pol.* 42.1–2.

[31] *Ath. Pol.* 55.2–3.

[32] See the references in LSJ s.v. ἑρκεῖος, especially Soph. *Ant.* 486–7, with L. R. Farnell, *The Cults of the Greek States* (Oxford, 1896–1909) I 54 and V 363. Philochoros *FGrH* 328 F 67 relates an incident in (?)306/5 when a dog got up onto the Akropolis, entered the precinct of Pandrosos, and 'jumped up onto the altar of Zeus Herkeios which was under the olive tree'. The spatial sense clearly predominates here.

[33] F 381 Rose = *Ath. Pol.* F 1 ed. Budé.

Apollo was named Patroos by them.'[34] Given that it was Pythian Apollo who was Patroos for Athens,[35] that Solon's links with Delphi must be historical in some sense or other,[36] and that Solon himself gives us our first evidence for the 'Ionian' aspect of Athens,[37] Jacoby[38] may well have been right to suggest that the public cult of Apollo Patroos was created by Solon. Anyway, whether then or later Athenians came all to share a cult whose very name as well as under-lying myth reflected descent as the dominating definition of the community.

Descent, then, is built into the institutions of the state. Yet, para-doxically, just because it is so firmly built in, and because procedures in deme, phratry, or tribe emphasize it so prominently, one gets a distinct sense of siege, of barricades being manned, of determined resistance to constant pressures from outside. In itself that is not surprising. There is no difficulty in explaining why the Athenians of the classical period were concerned to maintain a high boundary wall round the citizen body. Citizenship was a valuable privilege, both economically and politically, and became more so as Athens' power grew in the fifth century and as the perquisites of citizenship became more valuable, more frequent, and more pervasive: to open citizen-ship to all who wanted it would devalue it unacceptably. So the exist-ence of strict rules and of a sense of siege is no problem. What does need explanation is why those rules took the form they did, especially when, as we shall see, archaic Athens took a very different view of how and where the boundaries should be drawn, when alternative formulations on different principles surfaced intermittently in the classical period, and when the Hellenistic period saw a major shift towards a different principle.

Moreover, two other phenomena need to be taken into account. First, the breakdown of these rigid descent rules does not correlate with the decline in the relative value (in the Aegean, in Greece gener-ally, or in Athens herself) of the citizenship. *Isoteleia* survived as a status worth recording on gravestones, till the first century B.C. on Kirchner's datings.[39] Consistently, I know of only three marriages

---

[34] Cf. also Plato, *Euthyd.* 302 c–d.

[35] Dem. 18.141, Harp. s.v. Ἀπόλλων πατρῷος: L. Deubner, *Attische Feste* (2nd edn Darmstadt, 1966) 198.

[36] W. G. Forrest, *BCH* 80 (1956) 39 ff. and 48 ff.

[37] F 4a West.

[38] CQ 38 (1944) 70 and 72–3 = his *Abhandlungen zur griechischen Geschichtschreibung* (Leiden, 1956) 251 and 254–5.

[39] 2nd century B.C. – *IG* ii² 7862, 7872, 7876: 2nd/1st centuries B.C. – *IG* ii² 7867: 1st century B.C. – *IG* ii² 7866, 7878.

between citizen and non-citizen which are recorded on gravestones[40] before the second century B.C. In contrast, at least 17 such marriages are recorded on second-century tombstones,[41] and from the turn of the first century B.C. the custom was frequent. Again, it was not until the middle of the second century B.C. that political roles, especially as envoys, were entrusted to immigrants on any major scale, and even so it looks as if those concerned became citizens first.[42] Nor was the ephebate opened to *xenoi* ['foreigners'] till shortly before 119/8.[43] Be it said, thought, that when descent-group rules of citizenship did break down they were breached comprehensively and deliberately, and we can approximately say when.

Secondly, the rules generated obsessions, anxieties, and insecurities. If, as most do, we accept the historicity of a process[44] by which, in 445/4 in the wake of a general distribution of corn, 4760 persons were disfranchised as 'illegitimately enrolled' *parengraphoi*,[45] we have some idea of the possible scale of vulnerability. It comes as no surprise to find, as a frequent theme in Euripides, the reception of strangers on Attic soil and the extent to which, and the ways in which, they are either exposed as *xenoi* (e.g. *Medeia*) or accepted within the community (*HF*, *Hik.*, *Herakl.*), or recognized as being truly Athenians (Theseus in the lost *Aigeus*, or, clearest of all, Ion in *Ion*): the xenophobia, and neurosis about status boundaries, which are expressed by the chorus in *Ion* are more starkly put than is dramatically necessary:[46] and this must be one reason for the continuing popularity of the Medeia theme in tragedy and art. So, too, notoriously, it becomes a recurring theme in Old Comedy to

---

[40] *IG* ii² 9152, 9662, and 10097. I exclude from consideration ii² 6727, since relationships are not specified and the nationality of [Arch]ebios Protophanou is lost. I also exclude the documents ii² 8088, 8527, 8768, and 8875, dated variously by Kirchner after 317/6 and after end 4th century B.C., since knowledge of them comes solely from Koumanoudis' copies.

[41] *IG* ii² 7379/8693, 8092, 8377, 8581, 8693, 9027, 9054, 9198, 9217, 9679, 9895, 9968, 9975, 10204, 10206, 10304, 10452. I have not attempted to track down evidence published since 1940, but should be very surprised if the picture were to be substantially changed.

[42] E.g. Karneades of Kyrene, envoy to Rome in 156/5, was Azenieus by 162 (*IG* ii² 3781: *PA* 8527).

[43] Pélékidis 186 ff. and 184 (table).

[44] Whether formally as *diapsephismos* [vote on individuals: equivalent to *diapsephisis*, above] or no does not matter here.

[45] Philochoros, *FGrH* 328 F 119: Plut. *Perikles* 37.4. See Jacoby's endless note *ad loc.* or (much crisper) A. W. Gomme, *The Population of Athens in the Fifth and Fourth Centuries B.C.* (Oxford, 1933) 16 f. Admittedly, it is quite unclear how the figure is reached, and Philochoros' underlying premiss, that there were 19,000 citizens prior to the disfranchisements, is untenable.

[46] Especially lines 722 and 1048 ff. I am very grateful to Professors Helen North and Judy Hallett for drawing my attention to the Euripidean evidence.

denigrate politicians by impugning their status as proper citizens.[47] The practice need have been no more than a game, and had certainly become so by the time of the exchange of insults between Demosthenes and Aischines, but the underlay is a lot more serious than that.

Similar anxieties can be seen in the fourth century, and reflect the continuing importance of status-boundaries. In 346/5, out of the blue, a decree of one Demophilos ordered all the demes to scrutinize their membership lists in a *diapsephismos*.[48] We do not know why, though some demes were certainly corrupt in admitting citizens improperly,[49] and it may be that several scandals had broken simultaneously. We are told that many were disfranchised as a result,[50] and two extant speeches arising out of disputed enfranchisements shed some light on current attitudes. The speaker of the longer speech, Demosthenes 57, was vulnerable partly because of existing quarrels and factions within the deme of Halimous, but mainly because his father had spoken with a foreign accent and his mother had been a wet-nurse and sold ribbons in the Agora.[51] In the briefer speech, Isaios 12, the speaker, half-brother of the man whose status was in question, produces among much family detail the illuminating comment that their father had no need to pass off a non-citizen as his adoptive son: 'You will find that all who do such things are compelled to adopt non-citizens either because they have no legitimate children or through poverty, in the hope that they may get some assistance from the adoptees who through them have become Athenians.'[52]

Another contemporary speech tells us even more. Demosthenes 59 turns on the career of the famous hetaira Neaira, daughter of a freedwoman of Charisios of Elis. By 380 she had begun her career, which took her, being bought and sold by successive lovers, from Athens to Korinth, to Athens, to Megara, then back to Athens in 371/0 under the protection of the politician Stephanos.[53] One of her daughters was given in marriage by Stephanos, as if (a) she were his and (b) she

---

[47] Kleon and Hyperbolos are the clearest examples, but there are many others. I am grateful to Mr. Philip Manville of Yale for reminding me of the relevance of the practice.

[48] Aischin. 1.77 and schol, 86, and 114: 2.182: Isaios 12 with Dionysios, *Isaios* 17: Harp. *s.v.* διαψήφισις: Dionysios, *Deinarchos* 11: Dem. 57: Wyse 714 ff.: A. Diller, *TAPA* 63 (1932) 193 ff.: A. W. Gomme, *CP* 29 (1934) 123 ff.

[49] See references *ap*. Jacoby, Commentary to *FGrH* 324 F 52, note 9.

[50] Dem. 57.2.

[51] Dem. 57.42 and 45: cf. also 18 ff. (on the father) and 30 ff. (on the mother).

[52] Isaios 12.2.

[53] Her position in Stephanos' household will have been like that of Aspasia in Perikles', or that of Chrysis, the Samian girl in Menandros' *Samia*, who is free (577) but foreign, cannot be *engyete*, and can be thrown out at will (369–398).

were a citizen, to a citizen, Phrastor of Aigilia, along with an enormous dowry of 3000 drachmai. However, Phrastor, described as 'a peasant who made his living parsimoniously' (§50), threw her out after a year, and the members of his *genos* refused to accept the legitimacy of his son by her. Nonetheless, she did better the second time, being given in marriage by Stephanos, again as his legitimate daughter, to no less a person than the Archon Basileus, one Theogenes, to whom Stephanos was currently serving as assessor.

Now, Apollodoros brought the case because of his political *inimicitia* ['enmity'] with Stephanos, and brought it against Neaira on the grounds (a) that she was not a citizen (which was clearly a justified allegation) and (b) that she was married to Stephanos (which Stephanos denied, and for which Apollodoros produced no convincing evidence). But for the political dimension, Stephanos would very probably have got away with it, for he chose his sons-in-law with care. The position of each made it foolish for him to enquire too closely into the status and legitimacy of the woman being offered to him as wife – Phrastor because he was a poor peasant being offered via the dowry a bribe to keep quiet, Theogenes because, though a poor man inexperienced in public affairs, he had suddenly become Basileus by the luck of the draw and needed a wife to perform the Basilinna's rituals on behalf of the State. We are in a twilight zone where the strength of ambitions to gain recognition of one's citizen status is evident both from the tactics and subterfuges of Neaira and Stephanos to gain it for Phano and from the sanctions, pressures, and political blackmail being used against them. Most revealing of all is the attitude of Apollodoros, himself the son of an ex-slave, citizen by decree of the State, and quite neurotically status-conscious both in this speech and elsewhere. His speech is a very important document indeed, not just for the demi-monde of the fourth-century hetairai [prostitutes] for which it is usually quoted, but as an exemplification of deep status-anxiety on all sides.

Moreover, such anxieties took new forms in the wake of the Makedonian occupation of Attika in 322. In the convulsions, (1) in 322 the full citizenship was confined, on Antipatros' orders, to those who owned property worth more than 2000 drachmai: 9000 remained as citizens, and either 12,000 or 22,000 were disfranchised.[54] (2) An edict of Polyperchon re-enfranchised them all as

---

[54] Diod. 18.18.4-5 (giving the figure 22,000): Plut. *Phokion* 28 (giving 12,000). Since Demetrios' census counted 21,000 citizens in 317 (Ktesikles *ap.* Athen. 6.272c) it is slightly more likely that Plutarch was right, but Gomme, *Population of Athens* 16–18, disagrees.

from 30 Xandikos (March) 318,[55] but (3) early in 317 the edict of
Kassandros which established the regency of Demetrios of Phaleron
also specified a minimum property qualification of 1000 drachmai
for citizenship.[56] (4) Though we have no direct evidence, that qualification was presumably abolished when democracy was restored in
307/6.[57]

Of course these measures, save for the last, were Makedonian
fiats, designed to secure Athenian allegiance, and therefore tell us
nothing by themselves about Athenian attitudes. Fortunately, one
contemporary source does. If one stands back from the wild complexities of Menandros' plots, they can be seen to share one primary
characteristic – an intense, even obsessive awareness of the status-
boundaries separating citizen from foreigner, citizen from slave,
well-born from low-born, legitimate from illegitimate, wife from
concubine, wealthy man from poor man from beggar. Plot after plot
is exploring this sensitive area and mediating a transition from one
status to another – always, of course, in the fantasy, in an upwards
direction. For example, the cardinal fact of *Heros* and *Epitrepontes*
is that young man rapes girl, and they subsequently marry without
knowing that the other was the person involved, while the children
born of the rape are exposed. However, they then turn up, to cause
embarrassments and suspicions till the heavy use of the *gnorismata*
['tokens of recognition'] motif makes everything straightforward
again between virtuous wife, mortified and repentant husband, and
(after all) legitimate children. Or again the *Sikyonios*, where Stratophanes is in love with Philoumene but (a) he though rich is a
Sikyonian and therefore a foreigner, and (b) she, though upper-class
Athenian by origin, had been kidnapped and sold as a slave, and
though Stratophanes knows her real status it will be hard to get it
publicly recognized. Difficulty (a) disappears when it emerges that
Stratophanes was 'really' an Athenian all the time: difficulty (b)
vanishes when Stratophanes' parasite Theron tries to find someone
to impersonate her father and just happens, as it were, to stumble
upon the one man, Kichesias, who can perform that role without
pretence. Since so much depends on citizenship, while for fifteen
years of Menandros' adult lifetime Athens was powerless to determine her own citizenship criteria, his obsession with the theme is
understandable: he was dealing with something of crucial contem-

[55] Diod. 18.56.
[56] Diod. 18.74.3.
[57] Thus W. S. Ferguson, *Hellenistic Athens* (London, 1911) 95.

porary importance. Of course, in his fantasies things come right in the end without the need for action and change, since the plots consist of discovering what is the case, which is what the participants want. In that sense Menandros is deeply escapist, since for the facts once discovered *not* to be as the participants want them to be would constitute a recipe for neurosis, tragedy, or revolution.

So much for the effect of the citizenship rules in their classical formulation, pervasive not just in decisions taken in public life but also in the consciousness of individuals. To go further, we need to be more formal, and to distinguish between [A] the inhabitants of a particular area or community, and [B] those who are citizens of that community in Aristotle's sense of sharing the holding of office and the administration of justice. No ancient society was prepared to define [B], the office-holding class, by identifying it with [A], even if it were amended to 'free adult males' by the exclusion of women and chattel slaves. The perpetual challenge was therefore to define a subsection of [A] such that it and [B] could be mutually defining categories. In Athenian terms we have to consider three possibilities:

1) those who were in the segmental descent groups that mattered (*gene*, phratries, and demes):
2) those who perform military and other essential roles on behalf of the State: and
3) those who have economic resources above a certain level.

Other possibilities obviously exist (e.g. those who are descended from gods: those who live in particular areas) but need not concern us.

In these formal terms, *Archaic Athens* (by which I mean *imprimis* the social structure and values encapsulated in Solon's legislation) cares mainly about defining class [B], the office-holders, moves strongly away from defining it in terms of a version of criterion (1) and towards defining it in terms of criterion (3) (wealth), and seems to think in terms of a highly permeable, perhaps non-existent, boundary between class [A] on the one hand and citizenship by criteria (1) and (2) on the other. *Classical Athens* still cares mainly about defining class [B], but does so purely in terms of criterion (1) (descent) (that amalgamation *being* citizen status), allows permeable boundaries between class [A] and criteria (2) and (up to a point) (3), but differentiates rigorously between class [A] and the subsection defined by criterion (1), and rejects suggestions of defining class [B] in any other way. *Hellenistic Athens*, in contrast, seems to move back towards defining class [B] in terms of criteria (2) and (3).

To expand these telegraphic remarks: it should be non-controversial that the replacement of Eupatridai ['well-born'] by Pentakosiomedimnoi ['five-hundred-bushel men'] represents a shift, in the definition of those entitled to hold office, away from a descent-group definition to a definition in terms of economic resources. More tricky, in a Solonian context, is to argue that the boundary between 'free residents' and 'citizens' became, or remained, permeable. The case rests mainly on a passage in Plutarch's *Solon*: 'His law concerning naturalized citizens is a surprising one, because it granted naturalization only to those who had been permanently exiled from their own country, or who had emigrated with their families to practise a trade. Solon's object here, we are told, was not so much to discourage other types of immigrant as to invite these particular categories to Athens with the assurance that they could become citizens there. He also judged that one could safely rely on the loyalty of men who had been compelled to leave their country, and also of those who had left it with a definite end in view.'[58] This tradition bristles with problems. Briefly and dogmatically put, I wish to maintain (a) that we have no good reason to reject Plutarch's report of this law, and (b) that enfranchisements probably were made under it. The case for (a) is not, I grant, watertight. Plutarch does ascribe to Solon some laws of dubious authenticity,[59] and we can only explain its transmission on the assumption that it was included among 'the laws of Solon that they no longer use'.[60] Yet, as we can see from *Ath. Pol.*, the texts of at least some laws in that category were available to fourth-century scholars, while the main motive for invention does not apply: precisely with this law[61] we are not dealing with a later adaptation of Wortlaut [the wording] to meet changed conditions but with a law which had been totally superseded and was capable of causing 'surprise' to Plutarch or his source. Tentatively, I take the law as genuine. The case that enfranchisements were made under it is fragile too. It depends partly on what most scholars accept, that there were craftsmen immigrants to Athens in the sixth century,[62] partly on noting that Plutarch's law does not envisage metic status but citizen

---

[58] 24.4, tr. I. Scott-Kilvert.
[59] Cf. E. Ruschenbusch, *Solonos Nomoi* (*Historia* Einzelschriften 9 [1966]) 46 f.
[60] *Ath. Pol.* 8.3.
[61] F 75 Ruschenbusch (p. 98). The word πανεστίοις ['with all the hearth, i.e. household'] in Plutarch's text seems to be a *hapax* [unique occurrence of the word] but I see no means of telling whether that fact tells for or against genuineness.
[62] Cf. most recently D.A. Jackson, *East Greek Influence on Attic Vase-Painters* (Hellenic Society Supplementary Papers 13 [1976]) 80 ff. Add the graffito of a sixth-century Megarian in Athens: M. Lang, *Graffiti in the Athenian Agora* (Agora Picture Book 14 [1974]) no. 18.

status and uses the word μετοικιζομένοις ['migrating'] of a process of change of domicile, not of status as residents, and partly on the evidence from the Kleisthenic period that there were such people whose status caused problems.

To them, and to the classical period, I now turn. I am concerned here partly with *how* and *when* the classical pattern emerged, and partly with the alternatives which were rejected, leaving the *why* of the matter till last. The first problem is dating the emergence of metic status. By this I mean not the *de facto* [actual] presence of *xenoi* in Athens but the formalization of their status as permanent residents with obligations and limited rights: to pay the *metoikion* [tax levied on *metoikoi*, 'migrants', i.e. non-citizen residents], to have access to certain festivals, to be registered with the polemarch and to be liable for military service, and to be excluded from the political process and from property-owning. To go backwards: metics as such are serving by 431 as hoplites, and are participating as such in Lenaia, probably from *ca.* 440.[63] In his later plays Aischylos was using words such as *metoikos, metoikein* freely,[64] but we have no evidence here that metic status was regularized by then. So too, for obvious reasons, we can place no weight on the way in which the Themistokles Decree speaks of foreigners in Athens.[65] To go back further brings us hard up against the intractable difficulties of determining whether Kleisthenes' reforms did or did not put into the tribes and into the citizen body all the free residents of Attika, including those whose correlates 60 years later were being classed as metics. The case turns, notoriously, on the Aristotelian tradition about the *neopolitai* ['new citizens']. *Ath. Pol.* knows of a *diapsephismos*, passed in the wake of the expulsion of the tyrants, which excluded some Peisistratid supporters who were 'of impure descent' (τῷ γένει μὴ καθαροί, 13.5). The author also claims that Kleisthenes broached his tribal reforms, 'offering the citizenship (?) to the people' (ἀποδιδοὺς τῷ πλήθει τὴν πολιτείαν, 20.1: the translation is disputed), that they were adopted 'in order that more might share in the citizenship' (ὅπως μετάσχωσι πλείους τῆς πολιτείας, 21.2), and that appellation by demotic was adopted 'to prevent people addressing them with a patronymic and thereby exposing the new citizens' (21.4). Aristotle *seems* to reflect the same tradition in saying that at Athens after the expulsion of the tyrants Kleisthenes 'put into tribes many foreigners

---

[63] Thuc. 2.31.2: Davies, *JHS* 87 (1967) 34: D. M. Lewis, *Hesperia* 37 (1968) 380.
[64] See G. Italie, *Index Aeschyleus* (Leiden, 1964) *s.vv.* μετοικέω, μετοικία, μέτοικος.
[65] ML 23, lines 7 and 30–1.

and slave metics'.[66] The tradition has long been a battleground,[67] for it differs so noticeably from Herodotos' account, though the latter is the basis of *Ath. Pol.*'s narrative, that Jacoby roundly declared that the whole tradition was a fourth-century invention.[68] I should normally have much sympathy with such a view, and have no doubt that we have to do with fourth-century re-working, but for various reasons am reluctant to deny the existence of a historical kernel. First, the decrees which are suspected of being fourth-century fabrications or re-creations all share the characteristics of displaying the generosity and patriotism of the Athenian people in Panhellenic affairs and in a favourable light:[69] neither characteristic is to be seen here, either in fact or in presentation. Secondly, as we can see, the tone and direction of the tradition go directly against classical Athenian views on citizenship, while Kleisthenes is called in aid in fourth-century publicistic, but his role there (as in 411) was as the founder of democracy acceptable to conservatives.[70] Again, I should not wish to argue that the putative *neopolitai were* Kleisthenes' support, or to deny that *Ath. Pol.* has redirected and misinterpreted Herodotos' account. The point is, rather, that it is agreed that *Ath. Pol.* or his source had additional material about the Kleisthenic period – dates, detail about the tribal reforms, the Leipsydrion skolion – which he incorporated into a basically Herodotean narrative. The same is evidently the case for the motif of enfranchisement. His statement at 13.4 concerning support for Peisistratos is buttressed by a *semeion* ['sign'], namely the purifying *diapsephismos*. That is to say, his evidence *consists of* the *diapsephismos*, from which he is making an interpretative inference. Similarly, the motives which

---

[66] Arist. *Pol.* 1275 b 35 ff.: οἷον <ἃ> Ἀθήνησιν ἐποίησε Κλεισθένης, μετὰ τὴν τῶν τυράννων ἐκβολήν· πολλοὺς γὰρ ἐφυλέτευσε ξένους καὶ δούλους μετοίκους. The last word is commonly regarded as a gloss, but ξένος μέτοικος is certainly good fifth-century language. Cf. Ar. *Knights* 347, Soph. *O.T.* 452, and Harrison I 188.

[67] G. Busolt, *Griechische Geschichte*, II² (Gotha, 1895) 409; K. J. Beloch, *Griechische Geschichte*², I. 1 (Strassburg, 1912) 396 n. 2; H. T. Wade-Gery, *Essays in Greek History* (Oxford, 1958), 148 ff. (= *CQ* 27 [1933] 25 f.); C. Hignett, *A History of the Athenian Constitution* (Oxford, 1952) 132 ff.

[68] Commentary on Androtion, *FGrH* 324 F52, pp. 158 ff. He is followed by J. Day and M. Chambers, *Aristotle's History of Athenian Democracy* (Berkeley and Los Angeles, 1962) 117 f.

[69] To the list dressed by C. Habicht, *Hermes* 89 (1961) 17 ff., add the Congress Decree (R. Seager, *Historia* 18 (1969) 129 ff.), the decree for Aristeides' children (*APF* **1695, IV**), the decree for the sons of Hippokrates of Kos (Hippokr. ed Littré, 9, IX, p. 401), and, I now begin to think, Anytos' decree for Herodotos (*PA* 1321) and Plutarch's version of the Megarian decrees. I shall discuss the point in greater detail elsewhere.

[70] Isok. 7.16 and 59: *Ath. Pol.* 29.3. See K. Jost, *Das Beispiel und Vorbild der Vorfahren bei den attischen Rednern und Geschichtsschreibern* (Paderborn, 1936) 131.

he gives Kleisthenes at 21.2 and 21.4 are each followed by a 'whence' (ὅθεν) introducing what for him counts as supporting evidence for the interpretation – at 21.2 the existence of the slogan 'not to make tribal distinctions' (μὴ φυλοκρινεῖν), at 21.4 the creation and continued use of demotics.

In sum, then, the argument is that Aristotle and *Ath. Pol.* did have some fragments of extra evidence; that though these led them to an unHerodotean view of Kleisthenes which most of us would regard as a misinterpretation, the evidence remains evidence; that there were people in Attika in 510 who had been made citizens under Solon's enfranchisement law; that they were among those deprived of citizenship by a *diapsephismos* after the end of the tyranny; that those same people were re-enfranchised and enrolled in demes in the course of Kleisthenes' legislation; and that nothing in the evidence suggests that there were in Athens about 500 B.C., say, any free men who were not citizens. If I am wrong about this, then the chronological focus for the emergence of metic status has to be considerably broader: but if I am right, then we can see the legislation as the pivot round which Athenian concepts of citizenship were drastically realigned. On the one hand Kleisthenes was being Solonian, keeping the boundaries open between class [A] (the inhabitants) and its sub-sections by actually equating class [A] with that sub-section of it defined by criterion (1) (though perhaps *hoc tantum* ['this only'] and certainly not without a struggle): and this was possible because he was still being Solonian in not significantly changing or enlarging society's definition of the office-holders (still basically defined by criterion (3), of wealth). On the other hand the formalization of citizenship round the demes and in terms of the present demesmen and their descendants meant that the equation of class [A] with its sub-section was momentary, and that in the absence of gerrymandering, corruption, or new legislation, all other residents were *xenoi*. Once matters had taken such a turn, we can see how the broadening of the criteria for office-holding (to the point where class [B] came to be defined in terms of criterion (1) of descent, taken as a base-line), the increasing value of citizenship outside Attika, and the influx of *xenoi*, created pressure at the margins: at which point Perikles' citizenship law, closing the one remaining loophole, makes perfect political sense.

We can now look at the alternative in more detail. First, those in the air, or on paper, in the late fifth century. I catalogue them summarily. (1) The oligarchic programme of 411 specified, *inter alia* [among other things], that 'not more than 5000 should take part in public affairs, and these were to be those most able to contribute with their moneys and their bodies'.[71] (2) Just after the restoration of democracy in autumn 403 one Phormisios proposed that citizenship should not be for all, but for those who posses land: and our source adds that about 5000 persons would have been disfranchised had the proposal gone through, as it evidently did not.[72] (3) In the same context a decree of Thrasyboulos offered citizenship 'to all those who had come down together from Phyle' (though some, we are told, were 'plainly slaves'), and/or offering '*isoteleia* to all who fought with them even if they were *xenoi*'. However, the decree was indicted successfully on a *paranomon* [illegal proposal] charge by Archinos.[73] (4) Instead, and also in the same context, a decree of Archinos gave monetary and ceremonial honours to those who took part in the capture of Phyle.[74] (5) Also in the same context a law proposed by Aristophon re-enacted Perikles' citizenship law.[75] (6) Also in the same context Nikomenes proposed what was in effect a rider to (5), providing that the law was to apply only to those born (*or* coming of age: our source is opaque) after 403/2.[76] (7) Also in the same context or soon after, a decree of Theozotides granted public maintenance to the sons of those Athenians who died a violent death in the oligarchy while helping the democracy, but it excluded illegitimate or adopted sons from the privilege.[77] (8) Probably in 401/0 a further decree of Archinos seems to have re-enacted the graduated privileges, of citizenship or *isoteleia*, to the partisans of Phyle in much the same terms as the decree of Thrasyboulos (no. (3) above) which Archinos himself had had rescinded.[78] (9) In 396/5 a decree of the phratry of the Dekeleieis laid down: 'Whoever have not yet been scrutinized according to the Nomos of the Demotionidai, the Phrateres shall make scrutiny of them forthwith, after swearing by Zeus Phratrios, carrying their votes from the altar. Whoever seems, not being a Phrater, to have been introduced, his name shall be expunged by the priest and the Phratriarch from the list which is

---

[71] Thuc. 8.65.3. Cf. also Thuc. 8.53.1 and 3, and *Ath. Pol.* 29.5, with P. J. Rhodes, *JHS* 92 (1972) 115 ff.

[72] Lysias 34, with Dionysios' introduction (*Lysias* 32). It is not clear how Dionysios knows the figure of 5000, whether from the portion of the speech which he does not quote, or from the account of an Atthidographer: nor is it clear how either of them would have known.

[73] *Ath. Pol.* 40.2: Xen. *Hell.* 2.4.25.

[74] Aischin. 3.187: *Hesperia* 10 (1941) 287 no. 78.

[75] Dem. 59.16 and 52: Athen. 13.577 b–c.

[76] Schol. Aischin. 1.39.

[77] *P. Hibeh* I no. 14: R. S. Stroud, *Hesperia* 40 (1971) 280 ff., esp. 297 ff.

[78] Tod *GHI* II 100 = D. Hereward, *BSA* 47 (1952) 102 ff. In his comments at Princeton Professor Badian cast strong doubt on the current interpretation of this document.

in the archives of the Demotionidai and from the copy': and so on, specifying procedure at great length and detail.[79]

Apart from the enfranchisements made under (8), the net result of this barrage of legislation was to re-establish the post-451 status quo. All attempts to redefine class [B] in economic status terms, or in terms of service to the State (i.e. by forms of criteria (2) or (3)) were rejected, and its definition in descent-group terms was ostentatiously reaffirmed. As we have seen, the same thing was to happen again after the convulsions of the late fourth century, and we have to wait till 167/6 for any evidence that Athens was prepared off her own bat to redefine her citizenship qualifications. The evidence consists of a waspish remark of Polybios, in a context, of 167/6 B.C., about the Athenian claim to the territory of Haliartos: 'to make their own country common to everyone, while destroying that of others, would not seem to be in accord with the city's traditions.'[80] As known instances show, we have to do not just with the annexation of Delos, Lemnos, and Haliartos, but with a deliberate admission of *xenoi*. Two routes in are detectable. First, we know that *xenoi* were admitted to the ephebate, at Delos between 150 and 140 and at Athens between 128/7 and 119/8.[81] Given that in many other Hellenistic cities the ephebate became the, or a, criterion of citizenship,[82] analogy suggests the same possibility for Athens, and there is a rough correlation between the disappearance of *xenoi* ephebes at some date after 39/8[83] and the restrictions imposed by Augustus in 21 B.C. However, and secondly, Augustus' action in that year was to forbid the Athenians from making anyone a citizen for money.[84] The example of Atticus[85] is proof enough that what Augustus was prohibiting had taken place, even if we cannot certainly name other men thus enfranchised or say whether the procedure was regular, with a fixed tariff, or occasional.

More to the point, this was not a practice new in the second century B.C. Louis Robert has collected instances from Phaselis at

[79] *IG* ii² 1237, with Wade-Gery, *Essays in Greek History* 116 ff.

[80] Pol. 30.20.6.

[81] *I. de Délos* 1922 ff. for Delos. For Athens *Hesperia* 24 (1955) 228 ff., of 128/7 (archon Dionysios) has no *xenoi*: *IG* ii² 1006, of 123/2, is broken: and *IG* ii² 1008, of 119/8 (archon Hipparchos) does have *xenoi*. See Pélékidis 186 ff.: O. W. Reinmuth, *TAPA* 79 (1948) 219 ff.: and D. Geagan, *The Athenian Constitution after Sulla* (*Hesperia* Supp. 12 [1967]) 76.

[82] See Pélékidis 188 f.

[83] They are listed in *IG* ii² 1043 of 39/8 (archon Menandros) but not, e.g., in *IG* ii² 1963. *IG* ii² 1965, which has Milesians and other *xenoi*, will then have to be dated before 21 B.C.

[84] Dio 54. 7.2. I note, but do not pursue here, P. Graindor's argument that Augustus' action is better dated *ca.* 31 (*Athènes sous Auguste* [Cairo, 1927] 16 ff.).

[85] Nepos, *vita Attici* 3.2.

an unknown date, from Achaia, Ephesos, Aspendos, Thasos, and Byzantion, as well as from elsewhere in the Roman period.[86] Tariffs vary, as do the criteria for eligibility, but the idea would certainly have been accessible at least to fourth-century Athens. Moreover, some of the enfranchisements that fourth-century Athens did permit herself reflect the same thinking. Some admittedly reflect rather criterion (2) (service to the State), such as those of the diplomat Herakleides of Klazomenai (*PA* 6489) or of the commanders Phrasierides and Charidemos,[87] but others are purely financial. The enfranchisements of the banker Pasion and his son Apollodoros must come into this group, as do those of the bankers Epigenes and Konon, Chairephilos the salt-fish seller and others during the corn-shortage of the 320s.[88] It is clear from the parallels elsewhere in Greece that the attractions of the practice were above all fiscal, since cities thereby got much-needed extra revenue. Just so the Byzantines acted, 'in need of money' according to [Aristotle's] *Oikonomika*,[89] but if the practice was acceptable to a late Hellenistic Athens chronically in debt even though her military expenses were by then minimal, we ask all the more why it was not adopted more systematically during Athens' endemic financial crises after 413.

Again, the other alternatives were attractive and had logic behind them. The formulation 'those able to help the state with moneys and bodies' emanates indeed from oligarchic circles in 411, but by itself it is not a formula for oligarchy. It could and did encompass the award of citizenship to Phrynichos' assassins in 409,[90] or the post-403 enfranchisements for services rendered proposed by Thrasyboulos and later by Archinos (nos. (3) and (8) above). The same principle, at the level of manumission, rather than of enfranchisement, for military services to be rendered, can be seen in the freeing of slaves to row at Arginousai[91] and possibly at Aigospotamoi too,[92] or in Hypereides' proposal after Chaironeia to manumit 150,000 slaves in the silver mines and the rest of the country 'so that the free should not be slaves' and 'so that all in unity of purpose might fight for the country'.[93] Even the Old Oligarch recognized the logic of the

---

[86] L. Robert, *Hellenica* I (Limoges, 1940) 37–41.
[87] *APF* 14976 and 15380.
[88] Deinarchos 1.43: *APF* 15187.
[89] 2.2.3, 1346 b 13 ff.
[90] ML 85, lines 15 ff. For the problems about Agoratos see ML's commentary.
[91] Xen. *Hell.* 1.6.24: Hellanikos, *FGrH* 323a F 25: Ar. *Frogs* 190 and 693 with schol.
[92] Or whatever naval battle it was that is commemorated by *IG* ii² 1951.
[93] Hypereides F 27–29. It is not quite certain that he envisaged slaves as fighting, for the words 'so that all in unity of purpose might fight for the country' are applied to the *atimoi* ['deprived of rights']: but it is hard to see what other purpose Hypereides can have had in mind.

argument that since 'it is the *demos* which drives the ships and gives the city its power, ... it is just for all to share in allotted and elected office, and that any citizen who wished should be able to speak.'[94] So too the speaker of Lysias 34 argued against Phormisios' proposal by saying that it would exclude 'many hoplites and cavalrymen and archers, by retaining whom you will protect the democracy more securely, will defeat your adversaries more, and will be more useful to your allies'(§4).

The timocratic criterion also had attractions, though of a different order. We are told, for example, that the immediate motive of those who imposed it after 322 was not to concentrate attention on the hoplites (which was the last thing Antipatros, Kassandros, or Demetrios wanted) but to rid the State of the 'troublesome and warlike'.[95] However, especially with Demetrios and his links with Theophrastos and Aristotle, we also have to see some reflexion of Aristotle's theory of citizenship as developed in *Politics* book 3, where he moves from a functional definition of citizenship in terms of sharing permanently in the administration of justice and the holding of office, through an exploration of the nature of the good citizen, to an exploration of the problem posed by the existence of *banausoi* ['artisans']. To the question 'Are they citizens?' he ultimately replies, 'The truth is that we cannot include as citizens all who are necessary conditions of the State's existence': 'the best form of state will not make the mechanic a citizen.'[96] Though the pogrom of 306 against Theophrastos and the philosophical schools is readily understandable,[97] theories of citizenship which would make 'full citizen' and 'those who display virtue (ἀρετή) and/or have the necessary leisure and skills' mutually defined groups were and are extremely hard to rebut on their own ground.

The descent-group criterion of citizenship, then, was under pressure and attack from many sides. It lasted so long, I think, not because it was natural and logical, or because it was uncontentious, but because it represented the least troublesome compromise among violently opposing forces. Against the criterion of 'service to the State' it was objective, relying on the establishable facts of descent, while 'service to the State' was ambiguous, depending on the mode of service, or the nature of fighting equipment, which was selected as

---

[94] [Xen.] *Ath. Pol.* 1.2.
[95] Diod. 18.18.4.
[96] Arist. *Pol.* 3.5.2–3, 1278 a 3 and 8.
[97] Cf. too how anger caused by the deprivation of citizenship fuelled the lynching of Phokion in 317 (Diod. 18.66.6).

the criterion. Against oligarchic pressure it gave a guarantee of status and privilege even to those who had no other goods or skills or claims to honour. Against outsiders it ensured that those statuses and privileges remained economically and politically valuable, and pressure from outsiders could just be accommodated inside the descent system providing that the inflow remained only a trickle. Time and time again, interest in its continuance was stronger than interest in its overthrow. Its erosion came only when, with the disappearance of pay for public service at a date not closely determinable in the third century B.C. and the decline in importance of decisions taken in the assembly, the lower boundary of citizen status ceased to be identical with the lower boundary of the actual class of serious office-holders (lists of Councillors notwithstanding), so that other factors – especially, I suspect, fiscal – could count more. Whether, on the other hand, we should be right in attributing the creation of the classical system to the same forces as those which kept it in being once created is another question.

2 How Did the Athenian Ecclesia Vote?*

MOGENS HERMAN HANSEN

I

In classical Athens two kinds of voting were employed: the assembly voted by a show of hands and the popular court by ballot. The vote by ballot is known in every detail thanks to the account given by Aristotle in the *Constitution of Athens* 68–69 and to the discovery of several bronze *psephoi* [ballots] of the classical period. The *cheirotonia* ["show of hands"] however, is described neither by Aristotle nor by any other contemporary author and, although in this case archaeological evidence seems to be ruled out, it is in fact the excavations of the Pnyx which constitute the basis of the two most recent discussions of the subject by A. L. Boegehold and E. S. Staveley.[1] In discussing the Athenian voting procedure we are once

---

* Originally published in *Greek, Roman and Byzantine Studies* (Duke University, Durham, North Carolina) xviii 1977, 123–37; republished with addenda (here pp. 55–61) on pp. 103–21 of M. H. Hansen, *The Athenian Ecclesia: A Collection of Articles, 1976–1983* (Opuscula Graecolatina vol. 26. Copenhagen: Museum Tusculanum Press, 1983. Copyright © Mogens Herman Hansen and Museum Tusculanum Press); reprinted with the permission of the author, *Greek, Roman and Byzantine Studies* and Museum Tusculanum Press. Obeli † *in the outer margin* of the main text refer to the addenda.

[1] References in this article, hereafter cited by author's name and page number, are to: A. L. Boegehold, "Toward a Study of Athenian Voting Procedure," *Hesperia* 32 (1963) 366–74. C. G. Brandis, "Ἐκκλησία," *RE* 5 (1905) 2163–2200. G. Busolt and H. Swoboda, *Griechische Staatskunde* I–II (München 1920–26). J. Delz, *Lukians Kenntnis der athenischen Antiquitäten* (Freiburg 1950). E. B. England, *The Laws of Plato* I–II (London 1921). K. von Fritz and E. Kapp, *Aristotle's Constitution of Athens and Related Texts* (New York 1950). D. J. Geagan, *The Athenian Constitution after Sulla* (*Hesperia* Suppl. 12, 1967). G. Gilbert, *Handbuch der griechischen Staatsalterthümer* I (Leipzig 1893). M. H. Hansen, "How Many Athenians Attended the *Ecclesia*?," *GRBS* 17 (1976) 115–34 [= *The Athenian Ecclesia*, 1–23]. Hansen, "The Duration of a Meeting of the Athenian *Ecclesia*," *CP* 74 (1979) 43–9 [= *The Athenian Ecclesia*, 131–8], Hansen, *The Sovereignty of the People's Court in Athens in the Fourth Century B.C. and the Public Action against Unconstitutional Proposals* (Odense 1974). E. Koch, "Χειροτονεῖν," *RE* 3 (1899) 2225–26. K. Kourouniotes and H. A. Thompson, "The Pnyx in Athens," *Hesperia* 1 (1932) 90–217. J. H. Lipsius, *Das attische Recht und Rechtsverfahren* I–III (Leipzig 1905–15). W. A. McDonald, *The Political Meeting Places of the Greeks* (Baltimore 1943). G. R. Morrow, *Plato's Cretan City* (Princeton 1960). D. J. Mosley, *Envoys and Diplomacy in Ancient Greece* (*Historia* Einzelschriften 22, 1973). J. E. Neale, *The Elizabethan House of Commons* (London 1949). J. H. Oliver, *The Sacred Gerousia*

more faced with the curious fact that the working of the people's court is abundantly attested, whereas the *ecclesia* [assembly] is shrouded in mystery because of the silence of our sources. If the scanty evidence, however, is combined with an *a priori* [from cause to effect] argument, it should be possible to reconstruct a fairly reliable picture of how the Athenians passed their decrees and elected their officials.

In the orators the vote taken by the people is described either with the verb *psephizesthai* ["to ballot"] or with the verb *cheirotonein* ["to show hands"]. Whereas *psephizesthai*, in the fourth century at least, must be interpreted metaphorically,[2] we have sufficient evidence that *cheirotonein* has to be taken in the literal sense of the word. In Aristophanes' *Ecclesiazusae* (262–65) the women are reminded that on the Pnyx they have to raise their arms instead of (as usual) their legs; and Xenophon (*Hell.* 1.7.7) provides us with the valuable information that the majority was assessed by surveying the assembly: he tells us that the first *ecclesia* hearing the trial of the generals was adjourned because it was too late to see the hands. Several sources state that the *cheirotonia* took the form of a diacheirotonia [choice between alternatives]. When the people voted on a single proposal, first the ayes and then the nays were asked to raise their hands;[3] and similarly, when the choice was between two proposals, the chairman asked first for those supporting proposal A and then for those supporting proposal B.[4] So the voting was conducted by stages, and this is sufficient proof that the citizens raised their hands while seated and that no kind of division was applied. It is apparent from Lysias 12.75 that a citizen might abstain from voting, but the number of abstentions was probably not assessed, since all sources dealing with *diacheirotonia* mention only *two* successive stages.

So far we are on safe ground. The difficulties accumulate when we

---

(*Hesperia* Suppl. 6, 1947). H. Ryffel, *Die schweizerischen Landsgemeinden* (Zürich 1903). J. F. Sly, *Town Government in Massachusetts* 1620–1930 (Cambridge [Mass.] 1930). E. S. Staveley, *Greek and Roman Voting and Elections* (London 1972). W. Stauffacher, *Die Versammlungsdemokratie im kanton Glarus* (Zürich 1963). A Wilhelm, "Neue Beiträge zur griechischen Inschriftenkunde," *SBWien* 183 (1921) 1–79. Wilhelm, "Zu griechischen Inschriften," *Archäologisch-epigraphische Mitteilungen aus Österreich-Ungarn* 20 (1897) 79–82. The scattered publications of the bronze *psephoi* are collected by Boegehold 366 n.1. All the *psephoi* are dated by letter forms to the fourth century B.C.
  [2] When describing decisions made by the *ecclesia* the verb *psephizesthai* is often used synonymously with *cheirotonein*, e.g., Isoc. 8.52.
  [3] Dem. 22.5 and 9, 24.20, 59.4–5; Aeschin. 3.39. The councillors: Arist. *Ath. Pol.* 49.2; *IG* II² 223 A 5.
  [4] *IG* I² 57 .5ff; Xen. *Hell.* 1.7.34; Dem. 24.33 (the *nomothetai* ["law-enacters," the body which in the fourth century enacted *nomoi*, "laws"]); Dem. 47.43 (the councillors).

seek to know the officials in charge of the *cheirotonia* and the method
of assessing the majority. Concerning the fifth century we are (as
usual) almost ignorant of the procedure. The only relevant source
is Arist. *Ath. Pol.* 30.5, a paper constitution of 411 B.C. prescribing
that a board of five councillors chosen by lot be entrusted with the
cheirotoniai. Under the democratic constitution it may be assumed
that the *prytaneis* ["presidents," the fifty councillors from one tribe]
were responsible for deciding the outcome of the vote, but the
assumption is no more than an argument from analogy with the
following period.[5] The fourth-century evidence is more satisfactory:
from about 380 the *ecclesiai* were presided over by the nine *proedroi*,
and two sources state that the vote was conducted and the show of
hands assessed by this board of councillors (Aeschin. 3.3; Arist. *Ath.
Pol.* 44.3).

In most treatments of the Athenian voting procedure it is
cautiously suggested without any discussion of the problem that
an exact count of the votes might possibly be omitted in a *procheirotonia* or when a proposal was passed by an overwhelming majority.[6]
But it is taken for granted that usually the votes were counted with
precision, and the main source οἱ πρόεδροι ... τὰς χειροτονίας
κρίνουσιν (*Ath. Pol.* 44.3) is unhesitatingly rendered by the phrase
"the *proedroi* ... count the votes" (von Fritz/Kapp 118; Boegehold
373). It is admitted that the count of several thousands of hands is
no simple task, but the inference has been that the Athenians attending the *ecclesia* must have been ordered into groups on the Pnyx and
that each of the tellers must have been responsible for the count
of one of the sections of the auditorium. This has led to the further
inference that the citizens were grouped according to their tribes. So
there must have been ten tellers and, faced with the problem that the
proedroi numbered only nine, the solution has been to call in the
ἐπιστάτης τῶν πρυτάνεων ["foreman of the *prytaneis*"] as the tenth
enumerator.[7] Only slight evidence can be produced in support of this
elaborate reconstruction:

1. The assumption that the citizens were ordered into groups (the
ten phylae ["tribes"]) is based entirely on archaeological evidence

---

[5] We know that in the fourth century the *proedroi* ["chairmen," a board instituted early in
the fourth century] were responsible for (a) putting a proposal to the vote and (b) assessing the
majority. We have ample evidence that the *prytaneis* in the fifth century were responsible for
putting the proposals to the vote (e.g., Xen. *Hell.* 1.7.14–15), and by analogy we may assume
that they were entrusted with the decision on the outcome of the vote.

[6] Gilbert 332; Busolt/Swoboda 1002; Koch 2226; Boegehold 373; Staveley 86.

[7] Staveley 86; cf. Boegehold 374.

which is difficult to interpret. Describing the Pnyx of the first period (*ca.* 500–*ca.* 404), the excavators state that "a number of stele beddings cut in the rock surface suggest that the seating area was divided in some manner" (Kourouniotes/Thompson 104) … "It is uncertain whether we have to do with a formal arrangement according to which the citizens were required to seat themselves" (p. 105). In addition to the *a priori* assumption that the votes must have been counted, these cuttings are in fact the principal evidence for the theory proposed by Beogehold and Staveley. In my opinion too much has been based on the excavators' cautious statements and, even supposing that the auditorium was subdivided in some way or another, we need not draw the conclusion that this arrangement was based on the *phylae* and introduced in order to facilitate the *count* of the votes.

2. The evidence of the count of votes is even more doubtful. The only source which can be cited is a note on the *lemma* [phrase commented on] κατεχειροτόνησεν αὐτοῦ:[8] ἀντὶ τοῦ κατεψηφίσατο αὐτοῦ. καταχειροτονία δὲ καὶ ἀποχειροτονία διαφέρει. καταχειροτονία μὲν γὰρ ἐγένετο οὕτως. ἔλεγεν ὁ κῆρυξ· ὅτῳ Μειδίας δοκεῖ ἀδικεῖν, ἀράτω τὴν χεῖρα· εἶτα οἱ θέλοντες ἐξέτεινον τὰς χεῖρας, καὶ ἐκαλεῖτο τοῦτο πρῶτον καταχειροτονία. ἀποχειροτονία δὲ οὕτως· ὅτῳ μὴ δοκεῖ ἀδικεῖν Μειδίας, ἀράτω τὴν χεῖρα· καὶ ἐξέτεινόν τινες, καὶ ἐκαλεῖτο ἀποχειροτονία. λοιπὸν πάσας ἠρίθμουν τὰς χεῖρας καὶ ἑώρα ὁ κῆρυξ ποῖαι πλείους εἰσί, πότερον τῶν φασκόντων αὐτὸν ἀδικεῖν ἢ μή· καὶ ὅσαι ἂν εἴησαν πλείους εὑρεθεῖσαι, ἐκείνη ἡ γνώμη ἐκράτει.* In this comment on Demothenes' speech *Against Meidias* it is unequivocally stated that the votes were counted, but it is worth noting that the official responsible for the count is the *keryx* [herald]. This is inconsistent with the fact that, in the fourth century, the *proedroi* were entrusted with the assessment of the *cheirotoniai*. We know, however, that the *keryx* of the *boule* [council] and the *demos*, who in the classical period was an insignificant official, rose to prominence in the Roman period and

---

[8] Schol. Dem. 21.2 (Baiter and Sauppe). The same note is reproduced by several other scholiasts and lexicographers, cf. Photius, *Suda, Etym. Magn.*, *s.v.* κατεχειροτόνησαν αὐτοῦ ["they hand-voted him down"] and schol. Plat. *Axiochus* 368E.

* "'Hand-voted him down': Instead of 'balloted him down.' 'Hand-voting down' and 'hand-voting free' are different. Hand-voting down happened like this: the herald said, 'Whoever thinks Meidias is in the wrong, raise his hand'; then those who wished showed forth their hands, and this was originally called 'hand-voting down.' Hand-voting free was like this: 'Whoever does not think Meidias is in the wrong, raise his hand'; and some showed forth, and it was called 'hand-voting free.' Then they counted all the hands, and the herald saw which were the more numerous, those of the men saying he was in the wrong or not; and, whichever were found to be the more numerous, that opinion prevailed."

that he then ranked as one of the three most important officials in Athens.[9] The scholion is a comment on a passage in Demosthenes, but it cannot be adduced as reliable evidence for the conditions of the fourth century B.C. since it refers to institutions of the Roman period. Moreover, it is apparent from a decree preserved on stone that a proposal was put to the vote by the *proedroi* even in the third century.[10] So I conclude that the note found in the scholia and the lexica has no value at all even for the Roman period.[11]

3. Aristotle's famous comment on the Spartan voting procedure may indirectly shed some light on the Athenian *cheirotonia*. The Spartan voting *boei* ["by shouting"] is described as childish [*paidariodes*] *Pol.* 1271a10). The implication seems to be that the Athenian form of voting by a show of hands was the "adult" procedure. But on this assumption Aristotle's comment may be interpreted as an indication that the hands were counted: the Spartan way of voting is childish when compared with a *cheirotonia* because it is impossible to *count* the votes. In my opinion, however, there is an important difference between the Spartan and the Athenian voting procedure even when the majority in a *cheirotonia* was assessed on a rough estimate only. The right explanation of Aristotle's scornful remark may be that by voting *viva voce* [orally] a person may assume more than one vote by shouting loudly. If, for example, a proposal is supported by 1000 citizens moderately in favour of the scheme, but vehemently opposed by 800, the "nays" may have it simply by shouting more energetically than the "ayes". Accepting the principle "one man, one vote," one can describe the Spartan system as childish compared with the Athenian, although neither of the voting procedures entails a count of the votes.

II

Thus we are left with an *a priori* argument as the principal basis for the assumption that a *cheirotonia* in Athens entailed a count of the

---

[9] Geagan 104–06.

[10] Geagan 89; Oliver, nos. 31 and 32.

[11] In *Hermotimus* 16 Lucian suggests that a *cheirotonia* was decided either by estimating or by counting votes: ΛΥΚ: πόσῳ τινὶ πλείους τῶν Ἐπικουρείων ἢ Πλατωνικῶν ἢ Περιπατητικῶν; ἠρίθμησας γὰρ αὐτοὺς δηλαδὴ καθάπερ ἐν ταῖς χειροτονίαις. ΕΡΜ: ἀλλ' οὐκ ἠρίθμησα ἔγωγε, εἴκαζον δε [LYCINUS How many more (Stoics are there) than Epicureans or Platonists or Peripatetics? Evidently you counted them as in shows of hands. HERMOTIMUS No, I did not count; I estimated.] Lucian's information, however, hardly has any value as a source for this problem. First, it is not stated whether the reference is to an *ecclesia* or a *boule*. Second, assuming that Lucian has an *ecclesia* in mind, we do not know whether he refers to the Athenian *ecclesia* attended by several thousand citizens or to an *ecclesia* in a small *polis*. Third, Lucian's casual references to the Athenian *ecclesia* in the classical period bristle with misunderstandings and anachronisms. Cf. Delz 115–50.

hands. But this argument is contradicted by another *a priori* argument based on a careful consideration of how the Athenian *ecclesia* worked. I have argued elsewhere[12] that the meetings of the Athenian *ecclesia* were usually attended by 6000 citizens. In Boegehold's and Staveley's reconstruction each of the tellers must have counted a total of *ca.* 600 hands by two stages, first the ayes and then the nays, and afterwards the board must have had a short conference to add up the figures obtained by each of the *proedroi* and the *epistates* [chairman]. Such a procedure must have consumed at least a quarter of an hour. It is apparent from Aristotle's *Constitution of Athens* that the agenda for a simple meeting of the *ecclesia* comprised at least nine items.[13] Moreover, some of the proposals must have entailed several *cheirotoniai*: first a *procheirotonia* ["preliminary show of hands"],[14] then a vote on the main proposal and finally a vote on one or more amendments. Suppose that one of the decrees was an alliance prescribing that ten envoys be forthwith elected from among all the Athenians.[15] Such a decree would require a minimum of eleven successive *cheirotoniai*. A total of twenty-five *cheirotoniai* is in my opinion a moderate estimate of the votes that had to be taken during a single session. In the electoral ecclesia, for example, the Athenians must have voted at least sixty times. If all or most of the *cheirotoniai* resulted in an exact count of the hands, the time consumed by the voting procedure itself would amount to something between five and ten hours, which is impossible even on the assumption that a session of the *ecclesia* occupied an entire day. I have argued elsewhere that a meeting of the assembly did not usually fill more than a part of the day.[16] The necessary implications are that the majority was assessed on a rough estimate of the hands raised and that an exact count of the votes was carried out either exceptionally or never at all.

This conclusion is supported by an argument from analogy. From various places and various periods we have examples of votes taken in large assemblies resembling the Athenian *ecclesia*: the decisions are always made, in the first instance, on a rough estimate of the majority, and if an exact count is required in cases of doubt, the

[12] Hansen, *GRBS* 17 (1976) 129–30.
[13] Arist. *Ath. Pol.* 43.6: three items on religious matters, three on foreign policy and three on domestic policy. This minimum program was fixed for two of the four *ecclesiai* held every prytany. The agenda for the *ekklesia kyria* [the "principal assembly" of each prytany] was considerably longer.
[14] Harp. *s.v.*; Dem. 24.11; Aeschin. 1.23; Arist. *Ath. Pol.* 43.6 [For Hansen's view of the *procheirotonia* see his *The Athenian Ecclesia* 123–30.]
[15] Mosley 56.
[16] Hansen, *CP* 74 (1979) 43–9 [= *The Athenian Ecclesia* 131–8].

procedure employed seems invariably to have been either a poll or
† some form of division.[17] To count the hands of several thousand
seated attendants is unparalleled and presumably impracticable.

Admittedly, counting and estimating are different only in degree
and not in kind, but a distinction is nevertheless apparent in several
important respects. Counting the votes is a slow procedure, but in a
close vote it inspires more confidence than a rough estimate, and the
line between a fair and a crooked assessment of the majority can be
sharply drawn, at least by the tellers themselves. An estimate of the
majority can be made in a moment, but in cases of doubt the show
of hands has to be repeated, perhaps several times; a biased teller may
easily persuade himself that the ayes or the nays have it, and protests
against the assessment are much more likely to be made, especially
in Athens where the *proedroi* were chosen by lot and served for
one day only; they were barred from reappointment until the next
prytany (Arist. *Ath. Pol.* 44.3), and so it must have been impossible
for them to acquire any particular ability in estimating the majority.

III

After this preliminary investigation we must return to the sources.
Whereas the assumption that the votes were counted is unwarranted
by the literary evidence, it is in fact possible to adduce some important passages in favour of the opposite view, namely, that the
† majority was estimated.

1. Most important is Aristotle's statement in the *Constitution of
Athens* 44.3 that the *proedroi* were responsible for the *cheirotoniai*.
The text runs as follows: οἱ δὲ (ἐννέα πρόεδροι) παραλαβόντες
(τὸ πρόγραμμα) τῆς τ' εὐκοσμίας ἐπιμελοῦνται καὶ ὑπὲρ ὧν δεῖ
χρηματίζειν προτιθέασιν καὶ τὰς χειροτονίας κρίνουσιν καὶ τὰ ἄλλα
πάντα διοικοῦσιν καὶ τοῦ[[τ']] ἀφεῖναι κύριοί εἰσιν.* As mentioned

---

[17] A few examples may serve. (a) In the Swiss *Landsgemeinden* (attended by several thousand citizens) the vote is taken by a show of hands and the votes are not counted (Ryffel
107–10, 314–15). The majority is assessed by the *Landamman* (Glarus, cf. Stauffacher
311–13) or by a board of *Weibel* (Obwalden, cf. Ryffel 315). In cases of doubt the show of
hands is repeated, and continued doubt may result in a count of the votes after a division of
the assembly. (b) In the New England town meeting (attended by a few hundred citizens) the
voting is usually *viva voce* and the majority is assessed by the moderator (Sly 152–53). (c) The
election of representatives to the House of Commons in the Tudor period was conducted by
the sheriff. The vote was taken by voice; and only when competition was close, the election
proceeded to assessment implying a division of the electors (*ca.* 1000–2000) but not any count
† of votes – or to the poll (Neale 87–88).
* "The (nine *proedroi*) after taking over the agenda take care of good order and put forward
the business to be transacted and judge the shows of hands and administer everything else and
have the authority to close the meeting."

above the Greek is usually rendered "the *proedroi* count the votes," but "to count" is a mistranslation of *krinein* ["judge"]. This verb implies some decision made by the *proedroi*, and the correct translation is "the *proedroi* judge the *cheirotoniai*."[18] Now the show of hands can only have involved a decision on the part of the *proedroi* if they had to estimate the majority instead of counting the votes.

2. Next comes a curious passage in the sixth book of the *Laws* where Plato prescribes that the officers of the army be elected by *cheirotonia* and that the vote be taken by the whole army (*ca.* 5000 men) under the supervision of the thirty-seven *nomophylakes*. The last section of the passage runs as follows: τὰς δὲ ἀμφισβητήσεις τῶν χειροτονιῶν μέχρι δυοῖν εἶναι· τὸ δὲ τρίτον ἐὰν ἀμφισβητῇ τις, διαψηφίζεσθαι τούτους οἷσπερ τῆς χειροτονίας μέτρον ἑκάστοις ἕκαστον ἦν (756в).* It is usually taken for granted that the votes had to be counted and that any protest against the *cheirotonia* would result in a recount, perhaps even in two recounts of all the hands.[19] Against this it can be objected, first that Plato nowhere says that the votes were counted, second that it is grotesque to provide for a double recount of all the hands, and third that it makes no sense to transfer the powers to the presiding board of officials (either the thirty-seven *nomophylakes* ["law-guardians"] or the *prytaneis*) after no less than three *cheirotoniai* all involving an exact count of *ca.* 5000 votes. On the other hand, if we assume that the majority was estimated by the presiding board, the elaborate procedure in cases of doubt is only natural, and we have in fact an exact parallel to the voting procedure adopted by some of the Swiss *Landsgemeinden* (n. 17).

Now the ideal state described in the *Laws* is certainly not Athens, but it is worth noting that Plato, especially concerning procedural details, has often modelled his Utopia on Athenian institutions. Plato's vocabulary for military officers shows that in this section of the *Laws* he has Athens in mind, and so his provisions for electing military officers are probably a more or less modified copy of the Athenian procedure.

3. One more indication that the votes were not counted can be

---

[18] *Krinein* is the verb used by Aristotle to describe the assessment of the majority, not only in this passage but also in his account of the constitution of 411 (*Ath. Pol.* 30.5; cf. above p. 42).

* "There may be up to two disputes about the show of hands; if somebody disputes it a third time, those to whom was entrusted the measuring of the show of hands on each occasion shall choose by ballot between the alternatives."

[19] England 557; Morrow 160.

obtained by comparing the *cheirotoniai* in the *ecclesia* with the *psephophoriai* [casting of ballots] in the *dikasteria* [law-courts]. In the courts the votes were always counted with precision, and accordingly we have some information on the exact number of votes cast by the jurors: Socrates, for example, was found guilty by a majority of sixty votes (Plat. *Ap.* 36A). whereas Aeschines was acquitted by thirty votes (Plut. *Mor.* 840C). Cephisodotus escaped capital punishment by three votes only (Dem. 23.167), and Hyperides (3.28) states that Aristophon was acquitted ἐν τούτῳ τῷ δικαστηρίῳ παρὰ δύο ψήφους ["in this law-court by two votes"]. Only a tie saved Leocrates from a sentence of death (Aeschin. 3.252), and even in inscriptions the exact number of votes cast is sometimes recorded (*IG* II² 1641B). Although the preserved speeches contain references to hundreds of decrees passed by the people in the assembly, we have not a single piece of information of the same kind concerning *cheirotoniai*, which points to the conclusion that exact figures were unknown. The only source where numbers are mentioned is Demosthenes' statement that Aeschines was elected *pylagorus* [delegate to the Amphictyonic Council] by three or four votes: προβληθεὶς πυλάγορος οὗτος καὶ τριῶν ἢ τεττάρων χειροτονησάντων αὐτὸν ἀνερρήθη (Dem. 18.149);* but this scornful remark must be grossly exaggerated and is useless as a source whether we assume that the votes were counted or not. Conversely, Thucydides reports that after the debate between Cleon and Diodotus the people overruled their former decision by a close vote: καὶ ἐγένοντο ἐν τῇ χειροτονίᾳ ἀγχώμαλοι, ἐκράτησε δὲ ἡ τοῦ Διοδότου (Thuc. 3.49.1).** The vague statement is in conformity with my theory, but no conclusion can be drawn since it is most unlikely that Thucydides would have informed us of the exact figures even if they were known.

4. So far I have dealt only with *cheirotoniai*. We have in fact some evidence of the counting of votes cast by the people in the assembly. Citizenship decrees had to be ratified by a vote taken among 6000 citizens (Dem. 59.89), and similarly a quorum of 6000 was required in order to grant an *adeia* ["immunity"] (Dem. 24.45) or to allow the *nomothetai* to pass a *nomos ep' andri* [law affecting a specified individual] (Andoc. 1.87). Here an exact count of the votes was necessary, and the crucial point is that *cheirotonia* in these cases was

---

* "This man was nominated as *pylagorus* and when three or four men had raised their hands he was declared elected."
** "And in the show of hands they were very close, but the (proposal) of Diodotus prevailed."

replaced by a vote taken by ballot.²⁰ ἐὰν μή ἑξακισχιλίοις δόξῃ κρύβδην ψηφιζομένοις ["unless it is decided by six thousand in a secret ballot"] is the statutory requirement of all the laws prescribing a quorum. The reason may be that voting by ballot is secret whereas the voters reveal their position in a *cheirotonia*. But we must not forget that citizenship decrees in the first instance were passed by a show of hands and only *ratified* by the *psephophoria*.²¹ So a citizen would in any case have revealed his stand in the first vote, and accordingly secrecy cannot have been the primary concern. It is tempting to suggest that *psephophoria* was prescribed because it was the only possible way of counting the votes.

Additional evidence of this view can be found in some decrees published on stone in the Hellenistic and Roman periods. In a few decrees of the first century B.C. passed by ballot a count of the votes is recorded towards the end of the inscription: τῶν ψήφων αἱ πλήρε]ις αἷς ἐδόκει τὴν ἐγφερομένην γνώ[μην κυρίαν εἶναι ——] τριάκοντα πέντε, αἱ τετρυπημένα[ι αἷς οὐκ ἐδόκει οὐδεμία.²² The usual form of voting in the *ecclesia* was still *cheirotonia*, but in this case the vote is described in the following way: [ὁ πρόεδρος· ὅτῳ δοκεῖ κύρια εἶναι τὰ ἀνεγνω]σμένα ἀράτω τὴν χεῖρα. πάντες ἐπῆραν. καὶ ὅτῳ [μὴ δοκεῖ κύρια εἶναι ἀράτω τὴν χεῖρα. οὐδεὶς ἐπῆρεν.]²³ The difference is significant: although in both cases all voted for the proposal and none against, the exact number of ayes is only recorded in connection with the vote taken by ballot. So it is most unlikely that the hands were ever counted in a vote taken by a show of hands.

This conclusion is confirmed by a study of inscriptions from other parts of Greece, especially from the cities of Asia Minor: Colophon, Magnesia, Miletus, Iasus, Halicarnassus, Theangela and Cnidus. Whenever exact figures are recorded, the vote is invariably by ballot.²⁴ The only problematical example is an inscription from

---

²⁰ In addition to the *nomoi* prescribing *psephophoria* we have one example of a decree ordering that an *ecclesia* take the vote by ballot instead of by a show of hands, namely Callixenus' decree ordering the execution of the generals in 406 (Xen. *Hell.* 1.7.9).

²¹ Hansen, *GRBS* 17 (1976) 125–27.

²² ["The solid ballots, voting that the proposal brought forth should be valid, —— and   † thirty-five; the hollow, voting against, nil."] *IG* II² 1053 lines 11–13. Cf. *IG* II² 1051 and 1353; Ἐφημερὶς Ἀρχαιολογικὴ 1884, 167–68 line 3, where the exact figures are preserved: 3461 voted for and 155 against the proposal. Cf. further *IG* II² 1343 line 44.

²³ ["The chairman: 'Whoever judges what has been read out to be valid, raise his hand.' They all raised. 'And whoever judges that it is not valid, raise his hand.' Nobody raised."] Oliver, no. 31 lines 30–32. The restorations proposed are secured by *SIG*³ 1109.20–24 and by *IG* II² 2090.

²⁴ DELPHI: *Fouilles de Delphes* III. 1 no.294 lines 2–3 (454 *psephoi*); *BCH* 19 (1895) 7 lines 21–23 (= Michel 995) (182 *psephoi*). ANAPHE: *IG* XII.3 249 line 39 (95 *psephoi*).

Cnidus where the form of voting is described as *cheirotonia*, but the votes cast are called *psaphoi*.[25] The passage is discussed by Brandis (2194), who, rightly in my opinion, suggests that *cheirotonia* in this context does not mean more than "vote" whereas *psaphos* is the significant word showing that the vote was taken by ballot. Two inscriptions from Halicarnassus record the respective numbers of 4000 and 1200 *psephoi*. These figures are probably rounded. By way of contrast it is worth noting that the Athenian decrees discussed above seem to record exact numbers. Moreover, Aristotle's description of the table for counting pebbles (the ἄβαξ τρυπήματα ἔχων ["board which has holes"], *Ath. Pol.* 69.1) indicates that when the Athenians had to take a vote by ballot, they practised an exact count of all votes cast.

5. If I am right in maintaining that a *cheirotonia* was decided by the *proedroi* (and before *ca.* 380 B.C. by the *prytaneis*), it is unbelievable that their decisions were always allowed to pass unchallenged, and it would indeed be strange if objections against the result of the voting had left no traces in our sources. Now three passages can be adduced which are, in my opinion, best explained as protests against the presidency's assessment of the majority in a show of hands.

a. When the eight generals were put on trial in 406, Euryptolemus tried as a last resort to prevent the passing of Callixenus' *probouleuma* [preliminary resolution of the council] by making a counterproposal, but without success. Xenophon gives the following account of the incident: τούτων δὲ διαχειροτονουμένων τὸ μὲν πρῶτος ἔκριναν τὴν Εὐρυπτολέμου· ὑπομοσαμένου δὲ Μενεκλέους καὶ πάλιν διαχειροτονίας γενομένης ἔκριναν τὴν τῆς βουλῆς (*Hell.* 1.7.34).* The crucial word ὑπομοσαμένου may be interpreted as

COLOPHON: *Inschriften von Priene*, ed. Hiller von Gaertringen (1906), 57 lines 20–21 (1023) [?] *psephoi* [?] restored by Wilhelm, *SBWien* 183.7. MAGNESIA: *Inschriften von Magnesia*, ed. O. Kern (1900) 92a (4678 *psephoi*); 92b (2113 *psephoi*); 94 (3580 *psephoi*). MILETUS: *SIG*³ 683 line 66 (*psephoi* for: 584; against: 16). IASUS: *REG* 6 (1893) 170 line 23 (*psephoi* [?] for: ?; against: 4). HALICARNASSUS: Michel 455 (4000 *psephoi*); *BCH* 14 (1890) 95 line 4 (1200 *psephoi*). THEANGELA: *IG* XI.4 1054 b lines 21–22 (620 *psephoi*); CNIDUS: *Inscr. Brit. Mus.* 783 line 22 (*psephoi* for: ?; against: 0); *SIG*³ 953 line 86 (*psephoi* for conviction: 78; for acquittal: 126). Cf. Brandis 2193–96; Busolt 446 and 454; Wilhelm, *SBWien* 183. 4–9, *Archäologisch-epigraphische Mitteilungen aus Österreich-Ungarn* 20.79–82.

[25] *Inscr. Brit. Mus.* 788; ἐκυρώθη χειροτονίᾳ ἐν βουλᾷ· ἐκυρώθη καὶ ἐν τῷ [δ]άμῳ χιροτονίᾳ· ψᾶφοι αἷς ἔδοξε κυροῦν .... αἷς δὲ μή, οὐδεμία. ["It was ratified by *cheirotonia* in the council; it was ratified also by *cheirotonia* in the people (i.e. assembly); *psephoi* by which it was resolved to ratify ... by which not, nil."]

* "When they voted by show of hands between the alternatives, Euryptolemus' (proposal) was first judged (to prevail); but, when Menecles objected under oath and the show of hands was taken again, the council's (proposal) was judged (to prevail)."

a *hypomosia* [objection under oath] in a *graphe paranomon* [prosecution for making an illegal proposal] raised by Menecles against Euryptolemus,[26] but in this case it would be unconstitutional to pass immediately to a second vote on Callixenus' *probouleuma* instead of awaiting the jurors' hearing of the *graphe paranomon*. It is of course possible that we are faced with one more unconstitutionality committed during this notorious session of the *ecclesia*, but we must not forget that *hypomosia* is the technical term for various types of demurrer.[27] A more likely interpretation of ὑπομοσαμένου is that the enemies of the eight generals, because of the *prytaneis*' earlier attempt to stop the trial, were suspicious of their assessment of the majority and, quite constitutionally, demanded a second *cheirotonia*.

b. The second source is a malignant joke in Aristophanes' *Plutus*. When Cario relates how Plutus was led to Asclepius' sanctuary in order to recover his sight, the woman asks whether other suppliants were present. Cario answers that he saw, among others, the purblind politician Neocleides. But the god prepared for him a terrible unguent which, when rubbed in his eyes, blinded the wretched fellow totally. In reply to Neocleides' cry of pain the god maliciously remarked: ἐνταῦθα νῦν κάθησο καταπεπλασμένος, ἵν' ὑπομνύμενον παύσω σε τὰς ἐκκλησίας.[28] If there is a point in Aristophanes' story, it must be that Neocleides' total blindness in future will prevent him from lodging sworn objections against the decisions made by the *ecclesia*. Now even a blind man can listen to a debate and bring a sworn indictment against a decree which, in his opinion, is unconstitutional, but only a man in possession of the faculty of vision can protest against the presidency's declaration of the result of a show of hands. So ὑπομνύμενον in *Plutus* 725 is presumably to be taken in the sense suggested above for Xen. *Hell*. 1.7.34. I admit, however, that my interpretation is highly conjectural and may be questioned.

c. In the opening of the speech *Against Ctesiphon* Aeschines complains bitterly of the general decay of the democratic institutions due to the corruption of the politicians and the carelessness of the people. His point is that the *graphe paranomon* heard by the jurors is the only safeguard of democracy still left. One of Aeschines' complaints is connected with the declaration of the vote in the *ecclesia* ... ἂν δέ τις τῶν ἄλλων βουλευτῶς ὄντως λάχῃ κληρούμενος προεδρεύειν, καὶ τὰς ὑμετέρας χειροτονίας ὀρθῶς ἀναγορεύῃ,

---

[26] The interpretation I proposed in *The Sovereignty*, Catalogue no. 3, p. 29.

[27] Lipsius 393 and 902.

[28] ["Now sit there (with your eyes) plastered, so that I can prevent you from objecting under oath in the assemblies."] Ar. *Plut*. 724–25. ἐπομνύμενον manuscripts: corrected by Girardus.

τοῦτον οἱ τὴν πολιτείαν οὐκέτι κοινήν, ἀλλ' ἤδη ἰδίαν αὐτῶν
ἡγούμενοι, ἀπειλοῦσιν εἰσαγγελεῖν ... (Aeschin. 3.3).* This passage can be interpreted only as an accusation against some *proedroi*
of having been bribed to tamper with the result of the *cheirotonia* for
which they were responsible. They may have done so by intentionally miscounting the votes, but the accusation of fraud is much more
understandable if the board of *proedroi* was empowered to estimate
the majority. Furthermore, one of the reasons for the frequency of the
graphe paranomon may have been the difference between the form
of voting in the assembly and that in the courts. A politician may
sometimes have refused to accept a defeat in the *ecclesia* because he
was suspicious of the *proedroi's* assessment of the majority, and
accordingly he may have found some reason for bringing an indictment against the decree passed and for having the case referred to the
jurors, who voted by ballot.

†   6. Finally, the theory proposed is neither proved nor disproved by
the archaeological evidence. The stele beddings cut in the rock forming the seating floor of the Pnyx of the first and of the third period
were tentatively interpreted by Kourouniotes and Thompson as evidence of subdivisions of the auditorium. Accepting the excavators'
suggestion, Boegehold and Staveley assumed a division (both of Pnyx
I, II and III) into ten sections and argued that the arrangement must
have been adopted in order to make an exact count of the votes possible. I have no objection to the view that the stone beddings are
evidence of subdivisions of the auditorium (parallels can be found in
other Greek cities),[29] but I would prefer a different interpretation.
Not only when the votes are counted, but also when a board of
officials has to assess the majority on a rough estimate, it is reasonable to make each of the members responsible for the estimate of the
majority within a well defined section of the assembly.[30] In fourth-
century Athens the seating floor of Pnyx II and III could have been
divided into, e.g., nine sections so that each of the *proedroi* was
responsible for one section. After the *cheirotonia* the decision on the
result of the vote was presumably made, in cases of doubt, by a vote
taken among the nine *proedroi* themselves. On this theory there is no
reason for inventing a tenth vote-counter added to the nine *proedroi*

* "If any of the other councillors is actually picked by lot as *proedros,* and rightly
announces (the results of) your show of hands, this man is threatened with an *eisangelia*
('impeachment') by those who no longer regard the citizenship as a common possession but as
their own property."
   [29] McDonald 61–62.
   [30] In Glarus, for example, when the *Landammann* is in doubt, he calls four members of the
Regierungsrat, each of whom is entrusted with the assessment of roughly a fourth of the *Ring.*
Cf. Stauffacher 311.

in order to reach "the logical number for the sections" (Boegehold 374). Quite the contrary, the point of the whole system may have been to have an uneven number of members serving on the board which assessed the majority.

7. The theory that the auditorium of the *ecclesia* was divided into *ten* sections is based on the assumption that the Athenians in the assembly were grouped according to their *phylae* ["tribes"]. Staveley favours this view and adduces some evidence which may support his contention (81–82). Boegehold is much more cautious. He is well aware that the theory entails a somewhat strained interpretation of several passages (Ar. *Eccl.* 289ff; Thuc. 6.13.1; Plut. *Per.* 11.2). He suggests instead (374) a division into ten random groups, and his only argument for *ten* groups is that ten seems to be the logical number.

In my opinion the problem is decisively settled by Aeschines 2.64–68, where a certain Amyntor gives evidence that he, during the assembly held on 19 Elaphebolion 347/6, was seated next to Demosthenes, who showed him a proposal drawn up in writing and discussed with him whether he should hand it over to the *proedroi.* Now Amyntor is of Erchia (Aegeis II) whereas Demosthenes is of Paeania (Pandionis III). It is of course possible that each *phyle* occupied a fixed section of the *ecclesia* following the official order of the tribes, in which case Pandionis was next to Aegeis; but Demosthenes always placed himself beneath the *katatome*,[31] so that he must have been barred from speaking to any citizen from another *phyle.* Furthermore, if the *phylae* were placed according to their official order, the two *phylae* occupying the area beneath the eastern and western *katatome* must have been Erechtheis (I) and Antiochis (X) but never Pandionis (III). Admittedly, Demosthenes was a councillor in 347/6 (Aeschin. 3.62), but he was not a *prytanis* during Pryt. VIII (*IG* II² 212),[32] and there is no evidence that a special area was reserved for the 450 ordinary councillors. Moreover, assuming that the ordinary citizens were grouped according to their *phyle* in the assembly, we must *a fortiori* [arguing from the stronger point] conclude that the same division applied to the councillors. The

[31] Hyp. 1.9; that *katatome* designates the scarps of Pnyx II and III is convincingly suggested by Colin in the Budé edition of Hyperides (250 n.1).

[32] The *phyle* holding the eighth prytany was Aegeis (II). This is a very strong indication that Amyntor cannot have been a councillor, for in that case he would have been among the *prytaneis*, for whom a special area was reserved in the *ecclesia*, and could not have been seated beside Demosthenes. Nor does Aeschines offer any basis for assuming that Amyntor was a councillor. The most likely interpretation of Aeschines is that Demosthenes as a councillor and Amyntor as a private citizen had taken their seats where they pleased.

passage Aeschin. 2.64–68 is incompatible with the theory that the
Athenians were grouped according to their tribes, and accordingly
the theory must be dismissed.

The discussion between Demosthenes and Amyntor took place
late in the year 347/6. During the following year (346/5) the
† Athenians passed a law by which one of the ten *phylae* was entrusted
with the maintenance of order during the meeting (Aeschin. 1.34).
The law was indicted as unconstitutional, but it must have been
upheld by the court since Aeschines fifteen years later refers to the
institution as a fact (Aeschin. 3.4). The obligation was binding on
all members of the *phyle* attending that particular meeting of the
assembly, and it may have entailed a system by which the area around
the *bema* [platform] was reserved for the members of the *phyle*
responsible for the maintenance of order during the session.

IV

I conclude with a short outline of how the Athenian *ecclesia* voted
in the fourth century B.C. Apart from the basic proposal (that the
proedroi made a decision on the result without any exact count of
the votes), my description is conjectural, and some details are little
more than guesswork. I believe, however, that my reconstruction is
on the right lines and more in accord with the evidence than earlier
accounts of the subject.

In the Athenian *ecclesia* the vote was usually taken by a show of
hands. The board of officials responsible for the declaration of the
result was that of the nine *proedroi*, who made their decision on a
rough estimate without counting the votes. If they were in doubt,
they probably took a vote among themselves and the majority
decided the question. Possibly the seating floor of the Pnyx was
subdivided into nine sections, and each of the *proedroi* was responsible for estimating the majority within a section. After the *proedroi*'s
declaration of the result, any citizen was entitled to lodge a sworn
objection against the decision, whereupon a second vote was taken,
once more by a show of hands and once more without any exact
count of hands. We are totally ignorant of the procedure adopted if
† even the second *cheirotonia* was questioned. If the *ecclesia* had to
vote for a third time, the vote was perhaps taken by ballot.[33] An exact

---

[33] If so, it probably had to be postponed until the meeting was closed or until the next meeting of the assembly. The description of the *psephophoria* in connection with citizenship decrees
in Dem. 59.89–90 indicates that a vote by pebbles was usually taken at the beginning of a meeting when the Athenians ascended the Pnyx (προσιόντι τῷ δήμῳ ["to the people as they

count of the hands raised was presumably impracticable, and no source supports the assumption that any kind of division was practised in the assembly. Another possibility is that the decision was left to the board of *proedroi* or to the *prytaneis*, but nothing is known and I prefer to desist from further speculations.   †

ADDENDA

41: On *diacheirotonia* cf. M.H. Hansen, "Athenian *Nomothesia* in the Fourth Century B.C. and Demosthenes' Speech against Leptines," *ClMed* 32 (1980) 94 with note 5 (to which I can add *IG* II² 28.14).

46: After the completion of this article I have attended the *Landsgemeinde* held in Sarnen, Obwalden (24.4.1977, 26.4.1981) and in Glarus (1.5.1977). Both from personal experience and from interviews with the local officials I am now convinced that an exact count of the hands in an assembly attended by 3000–6000 voters is simply impossible.

46 n. 17: [Additional note written by Dr Hansen for this book.] The Swiss *Landsgemeinde*, introduced in the thirteenth century and still existing in one canton and one half-canton, offers in many respects a striking parallel to the Athenian *ecclesia*, and my studies of this institution have helped me to get a better understanding of the proceedings in a political mass meeting. The *Landsgemeinde* meets once every year and every adult citizen has the right to speak and vote. The *Landsgemeinde* is entrusted with the passing of major political decisions and with the election of the cantonal government, the judges and other cantonal officials. In the *Landsgemeinde* cantons there is also a popularly elected parliament, but it is only empowered to prepare all the proposals to be debated and voted on by the people in assembly. Its competence to make final decisions is, with a few exceptions, restricted to matters of minor importance.

When I studied the *Landsgemeinde* in the 1970s and 1980s five were still left: in Glarus, Appenzell-Auserrhoden, Appenzell-Innerrhoden, Obwalden and Nidwalden. Three were discontinued in the 1990s and those in Glarus and Nidwalden are the only two still in operation.

arrive"]). It would no doubt have been too complicated in the middle of a meeting to let the whole people pass by the voting urns and back again to their seats (cf. Hansen, *GRBS* 17 [1976] 127). In 406 the *ecclesia* hearing the trial of the generals probably concluded with the passing of the sentence by ballot (see above, n. 20).

My comparative study of the Athenian and the Swiss assemblies was published in 1983 in an article entitled "The Athenian *Ecclesia* and the Swiss *Landsgemeinde*," in M. H. Hansen, *The Athenian Ecclesia: A Collection of Articles* (Copenhagen), 207–29. In this article I focus on six aspects of political mass meetings where the study of the *Landsgemeinde* can provide us with a better understanding of the Athenian institution, namely (1) the space required by a crowd attending a major political meeting; (2) the vote taken by show of hands; (3) the frequency of unanimous decisions; (4) the duration of a popular assembly, and the proboulectic procedure by which all items on the agenda have to be prepared by a council or parliament; (5) the distinction between decrees (passed by the people in assembly) and laws (passed by referendum); (6) the absence of political parties. Peter Rhodes has allowed me in this collection of articles to reprint below that part of the article which deals with the vote taken by show of hands [from *The Athenian Ecclesia*, 213–15].

The Athenian *ecclesia* voted by a show of hands. There has been much speculation how the hands were counted in cases of doubt. The answer seems to be that they were never counted. The majority was assessed on a rough estimate. That is what our only explicit source says: the nine *proedroi* (who preside over the *ecclesia*) *judge* the votes taken by a show of hands (Arist. *Ath. Pol.* 44.3), and this piece of information is strongly supported by a study of the voting procedure in the Swiss *Landsgemeinden*. In all five cantons the citizens vote by a show of hands. The *Landammann* asks first the supporters and *ca.* 15 seconds later the opponents of a proposal to raise their hands. The hands are never counted. It is simply impossible, and if it had been possible it would have been too time consuming. The presiding officials assess the majority on a rough estimate only. The voting procedure is basically the same in all five *Landsgemeinde* cantons, and I will describe in more detail the methods practised in Obwalden and in Glarus.

In Obwalden the majority is assessed by a board of eight *Weibel* who stand on a platform raised *ca.* 1 meter above the ground. When both phases in a show of hands are over, each *Weibel* makes his decision about the majority and reports to the *Landammann*. If six or more *Weibel* agree on the outcome of the vote, the matter is definitively settled, and the *Landammann* proclaims the result. The whole procedure is over in about one minute. If less than six *Weibel* agree, the show of hands is repeated. If the second show of hands is equally ineffective, the *Landammann* orders a division: all citizens must leave the *Landsgemeindeplatz* through two entrances, one for the ayes and one for the nays, and an exact count is made, abstentions excepted. But this happens, on average, only once in a decade, most recently in 1973 and in 1982.

In Glarus the *Landsgemeinde* is regularly attended by 5000–8000 citizens and a division is impracticable. During six hundred years the votes have never been counted. Furthermore, the assessment of the show of hands is entrusted to the *Landammann* alone. He stands in the centre of the assembly on a small wooden platform. During both phases of the show of hands he looks all the way round and then he makes his decision on the outcome of the vote. If he is in doubt the show of hands is repeated. If he is still in doubt after the second show of hands, four senior members of the *Regierungsrat*, the government, are called to the central platform. In a third show of hands each *Regierungsrat* overlooks a quarter of the assembly and reports to the *Landammann*. But the decision rests with the *Landammann* alone, who for a third time has surveyed the entire assembly. There is no appeal against his verdict and, as far as I have been told, his decision has never been questioned. On average, the four senior members are called to the platform only once every second or third year.

In elections the people, in all five cantons, sometimes have to make a choice not between alternatives but between, say, four named candidates. The procedure is the following. In a first round the people are invited to vote on one of the four candidates. After this fourfold show of hands, the candidate who obtains the fewest votes is excluded and a threefold show of hands follows. Again the least successful candidate is eliminated, and after a final show of hands, the candidate who wins the majority is declared elected. The whole procedure takes only five minutes or so. With some variations a similarly speedy procedure can be assumed for the Athenian *ecclesia*.

46: I have found one more source which supports my assumption that the hands were not counted but estimated. In Ar. *Vesp.* 655–57, Bdelycleon exhorts his father to come up with a rough calculation of the *phoros* [tribute]: ΒΔ. ἀκρόασαί νυν, χαλάσας ὀλίγον τὸ μέτωπον. καὶ πρῶτον μὲν λόγισαι φαύλως, μὴ ψήφοις ἀλλ' ἀπὸ χειρός, τὸν φόρον ἡμῖν ἀπὸ τῶν πόλεων συλλήβδην τὸν προσιόντα ...* MacDowell (*Aristophanes Wasps*, Oxford 1971) has the following comment on the passage: "*and first calculate roughly, not with counters but on your fingers*. This implies that for

---

* "BD. Listen, now, relaxing your brow a little. And first calculate roughly, not with counters but on your fingers, the tribute which comes to us from the cities in total ..."

exact calculations counters would normally be used." I will add
that the opposition between *psephoi* and *cheir* is a pun, referring to
the opposition between *psephophoria* and *cheirotonia*: "don't use
voting-discs, use your hand." The inference is that voting by show of
hands could only give a rough estimate of the majority and not an
exact count.

48: I can now add seven more examples of the exact count of votes
cast by the jurors: Phayllus was convicted by two votes in a *dike
kakegorias* [prosecution for slander] (Ar. *Vesp.* 1207); Speusippus
obtained less than 200 votes in a *graphe paranomon* against
Leogoras (Andoc. 1.17); Nicodemus was acquitted by four votes
in a *graphe xenias* [prosecution for being a foreigner when claiming
to be a citizen] (Isae. 3.37); Euaion was convicted by one vote in a
homicide trial (heard by a *dikasterion*?) (Dem. 21.75). Other inscriptions recording the number of votes are: *IG* II² 1646.8; *Hesperia* 16
(1947) no. 51.57ff.

49: In note 22, for Ἐφημερὶς Ἀρχαιολογική 1884 read: *IG* II² 1035,
cf. also Heliodorus *Aethiop.* 1.14. In note 24, after Iasus, read: L.
Robert, *Études anatoliennes* (Paris 1937) 451 (*psephoi* for: 70;
against: 4). Furthermore, add: Phygela: *SEG* IV. 513.11 (*psephoi*
for: 350); Cyrene: *SEG* IX.354.26 (white [votes]: for: 53). I owe the
last two references to P. J. Rhodes.

52: For a new and different interpretation of the subdivisions of the
auditorium cf. Pnyx III, cf. Hansen, *GRBS* 23 (1982) 244–9 = *The
Athenian Ecclesia* 28–33.

54: On *he proedreuousa phyle*, "the presiding tribe", cf. *GRBS* 23
(1982) 246–9 = *The Athenian Ecclesia* 30–3.

54: In Aristotle's *Politics* one interesting passage bears on this problem but does not refer explicitly to Athens : ὁποτέρων οὖν τὸ τίμημα
ὑπερτείνει συναριθμουμένων ἀμφοτέρων ἑκατέροις, τοῦτο κύριον.
ἐὰν δὲ ἴσοι συμπέσωσι, κοινὴν εἶναι ταύτην νομιστέον ἀπορίαν
ὥσπερ νῦν ἐὰν δίχα ἡ ἐκκλησία γένηται ἢ τὸ δικαστήριον· ἢ γὰρ
ἀποκληρωτέον ἢ ἄλλο τι τοιοῦτον ποιητέον (1318a37–b1).*

* "Therefore, whichever side's assessment is the greater when they are added up for each,
this shall prevail. If they turn out to be equal, this must be considered the same problem
as occurs now if the assembly or law-court is (evenly) divided: either it must be resolved by
allotment or something else of that kind must be done."

Commentators and translators follow Bonitz, *Index Aristotelicus*: ἀποκληρωτέον, "sorte decernendum est" ["it must be decided by lot"]. But "to make a decision by lot" is certainly not the usual meaning of ἀποκληροῦν. The meaning is rather "by lot to appoint one or a small number from a larger number of candidates." So Aristotle probably refers to a procedure by which a small number of voters is selected by lot and entrusted with the decision of an issue when even a repeated show of hands does not allow to decide where the majority is. Aristotle's piece of information is a good parallel to the provision Plato *Laws* 756 B, discussed above, 47.

55: An account of the Athenian voting procedure is not complete without a discussion of how the show of hands was used in election of magistrates, ambassadors and other officials. Especially the election of *strategoi* [generals] has attracted much attention, but most of the elaborate reconstructions proposed by e.g. H. T. Wade-Gery and E. S. Staveley must be rejected because they presuppose an exact count of the hands. By far the best treatment of the problem is M. Piérart, "A propos de l'élection des stratèges athéniens," *BCH* 98 (1974) 125–46, with references to earlier literature. Cf. also his *Platon et la cité grecque* (Bruxelles 1974) 242–44 (election of *strategoi*) and 291–95 (election of *astynomoi* ["city officers"]). Combining the little information we have, in inscriptions and speeches, of the Athenian procedure with Plato's description, in *Laws* 763 D–E, of the election of *astynomoi* in Magnesia, Piérart suggests the following procedure: the candidates were named only in the electoral assembly and there was no previous nomination. The election was conducted tribe by tribe. As soon as a candidate of the first tribe was proposed, the people would vote for or against the candidate. If he was rejected, another candidate would be named etc. The first candidate who got a majority would be declared elected and the procedure would be repeated for the second tribe etc. Piérart's reconstruction is basically accepted by P. J. Rhodes, "Notes on Voting in Athens," *GRBS* 22 (1981) 129–32, but Rhodes objects that it would be unfair to vote on the candidates one by one in the order they were named because, if the first candidate had a majority, no other candidate would be named and voted on. He suggests instead that all candidates were named *before* the voting began. This device, however, would not remove the unfairness effectively, for the Athenians would still have to take the vote on the candidates in a fixed order and stop the election as soon as the required number had obtained a majority so that the rest of the candidates had no chance. I suggest instead to adduce another passage from Plato's *Laws*, namely his description of the election of *strategoi* (755 C–D). Comparing this passage with the passage describing the election of *astynomoi* I hope to propose a more plausible reconstruction of the procedure. Let me first quote the two passages in question.

> 755 C–D: στρατηγοὺς μὲν ἐξ αὐτῆς τῆς πόλεως ταύτης οἱ νομοφύλακες προβαλλέσθων, αἱρείσθων δ' ἐκ τῶν προβληθέντων πάντες οἱ τοῦ πολέμου κοινωνοὶ γενόμενοί τε ἐν ταῖς ἡλικίαις καὶ γιγνόμενοι ἑκάστοτε. ἐὰν δέ τις ἄρα δοκῇ τωι τῶν μὴ προβεβλημένων ἀμείνων εἶναι τῶν προβληθέντων τινός, ἐπονομάσας ἀνθ' ὅτου ὅντινα προβάλλεται, τοῦτ' αὐτὸ ὀμνὺς ἀντι-προβαλλέσθω τὸν ἕτερον· ὁπότερος δ' ἂν δόξῃ διαχειροτονούμενος, εἰς τὴν αἵρεσιν ἐγκρινέσθω. τρεῖς δέ, οἷς ἂν ἡ πλείστη χειροτονία γίγνηται, τούτους εἶναι στρατηγούς ...*

> 763 D–E: δεῖ δὴ καὶ τούτους δυνατούς τε εἶναι καὶ σχολάζοντας τῶν κοινῶν ἐπιμελεῖσθαι· διὸ προβαλλέσθω μὲν πᾶς ἀνὴρ ἐκ τῶν μεγίστων τιμημάτων ἀστυνόμον ὃν ἂν βούληται, διαχειροτονηθέντων δὲ καὶ ἀφικομένων εἰς ἓξ οἷς ἂν πλεῖσται γίγνωνται, τοὺς τρεῖς ἀποκληρωσάντων οἷς τούτων ἐπιμελές, ...**

Four general observations on the method of election can be derived from these two sources: (a) candidates may be nominated before the electoral meeting but new candidates can always be mentioned during the session. (b) The naming of candidates alternates with the votes taken, and it is unlikely that the list of candidates closed before the voting begins. (c) Sometimes a candidate is named as a rival to another candidate. (d) The vote is by a simple show of hands, and the issue is either to accept/reject a candidate or to make a choice between two candidates.

If we apply these principles to the Athenian election of officials we can reconstruct two different procedures for the election of a board of ten: one procedure if the board has a member from each tribe and another procedure if the board is appointed from all Athenians irrespective of tribe. In both procedures a *probouleuma* is required for the election (Arist. *Ath. Pol.* 44.4). This *probouleuma* may or may not include a list of candidates, but other names can always be

---

* "*Strategoi* shall be nominated by the *nomophylakes* ('law-guardians') from the actual (membership of the) city, and shall be elected from those nominated by all those who have taken part in war in their age-groups and those who are taking part on each occasion. If anybody judges that a man who has not been nominated is better than a man who has, he shall name which man he nominates in place of which other, making this alternative nomination on oath. Whichever is chosen in a decision by show of hands between the two shall go forward for the election. The three who receive the largest show of hands, these shall be generals ..."

** "These men must be able and have the leisure to take care of public affairs. So each citizen may nominate the man he wants as *astynomos* from the highest property-classes; a choice between them shall be made by show of hands and (the list) reduced to those who have the most votes; and those whose duty it is shall pick three by lot ..."

brought up at the meeting. The two procedures may be reconstructed thus:

(a) A candidate from the first tribe is named and the people vote for or against the candidate. If he is rejected, a new candidate is named and the same form of voting repeated. If the first candidate is accepted, he is declared elected, unless a new candidate is named, in which case the people, by another show of hands, make a choice between the two candidates. The one who obtains the majority is declared elected, unless a new candidate is named, etc. When no more candidates are proposed, the winner of the last vote is proclaimed elected and the same procedure is repeated for the other nine tribes.

(b) Candidates are named, one by one, and after each nomination the people vote for or against the candidate. When ten candidates have been accepted a new candidate has to be named as a rival to one of the ten candidates already accepted, and the vote is now a choice between the new and the previously accepted candidate. If the new candidate wins, he replaces his rival. When no more candidates are proposed as rivals to the ten accepted candidates, the election is over.

These reconstructions are little more than guesswork based on the assumption that Plato, in the *Laws*, copied Athenian electoral Procedures. But I believe that they are on the right lines, and they show at least that even complicated elections can easily be made by a series of shows of hands without any exact count of the votes. Since each show of hands regularly is over in less than one minute, a board of ten can, in most cases, be elected in 15–30 minutes.

3 *Aristotle, the Kleroteria, and the Courts*[*]

STERLING DOW

Aristotle reserved for the concluding chapters of his *Constitution of the Athenians* an elaborate account of the procedure of the dikastic courts, which were then at the peak of their long development. Even a superficial reader must feel, as I think he did, that these minutely detailed chapters illustrate more clearly than any others the political genius of the Athenians: their fair and thorough democracy, their passion for logic and also for litigation, their suspicion of human nature, their fascination with luck, and their penchant for intricate machine-like institutions. The first step in the procedure of the dikastic courts was the selection of jurors. Hundreds, sometimes thousands, were chosen anew every day the courts sat. The selection was by lot, and the process of selection was the most important part of the whole procedure. The text of Aristotle's account of the

* Originally published in *Harvard Studies in Classical Philology* l 1939, 1–34; reprinted with the permission of the Department of the Classics, Harvard University. The meanings established here by Dow for *kleroterion* and other technical terms are incorporated in the Revised Supplement (1996) to LSJ.
Note. For their kind assistance the author wishes to thank Prof. W. S. Ferguson, Prof. T. L. Shear, Prof. H. A. Thompson, Mr. A. W. Parsons, Mr. E. Vanderpool, and Mr. G. F. Swift.
Figure. The isometric diagram on the page opposite shows the two kleroteria of some one tribe ready for the archon's allotment of dikasts [jurors]. At the left of the two kleroteria is shown in section the tube of the left-hand kleroterion before the releasing of the counters; the counters appear to the reader in their "chance" order, which of course is not as yet known to any of the participants. The two kleroteria stood against the wall of the court area, separated from each other by a few meters. In the wall between the kleroteria was the tribe's entrance into the area of the courts (below, Part III). The diagram shows the vertical columns of slots (*kanonides*, Part I), into which have been plugged the wooden tickets (*pinakia*) of dikasts who have presented themselves for allotment on the day in question (Part V). The height of each kleroterion with its base was doubtless about the height of a man; the width, judging by the specimens in *Prytaneis*, Nos. III and IV, was *ca.* 0.60 m. These and the other preserved kleroteria may all be Hellenistic, but the literary evidence leaves no doubt that all the essential details shown in the diagram are correct for Aristotle's time. Certain non-essential details are borrowed from the Hellenistic specimens. Not knowing yet just how cubes can have been used, I have drawn spheres in the tube. [A different release mechanism has been suggested by J. D. Bishop, *JHS* xc 1970, 1–14.] The mouldings also might be different in the fourth century.

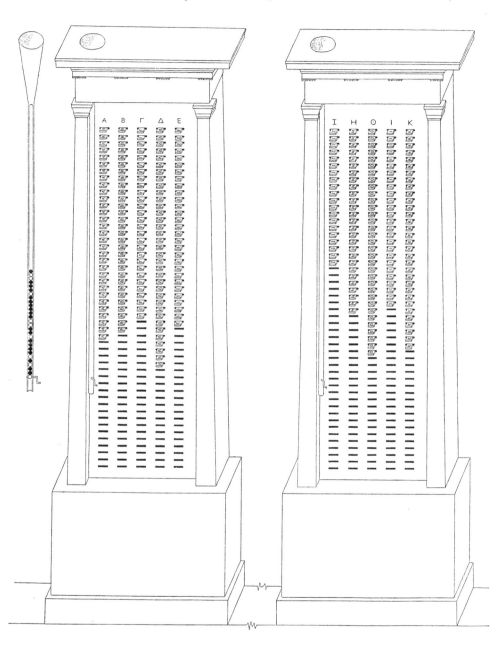

allotment, though full of restorations, has been improved until now it is almost letter-perfect.

The interpretation by modern scholars of that text, and of the allotment itself, is less happy. Down to 1937, the opinion was universally held that Aristotle's exposition has ambiguities and omissions serious enough to prevent a clear and full understanding of the process of allotment. Yet these chapters of Aristotle's undeniably have a tone of special clarity and fulness, of being meticulous and authoritative. In 1937 an object was identified which has a certain interest in this connection: the Greek allotment machine (*kleroterion*). The first publication indicated briefly what light the actual kleroterion seemed to throw on Aristotle's account.[1] Further study has tended to confirm and to supplement the first report. In Parts I–III of the present article, I have tried to examine all the evidence thoroughly; in Part IV, to make out the general plan of the courts; in Part V, to get at the essence of the dikastic allotment.

A short summary of the conclusions may be convenient. Two of the preserved allotment machines show that the columns of slots (*kanonides*), into which the jurors' tickets were inserted, were in the machines themselves, not in alleged "allotment rooms" (Part I, pp. 65–70). All the literary and epigraphical occurrences of the word are reviewed: *kleroterion* (*klerotris, klerotikon*) never means anything but "allotment machine," except in two erring lexicographers (Part II, pp. 70–6). Contrary to present opinion, the allotment for the courts did not take place in rooms, but outside the several entrances to the court-complex (Part III, pp. 76–80). The plan of the whole court-complex (*heliaia*) is thus reduced and simplified; a crucial word is restored in the text of the *Ath. Pol.*; the *kinklides* and *dryphaktoi* are located (Part IV, pp. 81–4). The hitherto unanswered question, Why did each tribe have *two* allotment machines? bears directly on the fundamental ideals and the practical exigencies of the dikastic allotments: to answer it, I have tried to visualize in precise detail the whole business of allotting (Part V, pp. 85–94 – this Part is meant to be intelligible if read separately – ; principal conclusions, pp. 93–4). The effect of the study as a whole is completely to vindicate Aristotle.

<hr/>

[1] S. Dow, *Prytaneis* (*Hesperia*, Supplement I, Athens, 1937), pp. 198–215, with photographs; summary by G. Klaffenbach, *Die Antike*, 14 (1938), 353–355. A summary will also appear in Pauly–Wissowa–Kroll, *Realencyclopaedie*, Supplementband VII, *s.v. Kleroterion* [columns 322–8]. – Fragments of three more kleroteria, discovered since 1937, do not alter the account.

PART I
THE GREEK ALLOTMENT MACHINE

Accepting views universally held, the new Liddell–Scott–Jones *Lexicon* gives three divergent meanings for the word *kleroterion*. The first of these meanings, *urn for casting lots* or *votes*, was illustrated recently by the above-mentioned identification of fourteen actual kleroteria preserved in Athens. Three had been excavated 75 years ago; one had lain on the Acropolis unrecorded until the inscription was partially copied in 1921; ten are from the current Agora Excavations. The identification is positive. That the kleroteria were used for performing allotments, not for voting, is beyond doubt; but instead of being urns, the objects (Figure, facing p. 63) are marble stelae. Trimmed to form *aediculae* [temple-shaped structures] somewhat like Athenian grave monuments, the kleroteria also bear slots, arranged in columns on the face proper of the stelae. The use of the slots, and in general the operation of the kleroteria, have been, I think, clearly made out. But although the object itself is understood, concerning the precise uses of the word *kleroterion* the facts have yet to be established.

The modern instrument for allotment naturally consists of a device for mixing numbered counters so thoroughly that when the counters are drawn out mechanically, or by a blind-fold attendant, the order will be determined by "chance" alone – that is, no one will be able to determine in advance which counter will be drawn first, which second, and so on, down to the last. The modern *kleroterion* is a device for mixing counters, and nothing more.

Prior to 1937, it had been generally supposed that the ancient allotment machine was equally limited in function.[2] If the word *kleroterion* seemed to imply something more, or something different, then it was almost universally supposed that in such uses the word had a second meaning, namely "place where allotments were carried out," that is, "allotment room."[3] Aristotle says that each tribe had two kleroteria, "in" each of which were bars or rows of

---

[2] The translation for this sense of the word was regularly "ballot box," "balloting urn," *urne, Losungsurne, urna in qua sortes conjiciuntur.*

On certain preserved leaden counters, thought to be *symbola* [tokens] used in the dikastic courts, a wide-mouthed, round-bodied vase or urn is depicted (Arist., *Ath. Pol.,* Sandys ed. 2, frontispiece, Figure 5, and p. 255). This vase was taken to represent a *Losurne* [allotment-urn] (Hommel, *Heliaia* [below, n. 4], p. 69).

[3] Or even, in a quite unlikely derivative sense, "public list (as of citizens) from which allotments are made." On this alleged meaning, see below, p. 74. There is no authority for U. Kahrstedt's interpretation in *Untersuchungen zur Magistratur in Athen* (Stuttgart, 1936) p. 26.

some sort called *kanonides*. Each tribe, then, would have two allotment rooms which contained *kanonides* and other equipment, as well as space where some 300 tribesmen could assemble for the allotments. This theory was first carried out in detail by H. Hommel in his study *Heliaia*.[4] The interior appointments of τὰ δύο κληρωτήρια [the two *kleroteria*], as suggested by his diagram (p. 141), permit a neat arrangement of the *kanonides*, urns, chests, allotment machines (also called *kleroteria*), and officials; there is scant room, however, for 600 men.

There were some grounds for the theory. It was difficult to imagine *kanonides* in anything like a modern allotment machine. Further, no one doubted that there ought to be halls of some sort in which the allotments took place; if so, Aristotle would mention them; hence they would have to be the kleroteria. The ending -*terion* can of course denote place as well as instrument, and in fact two lexicographers (below, p. 74) plainly stated that *kleroterion* meant a place.

Now the kleroteria actually surviving have only two functional parts, and in each part they have little resemblance to modern allotment machines. The ancient machines comprise no effective mechanism for mixing the counters, but only a simple tube for drawing them out one at a time.[5] Of interest for our present purpose is a second unexpected feature of the ancient klerotcria, namely the slots, arranged in vertical columns, cut into the face of the stele. These columns of slots, which are actually more prominent in the kleroteria than the allotment devices, vary in number: preserved examples show 1, 2, 5, [6], 11, and [12] columns. The number of slots cannot be fixed except in a few instances: one practically complete machine has only 12 slots (all in a single column); some if not most of the others seem to have had as many as 50 slots in each column.[6] For an understanding of Aristotle, Nos. III and IV (*op. cit.*, pp. 204–205) are of special interest. Each is inscribed: [one line missing] | ταμιεύοντος ἐπὶ τὰ πρυτανεῖα | Ἅβρωνος τοῦ Καλλίου Βατῆθεν.* The *prytaneia* were the deposits made with the state prior to lawsuits (*op. cit.*, p. 212, n. 3), so that these allotment machines are certainly to be connected with the law courts. Each of these two machines has five

---

[4] *Heliaia: Untersuchungen zur Verfassung und Prozessordnung des athenischen Volksgerichts, insbesondere zum Schlussteil der Ἀθηναίων Πολιτεία des Aristoteles* (*Philologus*, Supplementband XIX, Heft II, Leipzig, 1927).

[5] *Prytaneis*, p. 202; below, pp. 68, 89.

[6] Thus No. VI (*op. cit.*, p. 206) is proved to have been tall enough to have had at least 50 slots to a column.

* "The treasurer for the *prytaneia* being Habron son of Callias of Bate."

columns of slots. The number of slots to a column cannot be computed exactly; but the two fragments of No. IV, as is shown by the taper of the stele, must be separated *at least* far enough to allow 20 slots to a column, and the correct relative positions of the fragments seem to necessitate at least 22.[7] These are the minimal figures; the actual number of slots to a column may well have been as many as 60, or 300 in each machine.

Aristotle (64.2) tells us εἰσὶ δὲ κανονίδες [πέντε ἐ]ν ἑκάστῳ τῶν κληρωτηρίων.*[8] The dikasts of each tribe were divided into ten sections; each tribe had two kleroteria, and each kleroterion served for five sections. An *empektes* [inserter] was chosen by lot from each section, and he plugged the *pinakia* [tickets] of his section into one of the *kanonides*. Before the identification of the kleroterion, the *kanonides* were taken to be frames or bars of some sort,[9] five such separate frames or bars being mounted in each "allotment room" (*kleroterion*). On this hypothesis, one of two methods of choosing jurors can have been followed: (1) the first *kybos* drawn can have been taken to decide for the first five *pinakia* in the first *kanonis* (if the *kybos* was white, they were all to serve; if black, not); the second *kybos* would decide for the second five *pinakia in the same kanonis*; and so on. Thus it might happen that 30 or 40 of one section of the dikasts would be chosen, of another only 5 or 10; in any case the chances that equal numbers from each section would be chosen would be very small indeed. This procedure, however, would be the most expeditious *if* the five *kanonides* were all separate. The alternate procedure (2) would be to let the first *kybos* drawn settle for the first *pinakion in each of the five kanonides*, the second *kybos* for the second *pinakion* in each of the five *kanonides*, and so on. In this way the five sections for which any given kleroterion served would be equally represented in the day's courts. It would be somewhat awkward, however, to follow this procedure if the *kanonides*

---

[7] As shown in the photograph, *op. cit.*, p. 205, where the camera has distorted the perspective somewhat.

* "There are five *kanonides* in each of the *kleroteria*."

[8] The restoration of πέντε [five] is from 64.3, which says that each *kybos* [cube] drawn by the archon from the kleroterion decided whether five dikasts, whose *pinakia* were presumably juxtaposed in the *kanonides*, were or were not to serve in the juries on the day in question.

For the text of the *Ath. Pol.*, I have used (Blass–Thalheim–)H. Oppermann (Leipzig, Teubner, 1928).

[9] The translation was "bar," *tableau à rainures, Stange.* Sandys, in his ed. 2 of Arist., *Ath. Pol.* (London, 1912), p. 252, says the *kanonis* was "probably a wooden frame fitted with a number of 'straight rules' or parallel ledges (*kanones*) stretching horizontally across it" with grooves on the upper surface of each ledge to receive the *pinakia*.

were all separated; also, the chances for malpractice would be
increased.[10]

For a choice between procedures (1) and (2), we may turn to the
preserved machines, Nos. III and IV, each of which had five parallel
vertical columns of slots. If these columns of slots can be equated
with Aristotle's *kanonides*, the problem is solved in favor of procedure (2); but Nos. III and IV are *ca.* 180 years later than Aristotle,
and the long interval of time gives pause, especially if *kanonis* may
not properly be applied to a *vertical* column of slots.

In *Prytaneis*, p. 214, I conceded to previous translators of
Aristotle, whose rendering is adopted by Liddell–Scott–Jones, that
kanonis ought to mean "horizontal bar." In other places the word
occurs only seven times; in three of these it seems certainly to denote
horizontal objects. If, however, in the very period when the *Ath. Pol.*
was written, *kanonis* could mean "door-frame" (*IG*, II² 1672, line
155, of 329/8 B.C.), then horizontality is not necessarily implied in
every use of the word. In fact the word could denote a straight-edged
"ruler"[11] – i.e., it implied nothing as to verticality or horizontality.

Another consideration, unknown until the word *klerotikon*
was investigated, may now be brought forward. The riddle from
Euboulos (below, pp. 72–3) speaks of the allotment machine as being
"bored sharply through from top to bottom." From this it seems
clear that in Aristotle's day and before, the *kyboi* were poured down
a tube of some sort, as in the preserved machines. The tube being
used thus early, we gain a clue to the shape of the machines
mentioned by Aristotle. In allotting jurors according to his system,
the tube must be long enough to contain one *kybos* for each five
dikasts, which may mean as many as 60 or more *kyboi*. Hence
the tube must have been lengthy, as it certainly was in some large
kleroteria.[12] If then the *kanonides* were horizontal, the machine
would have been poorly designed. One part would consist of a frame
holding five horizontal rows of slots, each row capable of holding
some 60 tickets. The frame would have to be some two meters in
length, but its height might be less than one quarter of a meter –

---

[10] Among modern scholars, procedure (2) has been supposed to have been followed, but the
actual process could not be proved or visualized, although clearly the subdivision of each tribe
into ten *mere* [sections] points to an equal representation of all the 100 *mere* in the courts as
a whole on any given day.

[11] *Anth. Pal.*, VI 62: the meaning has been considered dubious, although Suidas supports
it. Apparently lexicographers have not noticed that in the very next poem, *Anth. Pal.*, VI 63,
the word *kanon*, occurring in a precisely similar context, where it certainly means "ruler," is
an exact synonym.

[12] E.g., *Prytaneis*, p. 208, No. X.

except for the tube, which would need to be about one meter tall. A long horizontal beam of wood or stone with a meter of tubing hanging from it would look ridiculous. Obviously, therefore, any machine with a tube will naturally have *vertical kanonides*, precisely as in the machines actually surviving.

In other words, there is no reason to suppose that the kleroteria known to Aristotle differed essentially from those now recovered. The dimensions of the slots are correct to allow *pinakia* of the size used before Aristotle's time to be plugged in.[13] The essential fact is that the slots are arranged in even rows horizontally (as well as vertically). If the slots did not form even horizontal rows, the argument from them would have no force, but since the slots do form even horizontal rows, the stones themselves suggest that the objects inserted into the slots were to be dealt with five at a time. Each *empektes*, then, inserts the *pinakia* of his section into the vertical column, which we may now call the *kanonis*, assigned to that section, filling the slots probably from the top down. The first *kybos* drawn by the archon, according to the proper procedure (2), settles for the (five) *pinakia* in the first horizontal row of slots, the second *kybos* for the second horizontal row, and so on.

In short, kleroteria Nos. III and IV have shown that the requirements of the text of Aristotle with respect to *kanonides* can be satisfied by two existing kleroteria bearing inscriptions connecting those kleroteria with the law courts. If, moreover, kleroteria Nos. III and IV do represent the arrangement of slots in the earlier kleroteria, then we learn from them a refinement of procedure not told us by Aristotle, but wholly in accord with all he does tell us: namely that each section (*meros*) of jurors within each group of five sections had exactly as many dikasts in the courts as every other section in that group. The chances of "packing" a court were thus reduced by just so much.[14]

---

[13] A *pinakion* recently published is typical: length, 0.118 m.; width, 0.021 m.; thickness, 0.002 m. (Vanderpool, *AJA* XXXVI [1932], 293–294). The slots average in width 0.03 m.; in height, 0.006 m.; in depth, 0.02 m.

There are only two other occurrences of *empektes*. *Etym. Magn. s.v.* has simply ὁ θεσμοθέτης ["the *thesmothetes*," one of the archons]. Hesychius *s.v.* is confused: ὁ τὰ δικαστικὰ γραμματίδια παρὰ τοῦ θεσμοφόρου λαμβάνων ὑπηρέτης, καὶ πήσσων εἰς τὴν κανονίδα ["the attendant who takes the judicial tablets from the *thesmophoros* (literally, 'law-bearer'; here probably an error for *thesmothetes*) and fixes them into the *kanonis*"]. For the curious mistranslation of *empektes* as "ticket hanger," and of *empegnysi* as "hangs," see *Prytaneis*, p. 214. The new (LSJ) *Greek Lexicon* still gives "one who sticks up judicial notices." The slots in the actual machines are precisely what the Greek words connote.

[14] This may seem an idle refinement, in view of all the other precautions against packing courts; but it is thoroughly Athenian in spirit, and the danger of having blocs of dikasts in the courts, especially if the issue was close, may have been very real. – Sandys (ed. 2, p. 249)

In the face of all this, it would seem unreasonable to speak any longer of separate frames or bars mounted in "allotment rooms." The identification of kleroteria Nos. III and IV has shown, by the forms of the stones themselves, that Aristotle in *Ath. Pol.*, 64.2–3 is speaking of machines, not of rooms. The kleroteria known to him doubtless resembled closely our Nos. III and IV.

PART II
KLEROTERION IN LITERATURE AND INSCRIPTIONS

Aristotle uses the word *kleroterion* five times:

1. εἰσιν - - - κλη[ρωτήρι]α εἴκοσι, δ[ύο τ]ῇ φυλῇ ἑκάστῃ* (*Ath. Pol.*, 63.2).

2, 3. εἰσὶ δὲ κανονίδες [πέντε ἐ]ν ἑκάστῳ τῶν κληρωτηρίων. ὅ[ταν δὲ] ἐμβάλῃ τοὺς κύβους, ὁ ἄρχων τὴν φυλὴν κληρ[οῖ κατὰ κ]ληρωτήριον** (64.2–3).

4, 5. τίθεται ἐν τῷ πρώτῳ [τ]ῶν δικαστηρ[ι]ω[ν] β′ κληρωτήρια, καὶ κύβοι χαλκοῖ, ἐν οἷς ἐπιγέγραπται τὰ χ[ρ]ώματα τῶν [δι]κ[ασ]τηρίων, καὶ ἕτεροι κύ[βο]ι, ἐς οἷς ἐσ[τι]ν τῶν ἀρ[χῶ]ν τὰ [ὀ]νό[μ]ατα ἐπιγε[γ]ραμμένα. λαχόντες [δὲ] τῶν δεσ[μ]οθετῶν δύο χωρὶς ἑκατέρων τοὺς κύ[β]ο[υς ἐμ]βάλλουσιν, ὁ μὲν τὰ χρώματα ε[ἰ]ς τ[ὸ] ἓν κλ[ηρ]ωτήριον, ὁ δὲ τῶν ἀρχῶν τὰ ὀν[ό]ματα [εἰς τὸ] ἕτ[ερ]ον*** (66.1).

In Passages (4) and (5) *kleroterion* has never been, and cannot be, taken to mean "room." We have seen that certain existing machines fit the requirements of (2), as well as of Athenian constitutional principles, so well that the meaning "rooms," which this passage has almost universally been taken to authenticate, must be abandoned. As to (1) and (3), there are serious arguments, deriving from the text of Aristotle by itself, which tend to prove that the meaning "rooms" should never have been considered. These arguments,

---

suggests that dikasts from each tribe were supposed to sit together in adjacent seats in the courts; doubtless they may have, and they may have cheered, booed, and voted together; but that could not be helped, and certainly it is unlikely that they or any other blocs were encouraged. The system was designed to prevent such blocs as far as possible.

* "There are twenty *kleroteria*, two for each tribe."

** "There are five *kanonides* in each of the *kleroteria*. Whenever he puts in the *kyboi*, the archon draws lots for the tribe on the *kleroterion*."

*** "There are placed in the first of the courts two *kleroteria*, and bronze *kyboi* on which are painted the colours of the courts, and other *kyboi* on which are inscribed the names of the officials. Two of the *thesmothetai* picked by lot put in the *kyboi* of each series separately, one putting the colours into one *kleroterion* and the other putting the names of the officials into the other."

four in number, together with a fifth from another source, are as follows. (I) The text of Aristotle, if *kleroterion* were ambiguous, would confuse any Greek reader not already familiar with the Heliaia. (II) According to the established, and erroneous, view of ante-1937, Aristotle, who in 63.2 is obviously enumerating the important articles of equipment, omits to state that there was a *kleroterion* (machine) in each *kleroterion* (room); i.e., he fails to mention the largest article of all, which first appears in 66.1 without any previous notice. This assumption is quite unnecessary. (III) His references, if interpreted as meaning "allotment rooms," are peculiar. He mentions that (63.2) εἴσοδοι δέ εἰσιν εἰς [τὰ] δικαστ[ή]ρια δέκα, μία τῇ φυλῇ ἑκάστῃ, καὶ κλη[ρωτήρι]α εἴκοσι, δ[ύο τ]ῇ φυλῇ ἑκάστῃ.* What he really meant to say, according to Hommel's theory, is that "there are 10 entrances into 20 allotment rooms, the rooms being grouped in pairs, each member of each pair sharing with the other member of the same pair a common ante-room, which is entered by one of the aforesaid entrances." (IV) The account of the actual process of allotment, as I shall show below, pp. 77–9, can be understood exactly as Aristotle has written it only if we drop all consideration of "rooms." And further, if we consider the evidence of excavations, (V) it may be doubted whether there was space in the Agora for a series of 20 rooms, each capable (with 10 ante-rooms) of holding some 300 persons in addition to a great or small open yard,[15] and the dikasteria themselves. No trace of any such series of 20 rooms, with or without the 10 ante-rooms, has been found at this writing, though to be sure no dikasterion has yet been identified.

The word *kleroterion* can therefore mean nothing but "allotment machine" in Aristotle. In other ancient authors there are several occurrences of the word. In Aristophanes, *Eccl.*, 681–683, it is a question of bringing kleroteria to the Agora, and of setting them up.[16] Here the word has been translated (Rogers) "balloting booths," as though some sort of small portable rooms were meant. The notion of allotment in a small room, out of sight of most of the participants, is contrary to the way the Athenians did things. Plainly as early as the *Ekklesiazousai* (*ca.* 393 B.C.), the use of a group of portable allotment machines was thoroughly familiar in Athens.[17]

---

* "There are ten entrances into the courts, one for each tribe, and twenty *kleroteria*, two for each tribe."

[15] There was some sort of open area before the courts themselves; Hommel, *Heliaia*, p. 140, Abb. 1, makes it much too large.

[16] *Prytaneis*, p. 215.

[17] Aristophanes used the word in his *Geras* also, where it was ambiguous to Pollux (see below).

Similarly there need be no doubt about the meaning in a fragment of Euboulos,[18] where two characters exclaim over "the things for sale together at Athens in one and the same place," one character mentioning groceries – figs, grapes, turnips, etc., – the other character interjecting (I preserve the order) "summoners," "witnesses," "law-suits" (a natural sequence; then), *"kleroteria," "klepsydrai* [water-clocks]" (note the association; finally), *"nomoi* [laws]" *"graphai* [prosecutions]" (which also belong together). Obviously allotment machines, like groceries and the other things named, could all be bought, sold, and moved about in a way that would be impossible for entire rooms. The order also shows that kleroteria were objects, in a class with water-clocks.

It will be convenient to insert here a riddle, also from Euboulos, and also preserved in Athenaeus:[19]

> ἔστιν ἄγαλμα βεβηκὸς ἄνω, τὰ κάτω δὲ κεχηνός,
> εἰς πόδας ἐκ κεφαλῆς τετρημένον ὀξὺ διαπρό,
> ἀνθρώπους τίκτον κατὰ τὴν πυγὴν ἕν' ἕκαστον,
> ὧν οἱ μὲν μοίρας ἔλαχον βίου, οἱ δὲ πλανῶνται,
> αὐτὸς ἕκαστος ἔχων θαυτοῦ, καλέων δὲ φυλάττειν.

ταῦτα δ' ὅτι κληρωτικὸν σημαίνει ὑμεῖς διακρίνατε, ἵνα μὴ πάντα παρὰ τοῦ Εὐβούλου λαμβάνωμεν.*

This riddle, which hitherto could not be explained, needs to be examined in terms of the existing allotment machines; *klerotikon* is obviously a variant for *to kleroterion.* The term *agalma*, in a vague sense, applies. The object stands high up – high enough so that many men, crowding around, could watch all the operations. It is pierced from top and bottom by a hole from which counters of some sort dropped. On the other hand, Athenaeus gives only a part of what Euboulos said, and the six existing machines with which definite dates are associated belong two centuries after the comedian's epoch. Thus it is impossible to say whether the machines known to Euboulos were actually "bored sharply clear through from head to foot" or whether, taking him less strictly, we should infer that they resembled the preserved machines, in which the hole from top to bottom was

---

[18] From the *Olbia*, preserved in Athenaeus, XIV, 640 B–C (= Kock, *CAF*, 74).

[19] I give the latest text, that of Gulick (Loeb Classical Library, Cambridge, Mass.; Athenaeus, vol. IV [1930], bk. X, 450 B–C), which makes sense throughout, as will appear. The one unsolved problem, *phylattein*, is not textual.

* "'There is an image standing high up, open at the bottom, bored sharply clear through from head to foot, giving birth at its bottom to men, one by one, of whom some have drawn the lot of life but others wander, each one having his own, calling out to beware.' You can determine that this indicates a *klerotikon*, so that we need not take the whole passage from Euboulos."

bored through part of the stone but was mostly a metal tube. Again, following the text closely, we should naturally suppose that the counters were inscribed with the names of the dikasts, which were drawn one by one; there is no mention, in what Athenaeus gives us, of *kanonides* and slots, and of *empektai*. There us no way of knowing how literally the riddle should be interpreted. The process of allotment in the time of Euboulos (*ca.* 378/7–? B.C.) *may* have been different from what it was in the time of Aristotle's *Ath. Pol.* (*ca.* 328–325). In the riddle itself there is one further clause which may be helpful: the rejected dikasts wander off, αὐτὸς ἕκαστος ἔχων θαὑτοῦ ["each one having his own"]. The explanation of this can hardly be doubtful. Nothing was so closely identified with a dikast as his juror's ticket, his *pinakion* which bore his name, patronymic, and demotic, the letter of his dikastic section, and two or three seals; dikasts' tickets have been found buried with their owners. After the allotment, in Aristotle's day, the rejected dikasts went away carrying their tickets. Hence it seems likely that in the time of Euboulos also the *pinakia* were somehow used in the allotment. They would not pass through the tube, which clogged at times with the dice themselves (below, p. 75). It may well be, then that slots, etc., were used, though Euboulos could not work them into his riddle – at least not into the part we have.

One further detail requires at least an attempt at explanation. Why did the still-born infants (= rejected jurors), when they wandered, call "Beware"? The explanation should recognize the dual aspect of the riddle. First as to the still-born infants: presumably they are ghosts – for which the expression *planontai* ["wander"] is appropriate. Deprived of the right to live, they may be thought of as murdered, thirsting for revenge, and hence calling out threateningly to beware. As to the rejected jurors, they too in their disappointment would be in an ill temper. Whether or not this explains *phylattein* ["beware"] it seems altogether likely that when jurors were rejected, they uttered some commonplace expression of disgust.

After due allowance is made for the fact that it is a riddle, and only partially preserved, the passage from Euboulos must be admitted as the most helpful literary reference next to Aristotle's. The mentions in Aristotle, *ca.* 50 years later, and the preserved kleroteria, some of them dated *ca.* 200 years later, are fully compatible with the theory that the essential element of dikastic allotment and of the kleroteria themselves had not changed since the days of Euboulos.

Other literacy references are more straightforward but less useful. The choice between the two meanings (machine, room) is not clear in Plutarch *Moralia*, 793d, ἡ πρὸς πᾶν μὲν ἀεὶ κληρωτήριον ἀπαντῶσα φιλαρχία ["the ambition for office which confronts every *kleroterion*"]. The comment of Phrynichos, κληρωτήρια· ἔνθα κληροῦνται οἱ δικασταί [*"kleroteria:* where the jurors are allotted"] (Bekker, *Anecdota*, 47, 13) was written in the time when Pollux also was wrong or uncertain as to the correct meaning. The sources of modern errors are this passage in Phrynichos, and Pollux (IX 44), λογιστήριον, ἵνα [οἱ] λογισταὶ συνεκάθιζον, κληρωτήριον, ἵνα οἱ κληρωταί.* Where verbal forms did not mislead him, Pollux could be correct. He has two lists of *skeue dikastika* [law-court equipment], the shorter of which (VIII 16) omits *kleroterion*, whereas the other (X 61) includes it at the end. The latter begins with five items, then adds οὕτω γὰρ τὰ Ἀττικά ["like this in Athens"], and concludes with eight more, of which the last reads: καὶ κληρωτήριον· εἰ γὰρ καὶ ἐπὶ τοῦ τόπου ἔοικεν εἰρῆσθαι τοὔνομα ἐν τῷ Γήρᾳ Ἀριστοφάνους, ἀλλὰ καὶ ἐπὶ τοῦ ἀγγείου ἂν ἐναρμό-σειεν.** (The use of *topos* ["place"] is to be remarked, since it is hardly the natural word to indicate a room.) All of the objects in the two lists are portable articles, and the lists as a whole reveal some knowledge of the courts.

The most notable fact in Pollux is his belief that kleroteria had been used only in Athens. The word occurs twice in inscriptions outside Athens.[20] In the famous Marmor Oxoniensis [Oxford Marble], Dittenberger, *OGIS*, 229, line 53, it is prescribed that the *exetastai* [examiners] of Smyrna (= *logistai* [accountants] in Athens?) are to allot to the *phylai* [tribes] (of Smyrna) all the names (of the Magnesians) which have been submitted (for citizenship in Smyrna), and are to inscribe them on the *kleroteria;* those who are thus inscribed are to have all the privileges of the other citizens. The meaning of *kleroteria* is obviously not *laterculi civitatum* ["citizenship tablets"] (as given in *OGIS*, commentary *ad loc.*), but "allotment machines." A permanent record is to be made on the machines themselves (which presumably were of stone) of the newly admitted citizens. That there existed a list of all citizens of Smyrna in *ca.* 243 B.C. inscribed on stone is highly unlikely. Such a record would require a large area of stone; it would also require constant revision,

---

* "*Logisterion*, where the *logistai* [accountants] sat together; *kleroterion*, where the *klerotai* [allotters]."

** "and *kleroterion:* for even if the work seems to be used of the place in Aristophanes' *Geras*, it would also be appropriate for the vessel."

[20] In Athenian inscriptions the word appears only in *Prytaneis*, Nos. 79 and 80, decrees which were each to be inscribed εἰς κληρωτήριον λίθινον [on a stone *kleroterion*].

the addition of those who came of age or otherwise became citizens, and the subtraction, by a symbol or by erasure, of those who died or otherwise ceased to be citizens. Hence such lists would ordinarily be kept on cheaper, perishable material. The reason for inscribing on stone the names of new citizens from Magnesia was to form a permanent authoritative record of their names under the headings of the tribes to which they had just been allotted; perhaps each tribe had its own kleroterion, as in Athens. There would be no erasure, e.g. of those who died subsequently, nor any addition, e.g. of their sons as the latter came of age; for the record of the originally admitted Magnesians would serve to authenticate the citizenship and tribal affiliations of their children.

This one inscription is sufficient to establish the fact that allotment machines were used outside Athens; machines of stone, capable, like *Prytaneis*, Nos. VI and VII, of receiving extensive inscriptions. At this writing, however, no actual kleroterion outside Athens has as yet been identified; and the second reference in an inscription cannot be held positively to substantiate the view that the Greeks generally made extensive use of them.

A lengthy inscription from Cyrene bears a set of Roman decrees dated 7/6 B.C. The text, published by G. Oliverio, in *Notiziario Archeologico*, IV (1927), p. 20, at lines 24–27, dealing with the selection of judges, reads σηκωθεισῶν τῶς | σφαιρῶν καὶ ἐπιγραφέντων αὐταῖς τῶν ὀνομάτων, ἐγ μὲν τοῦ ἑτέρου κλη|ρωτηρίου τὰ τῶν Ῥωμαίων ὀνόματα, ἐγ δὲ τοῦ ἑτέρου τὰ τῶν Ἑλλήνων κληρο[ύ]|σθω.* The use of kleroteria, which are clearly similar to those published in *Prytaneis*, since they use balls, not cubes, is notable; but the passage from Ausonius quoted by Oliverio shows that the Romans also used allotment machines. Hence nothing can safely be inferred as to Greek procedure. Hesychius seems to have understood that the word meant machine, since he writes κήτιον· μέγαν καὶ ᾧ τὰς ψήφους διωθοῦσιν ἐν τοῖς κληρωτηρίοις. καὶ ἐμετήριον ἀπὸ λαχάνου ἀγρίου, ὅπερ ἀντὶ πτερῶν καθίεσαν εἰς τὸ στόμα, κτλ.** In place of *psephous* ["ballots"], the technical word should be *kybous* (Aristotle, *Ath. Pol.*, 64.11; 65.2, 5) or later perhaps *sphairas* ["balls"], as in the inscription from Cyrene. If the counters were cubes, which would clog in the machine, the *ketion* would doubtless be needed frequently, but even spheres might need

---

* "When the balls have been collected and the names written on them, the names of the Romans shall be allotted from one *kleroterion* and those of the Greeks from the other."

** "*Ketion*: a large thing with which they push through the ballots in the *kleroteria*. And an inducer of vomiting, from a wild plant, inserted into the mouth instead of feathers, etc."

to be prodded. The *ketion* itself was probably a thin metal rod with some sort of hook on the end.

This exhausts the literary and epigraphical references to *klero-terion*. The conclusion is that the word always means "allotment machine", except in misinformed later writers.

The same is true of the variant form *klerotris*, which appears in Schol. Aristophanes, *Vespae*, 674, κηθάριον γὰρ πλέγμα ἐστὶ κανισκῶδες, ἐπιτιθέμενον τῇ κληρωτρίδι τῶν ψήφων, κτλ,* where it is clear that articles of equipment for dikasteria are being discussed. The *ketharion* was evidently a shallow wicker basket. The scholium to line 752 reads, τοῦ κήρυκος τὴν κληρωτρίδα προσφέροντος, ἔβαλον τὰς ψήφους.** According to the scholiast(s), therefore, the *klerotris* was the receptacle in which the dikasts deposited their *psephoi* in voting. The usual term for this receptacle, however, was *kadiskos* (Ar. *Vesp.* 853; Lys. 13, 37; Lyc. 149). The scholiast on line 674 offers an alternative explanation of *ketharion*: ἢ κηθάρια τὰ ὀξύβαφα, ἐξ ὧν τοὺς κύβους ἠφίεσαν. πλεκτὰ δὲ ἦν ταῦτα.*** If this suggestion is correct, the *ketharion* would be used to hold the dice, not in the dikasteria (where dice were not used), but in the allotment of dikasts. The dice would be poured from the *ketharion* into the *klerotris*, which would then be merely an alternate term for *kleroterion*, as the word itself suggests.

PART III
THE SUPPOSED "ALLOTMENT ROOMS"

The plan of the complex of dikasteria, called the *heliaia*, his hitherto been universally understood to contain a series of "allotment rooms." The finding that the meaning of *kleroterion* is properly "allotment machine" provides a different clue to the plan. Conceivably, however, there were allotment rooms (whatever their designation), rooms which Aristotle simply did not mention – after all, we are told very little of plans of the dikasteria themselves. The possibility cannot yet be dismissed, despite what has been stated above, that the lexicographers were right, that there were in fact allotment rooms, and that these rooms were designated as *kleroteria*.

The process of allotting dikasts was elaborate and lengthy. It

---

* "For the *ketharion* is a woven thing like a basket, which is placed on the *klerotris* of the ballots, etc."
** "When the herald brought in the *klerotris*, they cast their ballots."
*** "Or the *ketharia* are the saucers from which they let go the *kyboi*. These were woven."

is natural to suppose that during the allotment, the thousands of
dikasts were not forced to remain in the open air, exposed to the
elements, without seats and hence in disorder. Modern Athenian
topographers, reasonably enough, accepting the statement of lexicographers, regularly mention allotment rooms, locating them vaguely
in the Agora.[21] The most recent study of the Heliaia, that of Hommel
(above, n. 4), has carried out the implications of the meaning "allotment room" in minute detail; and his scheme might be correct in
general even though the translation of *kleroterion* is wrong. Thus
when Aristotle says that each tribe had two kleroteria, conceivably
he may *imply* that the allotment for each tribe was carried out in two
different rooms, rooms which the reader ought naturally to assume
without specific mention. These rooms would contain the equipment
(machines, urns, chests) mentioned by Aristotle, as well as space for
the officials, servants and at least 250 tribesmen. Since there were
ten tribes, the theory requires twenty rooms used for allotments.
Aristotle says that there was one entrance (*eisodos*) for each tribe;
hence the theory demands that each pair of rooms must have had
an ante-room, entered by the *eisodos*, and giving access by two other
openings (omitted by Aristotle, like the ante-rooms themselves) to
the two "allotment rooms." In short, if the theory as a whole were
correct, we should have to find, in addition to the area required for
the court-rooms themselves, space in the Agora for a complex of
thirty large rooms, capable of holding in all some 6000 citizens.

Aristotle's account begins (63.2) εἴσοδοι δέ εἰσιν εἰς [τὰ]
δικαστ[ή]ρια δέκα. There are ten entrances to the courts: i.e.,
Aristotle writes as if the *eisodoi* give immediate access, without
intermediate buildings, to the courts. Actually the chosen dikasts,
after passing through the tribal entrances, had to traverse *some* sort
of open space (which Aristotle does not mention),[22] and then had
to be admitted to the actual court-rooms (65.2). Hence in 63.2 the
exposition is compressed. It might be argued therefore that Aristotle
omits mention also of allotment rooms.

Aristotle next enumerates the various articles of equipment
for sortition: 20 kleroteria, 100 chests; other chests[23] to receive the

---

[21] Judeich mentions *die Losungshallen der Geschworenen* [the allotment-rooms of the
sworn (jurors)] as equivalent to *das Kleroterion*, and places them somewhere in the Agora
(*Topographie von Athen* ed. 2 [(Munich, 1931)], p. 347). References to the (similar) views of
Koehler and Wachsmuth, *ibid.*, p. 347, n. 1. In connection with the Heliaia, Judeich (p. 354)
omits mention of *das Kleroterion*.

[22] Hommel, *op. cit.*, p. 57, has conceived and proved for the first time the existence of this
open area.

tickets of the dikasts chosen; and two *hydriai* [water-pots]. Further, he goes on, staves, equal in number to the jurors required, are placed κατὰ τὴν ε[– $\overset{ca.\ 5-6}{---}$ –] ἑκάστην ["by each e——"]. The staves are to be given to the successful dikasts as they pass into the area between the entrances and the doors of the court-rooms themselves. The lacuna could be filled, as by Hommel, *op. cit.*, pp. 12 and 55–57, *e(xodon)* [exit], and that restoration is correct, *if* there were allotment rooms. Otherwise, by keeping the former restoration *e(isodon)* [entrance], we should have a significant fact: the staves, placed next each *entrance*, as Aristotle carefully specifies – the other equipment being placed, by inference, not immediately adjacent to the entrances, but near them – the staves are to be passed out before the dikasts enter the (first and only) *eisodos*: there is no other barrier before the door of the court-room itself is reached. This interpretation, of course, has yet to be proved.

The next significant clause is in 64.1: τὰ δὲ [κιβώ]τια τὰ δέ[κ]α κ[εῖται ἐ]ν τ[ῷ ἔμ]προσθεν [τ]ῆς εἰσόδου [κ]αθ’ ἑκάστην τὴν φυλήν.* The ten chests, one gathers, are placed squarely in front of the entrance. Now Hommel is obliged to place them five on each side of the entrance; that is, he is obliged to take Aristotle loosely at this point, since as many as 600 jurors may have to pass through the entrance before the allotting begins, and a row of 10 chests literally in front of the entrance would be inconvenient. If, however, we respect the text, we can conceive the chests being placed a few paces directly in front of the entrance; once the tickets from the chests begin to be inserted in the kleroteria, one of which presumably stood somewhere on either side of the entrance, the chests themselves can be removed, and free access will be given to the entrance. In other words, if the allotment is performed wholly outside the entrance, the chests will be out of the way before anyone is admitted at the entrance, the chests will be out of the way before anyone is a admitted at the entrance. This then is a useful detail to have settled, but by itself it hardly confirms us in altering the accepted opinion that there were "allotment rooms."

The procedure of allotment now begins. When the dikasts throw in their tickets, each into the chest on which is inscribed the letter which is on his ticket, the servant shakes up the chests and the archon draws from each chest one ticket. The owner of the ticket is

---

[23] Number not specified, because it would vary, depending on how many courts were to be filled.

* "The ten chests lie in front of the entrance for each tribe."

called a ticket-inserter, and he inserts the tickets into the *kanonis*. Thus Aristotle (64.1–2); but anyone who believes in allotment rooms must suppose an omission to the effect, "The servant shakes the chests up *and takes all ten chests into the allotment rooms*"; further, if there were two rooms, "*those lettered* A–E *go into the first room, and those lettered* Z–K *into the second*";[24] subsequently the archon must first draw five ticket-inserters in one room, then make his way through the crowd, draw five in the other room, and return to the first room.[25] Those who believe in allotment rooms must also assume that the dikasts, after throwing their tickets into the chests, or else after the chests have been taken into the rooms, themselves pass through the entrance. Aristotle, though he records their every other movement, says nothing of this movement of the dikasts. His account reads as if the whole process of allotment took place in front of the entrance, without any unnecessary comings and goings, at all times in view of all the parties concerned.

In sum, to suppose that there were allotment rooms is to suppose that Aristotle omitted to mention not only the rooms, but also several important details of the procedure of allotment; whereas without the assumption of allotment rooms, Aristotle's account appears to be clear and complete. This, then, is the decisive argument. There is no need to seek for space to accommodate 30 (or 10) "allotment rooms." In *Ath. Pol.*, 62.2 the text should therefore read (the staves were placed) κατὰ τὴν ε[ἴσοδον] ἑκάστην ["by each entrance"]. The chests are placed in front of the entrances, waiting to be filled with tickets; when the allotment begins, they are moved nearer to kleroteria, which are also *outside* the entrances. Here, out-of-doors, the allotment takes place.[26] The crowds may have overflowed in all directions; no special area need be provided for them. A fair amount of clear space before each entrance is all that is required.

---

[24] Aristotle is hardly likely to have omitted such a detail, since he specifies the moving of kleroteria into the first court-room (66.1).

[25] Part of these difficulties, but only part, could be overcome by assuming that there was only one allotment-room for each tribe.

[26] Thus Isocrates, *Areop.*, 54, πρὸ τῶν δικαστηρίων κληρουμένους ["allotted in front of the law-courts"] can be taken simply and literally, not (as by Colin, *REG* 30 [1917], 46, n.) "*avant l'ouverture des audiences* [before the opening of the sessions]."

For previous views on the place of allotment, see Hommel, *Heliaia*, p. 58, n. 136. A Greek lawyer, P. S. Photiades, came nearest to being correct.

PART IV
THE PLAN OF THE DIKASTIC COURTS

The elimination of the allotment rooms simplifies the current notion of the plan of the dikastic courts.

The actual plan can be determined, if at all, only by excavation. The excavated remains, however, will probably not be fully intelligible by themselves, and it may be useful to set down here the essential parts of the plan, and the proper relation of the parts to each other.

A study of the location of these courts belongs to the Agora Reports (*Hesperia*, in progress) rather than to the present study. It seems clear that the Heliaia was somewhere in or near the Agora.[27] Now it is generally assumed, as by Hommel, that the Heliaia was enclosed in such a way that no unauthorized persons could obtain access to the area before the doors of the court-rooms themselves; in other words, that the complex of court-rooms was accessible only through the ten tribal entrances.[28] There is no positive statement to this effect, but it is inconceivable that any dikast, once admitted at an *eisodos*, and carrying a staff which designated his court-room to all whom he met, was exposed to possible bribery in the Agora at large. That would be contrary to the intent of the whole system described in *Ath. Pol.*, 63–69. There would be in fact no meaning in "ten entrances" if they admitted dikasts, not to an enclosed area, but to the Agora in general – in which they were already.

When a given dikast, successful in the allotment, had drawn his lettered acorn *balanos*, and when his ticket had been placed in the chest which was to go to the appropriate court-room, he passed a barrier called the *kinklis*, where an attendant gave him a colored staff. After passing this barrier, he proceeded to the court-room (βαδίζει εἰ[ς τ]ὸ δικασ[τήριον, 65.2), encountering no other barrier until he reached the court-room door. The problem of where the *kinklis* was situated depends on whether or not there were allotment rooms: if so, then the *kinklis* was somehow associated with the

---

[27] Judeich, *Topographie*, ed. 2, p. 354, n. 2, with references; the exact location in the Agora there proposed is dubious. Professor T. L. Shear, Director of the Agora Excavations, has kindly permitted me to quote a letter from Professor H. A. Thompson, who writes that "from the area east and southeast of the Tholos have come many of the ostraka [potsherds used for voting in ostracisms] and exactly one half of the dikasts' tickets found in the excavations, and in this same region are numerous poros [coarse stone] blocks cut to support stone posts. Quite tentatively, then, the courts may be located in the southwest corner of the square." [Recent work locates one court in the south-west of the Agora, a major complex in the north-east: A. L. Boegehold et al., *The Athenian Agora*, xxviii (Princeton, 1995).]

[28] Conceivably the magistrates, litigants, witnesses, and servants used one or more other (guarded) entrances.

exit; if not, the *kinklis* was somehow associated with the "entrance" (*eisodos*). We have seen (pp. 77–9) that the *eisodos* opened directly on the area of the courts, not on a room; there was no *exodos*. Hence the *kinklis* may now be accurately located at or in the *eisodos* itself.

Aristotle does not provide a clear image of the *kinklis*. He merely says (65.1) that the successful dikast ἐ[ντὸς εἰσέρχετ]αι τῆς κ[ι]γκλ[ίδ]ος ["goes inside the *kinklis*"]. Entering within the *kinklis* must imply passing through the *eisodos* – through an "entrance"; Aristotle did not choose a more specific word such as "door" or "gate." Hence it might be thought that the whole enclosing barrier of the courts was a *kinklis* continuous except for openings which could appropriately be described only as "entrances." In that case *kinklis* would mean "latticed or grilled fence," and the courts would have to be imagined as enclosed by an open-work barrier. Clearly *kinklis* does usually imply an open-work barrier of some sort: Ps.-Dem. XXV 23 speaks of τὸ τὴν βουλὴν τοὺς πεντακοσίους ἀπὸ τῆς ἀσθενοῦς ταυτησὶ κιγκλίδος τῶν ἀπορρήτων κυρίαν εἶναι.*

This image of a long open-work grill about the courts should probably be rejected because in the bouleuterion [council-house] the *kinklis* was evidently some sort of swinging (latticed or grilled) gate, set in the main door.[29] Other uses of the word seem to imply a short grill-work, not a long fence.[30] The conclusion is that the simple tribal

---

* "The fact that the council of five hundred as a result of this weak *kinklis* is master of its secrets."

[29] Ar., *Eq.*, 640–1, κᾷτα τῷ πρωκτῷ θενὼν τὴν κιγκλίδ' ἐξήπραξα ["then, striking it with my bum, I shattered the *kinklis*"]. This was plainly (*pace* Rogers, note *ad loc.*) in the door of the bouleuterion, not in the *dryphaktoi*. There was no solid door (Ps.-Dem., XXV 23, given above). The *dryphaktoi* were a railing of some sort between the area of the members' seats and the rest of the floor; when the prytaneis were in a hurry to leave, they leaped over the *dryphaktoi* (Ar., *Eq.*, 675; see also Xen., *Hell.*, II, 3.50 and 55).

[30] *IG*, II², 1668 (of 347/6 B.C.), line 65: καὶ διαφράξει τὸ μεταστύλιον ἕκαστον ὀρθοστάταις δυοῖν λιθίνοις ὕψος τριῶν ποδῶν, καὶ ἐν τῶι μεταξὺ κιγκλίδα ἐπιθήσε[ι] κλειομένην ["and he is to fence across each gap between columns with two stone uprights three feet high, and insert between them a closing *kinklis*"]. The scholiasts on Ar. are inaccurate or vague: on *Eq.*, 641, τὴν θύραν, τὸ κάγκελον τοῦ δικαστηρίου. ἰδίως δὲ τὰς διπλᾶς θύρας οὕτω κλητέον, ἅς τινὲς δικλίδας φασίν ["The door, the barrier of the law-court. In particular this name should be given to the double doors which some call *diklides*"]; on *Vesp.*, 386, δρύφακτοι γὰρ ξύλινοι θώρακες, τὰ διαφράγματα, ἢ τὰ περιτειχίσματα, ἢ κιγκλίδες, περιφράγματα, τὰ νῦν ταβλωτὰ καλούμενα, τὰ τῶν οἰκοδομημάτων ἐξέχοντα ξύλα ["*Dryphaktoi* are wooden breastworks, the cross-fences or surrounding bulwarks or *kinklides*, surrounding fences, which are now called *tablota*, the projecting timbers of buildings"]. The lexicographers are inaccurate, but understand a door or gate: Pollux, 8, 124, αἱ μὲν οὖν δικαστηρίων θύραι κιγκλίδες ἐκαλοῦντο ["The doors of law-courts were called *kinklides*"]; [*Etym. Magn.*, *s.v.*, ἡ καγκελοθυρίς, θύρα δικτυωτή ["The doorway-barrier, a latticed door"].

The word appears also in Ar., *Vesp.*, 214, and in Fr. 18 (Blaydes); in *IG*, II², 4771; and in late authors, but not significantly for the present purpose.

entrances were controlled by swinging grills of wood or metal. Once in, the dikasts were reasonably well-insulated; temptations could not come from without.

The next step is to determine the character of the wall surrounding each court-room. It would not seem likely from Aristotle's account that outside spectators could witness the proceedings in the court-rooms; yet it is clear that large crowds actually could hear and see. The orators speak of them regularly, as though the phrase were almost technical, as "standing round about outside."[31] The implication of *exothen* [outside] is clearly that the public was not admitted to the court-room itself, but was allowed to see and hear from outside it, which must mean from over at least one (low) wall of the room. The use of *periistemi* [stand round] probably implies a low wall on three sides.[32] This barrier has usually been taken to be the *dryphaktoi*, which are thought of as a wooden paling or rail. Plutarch uses the word in precisely this sense, namely of a long outer circuit fence: τόπον τῆς ἀγορᾶς περιπεφραγμένον ἐν κύκλῳ δρυφάκτοις* (*Aristeides*, 7.5), but the scholiasts and the lexicographers[33] show that no exact definition survived the object itself. The *dryphaktoi* were doubtless wooden,[34] but they are hardly likely to have been merely part of the walls of the court. The *dryphaktoi* in the bouleuterion were clearly not part of the walls of that building (above, [n. 29]). Among the larger furnishings of the court, the *dryphaktoi* were the central feature: Aristophanes makes Bdeluklon cry out, If I die, θεῖναί μ᾽ ὑπὸ τοῖσι δρυφάκτοις** (*Vesp.*, 386); and again (830–831) ἄνευ δρυφάκτου τὴν δίκην μέλλεις καλεῖν | ὃ πρῶτον ἡμῖν τῶν ἱερῶν ἐφαίνετο;*** Such sentiments would hardly attach themselves to a mere barrier for keeping back the public. The

---

[31] Dem., XVIII, 196, πρὸς ὑμᾶς, ἄνδρες δικασταί, καὶ τοὺς περιεστηκότας ἔξωθεν καὶ ἀκροωμένους ["for you, gentlemen of the jury, and for those standing around outside and listening"]. Aeschines, II, 5, τις - - - τῶν ἔξωθεν περιεστηκότων ["one of those standing around outside"]. III, 56, ἐναντίον τῶν δικαστῶν - - - καὶ τῶν ἄλλων πολιτῶν ὅσοι δὴ ἔξωθεν περιεστᾶσι ["in the presence of the jurors and of the other citizens who are standing around outside"]. Isaeus, V, 20, ἐναντίον μὲν τῶν δικαστῶν, - - - ἐναντίον δὲ τῶν περιεστηκότων ["in the presence of the jurors, in the presence of those standing around"]. Kahrstedt, *Untersuchungen zur Magistratur*, p. 295.

[32] The fourth side, with the door, was probably higher, since the "entrance" (*eisodos*) had a lintel (*Ath. Pol.*, 65.2).

* "A place in the agora fenced round in a circle with *dryphaktoi*."

[33] Thus Hesychius *s.v.*, αἱ τοῦ δικαστηρίου θύραι ἢ κἀγκελοι, ἢ τὰ διαφράγματα, ἢ τὰ περιτειχίσματα ["The doors or barriers of the law-court, or the cross-fences, or the surrounding bulwarks"].

[34] Schol. Ar., *Vesp.*, 830.

** "Place me under the *dryphaktoi*."

*** "Are you going to call up the lawsuit without a *dryphaktos*, which was the first of the sacred things revealed to us?"

dryphaktoi should rather be imagined as railing the focal space where stood the archon, the three bemata, the urns for voting, and the water-clock. *Behind* the dikasts would be the low mud-brick walls of the room, walls not dignified by any special name.

It is notable that Aristotle (68.1) speaks of courts coming together "into the Heliaia": συν[έρχεται β΄ δικαστή]ρια εἰ[ς] τὴν ἡλιαίαν (Hommel, *Heliaia*, p. 24). This seems to imply that the Heliaia was included in the circuit wall, whether as the old Solonian court-room, or as a new room laid out to fit the old requirements, or perhaps as merely a name for a court sitting in any convenient large room. In the latter case, removable walls between lesser court-rooms may have enabled these rooms to be thrown together into a larger room of any desired size.

When one attempts to put the foregoing indications together, it becomes evident that much depends on the *peri-* of *periistemi*. If each and every one of the courts can be "surrounded" by the public on as many as three sides, then the fourth side must contain the entrance of the court. This entrance must open on an area accessible only to successful dikasts. The requirements could be satisfied by arranging the court-rooms at intervals along a sort of walled street. Outside the street, in the intervals between the courts, the tribal allotments would take place, and the successful dikasts would pass through entrances cut in the walls of the "street." Once in the street, they would have in view all the various court-room doors. So much results from taking *periistemi* literally. If, instead, the public could look over only one, or at most two, walls, then the court-rooms may have been built in a block forming one large solid rectangle. An outer wall, at an even distance of say 10 m. from the rectangle, may have been drawn about the whole. This circuit wall would contain the tribal entrances, outside of which allotments would take place. After the dikasts were in their courts, the public can have been admitted within the wall.

So much for the demands of theory.[35] Without violating these demands, the actual plan may well have been formed irregularly at different dates by building various rooms and connecting them with the complex. Thus some courts would remain more or less distinct, like the Batrachion and the Phoinikion seen by Pausanias (I 28.8). The Heliaia proper, a larger enclosure, may also have stood some-

[35] Hommel's diagram (*Heliaia*, p. 140), besides containing allotment rooms, allows too much free space in the middle, and in the case of all but two of the court-rooms, the public would have access to only one wall of each room.

what apart, and the name of the Trigonon suggests that the court so named was fitted into an awkward space (*ibid.*). A further complication is introduced by the inscription *Hesperia*, 5 (1936), No. 10, pp. 393–413, which mentions in lines 12–13 [δικαστήριον] πρῶτον τῶν καινl[ῶν] ["the first of the new courts"], and in lines 116–117 δικαστήριον τὸ μέσ[ον τῶl]ν ϙαινῶν ["the middle of the new courts"]. The natural interpretation here, as Professor Ferguson has suggested to me, is that three "new" courts are implied, presumably built in a block: *to proton, to meson*, and by inference *to triton* ["the third"]. This is not the only conceivable interpretation,[36] but at least it suggests the sort of thing which must have taken place.

The precinct and statue of Lykos[37] stood somewhere near, or probably in, the area, but only excavation can determine where.

PART V
THE ALLOTMENT OF DIKASTS

Aristotle, *Ath. Pol.*, 63.2: εἴσοδοι δέ εἰσιν εἰς [τὰ] δικαστ[ή]ρια δέκα, μία τῇ φυλῇ ἑκάστῃ, καὶ κλη[ρωτήρι]α εἴκοσι, δ[ύο τ]ῇ φυλῇ ἑκάστῃ, καὶ κιβώτια ἑκατόν, δέκα τῇ φυλῇ ἑκάστῃ, κτλ.* *One* entrance for each tribe is precisely what would be expected, since the allotment of dikasts took place outside the entrances,[38] the tribes being allotted separately, each outside its own entrance; and the successful dikasts filed one at a time each through his own tribal entrance. Likewise the number of chests *kibotia* is no mystery. The dikasts of each tribe were divided into ten sections, each designated by one of the ten letters A–K. Each dikast, as he arrived before his tribe's entrance, deposited his dikast's ticket in the chest bearing the same letter as the letter on his ticket signifying which section he belonged to. Hence there had to be *ten* chests for each tribe. The number of kleroteria was *two* for each tribe. *One* kleroterion for each tribe would seem suitable, or else *ten*. Why *two*?

This question has never been answered. Certainly there ought to be an answer, since the whole system of allotment, like much else in Athenian political institutions, was utterly logical. The inquiry may therefore be expected to lead us beyond mere considerations of equipment.

Hitherto students have thought that *kleroteria* in the passage

---

[36] Meritt, *Hesperia*, 5 (1936), 408.
[37] Ar., *Vesp.*, 389, 818, etc.
* "There are ten entrances into the courts, one for each tribe, and twenty *kleroteria*, two for each tribe, and a hundred chests, ten for each tribe, etc."
[38] Above, pp. 77–9.

quoted meant "allotment rooms," *Losungshallen, salles pour le tirage au sort.* The problem was therefore different for them; the main consideration in a hall would be space, and the crowds of dikasts, as many as 600 from each tribe, might each be handled most expeditiously if split into two "allotment rooms," each holding some 300 dikasts. Since it is now established that *kleroteria* can mean nothing but "allotment machines," and there were no "allotment rooms" at all (above, pp. 76–9), another form of the same solution might be considered, namely that a crowd of hundreds of dikasts milling around one machine would interfere with the proper witnessing of the procedure by all concerned. If only 300 were grouped about, then perhaps all could see satisfactorily. To this solution there is one telling objection, namely that the same considerations ought to have led the Athenians to set up five or even ten kleroteria for each tribe.[39]

Two other reasons of a practical sort are also not convincing. It might be thought, for instance, that kleroteria capable of allotting a whole tribe at once would be so heavy as to be practically immovable. There are two sufficient answers to this. One is, that the machines, once set up, never had to be moved. The other is, that the machines of Aristotle's day were movable.[40] Neither of these answers is known for a fact, but they have authority enough to serve.

The second practical reason which might be advanced is the technical difficulty of making a kleroterion with *ca.* 600 slots, and the consequent expense. The answer to this is that much larger kleroteria were produced.[41] It may be conceded that two lesser kleroteria were considerably cheaper to make than one kleroterion as large as both combined. This practical argument helps to explain why they did not make one large kleroterion, dividing it by a line on the front surface into two equal parts. The necessity which would have impelled them so to divide it has yet to be made clear.

More plausible would be a mathematical reason, if any could be

---

[39] In L. Whibley's *Companion to Greek Studies*, ed. 1 (Cambridge, 1905), W. Wyse wrote, in the days when the text of Aristotle was more imperfect than now, "The judges assembled at the allotment-chambers (*kleroteria*), one for each tribe (not, as might have been expected, one for each section)." Despite its three errors (which are unchanged in ed. 4 [1931], p. 475), this sentence shows the correct tendency of thought.

[40] In *Prytaneis*, p. 213, I suggested that Arist., *Ath. Pol.*, 66.1, which says that two kleroteria are set up in the first court when all the dikasteria are full, proves that the kleroteria of that time were portable, hence wooden. The kleroteria needed in the court were small, however, and presumably were different, then or eventually, from the kleroteria used to allot dikasts, which were bulky.

[41] *Prytaneis*, pp. 208–209, No. X clearly had 550 slots, and No. XI doubtless many more, perhaps 1000.

formulated. At first thought, it appears that a different kind of total might be reached, so that the system would be more flexible, when allotments were performed for five dikasts at a time (as in the actual kleroteria known to Aristotle and to us), rather than for ten dikasts at a time. For example, one thinks that courts totalling 750 dikasts could be filled on the former system; not on the latter, which results in even hundreds. This line of inquiry, however, appears to be mistaken. Twenty kleroteria allotting five dikasts at a time yield precisely the same totals as ten kleroteria allotting ten dikasts at a time. Courts totalling e.g. 750 were impossible: in either system, the total must always have been an even hundred dikasts, e.g. 700 or 800.[42]

The explanations which have been considered thus far have one feature in common. Though dealing with practicalities, all are general in nature: that is to say, none of them involves close attention to the actual process of allotment. Since none of them yields a satisfactory answer, it is natural to examine the only remaining aspect, namely the particular exigencies which might arise in the actual process of allotment. About certain of these exigencies Aristotle is silent. Modern students, failing to visualize the whole process, have failed to realize the existence of these exigencies. At the present time, with actual kleroteria at hand to assist the imagination, a better understanding of the whole situation ought to be, and I think is, within reach.

The ten Athenian tribes may have been approximately equal in size when Kleisthenes constituted them, but inequalities were bound to arise, and there was no way of obviating them. Our figures suggest that in fact there came to be, in the course of time, some inequalities.[43] Whether admission to the body of dikasts was controlled so as to keep the numbers of dikasts in each tribe approximately equal, we do not know; it seems likely that the effort was made. We do know (*Ath. Pol.*, 63.4) that each tribe was divided into ten sections, and that these sections were kept approximately equal to each other within each of the tribes. The intent embodied in the system as a whole was plainly to create 100 approximately equal divisions of the body of dikasts; and to order the allotment in such a

[42] See further, below n. 45. The full complement of dikasts for a court seems regularly to include an odd man, to obviate a tie (Arist., *Ath. Pol.*, 53.3; 68.1.). How this odd man was selected we do not know. He was probably not the presiding magistrate.

[43] A. W. Gomme, *The Population of Athens in the Fifth and Fourth Centuries B.C.* (Oxford, 1933), p. 50 assembled the data. Among preserved names, he counted (to take the extremes) 979 in Aiantis, 1540 in Aigeis. Chance plays so large a role, however, that not much argument can be based on these figures. A rough count shows that *Prytaneis* brings the total for Aiantis to 1103 without adding a single citizen to Aigeis.

way that a precisely equal number of dikasts would be admitted to the courts as a whole (but not to the various individual courts) from each of these 100 divisions on every day when the courts sat.

For our present purposes, the essential fact is that the ten sections of each tribe were approximately equal on the official rolls. This does not mean, however, that precisely equal numbers of dikasts from each section presented themselves for the allotment every morning when the courts were to sit. There was no compulsion on a dikast to attend, apart from the attraction of the three-obol fee. Presumably a man who removed his residence e.g. from Athens to Sounion still retained his ticket, though he seldom attended. How great the discrepancies between sections in actual daily attendance may ordinarily have been, we do not know. If, merely to illustrate, we may take 5000 as a round number for the whole body of dikasts in the period when *Ath. Pol.* was written,[44] then each section would normally contain about 50. On any given day, the attendance might, I suppose, fall as low as 25 or even 20 in some sections.

In order to construct a typical, or at least a possible, situation, let us suppose that on some given day two courts of 500 dikasts each are to be filled, so that in all 1000 dikasts are required, which means 100 dikasts for each tribe, or precisely 10 dikasts from each of the 100 sections.[45] It may be assumed, for purposes of this discussion, that at least 20 dikasts will appear on the given day in every single section.[46] It may also be assumed that the numbers of dikasts who

[44] Gomme, *Population*, estimates that there were about 28,000 citizens at this time. The number of dikasts is quite uncertain. Since there was no upper limit, such as the 6000 of the fifth century, the number nominally enrolled as dikasts may have been as high as 10,000, of whom only a minority were active.

[45] We do not know how many jurors were empanelled on a typical day in the fourth century. As few as 200 are contemplated in Dem. *Mid.*, 223: ἐάν τε διακοσίους ἐάν τε χιλίους ἐάν θ᾽ ὁπόσους ἂν ἡ πόλις καθίσῃ ["whether two hundred, or a thousand, or whatever number the city convenes"]. Certainly 1000 was not the upper limit; it may be taken as a large number, or more likely as typical. The number 200 has been taken as the smallest number which were or could be empanelled (Sandys, *Ath. Pol.*, ed. 2, p. 204 and refs.). The inference was bold but correct, as can now be proved by visualizing the process of allotment. As will be shown in this Part, actually there had to be two allotments of the dikasts who presented themselves. The first allotment had to be performed by ticket-inserters, and the ticket-inserters were *ex officio* [by virtue of that office] chosen to serve that day in the courts. There were 100 ticket-inserters. The whole body of dikasts was divided into 100 parts. These 100 parts had to be equally represented in the day's session, and the ticket-inserters, though they fulfilled this condition, were too simply chosen (below) and collusion might result in a packed jury. Hence more dikasts had to be chosen, and to keep the representation of the 100 sections even, at least 100 had to be chosen. Hence 100 ticket-inserters plus 100 other dikasts (the latter chosen by double allotment, below) made up a day's panel of minimum size. Hence also all panels contained even hundreds (p. 86).

[46] Aristotle says nothing of possible deficiencies. Probably the thesmothetai, in deciding the sizes of the various courts, took into account the nature of the cases, the weather, the military situation if any, and the state of the crops; and then fixed the total number of dikasts required

present themselves will not be the same, unless by mere coincidence, in any two sections within one tribe. In conformity with these assumptions, a set of figures for one tribe may be drawn up sufficiently representative, so far as one can guess, to serve as a basis for discussion. Let us suppose that from the first section, A, 32 dikasts present themselves, from B, 31, and similar numbers from other sections, one section (say Δ) having as many as 36, and one (say Z) as few as 21. From each of these sections 10 dikasts are to be chosen by lot.[47]

Each dikast, when he arrives in front of his tribal entrance, throws his ticket into that one of the ten lettered chests which bears the letter of his section, the letter which is inscribed on his ticket. A signal (*semeion*) of some sort,[48] presumably a blast on trumpets, presently signifies that no more tickets are to be accepted, and that the process of allotment is about to begin. At once a servant carries the ten chests to where the archon[49] is standing, at one side of the entrance for his tribe and near one of the two kleroteria, the other of which is presumably on the other side of the entrance. The servant shakes each chest, so that the tickets deposited last will not necessarily be uppermost. He then presents the chests in turn to the archon, who draws one ticket at random from each chest. The ten dikasts in each tribe whose tickets are thus drawn are called ticket-inserters (*empektai*). Their first duty is to insert the tickets from their chests into the vertical columns of slots (*kanonides*, above, pp. 67–8) in the two allotment machines (*kleroteria*). Each allotment machine has five vertical columns of slots: in the two machines together there are ten, so that each section of the tribe has its own column of slots (*kanonis*).

The ticket-inserter from section A begins the work. We are supposing that 32 dikasts from section A presented themselves for the allotment. There are now 31 tickets in the chest, since the ticket-inserter's own ticket, drawn out by the archon, has been set aside as that of a dikast already successful, without further allotment. The ticket-inserter from A draws the 31 tickets from the chest one by one, picking them at random, so that the very taking of them out of the

at something like half or one-third of the number of dikasts likely to present themselves for the allotment. A deficiency in any given section on any given day was probably not remedied: there was no inner necessity why a court had to have its even hundreds. A deficient section would simply suffer the penalty of having too few votes.

[47] The account which follows is an expansion of Aristotle, *Ath. Pol.*, 63–65.

[48] Ar., *Vesp.*, 690; Hommel, *Heliaia* (*Philologus*, Supplementband XIX, Heft II), p. 51.

[49] The allotment was presided over by that member of the tribe who was one of the board of nine archons, the secretary to the thesmothetai serving for the tenth tribe (Aristotle, *Ath. Pol.*, 63.1). In the present article the presiding official is referred to, for simplicity, as the "the archon."

chests is in itself an allotment;[50] and as he removes each ticket, he inserts it in the first vertical column (*kanonis*) of the first kleroterion. The first ticket goes into the topmost slot, the second into the second slot, and so on, until the uppermost consecutive 31 slots are full, and the chest for section A is empty. Then the ticket-inserter from section B inserts the (31 − 1 =) 30 tickets from the chest of section B into the second column of slots; and so on, until all the tickets (save those of the ten ticket-inserters) of sections A–E have been inserted into the first kleroterion. Simultaneously the second kleroterion will have received the tickets of sections Z–K.[51]

The archon can now begin the allotment proper. As he surveys the two kleroteria, they will look as they do in the Figure facing p. 62, if we keep to the figures mentioned above for some of the sections, and if we fill in the others with intermediate numbers of tickets. (In no case do the exact figures given matter in the least – all that is sought for is general verisimilitude, with discrepancies of the magnitude that must have occurred.)

The dikasts are to be allotted five at a time. According to the way the first lot decides, the five dikasts whose tickets are in the first *horizontal row* of the first kleroterion will succeed or fail together; and so on throughout the *whole series of horizontal rows filled with five tickets each*. In the first kleroterion the archon counts 28 such full horizontal rows. Now since 1000 dikasts in all are needed, or 10 from each section, the archon must count out 9 dice (that is, ten minus one, to allow for the ticket-inserters) which signify success: these dice are white. Black dice signify rejection. The remaining groups of five out of the total of 28 are to be rejected, hence the archon counts out 28 − 9 = 19 black dice. He shakes up the 9 white and 19 black dice together in a container, and dumps them all into the cone at the top of the kleroterion. (The Figure shows the long tube, into which the dice fall, cut open to reveal to us what the participants themselves could not see: the order of the 28 dice.) The first die to be drawn, as it happens, will be black. Hence the five dikasts represented by the first horizontal row will be rejected. The next two

---

[50] Colin (*REG* 30 [1917], 50–51), has the archon draw the tickets from the chest and pass them to the ticket-inserters. *Ath. Pol.*, 64.2 and the logic of the whole procedure oppose this. The archon was not entrusted with both allotments.

[51] Thus two ticket-inserters were at work simultaneously, one at each kleroterion. There would not have been room for all five ticket-inserters to work simultaneously at each kleroterion. The inserting was an allotment; it had to be orderly.

It may be noted that all the preserved *pinakia* have the letter which denotes the section stamped at the left end. The reason for this uniformity was probably to enable the tickets to be inserted in the kleroteria with the letter-end uppermost and (since the slots are not deep) protruding. A quick inspection would then enable the archon to detect error or malpractice.

dice are white; hence the next two rows will be accepted; and so on.

When the first die is drawn and proves to be black, the first row of tickets, being thus rejected, will remain in their slots. When the second die, which happens to be white, has been drawn, the second row of tickets will be removed by the archon and shown to the herald. The herald will call out the names, and each dikast, as his name is called, will come forward and complete the process of admission to the area of the courts. (The tickets of the unsuccessful dikasts will be passed back to their owners by the ticket-inserters when the drawing is complete and the successful dikasts have disappeared within the entrance.) The whole process is repeated with the second kleroterion. Here, as before, 9 white dice, plus (20 − 9 =) 11 black dice will be required. In this way all of the dikasts from the tribe in question, whose tickets occur in *full horizontal rows of five tickets each*, will have been allotted. Those who succeed in this tribe, as in every tribe, will number (9 × 5 × 2 =) 90, + 10 ticket-inserters, = 100 dikasts. The archon's allotment, now completed, will have rejected in the first kleroterion, 19 × 5 = 95, and in the second kleroterion 11 × 5 = 55, in all 150 dikasts.

We come now to the problem of the tickets inserted in the slots of each machine *below the last full horizontal rows of five tickets each*. Of such tickets there are 13 in the first kleroterion, 38 in the second, in all 51. As to these tickets, Aristotle gives us no information, and hitherto no modern student has realized the peculiar exigency to which their position inevitably gives rise. A situation more or less similar must have recurred in all the 20 kleroteria on every day when the courts sat. It is hard to see how the Athenians, who were doubtless annoyed, could obviate this ragged edge in their otherwise perfect system. The suggestion may be offered that all of these 51 tickets must have been considered as rejected by their position itself in the *kanonides*. To cast lots for rows of four, three, two, or one would be to introduce an unadjustable set of figures into the calculations. Courts of even hundreds could not be made up efficiently on such a basis. Nor could tickets from sections heavily represented (such as Δ) be inserted into other columns without risk of letting into the courts a disproportionate number of men (i.e., more than 10) from section Δ. Hence all of these 51 dikasts are rejected without having had a chance at the archon's allotment. The various ticket-inserters, by drawing these tickets last, have rejected their owners. Undoubtedly this is a fault in the system. Moreover, the drawing by the ticket-inserters, when they inserted the tickets, was far from being a perfect form of allotment. Aristotle expressly states that the ticket-inserters were drawn by lot to avoid the malpractice which would result if the same men held the position permanently. One form of malpractice can easily be imagined, a form which would be reduced perhaps but not eliminated by allotting ticket-inserters. Without much effort, a ticket-inserter could, if he chose, recognize some few names on the tickets in the chest, and leave them until the last, inserting them at the bottom of the *kanonis*, where their position would probably exclude them from the archon's allotment. Such an action would doubtless be malpractice, but it could hardly be prevented. Even if such malpractice were rare, the principle remained that all dikasts had a right to be allotted according to the archon's dice. On every day the courts sat, numerous dikasts in all the tribes were victims, like our 51 dikasts, of an injustice, if not also of malpractice.

The remedy was obvious, however costly in time. The remedy would consist in allotting each section by itself. The procedure would be as follows. Taking section A by itself first, the archon would count out the 9 white dice as in the actual procedure, and mix with them $31 - 9 = 22$ black dice. Then he would pour the 31 mixed dice into the machine, and draw one die to allot each ticket by itself (not for five tickets together at a time), until he had allotted the whole of section A ticket by ticket, including the tickets below, as well as those above, the last full horizontal row. Next, coming to section B, he would mix, with the 9 white dice, $(30 - 9 =) 21$ black dice, and proceed as with section A, ticket by ticket; continuing thus through all ten sections. This procedure, which gives every single dikast the full benefit of two allotments (since malpractice by the ticket-inserter would be nullified), is an absolutely just system. It is the only absolutely just system, I think, which can be conceived.

Anyone could see that this procedure, namely individual allotment, was the perfectly fair system. Such a procedure was doubtless used for many other offices in Athens – offices for which applicants were far less numerous than those for the jury-courts. Consequently there must have been some compelling reason why the dikasts were treated with less than perfect fairness.

The explanation may be sought in the chief difference between the perfect procedure and the procedure actually used. This chief difference is the greater amount of time required by the perfect procedure. No lengthy argument is needed to prove that time was a serious factor in the sessions of the dikasteria.[52] The selection of ticket-insert-

---

[52] So much so that the dikasteria could not be convened on the day of an ekklesia: ἀδυνάτου δ᾽ ὄντος αὐθημερὸν ἐκκλησίαν ἅμα καὶ δικαστήριον γενέσθαι ["since it is impossible for the

ers and the insertion of all the tickets, 291 in our illustration, could not be finished in less than 10 or 15 minutes; this process could not be shortened. The time needed for the herald to call out all the (say 100) names of successful dikasts, for the (100) men named to come forward through the crowd, for each of them in turn to draw a *balanos*, and for each to show his *balanos* to the archon so that the archon might dispose correctly of each ticket, would be a long and irksome period. This process *could* have been shortened only by having several helpers of the archon, and several heralds. More will be said presently about this solution, which was not adopted and evidently was out of the question. Further time had to be spent in passing back the tickets to the unsuccessful dikasts. This was speeded up by having all ten ticket-inserters take part. On top of all this was the actual time for the trials, for the voting, for making payments. Time could be saved only in the actual allotting by the archon – in the process of reckoning the number of dice (which had to be counted with strict accuracy, else fearful confusion would ensue), and in the drawing of the dice. That is why not one but several dikasts were allotted at once.

The drastic solution to save time would have been to allot not five, but ten dikasts at once. It is puzzling at first to see why this solution was not adopted. In this matter the situation visualized in the Figure will again be of use. If all ten sections were allotted at once, only one kleroterion, with ten *kanonides*, would be needed. If we examine the situation in terms of the Figure, it will be apparent that *all* the dikasts (not merely those in sections Z–K) whose tickets were inserted below the 20th row would be excluded from the archon's allotment. Dikasts in nine sections, to the total number of 91, would be affected. The procedure with one kleroterion would thus add 40 men to the total of (13 + 38 =) 51 who, as we have seen, are excluded by the procedure with two kleroteria, i.e., with two sets of five *kanonides*. In general form, the situation may be expressed thus: allotment in one kleroterion (with ten *kanonides*) means that nine sections would suffer if only one section were markedly ill-represented; whereas, with two kleroteria (of five *kanonides* each), only four sections would suffer when one section was ill-represented.

In other words, the Athenians chose to compromise between the perfectly fair procedure (allotment of one ticket at a time) and

---

assembly and a court to meet on the same day"] (Dem., XXIV 80). Some trials were planned to take most or all of the day: εἰς τρία μέρη διαιρεῖται ἡ ἡμέρα, ὅταν εἰσίη γραφὴ παρανόμων εἰς τὸ δικαστήριον ["The day is divided into three parts when a *graphe paranomon* is brought into the court"] (Aeschines, III 197).

the drastically quick system (allotment of ten tickets at a time). The compromise logically took the form of selecting a mean between one and ten, namely allotment of five tickets at a time. Correspondingly, this form of compromise would ordinarily reduce the number of dikasts unjustly treated by something less than a half (in our illustration, from 91 to 51).[53] Hence two kleroteria. Or rather, hence allotment of five tickets at a time. One kleroterion with ten *kanonides* could have been used, the archon allotting five *kanonides* at a time. The reasons against this, and in favor of two kleroteria, were certain factors mentioned at the beginning of this inquiry, namely expense, and the advantage of splitting the crowd of dikasts into halves.

The same weighty consideration, namely the saving of time, explains also why one kleroterion was not used twice, so as to save the expense of a second kleroterion. In the procedure actually followed, the second kleroterion was all ready, without delay, for the archon's allotment long before he finished with the first kleroterion, since the second group of five ticket-inserters would long since have finished inserting the tickets in the second kleroterion. If there were only one kleroterion, additional time would be required for the first five ticket-inserters to pass back the tickets of those who were rejected in the first allotting; then the second five ticket-inserters would have to insert all the 100 + tickets, before the second allotment could begin.

The inquiry into the problem of why there were two kleroteria has thus brought into relief several facts not hitherto appreciated. (1) There were two allotments: besides the allotment with dice by the archon, there was the prior allotment which consisted of the insertion of tickets into the kleroteria by the ticket-inserters. (2) Inequalities of attendance brought it about that this prior allotment, in the procedure actually followed, unjustly excluded some, often many, dikasts from the archon's allotment. (3) The only perfectly fair procedure would have been time-consuming individual allotment. (4) Time was so important a consideration that injustice to a minority of dikasts (2) was countenanced to save minutes for the

---

[53] Theoretically on some days no dikasts might be affected, i.e. when, in each group of five sections, the two sections least well-represented were precisely equally represented. This is one possible extreme. The upper limit cannot, of course, be fixed, but it may be noted that if one section had 30 dikasts present, and all of the others had 60 each, then the system of two kleroteria would operate unjustly for only 120 dikasts, while 150 dikasts would be spared the injustice which would result from allotting the dikasts ten at a time (i.e. in one kleroterion, in which case all of the 120 + 150 = 270 would suffer).

majority. (5) Also to save time, a second kleroterion, otherwise unnecessary, was provided for each tribe. (6) Both time and justice would have been served if the functions of the archon could have been fulfilled by a group of five or ten officials, operating simultaneously five kleroteria with two *kanonides* each (if there were five officials), or ten kleroteria with one *kanonis* each (if there were ten officials). A solution apparently so reasonable, in that it obviated both delay and injustice, must have been rejected for strong reasons. In the actual system, much depended on the probity and accuracy of the archon. Apparently the archons were trusted, or rather were considered more trustworthy than any boards of five or ten men each which could conveniently serve. The avoidance of malpractice, which thus out-weighed both time and justice, was a cardinal principle in the procedure of allotting dikasts.

4 *Jury Pay and Assembly Pay at Athens**†

M. M. MARKLE

Thucydides (2.37.1) represents Pericles in the Funeral Oration as claiming that 'no poor citizen who has the ability to serve the state is prevented from doing so by the obscurity of his position.' If this claim were true, it would mean that jury pay, which amounted to two obols per day and was raised to three obols by about 425, had proved adequate to enable the poor to serve as jurors. Perhaps one could also argue that assembly pay, which quickly rose to three obols after its establishment in the beginning of the fourth century, was also sufficient to allow the poor to attend assemblies.[1] But objections can be made. Pericles' assertion is made in a speech composed for an occasion on which it was appropriate to praise Athens, and some of the other claims made in the speech are exaggerated or false. Thus the occasion, purpose, and contents of the speech would persuade some scholars that the orator is describing an ideal, rather than a real Athens.[2] In addition, jury pay in the late fifth century amounted to

---

* First published in *Crux, Essays Presented to G. E. M. de Ste Croix on his 75th Birthday: History of Political Thought* Vol. No. VI (1985), pp. 265–97, copyright © Imprint Academic, Exeter, U.K.; reprinted with the permission of the author and of Imprint Academic.

† I wish to thank Dr Geoffrey de Ste. Croix for the helpful discussions which we had whilst I was writing this article. He has, however, not read the article and thus must not be taken to agree with the views expressed. I offer it as a small return for our many years of friendship. I am also grateful to F. D. Harvey and Dr P. A. Cartledge for many helpful comments.

[1] *Jury pay* was instituted by Pericles, probably some time in the 450s: Aristotle, *Politics* 1274a8; *Ath. Pol.* 27. 3–5; for a recent discussion of the date, see P. J. Rhodes, *A Commentary on the Aristotelian* Athenaion Politeia (Oxford, 1981), pp. 339–40. It was at first two obols per day but was raised to three obols by Cleon in the 420s: Aristophanes *Knights* (424 BC) 51, 797–800; Schol. Ar. *Wasps* 88 (emended), 300; Schol. *Birds* 1541. For *assembly pay* see Arist. *Ath. Pol.* 41.3; Ar. *Eccl.* 180–88, 204–7, 282–4, 289–92 (*triobolon*), 300–10, 377–93. Some time between the late 390s and the 320s it was increased to one drachma for ordinary assemblies and one-and-a-half drachmas for principal assemblies, whilst jury pay remained three obols per session, according to Arist. *Ath. Pol.* 62.2.

[2] See e.g. E. Schwartz, *Das Geschichtswerk des Thukydides*[3] (Bonn, 1929), pp. 144–7 and 144, note 2; J. de Romilly, *Thucydides and Athenian Imperialism*, Eng. transl. (Oxford, 1963), pp. 130–40; H-P. Stahl, *Thukydides: die Stellung des Menschen imgeschichtlichen Prozess* (*Zetemata* XL [1966]), pp. 50–3, 77–9.

only half the pay of an artisan, and after the mid-fourth century only about a fifth. Ancient historians therefore argue that the rate would have been insufficient to attract citizens to leave their work to serve on juries and attend assemblies, but they disagree about the class of citizens who would have constituted the majority. Aristophanes' *Wasps* paints so vivid a picture of idle, aged jurors that it has led certain historians to view jury pay as intended to be a kind of pension for the elderly, and dole for the poverty-stricken, unemployed and lazy.[3] Others have inferred from statements made by the Attic orators, especially by Demosthenes, that the juries and assemblies which they addressed were composed of moderately well-to-do Athenians and that the poor did not attend in significant numbers.[4]

I will begin (I) by considering the former view. I will show that it is based on a misinterpretation of Aristophanes' *Wasps* and on a false notion of what the ancient writers mean when they speak of the poor. I will demonstrate that when the sources use the Greek words which we translate as 'poor', they refer to people who had little or no leisure, that is to those who had to work full time to support themselves and their dependants. Next (II) I will argue that jury and assembly pay was sufficient to allow citizens, who otherwise would have been compelled to work full time to support their households, to have leisure to serve on juries and to attend the assemblies. Finally

[3] For example, W. S. Ferguson, *Greek Imperialism* (Boston, 1913), p. 64, and C. A. Robinson, Jr., *Athens in the Age of Pericles* (Oklahoma, 1959), p. 33, compare it with the modern old-age pension; similarly A. W. H. Adkins, *Moral Values and Political Behaviour in Ancient Greece* (London, 1972), p. 120; E. Kluwe, 'Noch zum Problem: Die soziale Zusammensetzung der athenischen Ekklesia', *Klio* LIX (1977), pp. 45–81, on p. 46; T. Tarkiainen, *Die athenische Demokratie* (Zurich, 1966, transl. from Finnish original of 1959), pp. 137–8. C. Meier, *Die Entstehung des Politischen bei den Griechen* (Frankfurt, 1980), pp. 251–3, rightly stresses the participation of many Athenian citizens in political activities, but he somewhat discounts the importance of political pay in bringing about this situation. Nor can I accept entirely his view that craftsmen and traders (whom he seems to confuse with wage labourers) despised their work; see rather M. I. Finley, *Politics in the Ancient World* (Cambridge, 1983), p. 34; and further pp. 115–16 below.
[4] For example, A. M. H. Jones, *Athenian Democracy* (Oxford, 1957), p. 50; S. Perlman, 'Political Leadership in Athens in the Fourth Century BC', *Parola del Passato*, CXIV (1967), pp. 161–76, on p. 163; he adds that jury and assembly pay was 'certainly insufficient for regular upkeep', and doubts 'whether people who earned their living solely or mainly from their own work could spare the time once in nine days to attend the popular assembly'. K. J. Dover, *Greek Popular Morality* (Oxford, 1974), pp. 34–5, points to 'two possibilities: either the majority of the jurors addressed by the fourth-century orators were fairly prosperous … or, if they did not belong to the prosperous class, they liked to be treated as if they did.' He argues that jury pay which 'began as a means of drawing the poor into the administration of the state became an honorarium for people who did not lose by leaving their usual occupation for service on juries – and at the same time a subsistence allowance for those whose earnings were very low indeed.' He then forgets that he opted for the middle-class jury on the preceding page and states that it is impossible to determine which class predominated in late fourth-century juries.

(III) I will argue that those historians who maintain that Athenian juries and assemblies were composed predominantly of citizens of moderate property have misinterpreted statements made by the Attic orators. Contrary to their views, I will attempt to show that the orators are addressing juries and assemblies in which the poor, that is citizens who had no leisure, constituted the majority.

I

The picture drawn by Aristophanes in the *Wasps* is fixed indelibly in our imaginations, but the assumption that comedy presents an accurate account of a political institution is very risky. Aristophanes' purpose is to cause his audience to laugh, and he is very iconoclastic in his treatment of the Athenian democratic constitution.[5] One of his methods is to distort a subject by seizing upon a funny but recognizable characteristic and exaggerating it, like a modern political cartoon. I do not doubt for a moment that old, retired men in Athens found jury service exciting, and would queue up before dawn to ensure themselves of a place, but, as will become apparent in the discussion that follows, there is no reason to believe that they made up more than a small part of the six thousand jurors who were selected to form the panel from which jurors were drawn at need throughout the year. Moreover, Aristophanes sometimes seems to imply that these old men did not really need to depend on jury pay for their sustenance. From time to time jokes are made about the paltry amount of jury pay. Once it is claimed that if the session of the court is called off the chorus of jurors will have no money for food (303–11). But this too could be an aristocratic sneer. Perhaps the members of the chorus were like Philokleon. He preferred to wear old clothes and live off jury pay, but his son Bdelykleon wanted to support him in a life of luxury.[6] Clearly, the family had property. Aristophanes has drawn a caricature of the Athenian juror.

Some historians erroneously equate the poor with the unemployed, the lazy, those too old for work, the utterly destitute, all of whom would have abundant time on their hands and nothing better

---

[5] For Aristophanes on democracy, see the excellent discussion by G. E. M. de Ste. Croix, *The Origins of the Peloponnesian War* (London, 1972), App. XXIX, pp. 355–71.

[6] In Ar. *Wasps* 503–7 Bdelykleon wants his father Philokleon to give up his life of toil in the courts to live a noble life of ease. Thus, Philokleon does not serve as a juror for the money but rather for the excitement and interest in the activity. Philokleon, who says that he ate his fill of fried fish and paid his three obols to a fuller (1127–8), does not seem to have relied on his jury pay for life's necessities.

to do than attend juries. The assumed paltry pittance of jury pay
would thus provide them with sufficient means to keep body and soul
together. But these people would have made up only a tiny portion
of those whom the ancient writers designate as the poor. Indeed,
persons utterly without means were denoted consistently by different Greek words. The two words used most commonly by Greek
writers of the fifth and fourth centuries BC to designate the poor
are *hoi penetes* and *hoi aporoi*. The corresponding forms which
are employed to denote the condition of being poor, or poverty, are
penia and *aporia*. Though linguistically interpreted *aporia* translates
'without means' and thus might appear to denote a greater degree
of poverty than *penia*, the two words and their related forms are
employed indiscriminately, and indeed Aristotle's precise definition
of *aporia* excludes the notion that it means destitution.[7]

How, then, should these terms be defined? Aristotle, contrasting
oligarchy with democracy, says that democracy is the kind of government 'when men who do not possess much property but are
poor (*aporoi*)' are in control of the state (*Pol.* 1279b18–20). In other
words, he seems to equate the poor (*aporoi*) with those who do not
possess much property (οἱ μὴ κεκτημένοι πλῆθος οὐσίας). Therefore
the poor are not regarded as people utterly without property but
as those without much property. Other passages confirm this definition. In the *Politics* (1320a32–4), Aristotle, discussing the danger to
democracy of distributions of surplus revenues, says that the truly
democratic leader must see to it that the multitude be not excessively
poor (*lian aporon*). In other words, people without property and
without the means of supporting themselves who come to depend
on doles are not described as merely 'poor' (*aporon*) but as 'excessively
poor' (*lian aporon*). The word *penetes* is employed in a similar
manner. Speaking of the requirement among the Spartans that each
man must contribute to the common mess (*phidition*), Aristotle
states that 'some being very poor (*sphodra penetes*) and not able

---

[7] G. E. M. de Ste. Croix, *Class Struggle in the Ancient Greek World* (London, 1982), p. 53,
wrongly translates *tois aporois* at *Pol.* 1323a5 as 'the propertyless', but this translation is not
supported by Aristotle's usage. See *Pol.* 1279b19 with W. L. Newman, *The Politics of Aristotle*
(Oxford, 1902) III, p. 196, Again, at 1320a32 it would not be possible to translate λίαν ἄπορος
as 'too propertyless'; the word must mean simply 'poor'. On the other hand, the term *aporoi*
would *include* people without property, and it can refer *exclusively* to such people, e.g. 1320a
35 ff. Nor is de Ste. Croix's claim (*loc. cit.*) that *penetes* commonly indicates 'a less extreme
degree of poverty than *aporoi*' (cf. p. 144) borne out by such passages as Plato *Rep.* 552a (see
further note 9 below); Dem. 19.146, where it would be nonsensical to indicate a degree of
propertylessness; or Lys. 31.12, which indicates that the basic meaning of *a-poros* is 'without
sufficient property to serve the *polis*'. The English usage 'he is a man of means' is similar to the
positive form of such a statement, though to refer to a person 'without means' in English would
denote a really poor person.

to afford the expense lose their citizenship, and thus the common mess is not democratic, since it is not easy for the very poor (*tois lian penesin*) to participate' (*Pol.* 1271a30–5).[8] Other passages in the *Politics* explicitly attest that the poor (*hoi penetes*) had property: 'For the poor (*hoi penetes*) who do not share in the honours are willing to remain peaceful if no-one insults them or deprives them of their property' (*tes ousias*, 1297b6–8), and 'For the ox replaces a slave for the poor' (*tois penesin*, 1252b12).

Use of the words *penia* and *aporia* and their related forms by other ancient writers also shows that these terms can refer to people who have some property and are not utterly destitute. Herodotus (1.133.1; 2.47.3; 8.51.2) describes the poor (*hoi penetes*) as people who suffer from a scarcity of means (ὑπ' ἀσθενείης βίου) and thus cannot afford as expensive sacrificial offerings as the rich, or, from a lack of funds, are not able to remove their families from Athens in war. In Sophocles' *Philoctetes* (584) a trader who has dealings with the Achaean army at Troy describes himself as a poor man (*aner penes*). Socrates in Xenophon's *Oeconomicus* (11.4–5) implies that *penes* is a term which indicates the lack of 'many possessions' (πολλὰ χρήματα).

Other passages in Aristotle make the definition of these words more precise. Repeatedly, he stresses that it is the lack of leisure that characterizes the poor, and the having of leisure that qualifies the rich. Thus, 'the poor' includes, but is not co-extensive with, all those who must work full time to support themselves and their dependants, whilst the rich are those who do not need to work continuously to maintain themselves and their families. Discussing the Carthaginian belief that rulers should have wealth, Aristotle states that the poor are excluded because the poor man would not have the leisure to

[8] Two passages in the *Politics* at first sight seem to suggest that the poor (*aporoi*) have no property, but careful study shows that they cannot be so interpreted. At 1283a17ff. Aristotle writes: 'Thus, the well-born, free, and rich have good reason to claim the right to honour. For there must be free men who have rateable property (τίμημα φέροντας); for a city would not exist if it consisted entirely of poor men (*aporon*), any more than of slaves.' Again, discussing the devices which ensure the control of government by the propertied classes, he says 'with regard to the magistracies it is not permitted those who have rateable property (τοῖς ἔχουσι τίμημα) to decline by oath to serve, while it is allowed to the poor (*tois aporois*)' (1297a20). In both passages, however, the word for 'rateable property' (*timema*) characterizes those who are contrasted with the poor, and in the first those who have 'rateable property' are called rich (*plousioi*). In Athens, these are the people whose property would make them liable to such obligations as the special tax levy (*eisphora*). Thus the *aporoi* who are contrasted with these rich people would be those with too little property for assessment and would not include those without any property at all. *Pol.* 1270b9 exaggerates the degree of poverty among Spartiates: Aristotle says that 'very poor men (*anthropoi sphodra penetes*) often acquire the ephorate, who on account of their poverty (*dia ten aporian*) can be bribed'. This is inconsistent with the claim that the 'very poor' Spartans lose their citizenship.

govern well (ἀδύνατον γὰρ τὸν ἀποροῦντα καλῶς ἄρχειν καὶ σχολάζειν, *Pol.* 1273a21–36). With the poor Aristotle contrasts the best citizens (*hoi beltistoi*) who 'are able to have leisure (*scholazein*) and do nothing unseemly (*meden aschemonein*) either as rulers or private citizens'. By the phrase 'do nothing unseemly' he means that the best citizens are not obliged to engage in occupations as artisans, traders or shop-keepers that are unsuitable for the good life. Listing the various classes of common people, as distinguished from the nobles, Aristotle asserts a causal connection between having little property and lacking leisure: they include 'the class which has little property so that they are not able to have leisure' (καὶ τὸ μικρὰν ἔχον οὐσίαν ὥστε μὴ δύνασθαι σχολάζειν, 1291b17–30).

Use of the terms *penia* and *aporia* and their related forms by other ancient writers also indicates that the poor included people who had to work for a living and lacked leisure. Indeed the nouns *penia* and *penes* are derived from the verb *penomai* which means to 'labour'. Isocrates claims that poverty and need characterize those people who are obliged continuously to toil. Describing the hardships allegedly endured by the propertied classes in Athens in the discourse *On The Peace* (128), he contrasts them with the poor who, he says, are better off: 'Some are forced to describe and lament among themselves their poverty and needs (τὰς πενίας καὶ τὰς ἐνδείας), whilst others bewail the multitude of duties imposed on them and public services ... so that life is more of a torture for the propertied class than for those who must continuously work' (τοὺς συνεχῶς πενομένους). Moreover, Socrates in Plato's *Apology* (23c) seems to regard his 'measureless poverty' (πενία μυρία) as at least partly characterized by his lack of 'leisure to perform any service worth mentioning for the city'.

Persons without property and without crafts and occupations by which they could support themselves, the unemployed and the destitute, are not usually designated in Greek by the terms *penetes* and *aporoi* and their condition is not commonly described as *penia* and *aporia*.[9] Such people were called *ptochoi* and their condition *ptocheia*, words best translated as 'beggars' and 'beggary'. Plato, describing the patterns of lives which souls are invited to choose for

---

[9] I have found only one example (though there are no doubt others) of the use of *penes* and *aporos* to characterize people who have no possessions: Plato (*Rep.* 552a) discussing oligarchy says that one of its weaknesses is that it 'permits a man to sell all his possessions and continue living in the city ... designated as indigent and poor (πένητα καὶ ἄπορον κεκλημένον)' – i.e. the propertyless are at the bottom end of the scale of persons characterized by *penia* and *aporia*.

a new cycle of human generation (*Republic* 618a), clearly distinguishes between lives which ended in poverty (*eis penias*) and
in beggary (*eis ptocheias*). Indeed, Plato excludes by law beggars
from his ideal oligarchic state (*Laws* 936b–c). He argues that the city
should not permit a man of quality to fall into utter beggary, but that
the ordinary person who suffers from hunger deserves no pity and if
he begs he must be driven out of the land. Of course, beggars would
be citizens in a radical democracy such as Athens, provided they
satisfied the birth criterion, but the ancient writers, especially
Aristotle (who nowhere uses the words *ptochos* or *ptocheia* in
his *Politics*), attribute to them no significant role in the city-state.
Aristophanes in *Ploutos* (537–54) has the character Penia draw a
clear distinction between the *penes* and the *ptochos*: 'the life of the
ptochos ... is to live having nothing, whilst that of the *penes* is to live
frugally, occupied with his work, having no surplus, but at the same
time lacking nothing.' Aristotle himself could not have given a more
precise definition, and indeed the account of the life of the *penes*
agrees with his assertions that such a person is characterized by lack
of leisure.

A client of Lysias aims to arouse sympathy among the jurors by
describing himself as poor in the sense of having no leisure from his
work. He pleads: 'I possess a trade that can give me only a meagre
subsistence. I work it myself with difficulty, and I am not yet able to
acquire someone to take it over' (Lysias 24.6). Lysias' client is poor
not because he lacks slaves but because he lacks leisure. A person
could be poor and still own one or more slaves, provided that he was
compelled to work full time beside his slaves and had virtually no
leisure. Many of the poor in Athens owned slaves. In a speech
composed by Lysias for a resident alien accused by his slaves of sacrilege, the speaker argues (5.5) that false testimony of slaves who hope
to gain their freedom should be 'the concern of everyone in the city;
for these (the accused) are not only ones who have slaves, but everyone else has them'. The argument would lose all force if it was known
that significant numbers of Athenians did not own a single slave.[10]
It was the lack of leisure which characterized the poor.

---

[10] For evidence of slave-owners working alongside their slaves for the same rates of pay, see
IG I³ 476. 221–31; for the correct translation, R. H. Randall, 'The Erechtheum Workmen',
AJA LVII (1953), pp. 199–210. The slave's 'pay' was of course pocketed by the master: see
M. I. Finley, *The Ancient Economy* (London, 1973, rev. 1975), p. 80. That very large numbers
of Athenians owned slaves, see A. H. M. Jones, 'Slavery in the Ancient World', *Econ. Hist.
Rev.* 2nd ser., IX (1956), p. 185 (republ. in *Slavery in Classical Antiquity*, ed. M. I. Finley
[Cambridge, 1960], p. 1) and de Ste. Croix, *Class Struggle*, pp. 143–6 (later parallels). On
p. 144 he cites additional evidence of slaves being owned by 'men described as 'poor (*penetes*)'
in antiquity.

Thus, when Pericles says in the Funeral Oration that no one is prevented by *penia* from serving the state, he is claiming that people who must work full time to support themselves and their dependants are enabled by political pay to take time off from their occupations to perform public service and attend festivals. What evidence, then, is there to show that political pay was sufficient to enable these workers to serve the state?

II

The effectiveness of pay for public service is indicated by the strong oligarchic opposition to the practice. When the oligarchs of 411 set about to overthrow the democracy they abolished all pay except for 'those serving on campaign' (τοὺς στρατευομένους).[11] Surely, their aim was to make it impossible for the poor to serve on juries, perform as magistrates, and attend the Council of Five Hundred. Later, after the fall of the extreme oligarchy of the Four Hundred, control of the state was given to the Five Thousand, but once more the assembly decreed that no one was to receive pay for holding office.[12] This prohibition also must have included a prohibition of jury pay. Since control of the state was given to 'the Five Thousand, ... as many as provide arms', i.e. to the hoplite class, it would have been contrary to this intention to provide pay for the *thetes* [the lowest of the four property-classes] to attend juries and so enable the poor to exercise judicial control over the magistrates. Thus both moderate and extreme oligarchs opposed political pay.

Isocrates and Plato in their attacks on political pay for office attest to its effectiveness. Isocrates in the *Areopagiticus* (7.54) admits that wages for jury service provide the necessities of life for many Athenians. In the same pamphlet (24–7) he exaggerates the amount of money the people earn from public service by claiming that 'they administer their own property from the public funds' and he recommends the past when 'those who had leisure and sufficient property were in charge of public affairs'.[13] Plato implies the effectiveness of

---

[11] Thuc. 8. 65.3. Arist. *Ath. Pol.* 29. 5 records that an exception was made for the nine archons and for those who served as *prytaneis* ['presidents', the fifty councillors from one tribe], and that the cancellation of pay was to continue for the duration of the war.

[12] Thuc. 8. 97. 1; Arist. *Ath. Pol.* 33. 1. See G. E. M. de Ste. Croix, 'The Constitution of the Five Thousand', *Historia* V (1956), pp. 1–23, and *Class Struggle*, pp. 605–6 (replying to P. J. Rhodes, 'The Five Thousand in the Athenian Revolutions of 411 BC', *JHS* XCII (1972) 115–27). Thucydides thoroughly approves of this constitution which he judges 'a reasonable mixture, a fair blend, of the interests of the Few and the Many' (8.97.2, as interpreted by de Ste. Croix, *Hist.* 1956, p. 6).

[13] This passage has been taken by M. H. Hansen, 'Misthos for Magistrates in Classical

political pay when he argues in the *Republic* (345e) that 'no one is willing to hold office voluntarily, but they demand pay', and he cites the institution of pay for magistrates as support for his argument that one who holds office benefits the ruled and not himself (346a). Plato shows his opposition to state pay when he states that 'the good are not willing to rule for the sake of money ... For they do not wish by collecting pay openly for office to be called hirelings (*misthotoi*)' (347b).[14] Plato, like Isocrates, exaggerates the effect of pay for public administration. In the *Gorgias* he writes that Pericles 'made the Athenians idle, cowardly, garrulous and lovers-of-money by establishing state pay' (515e).

Isocrates and Plato are so tendentious that strict interpretations are not likely to find general agreement. Aristotle provides much stronger evidence that political pay permitted the poor to participate in public service. The *Politics* is a work of much greater value to the historian who is seeking an accurate account of ancient political institutions than the writings of Plato and Isocrates. Plato described the authoritarian and hierarchical states which he envisaged as ideal, and regarded actual forms of government, including democracy, to be so flawed as to be utterly unacceptable. Isocrates falsified history to create propaganda for an Athenian state more devoted to the interests of the propertied classes. In contrast, Aristotle and his pupils conducted careful research into one hundred and fifty-eight existing constitutions in preparation for the writing of the *Politics*. Aristotle asserts that he hopes to study in the light of these constitutions 'what sorts of influence preserve and destroy states ... and to what causes it is due that some are well and others ill administered' (*EN* 1181b15–20, trs. Ross). For this reason the accounts of political institutions given in the *Politics* must be taken seriously and should not be rejected unless there is strong evidence to the contrary.

Aristotle clearly shows the effectiveness of state pay. With reference to the complete kind of democracy, he states: 'all citizens take part in this sort of government because of the predominance of the masses, and they participate and exercise their citizen rights because even the poor (*tous aporous*) are able to have leisure by receiving pay (*misthos*)' (1293a3–7). In this passage Aristotle observes generally

Athens', *Symbolae Osloenses* LIV (1979), p. 21, note 34, to refer to perquisites of office and not to money earned from public service; but V. Gabrielsen, *Remuneration of State Officials in Fourth-Century B.C. Athens* (Odense, 1981), pp. 89–93, argues rightly that τὰς ἐκ τῶν ἀρχείων προσόδους should be translated as 'incomes derived from public offices'.
[14] For prejudice against working for money, see Xen. *Mem.* 2.8, with de Ste. Croix, *Class Struggle*, pp. 181–2.

that pay allowed the poor to have the leisure to participate in the government, and he presumably means that it permitted them to attend both juries and assemblies.[15] When he refers to the 'complete kind of democracy' he must be describing not only the Athenian constitution but other Greek democracies which enabled the poor to participate by offering pay.[16] Moreover, his careful study of the history and development of the various constitutions would indicate that his general observations do not apply only to the years during which he composed the *Politics* but are valid for the entire period in which the institution described existed. Thus, when he says that the poor were able to have leisure to take part in government by receiving pay, he means that political pay in Athens was effective from the time of its establishment by Pericles in the 450s (note 1 above).

Perhaps even more reliance can be placed on Aristotle's treatment of assembly pay, since, at least in Athens, that was a fourth-century institution. He writes: 'Also the power of the Council is weakened in democracies of the sort in which the people in assembly deals with everything itself; this usually happens when there is a plentiful supply of pay for those attending the assembly, for having leisure they meet often and themselves make all decisions' (*Pol.* 1299b38–1300a4). The main point of this passage is that assembly pay makes it possible for the people to have the leisure to attend meetings. Apart from this, nothing in the passage is inconsistent with what we know about the Athenian assembly from other sources. Of course, there may have been occasions in Athens when the supply of money for political pay was not plentiful. Demosthenes (24. 96–9) describes the circumstances which will bring about such a crisis, but he does not indicate that the situation ever actually occurred.[17] Aristotle, however, would allow for such an occasion: he says '*when (hotan)* the supply of pay is abundant for those attending the assembly, they have the leisure to attend often'. Did the Athenians have frequent assemblies? They held four regular assemblies each prytany which amounted to forty

---

[15] cf. 1275a22–3, b6–7 where Aristotle defines the citizen, especially in democracies, as one who participates in *krisis* [judging] and *arche* [ruling].

[16] De Ste. Croix, *Class Struggle*, pp. 289–90, is certainly right that political pay was not limited to Athens but had been established in a number of other democracies by the fourth century. For detailed argument, see his 'Political Pay outside Athens', *CQ* n.s. XXV (1975), pp. 48–52.

[17] Thuc. 6.24.3 says that 'the vast multitude and the common soldier' voted for the Sicilian expedition 'to gain immediate paid employment and to add enough to their empire that they would have pay permanently' (*aidion misthophoran*). This passage might imply that there was not always enough pay in Athens to satisfy the people. Alternatively, *aidion* could mean 'indefinitely, for evermore'; or else the reference could be to insufficient public works providing employment; neither of these interpretations would permit the inference that funds were ever so short that the state business could not be conducted.

sessions prescribed by law per year, and, moreover, as many additional assemblies would be summoned as urgent state business warranted.[18] Aristotle himself would have observed Athenian democracy in practice in the second quarter of the fourth century during his period of study at the Academy under Plato, and could have made enquiries from those who had been active in politics in the previous generation. For this reason, scholars who doubt his authority for the fifth century ought to provide very strong evidence for rejecting his views on the fourth century. I will argue that other evidence does not oppose his judgment.

Assembly pay was introduced in the 390s at the low rate of one obol per meeting, but as early as 393 BC it had risen to three obols. This rate, precisely the same as jury pay in the late fifth century, at first seems to have been effective. By the 320s, however, assembly pay had risen to one drachma for ordinary assemblies and one and a half drachmas for principal assemblies, whilst the three-obol jury pay remained the same (note 1 above). I am primarily interested in the three-obol rate in this paper and I shall argue that this rate compensated a worker sufficiently to allow him to leave his occupation for a day and attend juries and assemblies.

In addition to the testimony of Aristotle in the *Politics*, Aristophanes in the *Ecclesiazusae* indicates that assembly pay achieved its aim. The half-chorus of country women exclaim: 'We must push aside the men [who have come to the assembly] from the city. Previously they sat babbling in the market place when assembly pay was only one obol, whilst now that it is three obols they are an exceeding nuisance' (300–3, 308–10). Of course, the danger of inferring anything about a political institution from comedy is that the entire presentation of it may be a cartoon, and in all respects distorted.[19] Thus, there is a remote possibility that the Athenian

---

[18] M. H. Hansen and F. Mitchel, 'The Number of Ecclesiai in Fourth-century Athens', *Symbolae Osloenses* LIX (1984), pp. 13–19, argue that the four regular assemblies per prytany were an innovation of *c*.350 BC. Hansen, 'How Often did the *Ecclesia* Meet?', *GRBS* XVIII (1977), pp. 43–70, also argues that during the period 355 to 322 BC the number of assemblies which could be held in Athens was restricted to four each prytany, (including emergency meetings), but he does not persuade Rhodes, *Commentary on* Ath. Pol., pp. 521–2. Hansen has now republished his article in his *Athenian Ecclesia* (Copenhagen, 1983), pp. 35–62, with addenda, pp. 63–72. His theory depends on the assumption that the two assemblies held on the 18th and 19th of Elaphebolion 347/6 counted as only one meeting on the ground that they proceeded from 'only one of the four summonses' (*Ath. Eccl.* addenda, p. 71). This assumption seems very unlikely: any need for more assemblies in a prytany could presumably be satisfied merely by naming more than one date in a summons. I suppose we are also called upon to assume that the people who met on the 18th and 19th were only paid for one meeting!

[19] See Dover, *Greek Popular Morality*, pp. 18–22; cf. also note 5 above.

assembly was never crowded at all and that Aristophanes is joking
about assembly pay which was in fact a total failure. Nothing in
the play, however, supports this interpretation. The humour of the
comedy turns continually upon the assumption of the role of men by
women, and the joke in the passage quoted above is that the women
from the country support the masquerade by referring to, and
describing, the half-chorus of women from the city as men. Though
the passage is humorous, there is no reason to doubt the assertion
that the three-obol assembly pay attracted a large attendance. Indeed,
much of the humour in the play seems to depend on the fact that
unless one made haste and arrived early one would not receive the
pay (282–4, 289–92, 376–82). Such situations would indicate that
pay produced quickly a full house, and consequently one had to
arrive early to gain admission.[20]

The kinds of citizens who predominated in the Athenian assembly
were craftsmen, traders, and farmers, and these persons required
some compensation for loss of earnings when they took time off from
their occupations to attend the assembly. It is such people as these
whom the ancient writers characterize as 'poor' (*penetes, aporoi*).
Socrates, attempting to persuade Charmides, a young aristocrat, to
speak before the Athenian assembly, argues that he should not fear
to address an audience composed of his inferiors, and as examples
Socrates names 'the fullers, shoe-makers, carpenters, blacksmiths,
farmers, merchants, or traders in the market who think only of
buying cheap and selling dear' (Xen. *Mem.* 3.7.6). Plato has Socrates
give a similar description of the Athenian assembly: 'anyone may
stand up and offer advice, whether he be a carpenter, a blacksmith,
a shoe-maker, a merchant, a ship-captain, wealthy, poor, noble, base-
born ...' (*Prot.* 319d). The evidence that the three-obol assembly
pay was sufficient to attract the poor to attend assemblies in the early
fourth century would indicate that the same amount would have
been adequate as jury pay.[21]

---

[20] Hansen has shown that in the fourth century 6,000 was 'a normal attendance' at ordinary
meetings of the assembly and 'at the principal meetings even more citizens were present due to
the importance of the matters discussed and to the additional fee of half a drachma'. See his
'How Many Athenians Attended the *Ecclesia*?, *GRBS* XVII (1976), pp. 115–34 (= *Athenian
Ecclesia*, pp. 1–23, with addenda); the quotation is from p. 130 (= p. 16). Hansen also
concludes from his study of the excavation of Pnyx II and from inferences based on
Aristophanes' *Ecclesiazusae* that 6,000 was the regular attendance at the assembly during this
period, and 'that regularly at least some citizens were refused admission because the "house"
was full'. See his article 'The Athenian *Ecclesia* and the Assembly-Place on the Pnyx', in *GRBS*
XXIII (1982), pp. 241–9 (= *Athenian Ecclesia*, pp. 25–34, with addenda); my reference is to
pp. 243–4 (= pp. 27–8).
[21] Apart from pay, assemblies and courts each had peculiar aspects which might attract or
discourage attendance. The agenda of the assembly was publicized in advance, so one would

Comparison of jury pay with military pay also supports the view that three obols was enough to permit the worker to leave his occupation for jury service. In spite of Andrewes' recent argument in the *Commentary* on Thucydides VIII, I would still accept the view of Pritchett that 'the Athenian citizen-soldier or -sailor in the second half of the fifth century was normally paid no more than three obols, from which he must buy his rations.'[22] Thucydides (8.45.2) represents Alcibiades as claiming that the Athenians 'for a considerable time ... have paid three obols to their own sailors' in order to persuade Tissaphernes to reduce the pay of the Peloponnesians, and I think that it is unlikely that Alcibiades would lie about Athenian *misthos* since the rate must have been generally known: had he done so, he done so, he would have been offering the satrap an ineffective argument. The rate of a drachma per day for the sailors setting forth on the expedition to Sicily is certainly given in a context in which Thucydides is stressing all arrangements and preparations as exceptional (6.31.3).

Little is known about the methods of recruitment for the fleet in Athens, but surely if citizens had needed to be persuaded by special concessions,[23] some indication would be found in the sources. The state was forced to resort to conscription of ships' crews only twice in the fifth century (in 428 and 406), and both occasions were emergencies in which the main Athenian fleet was away from the city and an additional fleet had to be manned (Thuc. 3.16.1; Xen. *Hell.* 1.6.24). Hope for plunder would have attracted some Athenians to volunteer, but such expeditions would have been too uncertain to draw the poor away from their work. Naval pay alone would have persuaded them, and from their pay they were required to purchase

---

know what was to be discussed; on the other hand, the elaborate system of lot for selecting jurymen for the courts meant that one could not predict what case one would have to judge (it might be something very tedious), or whether one would be called to serve at all. Much of the business of the assembly was routine, and it is in the nature of meetings that most of the people who stand up and speak are frightful bores; at least, in the courts the adversary situation offered an excitement of its own, as is clearly shown by Aristophanes' *Wasps*, and the speeches must usually have been composed by orators skilled in arousing the interests of jurymen. On the whole, even with the lack of predictability, the courts must have been much more interesting than the regular assemblies. For publication in advance of the agenda of the assembly, see Hansen, *GRBS* XX (1979), p. 47 (= *Athenian Ecclesia*, p. 39). For allotment of jurors, Arist. *Ath. Pol.* 63–5; cf. Hansen, 'How Often Did the Athenian Dicasteria Meet?', *GRBS* XX (1979), pp. 243–6–150 to 200 days per annum, in his opinion.

[22] A. W. Gomme, A. Andrewes and K. J. Dover, *A Historical Commentary on Thucydides*, V (Oxford, 1981), pp. 97–9; W. K. Pritchett, *Ancient Greek Military Practices*, I (University of California, 1971, reissued in 1974 as *The Greek State at War*, I), pp. 3–24; the quotation is from p. 24.

[23] Cf. the early Roman consuls' difficulties in persuading the people to respond to a call to arms, e.g. Livy 2.27.10.

their food while on campaign, at occasionally inflated prices.[24] The three obols which they received as a daily wage must have been sufficient for them to support themselves and still have some money left over for savings. Otherwise, it is hard to imagine why no difficulty was experienced by the state in finding rowers for the fleet in the fifth century (Thucydides 1.142–3; cf. 121).

The contrast with the fourth century is instructive: almost all the major Athenian naval campaigns from 389 to 341 suffered from lack of money, and the situation was so bad that conscription of thetes for the fleet became a frequent practice from about 362.[25] The orators frequently complain in this period that the Athenians cannot man their ships because of the inadequacy of naval finance and insufficient contributions from their allies. The generous amount of naval pay in the late fifth century is also indicated by comparison with the ten drachmas per month recommended by Demosthenes in the *First Philippic* (4.28) as *siteresion* for a standing force against Philip in 351; he argues that these soldiers will gain their *misthos* from booty. Thus two obols per day are reckoned as sufficient for sustenance in the mid-fourth century.

Finally, comparison of the three-obol daily wage for jury service with the cost of living in late fifth-century Athens indicates that the rate was sufficient to allow all the poor to take part. The most important food in the diet of the poor was barley. Bread made from wheat, no doubt, was preferred and eaten by the poor on special occasions, but their daily fare would have been *maza*, bread made from barley, or *alphita*, barley groats. The juror from the chorus of the *Wasps* complains: 'From this paltry wage I must buy barley groats and firewood and relish for myself and two others' (300–3). Evidence on prices of the necessities of life, such as barley, wheat, olives, wine, etc., shows that the juror could have fed himself, his wife, and two children and still have had a half-obol left over from his pay. The nutritional value of wheat and barley by weight (not by dry measure or volume) is closely equivalent: wheat contains only 1% more of digestible protein.[26] The prices of these commodities,

---

[24] For the attraction of naval pay, see Thucydides 6.24.3 (see note 17 above), and for need for troops to purchase food from their pay, see Pritchett, *Military Practices*, I, pp. 23–4.

[25] For lack of money in Athenian naval campaigns, see de Ste. Croix, *Class Struggle*, pp. 293, 607 note 37; for conscription, pp. 207, 581 note 8.

[26] For the nutritional value of wheat and barley by weight, see F. B. Morrison, *Feed and Feeding* (Ithaca, N.Y., 1954), pp. 1114 and 1128. Part of the reason the ancients placed a greater value on wheat than on barley was because they priced these cereals by dry measure rather than by weight, and they would have noted that a larger measure of barley than of wheat would have been required to make the same amount of bread. They also believed that bread made from wheat was more nourishing, digestible, and generally superior to bread made from

however, are given in the ancient sources not by weight but by dry measure and an error can be made in the computation of necessary daily rations unless one keeps in mind the fact that a *medimnos* of wheat weighs considerably more than the same measure of barley.

Foxhall and Forbes (see note 26) have observed correctly that 'the ancient sources never mention distributions of whole barley for human consumption; instead only handouts of *alphita* are known, that is, coarse barley flour with the inedible hulls removed' (p. 44). With regard to necessary daily rations, therefore, the ratio of the weight of wheat per unit of volume to the weight of barley meal (*alphita*) per unit of volume is most relevant to the ancient diet. Foxhall and Forbes have selected median weights per unit of volume for grains, 'derived from both modern grain samples and the weight/ volume ratios for wheat given by Pliny.' They have also taken account of von Wersch's measurement of the weight of wheat from modern Messenia which 'falls somewhere in the middle of Pliny's range', and I accept their recommendation that this should be considered the most likely median weight of wheat in antiquity. According to their estimates, therefore (p. 43), 0.772 kilogramme of wheat and 0.643 kilogramme of barley meal are each equivalent to a litre measure. Thus, a litre of wheat weights about 1.20 as much as a litre of barley meal.

This factor is important in calculating nutritional equivalents of wheat and barley because some of the most reliable estimates in the ancient sources for daily consumption of adult males are in terms of *choinikes* of wheat. Herodotus (7.187) reckons the provisioning of Xerxes' army on the assumption that each man would receive no more than a *choinix* of wheat per day. Polybius (6.39.13) gives independent confirmation when he records that the Roman soldier was allowed two-thirds of a *medimnos* (32 *choinikes*) of wheat per month, or slightly more than one *choinix* per day. (For further evidence see Appendix.) Thus the two Attic *choinikes* of barley meal which the Athenians allowed to be sent to the Spartans blockaded on Sphakteria were a very generous allowance, and should not

barley (Diphilus *ap.* Athen. 3. 115c–d; Arist. *Probl.* 927a17–19). The poor, however, could not afford a *choinix* of wheat per man per day nor two *choinikes* of barley, since that amount would normally cost the same as a *choinix* of wheat; instead, they would have discovered by experience that a *choinix* and a quarter of barley would satisfy their daily needs as well, if not as pleasantly, as a *choinix* of wheat. (For relative prices of wheat and barley see Appendix.) The editors [of the original publication] have drawn my attention to the excellent and important article by L. Foxhall and H. A. Forbes, 'Σιτομετρεία: The Role of Grain as a Staple Food in Classical Antiquity', *Chiron* XII (1982), pp. 41–90, whose study of grain measurement and the ancient diet is much more thorough than mine. I rely on their estimates of weight to volume ratios of ancient wheat, barley and barley meal.

be regarded as the average daily consumption of an adult male.[27] Since the same measure of wheat weighs 0.2 more than barley meal, 1.2 *choinikes* of barley meal would be a sufficient ration for an adult male.[28]

Foxhall and Forbes point out that according to UN Food and Agriculture Organization standards, 'a man aged 20–39, weighing 62 kg, would require ... only 2853 calories per day if he were moderately active', and they argue this would be a man of average size in ancient Greece. According to their Table 3 on page 86, 1 *choinix* of barley meal (*alphita*) would provide 2320 calories; 1.2 *choinikes* of barley meal would therefore provide 2784 calories, or 98% of the daily requirements of a 'moderately active' man who was attending assemblies or juries. Foxhall and Forbes indicate that 'cereals and starches as a whole rarely comprise more than 75% of total calories, on average, even in poor, Third World countries where a great deal of grain and starchy foods are consumed' (p. 56). Thus the assemblyman or juryman would be most unlikely to consume as much as 1.2 *choinikes* of barley meal per day, if he supplemented his cereals with other kinds of food. The amounts which the ancient sources give for standard daily rations are for very active, or exceptionally active, men, such as soldiers and labourers. Thus, the amount of barley meal which it is assumed that our citizen and his family would consume per day is a maximum.

The price of wheat, though it fluctuated in times of great plenty or scarcity, averaged about six drachmas per *medimnos* in the late fifth and fourth centuries BC. Barley usually sold for half the price of wheat, i.e. for three drachmas per *medimnos*.[29] Since rations are given as barley meal (*alphita*), not as hulled barley (*krithai*), it is

[27] Thuc. 4.16.1. In addition to barley groats and wine, the Spartans were allowed daily portions of meat, which Athenians would not normally have eaten. To judge from the comic writers cited by Athen. 10.417b–c, the Athenians were thought to eat little in comparison with Thebans and other Boeotians (417c–18b) and Thessalians (418b–e). To these nations we must add the Spartans: the Athenians, who allowed them two *choinikes* of barley meal, permitted their attendants only half that amount, surely on the assumption that the latter could live on one *choinix* of barley meal per day (cf. Foxhall and Forbes, 'Σιτομετρεία', p. 55). The armistice, during which the Spartans were allowed these rations, lasted only twenty days, and during the remaining 52 days food had to be smuggled across. Though some grain and other food was found on the island when the Athenians captured it, the Spartan commander must have issued subsistence rations for many days as a necessary precaution (Thuc. 4.39). These circumstances might partly explain the pitiful condition of Spartan prisoners from Sphakteria as represented by Aristophanes (*Clouds* 186 ff.; cf. Thuc. 4.41).
[28] *Contra* J. A. O. Larsen, 'Roman Greece', in *An Economic Survey of Ancient Rome*, IV, ed. Tenney Frank (Baltimore, 1938), p. 413.
[29] W. K. Pritchett, 'Attic Stelai, II', *Hesperia* XXV (1956), pp. 196–8 (wheat), 186 (barley). Although Pritchett says barley was usually half the price of wheat, he states that the most common price was 4 dr. per medimnos. For further evidence, see Appendix below.

necessary to estimate how much more a *medimnos* of barley meal would cost than the same volume of hulled barley. Foxhall and Forbes, who stress that more experimentation is needed, found that after sifting and winnowing barley, 'the volume of flour was still 70% of the original volume of grain, although the weight was only 60% of the original weight' (pp. 75–9, at p. 78). If the 30% contraction in volume is normal, then 1.3 *medimnoi* of barley would be required to make 1 *medimnos* of barley meal. Thus, when barley was selling for 3 drachmas (18 obols) per *medimnos*, an additional 0.3 *medimnos* would cost 5.4 obols, making a total of 23.4 obols. Aristotle (*Ath. Pol.* 51.3) attests that the grain-guards in the Peiraeus and the city ensured that the millers sold 'barley meal (*alphita*) in accordance with the price (which they paid) for hulled barley (*krithai*)'. None of the sources say what amount of profit was allowed by law to the millers, but I estimate that it would have been about half an obol per *medimnos*. Such a profit would make the usual price of barley meal about 24 obols (4 dr.) per *medimnos*. Some support for this conclusion is found in the only attested prices for barley meal (*alphita*): an inscription from Delos of 282 BC records a price for one month of 4 drachmas per *medimnos*, but the following month it rises to 5 (*IG* XI ii 158A. 48–50). The former, however, may have been the usual price, since price rises during this year were probably caused by war.

On this basis it is possible to calculate the cost of barley meal for a family of four in fifth- and fourth-century Athens. Four drachmas or 24 obols divided by 48 would give the price of a *choinix* of barley meal as 0.5 obol, and an additional 0.2 *choinix* would cost 0.1 obol. Thus the daily ration of barley meal for a man would cost 0.6 obol. Three-quarters of this amount, or 0.45 obol, would seem to be the cost of the barley meal ration for the man's wife, and half for two children would cost 0.6 obol.[30] Thus 1.65 obols would provide a family of four with the most essential part of their diet.

Of course, man does not live by bread alone, but the other kinds of food in Athens at the end of the fifth century BC were so cheap that

---

[30] For rations for women and children, see Larsen, *loc. cit.* (note 28 above); I prefer Larsen's three-quarter ration for women to J. K. Davies' estimate (handout for his Oxford lectures, 'The social and economic structure of Athenian society') of half-rations for women on the grounds that the *trophe* [sustenance] for a female slave was half that of a male labourer in *IG* XI 161 A. 83–4 (Delos, 279 BC). *Trophe* is no basis at all for estimating how much barley or wheat the female would have eaten (see Appendix below, p. 128). The two obols per day which she received would have purchased her 5 1/3 *choinikes* of barley, if the normal price of three drachmas per *medimnos* prevailed. IG XII vii 515 shows that boys received half the ration of men, or half a *choinix* of wheat per day, on Amorgos at the end of the second century BC.

they are hardly worth reckoning. Plutarch tells that Socrates led a friend who was complaining how expensive the city was to the various markets to show him how cheap the necessities of life were.[31] Olives cost only two drachmas per *medimnos*; dried figs were the same price. A *kotyle* (0.3 litre) of honey cost three obols, but the amount needed for a daily sweetener would have been only about fifty millilitres, costing about half an obol. The price of olive oil was half an obol per *kotyle*, and a small daily ration is given as ⅛ *kotyle*, which would cost only 1/16 obol. In addition to these early fourth-century prices, the cost of wine can be reckoned from remarks of Demosthenes as three and four drachmas per *metretes*. An amphora or *metretes* (39.39 litres) held 144 *kotylai* and one *kotyle* is equivalent to 0.2736 litre. In an Egyptian papyrus of 226 BC, four *kotylai* of wine are given as a daily ration to a horse-driver, but none is allowed to a groom.[32] Among the poor wine may have been a luxury enjoyed only by the head of a household, and so four *kotylai* (one litre) would be sufficient. At three drachmas per *metretes*, four *kotylai* of wine would cost exactly half an obol, and at four drachmas 0.664 obol. Therefore, a family of four could have been fed on about two-and-a-half obols per day during the fourth century BC. At the sacrifice of about half their wages artisans could leave their work and participate in jury service at pay that would still enable them to provide themselves and their families with the necessities of life.

III

Finally, I would like to consider the views of those scholars who maintain, like Jones (note 4 above), that juries and assemblies 'consisted predominantly of middle-class citizens rather than of the poor'. I am not persuaded by their arguments. The passages in the Attic orators cited by these historians to show that the persons addressed must be well-to-do can be interpreted merely as attempts by the speaker to flatter or entertain his audience. Such flattery and entertainment were often essential to his strategy in winning his case. Poor Athenians would have liked to be addressed as if they were

[31] Plut. *Mor.* 470f. Cf. Xen. *Mem.* 3.14.1, which shows that some were mean about buying *opsa* (non-cereals), however cheap.

[32] For prices of olives and dried figs, see Pritchett, 'Attic Stelai II', pp. 184 and 191. For prices of olive oil and honey, *IG* II² 1356 (beginning of fourth century), 7–8, 13–4. In Egypt in 226 BC a groom received ⅛ *kotyle* as his ration of olive oil, whilst a horse-driver got ¼: *The Flinders Petrie Papyri* II, ed. J. P. Mahaffy (Dublin, 1893), xxv (a) and (b). For prices of wine, Pritchett, pp. 199–203, esp. p. 201. (That *metretes* and *amphora* are equal measures is shown by *IG* XI 287, 131–2.) For a daily ration of wine, *Petrie Papyri*, II, xxv.

prosperous. Pericles is made to say in the Funeral Oration that among the Athenians poverty was no disgrace but only failure to make the effort to escape from it (Thuc. 2.40.1). It was a compliment to the audience for an orator to speak as though all his listeners had succeeded in their ambitions. Thus, when Lysias in the speech before the assembly against Ergocles has the Athenians addressed as 'being oppressed by capital levies' (*eisphorai*) (28.3, cf.4), he is most probably appealing directly to only a very small part of his audience, i.e. those who had sufficient property to qualify for payment of the tax. But his strategy was to speak as if the entire assembly were subject to this tax: in this way he could flatter the poor and create in them a fellow-feeling with those oppressed with payments of *eisphora*. Most of this speech would have appealed to an assembly consisting of both the propertied citizens and the poor, and there is some indication that the poor predominated. The orator repeatedly stresses that the defendant and his associates have made themselves rich at the expense of the Athenian people, and he indicates that he is referring to the *majority* of the Athenians. He begins by saying that even if Ergocles 'should perish many times he would not pay a sufficient penalty to the majority of you (τῷ ὑμετέρῳ πλήθει)', for, in addition to his other wrongs, he, 'formerly a poor man, has become rich at your expense (ἐκ τῶν ὑμετέρων)' (28.1; cf. 28.2, 4, 13). The audience is clearly identified with the mass of the Athenians. Moreover, the speaker's great care to counter the anticipated defence that 'he (Ergocles) returned from Phyle and is *demotikos* [pro-democratic] and shared in your dangers' points to his concern about the favourable impression the defendant might make on the poor in the assembly by such a plea. He argues that those such as the defendant, 'who, returning from exile in the democracy, treat unjustly the majority of you (τὸ ὑμέτερον πλῆθος) ... are more deserving of your anger than the Thirty.'[33]

(a) Juries

Other passages in the orators can be erroneously interpreted to demonstrate that the juries in Athens consisted largely or wholly of citizens of moderate wealth. In Demosthenes' speech *Against*

---

[33] Lys. 28. 12–14. R. K. Sinclair, 'Lysias' Speeches and the Debate about Participation in Athenian Public Life' (Australasian Universities Language and Literature Association conference, Canberra 1983; unpublished), relies considerably on this speech, in contrast to Lys. 29 (*Against Philocrates*), to show that 'the war taxpayers ... constituted a substantial proportion of the citizens attending an average assembly' (pp. 10–11).

Timocrates, the speaker refers to Androtion's notorious collection of arrears of property tax 'which he ... exacted from all of you (πάντας εἰσέπραξεν ὑμᾶς) with the aid of this good man (Timocrates)' (Dem. 24.160). If this statement were taken literally it would indicate that all jurors were of the class of citizens subject to the *eisphora* [property tax]. In other words, it would mean that only those 6,000 citizens, out of a total of about 21,000, whose property of 2,500 drachmas or more obligated them to pay the special tax levies, were members of the jury.[34] In fact it should be interpreted merely as a method employed by Demosthenes to urge the majority of jurors to identify with the feelings of a minority. Numerous other passages in this speech indicate that the jury consisted predominantly of the poor. The speaker commends the jurors and identifies them with 'the many'. He asks, 'Who, therefore, alone is a righteous and sure guardian of the laws?' and he answers, 'You, the many ...' (24.37). Again the speaker maintains that Timocrates' law will ultimately lead to the ruin of state finances and the consequent loss of political pay. He argues that without money the assembly cannot meet and the juries cannot be held. Though the speaker admits the possibility of carrying on without pay, he stresses that this would be a terrible situation (*deinon*, 96–9). He goes on to argue that the defendant should be punished because he was the sort of man who would exact the full penalties from a poor man found guilty of peculation, yet would propose a law relieving rich ambassadors convicted of the same crime (112). Finally, he praises the generosity (*megalophrosyne*) of the jurors for not repealing laws which weigh most heavily on members of their own class – the poor.[35]

The poor in Athens regularly elected the rich, leisured and well educated to the chief positions in the state. Thus the Athenians expected the most influential speakers in the assembly and their

---

[34] For the number of citizens subject to *eisphora*, see Jones, *Athenian Democracy*, pp. 28–9; de Ste. Croix, 'Demosthenes' τίμημα and the Athenian Eisphora', *ClMed*. XIV (1953), p. 33. For my argument that people owning property valued at 2,500 dr. would have been free from the necessity of working to support themselves and their households, see Appendix below.

[35] Dem. 24.123. Jones, *Athenian Democracy*, pp. 36–7, includes the *Timocrates* among the speeches which he judges would not have been delivered before 'a really poor audience', citing (p. 143, note 82) sections 160 ff. But Jones's translation of διάκονον εἴ τις ἐχρῆτο at 197 ('distraining on a servant girl, if anyone employed one'), from which he infers that there might be *eisphora*-payers who did not employ a domestic servant at all, is manifestly incorrect. As de Ste. Croix has pointed out in his unpublished Oxford lectures *Athens and other Greek States: Society and the Economy*, it should be translated 'when they found someone (sc. an *eisphora*-payer) with a slave he was *specially fond of*, they even took *her* off too!': ἐχρῆτο is a euphemistic innuendo for sexual intercourse (cf. W. Wayte's commentary [Cambridge, 1882] *ad loc.*).

elected officials to differ in social position from the majority of the
citizens.[36] I cannot agree with K. J. Dover that it is 'remarkable to
find Demosthenes, in addressing a mass jury, adopting so super-
cilious an attitude to schoolmasters, clerks and decorators.'[37] In the
speech *On the Crown* (18.10) Demosthenes appeals to the judgment
of the jury that he is a 'much better man than Aeschines and from
a better family' in order to counter the prosecutor's attack on his
own personal life (Aeschin. 3.78, 162, 169–76). Demosthenes also
points out that he himself attended good schools and was able to
perform liturgies, whilst Aeschines was forced by poverty to help his
father by performing such menial tasks as 'sponging benches' in a
school (18.257–62, 265). The poor among the Athenian jurors are
not likely to have taken offence at their leaders uttering abuse which
ridiculed poverty and the humble occupations forced on people by
circumstances. Quite the contrary. These personal attacks were the
comic interludes which were a welcome break from the dull legal
arguments and pompous self-justification of the orators. The poor
loved to hear such abuse; Demosthenes himself refers to the jurors'
'delight in invective' (18.138; cf. Hyp. 2.7).

Moreover, it seems likely that the poor jurors accepted to some
degree the contempt of the wealthy for their humble occupations.
This does not mean that craftsmen were not proud of their work or
traders of their profits, but the ultimate goals of most people would
surely have been to acquire enough property to allow themselves to
be free of their work. Thus, again, they felt flattered when the orators
addressed them as if they had already attained their ambitions. In
Lysias' speech *For Polystratos*, the speaker, attempting to counter the
charge that his father was a kinsman of the hated Phrynichos, challenges anyone to attest this kinship and adds, 'The one (Phrynichos),
who was a poor man in the country, kept sheep, whilst my father was
being educated in the city' (20.11). Of course, Polystratos intended
merely to argue that his father and Phrynichos would not have been
associated, but he clearly implies that Phrynichos, because of his
servile occupation, was not so good a man as his (the speaker's)
father.

The same attitude of the jurors towards humble occupations is
implied in Demosthenes' speech *Against Euboulides*. Euboulides had

---

[36] Even Cleon and Cleophon, the most famous of the radical 'demagogues', came from the
upper classes: see de Ste. Croix, *Origins*, p. 235, note 7 (cf. 41–2); W. R. Connor, *The New
Politicians of Fifth-Century Athens* (Princeton, 1971), pp. 158–63; F. Bourriot, 'La famille et
le milieu social de Cleon', *Historia* XXXI (1982), pp. 404–35.
[37] Dover, *Greek Popular Morality*, p. 34.

appealed to such prejudice among the jurors when he had charged
that Euxitheos' mother had sold ribbons in the market-place and had
worked as a wet-nurse (Dem. 57.30–1, 35–6). Euxitheos, however,
attempting to arouse the sympathy of the jury, says, 'We admit that
we sell ribbons and do not live in the manner we would wish.'
Doubtless some of the jurors also worked in the market-place, and
would have preferred not to have been obliged to do so. Euxitheos
also says that Euboulides has broken laws 'which order that anyone
reproaching either a male or female citizen for working in the
market-place shall be liable for slander'. If there were indeed such
laws, then they represent efforts made by traders and shop-keepers
to counter the prejudices of the propertied class, which we find so
evident in our sources. Euxitheos also counters the charge that his
mother worked as a wet-nurse, a task normally performed by female
slaves, by pointing out that she did so 'when the city had suffered
misfortune and all people were faring badly' and he adds that at
present due to poverty 'many Athenian women … are serving as wet-
nurses' (35–6). The speaker narrates in detail the circumstances that
compelled his mother to take up this occupation: she was obliged
to support two children while his father was abroad on military
service, and his family was poor (40–2). Indeed, Euxitheos' frequent
appeal to poverty would itself indicate that he expects to find ready
sympathy in a jury largely composed of the poor (25, 30–1, 35–6,
40–2, 44–5, 52, 58). Perhaps most telling is the general observation:
'Poverty (*penia*) forces free men to do many servile acts' (*doulika
pragmata*, 45).

Some indication that the poor constituted a large part of the
jury that heard the speech *On the Crown* is found in Demosthenes'
discussion of his trierarchic law (18.102; cf. Aeschin. 3.222). He
stresses that it was aimed against the wealthy who were getting off
'with small expenses whilst citizens with moderate or little means
were losing their possessions', and states that his law 'stopped the
injustices perpetrated on the poor'.

I see no reason to believe that the increase in assembly pay from
three obols to one drachma for an ordinary assembly and one-and-
a-half drachmas for a principal assembly (see note 1 above) indicates
that jury pay, which remained unchanged at 3 obols, was no longer
sufficient to allow the poor to attend juries. Prices for basic foods did
not increase during this period, except in times of temporary scarcity
usually produced by greedy speculators, bad harvests or war (see
Appendix). No explanation is likely to find general agreement, but I
would favour in this case a non-economic reason. I suggest that the

adversary situation of the courts and its dramatic interest attracted the poor in considerable numbers at low pay, but the pay had to be increased to induce them to attend the comparatively boring assemblies (cf. note 21 above), especially since wages for skilled and unskilled labour had increased so much during this period. Whatever the explanation, speeches composed for jury trials from the late fifth century through to the third quarter of the fourth provide ample evidence that the poor continued to predominate in the juries.

The speaker who stresses the liturgies which he has performed seems to make his appeal more to the poor members of the jury than to the more wealthy. The poor were the beneficiaries of these public services (Ps.-Xen. *Ath. Pol.* 1.13). Thus in Lysias' *Defence against a Bribery Charge* the defendant emphasizes that he has performed liturgies with expenditure far beyond what was required by law (21.1–5). He points out that his accusers 'omit nothing to make you angry with your benefactors' (20). He says that he does not know anyone whom he would prefer to the present jurors on his case, since 'one ought to pray that the benefited should give their vote to their benefactors' (22). The distinction drawn by the defendant between himself as benefactor and the jury as the beneficiaries is strictly one of class: the jurors are the poor recipients of their patron's favours (cf. Dem. 21.153–74).

In the late fifth and early fourth centuries there are isolated indications that the poor played a large role in the juries. In Antiphon's speech *On the Murder of Herodes* the defendant complains that since he is charged with murder he ought to be tried before the Council of the Areopagus instead of before a heliastic court. Obviously fearful of alienating the sympathy of the jury by this complaint, he adds that it is not from his wish to avoid 'the mass of you' (τὸ πλῆθος τὸ ὑμέτερον) that he makes his objection (Antiphon 5.8; cf. 78). This phrase suggests that the jury of the heliastic court consisted of the multitude, i.e. largely of the poor. The motive of the prosecution in bringing the defendant before the heliasts is probably that the democratic jury will be less well disposed towards an oligarch, whose father was involved in the revolt of Mytilene, than the more conservative Council of the Areopagus (79).

Andocides in his speech *On the Mysteries* seems to make an appeal to a jury which consisted of a mixture of oligarchic sympathizers and of the poor. He says that it was a disgrace when during his exile his house was occupied by Cleophon the lyre-maker (note 36 above), but he hastens to add that his house, the oldest in Athens, has always welcomed anyone in need (1.146–7). Such methods of winning popular support were employed by Cimon in the 470s and 460s: he opened his orchards and offered free meals to the poor of his deme.[38]

The speeches of Demosthenes show that the poor continued to predominate in the juries in the second and third quarters of the fourth century. In his speech *Against Leptines*, which also contains a defence of the rights of the people and an appeal to democratic ideals, Demosthenes anticipates and tries to refute the argument of Leptines that his law will benefit the poor (20.2–4, 16, 18). He states: 'Perhaps Leptines may attempt to say ... that the public services now fall upon poor men, but that under his law the richest people will perform the liturgies.' He argues that the rejection of Leptines' law which cancelled exemptions from public services (liturgies) would not affect the poor adversely because, he says, 'those who have insufficient property are necessarily exempt from the requirement to perform liturgies' (19).[39] In this manner, Demosthenes attempts to prevent Leptines from deceiving the poor members of the jury into believing that they will benefit from the law.

Demosthenes' speech *Against Meidias* repeatedly appeals to the feelings of the poor jurors against the wealthy. Although the speech was never actually delivered (Aeschin. 3.52), Demosthenes would have included only those arguments which he considered would gain the support of the jury. He constantly stresses not only that Meidias has great wealth but also that he does not use it for the benefit of the people. He argues that if Meidias or anyone else 'so presumptuous and rich' is allowed to mistreat someone performing a liturgy, then no sensible person 'will be willing to spend a single drachma' in public service (21.66). He also points out that Meidias' wealth is the 'main cause of his insolence' and that 'to allow such a creature to remain so rich ... is to provide him with resources to use against yourselves' (98). He argues that in contrast to the rich the rest of the Athenians have no share in just and equal rights (112, 124). He argues that if Meidias were deprived of his property he would have 'to pay the penalty like the rest of us' (137–8).

One of the most effective appeals which a wealthy citizen could make to a jury composed of the poor was that he had expended his wealth generously on public services (cf. p. 117 above). For this reason, Demosthenes takes great pains to counter any such argu-

---

[38] Theopompus, *FGrH* 115 F 89 *ap.* Athen. 12.533a–c. On the 'politics of largess', see Connor, *New Politicians*, pp. 18–22, and *Theopompus and Fifth Century Athens* (Washington D.C., 1968), pp. 30–6.

[39] Jones, *Athenian Democracy*, p. 37, finds the *Leptines* 'a very strange speech to deliver to a poor audience', since not 'a word is said about the effect of the law on the masses'.

ments which Meidias and his rich associates have threatened that they will make (151–2). He compares his own record of performing liturgies with that of Meidias to show that the defendant has done relatively very little (154–7). He points out that Meidias' greatest expenditure is on luxurious living and says that he 'does not see how the mass of Athenians (*tous pollous*) are benefited by the property which Meidias retains for his personal luxury' (158–9). He warns the jury not to be deceived by Meidias' boast that he donated a trireme, and he narrates a story to show that Meidias' motive in doing so was to escape cavalry service (160–7). He points out that Meidias as paymaster of the state trireme, the Paralos, was corrupt and mean, and that as commander of the cavalry, in spite of his wealth, he led the processions on a borrowed horse (171–4).

Demosthenes addresses the jury as people of small means who must combine together to overcome their rich and powerful enemies (140). He argues that the jurymen, who are so strict in punishing a man of moderate means and a *demotikos*, should not pardon a 'rich and insolent man' (183, 201). He invites the jurymen, whom he characterizes as consisting of the multitude and *demotikoi*, to consider what treatment one of them would receive if he had offended a rich associate of Meidias and was brought before a court filled with wealthy men. He asks: 'Do you think he would obtain any pardon, or any consideration? … Would they pay any attention to the petition of one of the multitude? Would they not immediately say, "the cheat! the pest! Should he insult us and still breathe? If he is allowed to live, he should be happy"?' (209). Demosthenes continues to employ words which appeal to the class feelings of the jurymen as poor men against his rich enemies: 'they have many goods which no one prevents them from enjoying; so let them not hinder us from enjoying our common property, the security which the laws provide' (210). Finally, he claims that Meidias 'has insulted' the jurymen by calling them 'beggars' (*ptochous*, 211). Such a term would be really offensive to a jury of the poor (*penetes*) who worked full time to support themselves and had little or no leisure, but it would simply miss the mark if the jury consisted of citizens who owned a moderate amount of property.[40]

---

[40] Jones, arguing that this speech was designed for 'an audience of well-to-do propertied persons', states: 'it is noteworthy that Demosthenes finds it necessary to apologise for introducing a really poor witness, the arbitrator Straton, who is a hoplite' (*Athenian Democracy*, p. 36); but he misinterprets the passage by considering it out of context. Demosthenes summons Straton as a victim of Meidias' persecution, and his characterization of Straton as 'perhaps poor but not bad' is intended to stress that Straton had *formerly* had sufficient property to serve as a hoplite before his honesty had gained him the enmity of Meidias (21.95).

In Demosthenes' speech *Against Androtion* the speaker is obliged to tread a precipitous path. Androtion's collection of arrears of *eisphora* has angered some of the rich citizens who had attempted to withhold a portion of the amounts owed. The poor among the jurors would not be likely to feel much sympathy for these rich citizens who had avoided their taxes, and the presence of significant numbers of the poor in the jury is indicated by the argument which Demosthenes composed for his client Diodorus. Demosthenes takes care not to oppose Androtion's collection of arrears in the capital levies, but emphasizes the brutal and autocratic methods the defendant employed in this work (Demosthenes 22.51–8). He argues that such actions were detrimental to rich and poor alike. He asks a rhetorical question: '… what do you think, when a poor man, or even a rich man, who has had large expenses and perhaps in some way is short of money, climbs over a roof to his neighbours, or creeps under a bed to avoid being arrested and dragged off to prison … ?' (53). The method employed by Demosthenes is to create a common bond of interest between the rich man and the poor man: the person subject to the capital levy becomes 'poor' because he is short of money – an effective means to make this difficult case elicit sympathy from a jury composed largely of the poor.

Finally, Hyperides in his speech *In defence of Euxenippus* (dated between 330 and 324 BC) praises the democracy of Athens as 'magnanimous' and describes specific lawsuits to illustrate that Athenian juries are not motivated by class hatred against the rich but judge each case on its own merits (4.33–6; cf. 32).[41] This tribute would be intelligible only if the poor predominated in these juries.

Of course, there is no reason to doubt that some of the richest Athenians became members of the juries simply because they were interested in serving the state in that capacity, but it is not likely that they would have been numerous enough to influence the outcome of any particular case. At the trial of Demosthenes in 323, the orator whose speech was composed by Dinarchus asks: 'Are there some men in the court who were among the Three Hundred, when Demosthenes proposed his law concerning the trierarchs? Will you

Straton had refused to accept a bribe from Meidias to change his vote in a lawsuit, and due to the consequent machinations of Meidias he was deprived of citizenship and property. Thus Demosthenes apologizes for introducing a man who had become poor through no personal fault ('not bad'), but through the persecution of Meidias.

[41] For the date see G. Colin in the Budé *Hypéride* (Paris, 1946) p. 164. In 19–23, Hyperides assumes that the jurors are intensely anti-Macedonian. This feeling was characteristic mainly of the poor: Philip favoured the oligarchs (see, e.g., Dem. 10.4; M. M. Markle, 'Support of Athenian Intellectuals for Philip', *JHS* XCVI (1976), pp. 80–99, esp. 98–9).

not tell those (sitting) close to you that when he had received three talents he modified and re-worked the law in each assembly?' (Dinarch. 1.42). But such questions do not prove, as Jones maintained (*Athenian Democracy*, p. 37), that 'members of the Three Hundred, the richest men in Athens, frequently sat on juries'. Firstly, the method of allotment of jurors made it impossible for an orator to predict who would be judging his case (cf. note 21 above). Secondly, although by allotment a few one-time members of the Three Hundred might have gained admission to the jury of fifteen hundred who were hearing the case against Demosthenes (Dinarch. 1.107), they would have exerted only a negligible influence on the result of the trial. Indeed, the orator would have got his message across that Demosthenes had been bribed, even if no members of Three Hundred were present, and that was the chief purpose of the rhetorical questions. Elsewhere, Dinarchus indicates that the poor still predominated in the juries: in the speech *Against Philocles* the speaker tells the jurors that they must show all men that the 'mass of the people' (τὸ τοῦ δήμου πλῆθος) has not been corrupted along with some of the orators and generals (3.19).

(b) Assemblies

Next, what indications can be found in the speeches that the poor attended the assembly in large numbers? For the early fourth century very few speeches delivered before the assembly have survived. I have examined Lysias' speech *Against Ergocles* and have shown that the passages cited to show that the assembly consisted primarily of well-to-do citizens have been misinterpreted, and that other statements in the speech indicate that the poor predominated (pp. 112–13 above, with note 33). Most of Demosthenes' speeches on foreign policy stress what the orator considers to be in the best interest of all Athenians and avoid appealing to one particular class. Nevertheless, isolated passages show that the poor commanded the majority vote in the assembly. In his speech *On the Navy-Boards* Demosthenes speaks as if the poor in the assembly could determine by their vote whether those citizens whose property obliged them to pay the capital levy (*eisphora*) should do so (14.25–8). However, scholars have dismissed this evidence by arguing that this speech was delivered at an assembly held in an atmosphere of fear of war with Persia and that an unusually large number of poor would therefore have attended.[42]

---

[42] Jones, *Athenian Democracy*, p. 36; Perlman, 'Political Leadership' (note 4 above), p. 164.

The mood of the Athenians, however, at this assembly may not have been as Demosthenes represents it. He makes it clear that on the occasion of the speech there were no 'clear and unmistakable signs of the King's hostile intentions'; so perhaps his reference to 'the present fear' is a rhetorical exaggeration (14.2–4). In these early years of Demosthenes' career he had little influence in the assembly, and in his speech he may have exaggerated the war-scare simply to magnify his 'success' in overcoming it. The situation that he describes has an air of unreality. Fear of the Persian king is represented as having led the Athenians to desire to make what in modern military jargon is called a pre-emptive first strike against their powerful enemy. Demosthenes mentions rash orators who urge the Athenians to go to war against the Persians (14.8), and he repeatedly advises the assembly not to attack the Persians without justification and sufficient preparations (14.3, 10, 36–8). Surely there was no real probability that Athens would undertake a war with the Persian king at the very time when they had proved too weak to defeat their own rebellious allies supported by Mausolus of Caria. The speeches in this assembly may have amounted to no more than the usual displays of rhetoric by patriots such as Aristophon and Hegesippus against more conservative politicians such as Demosthenes was at this time. In any event, whether this assembly was exceptional or unexceptional, speeches of Demosthenes on other occasions indicate the predominance of the poor.

In the *First Olynthiac* he draws attention by circumlocution to the money held in the theoric fund which is protected by a 'writ against unconstitutional proposals' (*graphe paranomon*) from conversion to military purposes. The orator implies that the assembly ought to spend this money on campaigns, but refuses to propose the illegal motion. He says in criticism, 'you, however, without any compunction simply take the money for your festivals' (1.19–20).[43] Only the poor really needed this money for the festivals and it was also the poor who benefited from employment on the public works financed by this fund.[44] Demosthenes goes on to point out that the only alter-

---

[43] De Ste. Croix in his review of Buchanan's *Theorika* in CR n.s. XIV (1964), pp. 190–2, argues rightly that 'one must distinguish between theoric [festival] distributions and the theoric fund', and he shows that the fund was considerably larger than the annual distributions since it was used for financing public works.

[44] The allowance for the festivals, probably only the Dionysia and Panathenaea, had reached at least 5 drachmas per year for each recipient (Dinarch. 1.56; Hyp. 5.26), and the 5 drachmas may not have been the only payment for the year in question. This sum was not inconsiderable to a poor person who otherwise could not have afforded to take time off from his work to attend the festival, let alone have paid the admission price to the theatre

native source of money for military needs is for 'all men to pay the capital levy' (1.20). By the phrase 'all men' Demosthenes speaks as if the burden of *eisphora* will fall on the entire assembly, but in reality only those whose property was sufficient for this duty would be required to pay. He does not advocate this alternative, since at this point in his career he is not inclined to burden the propertied classes with military finance. In the *Third Olynthiac* he offers the same advice. He urges the people (*tois pollois*) to appoint *nomothetai* [a board of law-enacters] to repeal the laws related to the theoric fund, which he characterizes as 'those laws which distribute military funds as festival disbursements to men who remain at home'. Only if these laws are repealed, he says, will it be safe to give the best counsel to the assembly (3.10–13). Moreover, in this speech and in his speech *On Organization*, Demosthenes depreciates the public works financed by the theoric fund, but, knowing that his opposition to these projects which benefit the poor will not go down well with the assembly, he resorts to the irrelevant charge that the leaders responsible for these programmes have become rich at public expense (3.29; 13.30). Finally, in the *Third Olynthiac* he implies that the theoric fund is the only possible source for military finance (3.19).

In his speech *On Organization*, Demosthenes makes it clear that the question of distribution of public money is one of class: that the propertied class oppose such doles and the poor who need to receive them approve of them (13.1). That the theoric fund is a principal case of such distributions defended by the poor against the rich is shown by his statement: 'If you are going to regard a festival (*heorte*) or any pretext as a sufficient reason for receiving a hand-out ... unless you are careful you will come to realize that ... you have made a serious mistake' (13.2).

Probably not long after Demosthenes delivered the *Olynthiacs*, when an expedition was about to set forth from Athens for Euboea and Olynthus, the assembly voted on a resolution of Apollodorus 'whether the surplus money from administration should be employed for military finance or festival disbursements', and we are told that the decision was unanimous that it ought to be devoted to the former (Ps.-Dem. 59.4–8). Apollodorus was then indicted by Stephanus for making an illegal proposal, and the court convicted him and condemned the decree. These facts cannot be doubted: Theomnestus,

(Harpocration, s.v. θεωρικά [*theorika*], for the importance to the poor of the distributions). On the controversy over the date for the origin of the theoric fund, see P. J. Rhodes, *The Athenian Boule* (Oxford, 1972), p. 105 with note 6; Rhodes, *Commentary on Ath. Pol.*, pp. 514, 768.

the prosecutor of Neaera, who gives this account, reminds jurors in his own case that they were all witnesses on the occasion of the assembly. However, attempting to arouse the sympathy of the jury towards Apollodorus, Theomnestus attributes to him the most democratic motives for making his resolution. These we may justifiably doubt. We can only speculate that Apollodorus carried the assembly away with an impassioned speech, but the 'writ against unconstitutional proposals' was intended for precisely such a situation. The jury may, as Theomnestus asserts, have been deceived by irrelevant charges made by Stephanus, but it is equally possible that the interests of the poor were not promoted by giving up the festival disbursements and the public works programme.[45]

In the *Fourth Philippic* Demosthenes yields to the poor who control the assembly and reverses his policy with regard to the theoric fund. Once again, he introduces his advice on this subject by pointing out that it is one on which the classes are divided: he says, 'I think that, in the best interests of the city, I will be able to justify the complaints of the poor against the rich, and of the propertied classes against the needy.' Then he immediately proceeds to his recommendation: 'If we should remove from our midst the false charges which some unjustly make against the theoric fund, and the fear that it will not be maintained without some great harm, we would make no greater contribution towards solving our problems nor anything which would give greater strength to the entire city' (10.36). It is difficult to understand his purpose in making this concession. He goes on to say that now the revenues of the city are much greater than before – 'four hundred instead of one hundred talents'. Surely this increase would mean that the theoric fund which received 'the surplus money of the administration' (Ps.-Dem. 59.4) would be larger than ever before, and would thus be even more valuable a source for financing the war. Except for the assembly persuaded by Apollodorus, the poor had resisted all suggestions to convert the theoric fund for military use, and the conviction of Apollodorus would not have encouraged Demosthenes.

An alternative mode of financing the war was for the upper classes to perform trierarchies and pay the property tax levies (*eisphora*), and Demosthenes implies that the rich should not avoid these obligations on the grounds that revenues have increased, and that

[45] De Ste. Croix tells me that he interprets this reversal of the assembly's decree by a court as evidence that the jury was composed of persons of greater wealth than the members of the assembly, but I cannot agree with him.

hence the theoric fund is greater. He asks: 'Why, therefore, experiencing this (increase in revenues) do we reproach each other and employ it as a pretext for doing nothing unless we begrudge the poor the help they have got from good fortune?' (10.39). Demosthenes' use of the second person plural and the word 'poor' to designate other people shows that he speaks as a member of the propertied class. To advocate that the rich should shoulder the full burden of military finance is not inconsistent with the Trierarchic Law which Demosthenes carried about this time. Moreover, on the occasion of the *Fourth Philippic* Demosthenes was indulging in optimistic hopes (which proved to be ill-founded) that the Persian king would contribute greatly towards financing the Athenians in a war against Philip (10.31–4). It was not until war with Philip had actually broken out in 339/8 that the poor were willing, because of the need of money for military campaigns, to postpone construction of the arsenal and dockyards and give up receiving festival disbursements, both of which were financed by the theoric fund. At this time it was Demosthenes who drew up the successful bill that all this money should be used for military purposes (Philochorus *FGrH* 328 F 56a).

APPENDIX
Wages, prices, daily rations, and the cost of living in the late fifth and the fourth centuries BC*

Rates of pay by the day for labour are found in two inscriptions: the first from the late fifth century and the second from the end of the third quarter of the fourth century. These inscriptions show that wages for the same kinds of work increased considerably between these dates. In the building accounts of the Erechtheum from 409 to 407 BC, free men and slaves were paid for skilled labour, such as carpentry and masonry, at the rate of 1 drachma per day for each day that they worked (*IG* I³ 475, lines 54–6, 65–7, 67–71, 250–1, 253–6; *ibid.* 476, lines 33–7, 38–44). The architect and *hypogrammateus* (assistant secretary) were paid by the prytany rather than by the day: the architect received 37 dr. for the 36-day prytany and 36 dr. for the 35-day prytany, or slightly more than a drachma per day; the *hypogrammateus* received 30 dr. 5 obols for the longer prytany and 30 dr. for the shorter, i.e. 5 obols per day (6 obols = 1 drachma). Their advantage, of course, was that they received a salary and so were paid at these rates whether they worked every day or not (*IG* I³ 476. 59–63, 266–70).

In the Eleusinian building accounts from 329/8 to ?327/6, however,

---

* For a book-length collection of data see W. T. Loomis, *Wages, Welfare Costs and Inflation in Classical Athens* (Ann Arbor, 1998).

payment mostly to hired workers (*misthotoi*) for unskilled labour, such as carrying bricks, mixing mortar, breaking clods and working on the site, was at the rate of 1½ dr. per day (*IG* II² 1672.28–30, 32–4, 44–6); the one exception is that two sawyers are paid this rate for 'sawing wood', presumably unskilled sawing (159–60). For some semi-skilled and skilled labour, such as polishing doorposts in a temple (177–8) and tiling (110–11), the pay was 2 dr. per day, and for other skilled labour, such as brick-laying, wood-working, stone-dressing and plastering, 2½ dr. per day (26–8, 31–2). In these accounts, unlike those of the Erechtheum, no indication is given of the status of these workers: they are identified only by the designation 'hired labourers' or by the name of their skill. Moreover, the architect received a salary of 72 dr. for the prytany; thus he was paid at the rate of 2 dr. per day (11–12); he received the same rate in ?327/6, an intercalary year of 13 months, in which he was paid 780 dr. for 390 days (*IG* II² 1673.59–60).

Although wages and salaries were thus 2, and even 2½, times higher in the 320s than in the last decade of the fifth century, the prices of the most basic and essential foods – wheat and barley – did not increase during this period, except for temporary fluctuations in prices caused by bad harvests, wars, piracy, and perhaps seasonal shortages. In the Hermokopidai *stelai* of 414/13, prices for a *phormos* of wheat vary between 6 and 6½ dr (*IG* I³ 421. 137–9). It is possible that a *phormos*, which in Athenian law was recognized as a standard measure for grain (Lys. 22.5), is the equivalent of a *medimnos*. Since 6 dr. per *medimnos* is the most common price for wheat in the other sources, it is tempting to regard this price as prevailing as early as 414. But even if the equivalence of *phormos* and *medimnos* cannot be assumed, the price of wheat at the beginning of the fourth century was 6 dr. per *medimnos*. In an inscription of that date which contains a law concerning offerings to priests, ¹⁄₁₂ of a *medimnos* of wheat is priced at 3 obols, i.e. at 6 dr. per *medimnos* (*IG* II² 1356. 17, 21). (Surely no reliance at all can be placed on the low price of 3 dr. per *medimnos* of wheat in 393 which can be computed from Aristophanes' *Ecclesiazusae* 547–8: a complaint is made about having 'lost a sixth (of a *medimnos*) of wheat' which could have been purchased from the pay for attending the assembly (6 × 3 obols = 18 obols, or 3 dr. per *medimnos*): exaggeration of such a loss is most likely in comedy.)

The next price for wheat is found in a document dated half a century later, at a time of great scarcity. A decree carried some time during the years 340 to 330 honours the Heracleotes Mnemon and another (whose name is lost) for providing grain to the Athenians at 9 dr. per *medimnos* for Sicilian wheat and at 5 dr. for barley (*IG* II² 408. 10–15, κριθάς restored). Since these benefactors are commended for selling grain to Athens at almost twice the normal price, the prices which the Athenians would otherwise have been forced to pay must have been much higher; so this was a time of famine. In about 330, Chrysippus in his prosecution of Phormion says, 'when grain rose in price and reached 16 dr. (per *medimnos*), we imported more than ten thousand *medimnoi* of wheat, and measured it out to you at the usual price (τῆς καθεστηκυίας τιμῆς) of 5 dr. per *medimnos*' (Ps.-Dem. 34.39). Moreover, a decree praises Heraclides the Salaminian for 'giving' 3,000 *medimnoi* of wheat to the Athenians at 5 dr. per *medimnos* during the famine (ἐν τῆι σπανοσιτίαι) in the archonship of Aristophon, 330/29 (*IG* II² 360.8–10, 28–30; date: 54–6, 66–8).

The Eleusinian accounts for the year 329/8 (on which see also P. D. A. Garnsey in *Crux ... de Ste Croix*, pp. 62–75) record several prices for wheat and barley. 62 *medimnoi* of wheat sold for 6 dr. per *medimnos*, and 10 *medimnoi* sold for 5 drachmas per *medimnos* (*IG* II² 1672. 286–8). Also, 36 *medimnoi* of wheat with *epibole* (an extra) 10 *hemiekteia*, are valued at 221 drachmas, i.e. at 6 dr. per *medimnos*. Two prices are also recorded for barley: 3 dr. per *medimnos* (lines 282–3) and 3 dr. 5 obols (298). Finally, the decree honouring Heraclides the Salaminian shows that 5 dr. per *medimnos* for wheat was the normal price in 324 (*IG* II² 360, *passim*).

Prices for wheat and barley, however, could vary a considerable amount during a single year. In 282, the price of wheat changed from month to month: from 7 dr. it dropped to 6½, then to 6, then to 4½; then rose back to 7 dr. and finally shot up to 10. After this month, wheat seems no longer to have been available at a marketable price, and barley meal (*alphita*) was purchased, in amounts double those of wheat for the same number of recipients. In the first month barley meal was bought for 4 dr. per *medimnos*, and in the following two months at 5 dr. (*IG* XI ii 158A. 38–50; Delos). The prices during this year were probably affected by the war between Seleucus and Lysimachus. Prices could, however, vary a considerable amount in a normal year, in which no war was being waged, probably due simply to available supplies, which might be larger after a harvest, or after large shipments had arrived, than at other times. Variations in price could also result from differences in the quality of the grain. Prices varying by as much as a drachma in the course of a day could be explained thus (see G. R. Stanton, 'Retail Pricing of Grain in Athens', *Hermes* CXIII (1985), pp. 121–3). In the year 250, the accounts of the Temple-overseers on Delos show variations in the price of hulled barley from month to month: at first the price is 3⅙ dr. per *medimnos*; then it falls to 3 dr., then to 2⅔, then to 2⅓, and in the last recorded month only 2 (*IG* XI ii 287.59–71).

Evidence on daily rations is too abundant and offers too many problems of interpretation to be dealt with in a footnote; I therefore discuss the testimonies (other than those cited on p. 111 in note 30 above) in this Appendix. There is no reason to doubt that one *choinix* of wheat per day was an adequate diet for an adult male who was obliged to do hard physical labour. A treaty between King Attalos I of Pergamon and the people of the Cretan city of Malla (*c*.200 BC) requires that the latter maintain any auxiliary troops sent them by the king by paying each man an Aeginetan drachma per day and each officer 2 dr., and by providing each person with an Attic *choinix* (of grain), provided that they are not in enemy territory where they can exact their own provisions (P. Ducrey, 'Nouvelles remarques

sur deux traités Attalides', *BCH* XCIV (1970), p. 639). The kind of grain is
not specified by the treaty, but it would almost certainly have been wheat.
Again, regulations for giving a public feast in an inscription from Aegiale in
Amorgos (end of second century BC) require the overseers to measure out
one *choinix* of wheat for each man who attends and one half-*choinix* for
each boy (*IG* XII vii 515. 70–4). Foxhall and Forbes seem to me to be over-
cautious in their discussion of this inscription: they write that it is 'not
appropriate under such special, ceremonial circumstances to consider the
grain dispensed to be a proper ration' ('Σιτομετρεία', pp. 52–3). The fact,
however, remains that the ration given to each man under the regulations
governing the festival is the precise equivalent of the daily military ration
attested by the other sources; thus, the regulations recorded by this inscription strongly imply that a *choinix* of wheat for each man was an appropriate
ration for one day. Thirdly, rations for horse-drivers at 'Ptolemais at the
harbour' in Egypt in 226 BC consist of 'one *choinix* of fine bread (*artos
katharos*) for each'; ¼ *kotyle* of olive oil, and 4 *kotylai* of wine, whilst
the grooms receive each 'two *choinikes* of whole-wheat bread' (*artos
autopyros*), only ⅛ *kotyle* of oil and no wine at all (*Petrie Papyri* II, xxv,
a. and b.). I would interpret the double ration of cheaper bread (coarse,
whole-wheat, not barley) as meant to compensate the groom for the half-
ration of olive oil and the lack of wine ration.

On Delos in 282 BC craftsmen are given 10 dr. per month each, i.e. in a
month of 30 days, two obols per day, *eis opsonion* ['for food-purchase'],
and, in addition, 45 *choinikes* of wheat per month each, i.e. 1½ *choinikes*
each per day. During this year, when wheat has risen in price, and is perhaps
no longer available, each craftsman receives, in addition to his 10 dr. per
month [*eis opsonion*], 90 *choinikes* of barley per month, or 3 *choinikes* per
day (*IG* XI ii 158A. 37–50). I would like to make two points in interpret-
ing these rations. First, the 1½ *choinikes* of wheat per day for each craftsman probably includes a half-*choinix* for his wife, and the 2 obols per day
eis opsonion is too much for other food, such as oil, wine, fruit and vege-
tables, for one person, and so also includes an allowance for the craftsman's wife and children. Secondly, 3 *choinikes* of barley per day is more
than a man and his wife would need, but the craftsman is owed this amount
of barley, because when wheat was no longer available at a marketable
price, he must be paid the equivalent value of wheat in barley: barley had
only half the value of wheat, so the craftsman must be given twice as much
barley as he had received in wheat. In fact, the receipt of money *eis opsonion*
and of agreed amounts of grain constitutes the wages of these craftsmen.
Finally, 2 *choinikes* of barley are to be given to the cook by the archons
in charge of a sacrifice on Mykonos in c.200 BC, but this amount need
not be interpreted as a normal daily ration unless it is also assumed that the
cook would also eat in 1 day the loins and ham of 1 of the 2 pigs offered in
sacrifice, which, together with 3 *kotylai* of wine, were his other perquisites
(*SIG*³ 1024. 14–15).

The daily cost of living can be reckoned on the basis of prices of the foods most necessary for life and the daily rations which a person requires of those foods. On the other hand, the amounts of money paid to individuals for *trophe*, which is translated as 'sustenance', provide no guide to the cost of purchasing necessities. In the Eleusinian building accounts of 329 BC, public slaves (*demosioi*) were given 3 obols per day as *trophe*, but this would have purchased 4 *choinikes* of wheat at the current price of 6 dr. per *medimnos*, or 4 days' rations. Moreover, in the 320s, superintendents of ephebes (*sophronistai*) were given a drachma as *trophe*, whilst the younger ephebes themselves received 4 obols (Arist. *Ath. Pol.* 42.3), but the older men presumably did not eat $\frac{1}{3}$ more than their charges. Indeed, the drachma would have bought 8 days' rations of wheat at current prices. Even the 2 obols per day given as *trophe* to disabled persons having property valued at less than 3 *mnai* (*ibid.* 49.4) would have bought more than a day's supply of food.

These estimated daily costs of the necessities of life in Athens make it worth while to consider the economic class of the least wealthy, or poorest, of those obligated to pay the *eisphora*, whose property was valued at 2,500 drachmas. Would this amount of property liberate the owner from the need to work to support himself and his family? The answer to this question depends on answers to two other questions. First, how much of the property would yield a return? The portion of his house and furniture that he and his family occupied and employed would not produce income. Secondly, of what did the property consist? Slaves would probably yield a greater return than land or houses. It is a reasonable assumption that the value of the person's house and furniture was about 500 drachmas. Pritchett points out that 'the median value' of seven houses sold in Athens in 414 BC was 410 drachmas (*Hesperia* XXV (1956), p. 275). If the remaining property of 2,000 drachmas consisted of land or houses and yielded an annual return of 12% (an average of the rates referred to by Isaios 11.42 (8%) and Dem. 34.23 (16%)), it would produce 240 dr. or slightly more than 4 obols per day in an Athenian year of 355 days. If my estimate is correct that a family of four could buy the necessities of life for about $2\frac{1}{2}$ obols per day, then 4 obols per day would be sufficient for such a family to live quite comfortably.

If their property consisted of slaves, the annual return would probably be considerably more than 12%. Pritchett reports that the average price for 25 slaves sold in Athens in 414 BC was approximately 174 dr. each, and there is reason to believe this would have been the price for unskilled slaves (*ibid.* pp. 276–7). If the income-producing property consisted of 11 slaves who cost about 175 dr. each, and the owner exploited them as much as possible by finding them work at a drachma per day for 355 days, they could in theory produce a gross income of 3,905 dr. Obviously, in practice, such exploitation would not be possible: work could probably not be found for them every day, and illness, accident and death would take a toll.

Nonetheless, the profits from the exploitation of slaves must have been enormous, because the cost of maintenance of these 11 slaves would have been little in comparison with their earnings. A tunic for a slave cost 3½ obols, and so 2 tunics for each of the 11 slaves per year would cost about 13 dr.; a cloak cost 10 dr. 3 obols, and so the total cost of 11 cloaks would be 115.5 dr; 11 pairs of shoes at 6 dr. would equal 66 dr. So the total cost of clothing these slaves would be about 195 dr. per year (for prices, see Pritchett, pp. 204–6). Feeding these slaves would cost 0.6 obol per day each for barley meal, to which should be added another 0.2 obol for *opson* (see note 31 above), and thus the cost of feeding the 11 slaves for 355 days would be about 521 dr. The total cost of maintenance for the 11 slaves (apart from sheltering them) would thus be about 716 dr. per year. This amount subtracted from the theoretical maximum income from this crew would leave a net profit of 3,189 dr. This yield is theoretically possible, but in practice we might assume perhaps ⅔ of the maximum gross income possible, 2,605 dr. This amount minus the 716 dr. maintenance would leave a net profit of 1,889 dr. which would be a 98% return on the property of 11 slaves.

A person who owned property assessed at 2,500 dr. would probably have had land, houses, and 4 or 5 slaves, and to increase his wealth he may have chosen to work part of the time. Nevertheless, we must conclude that he falls into the group which can be regarded as rich by the definition derived from Aristotle's *Politics*, those who own sufficient property to free them from the need to work. After all, the *eisphora*-paying class were the upper 30% of the adult male citizen population of Attica in the fourth century.

Annual incomes of workmen in Athens are occasionally exaggerated by historians. This happens because they make the false assumption that a year's earnings can be determined by multiplying the number of days in a year by the daily rate of pay. So, for example, J. K. Davies, *Wealth and the Power of Wealth in Classical Athens* (New York, 1981), p. 28, gives the income of a skilled workman in the 320s as amounting to 700 dr. a year or more, citing Jones, *Athenian Democracy*, p. 135, note 1. Jones, however, does not give this figure as the annual income for a skilled workman, but merely notes that skilled men received 2 or 2½ dr per day. Davies seems to have simply multiplied 2 dr. by 350 days. This, however, produces a greatly exaggerated annual income. Artisans and labourers, who were paid only for the days they worked, did not work every day of the year. There were 40 assembly-days per year, and workers who attended the assembly would have received only 3 obols until the pay was raised to 1 dr. for regular assemblies and 1½ dr. for principal assemblies. In addition, probably only during the years 355 to 339 BC did workers receive some, probably small, compensation for their loss of earnings during the Dionysia and Panathenaia, when distributions were made from the theoric fund (see above, notes 43 and 44). But the festival days were many, and it is most unlikely that even the poor worked during them all. J. D. Mikalson (*The*

Sacred and Civil Calendar of the Athenian Year (Princeton, 1975), p. 201) estimates that the total number of festival days, if they all were known, 'would probably be only slightly less than one-half of all the days of the year'. Though he argues rightly that 'those of the lower economic strata would be less able to enjoy festival days as non-working days' (p. 203), it seems inconceivable that poor Athenian citizens never could have any holidays. Mikalson does not suggest this, but he points to evidence that a group of wage labourers at Eleusis worked for 40 successive days from Hekatombaion 4 to Metageitnion 13 (*IG* II² 1672. 32–3), and he states: 'They not only laboured on the monthly festival days in Hekatombaion and Metageitnion, but they even laboured through the Kronia, the Synoikia, and the splendid festival of the Panathenaia.' On the other hand, other skilled and unskilled labourers at Eleusis worked for fewer days in succession: during the same period of time that Mikalson's labourers worked 40 successive days, a stone-dresser and plasterer worked only 17 days (31–2); three brick-layers worked 25 days (26–8), and their unskilled assistants 25 days (28–30). Of course, these workers might have gone to other jobs for the remaining days of the first prytany, but comparison of the salary of the architect, who was paid by the prytany, with wages paid by the day would suggest that it was not expected that workers would normally work every day. One would expect that the architect in charge would be compensated for his greater skill and responsibility, and indeed he was by being paid a salary of 72 dr. for the prytany of 36 days (11–12). On a daily wage this would amount to only 2 dr. per day, a sum less than the 2½ dr. which some skilled workers under his charge received. The advantage enjoyed by the architect was that he received 2 dr. per day whether he worked or not. This arrangement strongly implies that it was not expected that the workers under his supervision would work every day.

Aristophanes (*Wasps* 660–3) indicates that apart from holidays on which the courts would not sit there were 300 working days in the year, but this number is certainly exaggerated (see end of note 21 above). I suspect that 250 would come closer to the number of days which an Athenian citizen would be obliged to work, and at a drachma per day this amount of labour would have produced an annual income of 250 dr. for unskilled labour in the late fifth century BC, about 4 obols per day. As has been argued, this income is sufficient to support comfortably a family of four.

5 Capital Punishment[*]

LOUIS GERNET

... Und auch an der Strafe ist so viel Festliches![**]
F. Nietzsche, *Zur Genealogie der Moral*
[On the Genealogy of Morality] II.6.

A certain number of allusions attest to the existence in ancient Greece of a form of capital punishment called *apotumpanismos*. Recently, Keramopoullos has produced a study on this form of punishment that is more than just another monograph.[1] Not only does his study break new ground, but it reexamines this topic as a whole and is, accordingly, a contribution to the history of penal law and ethnography. This book deserves more than mere mention; it should be studied carefully.

I

Until recently, scholars thought they knew what *apotumpanismos* was.[2] In fact, texts contemporary with the practice are not very explicit and provide us with little more than the term itself. In Lysias (XIII.56, 67, 68), Demosthenes (VIII.61, IX.61, XIX.137), and

---

[*] "Sur l' Exécution capitale: à propos d' un ouvrage récent" originally published in *Revue des Études Grecques* xxxvii 1924, 261–93, and reprinted in L. Gernet, *Anthropologie de la Grèce antique* (Paris: Maspero, 1968), 302–29 part III ch. iv, © 1968 François Maspero. This translation originally published in Louis Gernet, translated by John Hamilton and Blaise Nagy, *The Anthropology of Ancient Greece* (Baltimore: Johns Hopkins University Press, 1981), pp. 252–76 ch. x, © 1981 Johns Hopkins University Press; reprinted with the permission of Les Éditions La Découverte (successor to François Maspero) and of Johns Hopkins University Press.

[**] "And also in punishment there is so much that is festive!"

[1] A. Keramopoullos, ὁ ἀποτυμπανισμός· συμβολὴ ἀρχαιολογικὴ εἰς τὴν ἱστορίαν τοῦ ποινικοῦ δικαίου καὶ τὴν λαογραφίαν (Athens, 1923).

[2] J. H. Lipsius (*Das attische Recht und Rechtsverfahren*, p. 77, n. 101) restates the traditional opinion in translating it: "Tötung mit der Keule [killing with the club]." Thalheim (s.v. *Apotumpanismos*, in *RE*; K. F. Hermann's *Lehrbuch der griechischen Rechtsalterümer*[4], p. 141, n. 5) wants to correct it. He thinks that the *tumpanon* is a "*Maschine*" [machine] on which the condemned man is bound in order to be executed by cudgeling.

Aristotle (*Ath. Pol.* 45.1; *Rhet.*, II.5.1382b–1383a, II.6.1385a),[3] we merely find that *apotumpanismos* is a contemporary method of executing criminals. One of the references in the *Rhetoric*[4] could have furnished us with more precise information, since it pre-supposes a lengthy form of punishment, but no one took time to examine the text. For lack of anything better, scholars resorted to the witness of the lexicographers, and with this we often have to be satisfied. According to them, the word *tumpanon* (which, if it is connected to *tuptō* ["strike"], has an active force) refers to a kind of club used to execute the condemned man; this would then be the origin of the term in question.[5] But in fact the lexicographers date from a period that affords only a reconstruction based on conjecture, whereas the earliest texts are not very explicit, since they have no need to be for their contemporaries. Some vague survivals may have found their way into the works of lexicographers, who in general were quite diligent in copying one another. But in general they did what we would have to do: they rationalized about these terms – for better or worse.[6] In any case, modern writers were in general agreement with the view that the *apotumpanismos* was an execution carried out by blows with a club.

Following an archaeological discovery, however, Keramopoullos proposed a different interpretation of the practice. Excavations undertaken at the site of ancient Phaleron had twice (in 1911 and in 1915) unearthed a cemetery.[7] In the group of tombs discovered in 1915 – tombs that from the pottery found in them can be dated as belonging to the pre-Solonian era (probably the seventh century B.C.) – there was one that was most remarkable. It was a common grave

---

[3] There is nothing to be derived, at least on a first attempt, from the exclamation in Aristophanes' *Plutus*, 476: *ō tumpana kai kuphōnes* ["O tympana and collars!"].

[4] II.5. 1382b–1383a: οὐκ οἴονται δὲ παθεῖν ἂν ... οὔτε οἱ ἤδη πεπονθέναι πάντα νομίζοντες τὰ δεινὰ καὶ ἀπεψυγμένοι πρὸς τό μέλλον, ὥσπερ οἱ ἀποτυμπανιζόμενοι ἤδη ["people do not believe that something will happen to them ... nor do those who think that everything terrible has already happened to them and who have become coldly indifferent with regard to the future, like those who are now being subjected to *apotumpanismos*"]. See Keramopoullos, *op. cit.*, p. 24.

[5] See, in particular, Hesychius, s.v. τυμπανίζεται ["subjects to *apotumpanismos*"], Bekker, *Anecdota* I, p. 438, 12. In the *Suda*, one finds τύμπανα ... ξύλα, ἐν οἷς ἐτυμπάνιζον ["wooden *tumpana*, on which they performed *apotumpanismos*"], but it is quite possible that ἐν οἷς simply has an "instrumental" meaning. There are bits and pieces of truth in the rather confused gloss of schol. Ar., *Plut.*, 476.

[6] This is also seen in an entirely imaginary reconstruction of the history of the punishment: see Bekker, *Anecdota*, I, p. 438, 12: τὸ γὰρ παλαιὸν ξύλοις ἀνήρουν τοὺς κατακρίτους, ὕστερον δ᾽ ἔδοξε τῷ ξίφει ["In antiquity they executed the condemned with pieces of wood, but later they decided to do it with the sword"].

[7] *Arkhaiologikē Ephēmeris* 1911, pp. 246 f. (K. Kourouniotis); *Arkhaiologikon Deltion*, II (1916), pp. 13 f. (E. Pelekidis).

in which excavators found seventeen cadavers without any accompanying objects. Each was wearing an iron collar around the neck and clamps on the hands and feet. Certain observations led to the conclusion that the skeletons belonged to executed criminals: before their death, they had been placed on planks (some pieces of wood remain on the clamps). These were not slaves who were tortured. Their death was the intended result of the treatment given to all seventeen of them. Nor were they innocent victims of the ingenious cruelty of some brigands similar to modern-day terrorists. Such an interpretation would be false; it is not only improbable but impossible as well. There can be no question but that Keramopoullos was dealing with a form of capital punishment. Moreover, by process of elimination, he could determine that of all the known types of execution, the only one that fit this situation was the *apotumpanismos*.

Such a hypothesis needs justifying, and in his study Keramopoullos applies himself to the task with good results. He notes that the word *tumpanon* never has the meaning scholars usually attribute to it, and that by virtue of its very formation the word has a passive, not an active, force. Keramopoullos also examines the uses of the Latin term *tympanum*,[8] which allow the possibility of *tumpanon* and *sanis* [board] being synonymous. He finds the word *sanis* in a very characteristic form of torture mentioned by Herodotus,[9] Plutarch,[10] and especially Aristophanes, where the torture is described in great detail.[11] In Aristophanes' play, we find condemned prisoners being restrained for an indefinite period of time; they are fastened to a

[8] *Tympana (ostiorum)* ["panels" (of doors)] (Vitruvius, *On Architecture*, IV.6.4); *tympana*, in the sense of the solid drum of a wheel (Virgil, *Georgics*, II.444); etc.

[9] Herodotus (VII.33 and IX.120) describes the punishment inflicted on the Persian Artayctes, who was seized by the Athenians and given by them to the inhabitants of Elaeus for purposes of vengeance: πρὸς σανίδα διεπασσάλευσαν ["they nailed his extremities to a board"]; σανίδα προσπασσαλεύσαντες ἀνεκρέμασαν ["they nailed him to a board and hung him up"].

[10] Plutarch (*Per.*, 28) relates a story which on his own authority he claims is false and which he attributes to Douris of Samos: after the Samians had been defeated by Pericles, he ordered a certain number of them fixed to planks (σανίσι προσδήσας), where they remained for ten days; afterward their heads were bashed in. Keramopoullos gives us good reasons not to accept Plutarch's negative opinion.

[11] Aristophanes (*Thesm.*, 930–46, 1001 f.) describes the order of the prytany, which had met to establish Mnesilokhos' flagrant crime of impiety; Mnesilokhos is "fixed to a plank" by a Scythian archer (930–31, δῆσον ... ἐν τῇ σανίδι; 1012–13, πάντως δ' ἐμοὶ τὰ δέσμ' ὑπάρχει, ["the bonds are fully ready for me"]. From this comes the comparison with Andromeda, which is maintained throughout the scene (1031, ἐν πυκνοῖς δεσμοῖσιν ἐμπεπλεγμένη ["fastened in stout bonds"], 1054, λαιμότμητ' ἄχη ["throat-cut woes"]). Note the word *kremazein* ["hang"] (1028, 1053, 1110). On the object of the punishment itself, cf. 942 (τοῖς κόραξιν ἑστιῶν ["while I am providing a feast for the crows"] and 1028 f. (κόραξι δεῖπνον ["dinner for the crows"]); these are elements that Keramopoullos connects partially with the moment of agony (cf. 866–68).

board or pole with clamps similar to those found at Phaleron. This helps clarify an allusion in Aristophanes' *Equites* (1037–49), which in turn helps us understand our problem. Reference is made to a *pentesuringon xulon*, or a "wooden device with five holes," for which Cleon is destined according to the prophecy of the "sausage seller."[12] It is in fact the instrument of execution of *apotumpanismos*. A careful reading of pages 21–36 of Keramopoullos' study gives some indication of the compelling nature of his investigation of this whole subject.[13]

There emerges from the archaeological and literary evidence a rather neat picture of the *apotumpanismos*. First of all, it is a cruel punishment. The condemned man is stripped and fixed with five clamps to a pole that is set up in the ground.[14] No one is allowed to approach and bring the man help or relief of any kind *whatsoever*.[15] It is only a matter of waiting until he dies. The procedure in some way resembles crucifixion, except that in the latter the hands and feet are nailed, and the consequent loss of blood tends to cut short the punishment. What is more, one of the essential elements of the *tumpanon* is the iron collar, which because of the body's weight puts pressure on the lower jaw and thus adds significantly to the suffering. It is possible to imagine that the agony of the victim could last for several days.[16] That such a form of capital punishment was practiced in Athens should somewhat modify our ideas concerning the Athenian penal code. Inherited from a remote past, and probably

[12] The five holes correspond to the clamps that held the neck, the feet, and the hands. One can also see allusions to *apotumpanismos* in other works, such as Ar., *Eq.*, 367, 705, and Plat., *Rep.*, II.362. See also Dem., XXI.105 (*proselōsthai* ["nail up"]), which deals with an Athenian form of punishment.

[13] Let us admit, however, that a difficulty still remains in the composition of the word *apotumpanismos*; this interpretation is perhaps more satisfying than the traditional one, but the prefix is not what one would expect. It would not be too bold to give *apo* the same meaning as *ap-* in *apagein* ["lead away"], especially since there is a relationship between *apotumpanismos* and the *apagōgē* ["leading away", arrest: cf. pp. 145–7, below].

[14] As for the necessity of nudity, Keramopoullos makes an ingenious deduction *a contrario* [from the opposite] from Ar., *Thesm.*, 940 ff., where the case of Mnesilokhos, who was exposed in full dress, appears to be an exception. As for the position of the condemned being upright, this is fairly well attested in accounts by Herodotus and Plutarch, as well as in Aristophanes' scene (see nn. 9–11 above). Hesychius must have preserved some vague idea of the *apotumpanismos*, since he used the verb *krematai* ["is hung"] when speaking of the condemned in this form of punishment. [in fact Suidas, s.v. τυμπανίζεται ("subjects to *apotumpanismos*"), τ 1165 Adler].

[15] During the entire punishment scene of the *Thesmophoriazousai*, the archer keeps guard over Mnesilokhos; φύλαττε καὶ προσιέναι μηδένα ἔα πρὸς αὐτόν ["Keep guard and let no one go near him"] is the order enjoined on him by the prytany (932 f.).

[16] After death, the victim can remain exposed to wild beasts; even before he dies, this is the case. The *tumpanon* of the Samians remained in the upright position for ten days (Plut., *Per.*, 28).

introduced by Draco, whose criminal laws earned him his sinister reputation,[17] it was practiced throughout the classical period. Indeed, we can trace this form of capital punishment to the end of the fourth century B.C.

Understandably this practice had a powerful impact on the collective imagination. Keramopoullos shows this in a curious detail. He demonstrates that in depicting the punishment of Prometheus in a fashion that is quite different from Hesiod's, Aeschylus is actually conforming in the essentials to the traditional national image of *apotumpanismos*.[18] He also examines some formulas and certain gestures of imprecation, where he finds an allusion to this punishment; and he looks at practices of magic, such as the chaining of statues,[19] whose object is to cause such punishment. It is not our purpose to follow the author through his entire exposition, in which he sometimes goes too far. We limit our interest to (1) his confirmation of the importance of *apotumpanismos* as a punishment; and (2) his demonstration once again (through a specific example) that the penal code is one of the sources from which magical and religious representational forms spontaneously draw nourishment. What should be emphasized here is Keramopoullos' contribution to the history of a penal code as such. His study suggests certain points that could lead to one's not always being in total agreement with him.

II

Our interest is not in the punishment itself; as we have already noted, Keramopoullos gives a quite satisfactory account of this. It is appro-

[17] We would accept the author's view in the case of theft, the crime that particularly concerned Draco. Let us understand that he would have adopted a traditional and customary practice as a legal form of execution (see section III of this chapter). Without doing anything really new, he gave his approval to the practice, and this would have been enough to justify his fame for cruelty. As to whether the affirmation by Keramopoullos here appears to be a little arbitrary in terms of determining whether or not the *apotumpanismos* was the punishment anticipated by Draco for intentional murder, that is another question. It is true that a passage in Aeschines (II.181 f.: οὐ γὰρ ὁ θάνατος δεινόν, ἀλλ' ἡ περὶ τὴν τελευτὴν ὕβρις φοβερά· πῶς δὲ οὐκ οἰκτρὸν ἰδεῖν ἐχθροῦ πρόσωπον ἐπεγγελῶντος, καὶ τοῖς ὠσὶ τῶν ὀνειδῶν ἀκοῦσαι; ["It is not death that is terrifying, but to be insulted at one's end is fearful. How can it not be pitiable when one sees the face of an enemy laughing at one, and hears his insults with one's ears?"]) agrees nicely with the punishment in question and could be used if one had to relate it (as did G. Glotz, *La Solidarité de la famille dans le droit criminel en Grèce*, p. 309) to the punishment for murder. For nothing indicates that such a connection should be made (the connection with Dem., XXIII.68, would be insufficient). On the subject of the execution of murderers, we remain totally ignorant.

[18] Keramopoullos, *op. cit.*, pp. 61–66. The author admits that the depiction of the punishment of Prometheus could only have been represented by a mannequin.

[19] See C. Dugas, *BCH* XXXIX (1915), pp. 416 f.

priate to note, however – and there are certain indications of this in his work – that *apotumpanismos* as it has been described does not constitute a rigorously isolated type of punishment, nor is it one that is without some variations. In early times at least, the condemned man could be fixed to a pole with ropes.[20] In some cases there was flagellation,[21] and there were local variations in the positioning of the victim.[22] Finally, as we have noted in agreement with the author, there is probably a relationship between *apotumpanismos* and crucifixion. Later we will see the importance of this preliminary observation.

Apotumpanismos nevertheless remains a well-defined punishment at least in Athens (as a rule, Keramopoullos wants to associate it with Athens alone) from the seventh to the fourth century B.C. One could ask what its position was in the whole complex of Athenian law. If there were other kinds of capital punishment, what system determined which was to be used? Or *were* there any other forms of capital punishment? At the end of his review Keramopoullos denies any such variety. We know, however, that poisoning by hemlock was practiced in Athens during the classical period.[23] And we seem to have evidence that victims were hurled into the *barathron* [pit]. Still, the former practice appears only late in the classical period – at the end of the fifth century B.C. – so that we can for the moment put it aside. We can be even more radical than the author, since we have only to recall that poisoning did not constitute a type of execution in the proper sense; it must be seen as permitted but controlled suicide.[24] As for the *barathron*, Keramopoullos' view is strongly negative. He believes that this is not an independent form of execution, and admits

[20] Keramopoullos, *op. cit.*, p. 68; cf. S. Reinach, *Répertoire des vases peints grecs et étrusques* II.48.1.

[21] Keramopoullos, *op. cit.*, pp. 30 ff.; cf. Soph., *Aj.*, 108 f.

[22] In Aristotle's account (*Ath. Pol.*, 45.1) there is one word that attracts our attention: *kathēmenon* ["sitting"] (Λυσίμαχον ... καθήμενον ἤδη μέλλοντα ἀποθνήσκειν ["Lysimachus, already sitting and waiting to be put to death"]). One thinks of *sedet aeternumque sedebit* ["sits and will sit for ever": Virgil, *Aeneid*, VI. 617] ... Is there a trace of something that could relate to the punishment itself and to the position of the condemned? Such would hardly be the case if one saw in the "punishment" of Theseus the simple memory of an underworld iconography (see Paus., X.29.9), and in any case, the detail would remain a mystery. But perhaps it is fitting to place a question mark here.

[23] We cannot state with certainty that there were not other methods as well; it is a fact that very often the texts say nothing about the execution. It would be too much to say that execution was always accomplished by one of the methods we have seen in certain cases; we have already said that nothing is known about the execution of the murderer. Elsewhere the *xiphos* [sword] is used at least on occasion; it is attested for Sparta (Zen., VI.11) and for Athens (Lys., XIII.78).

[24] G. Glotz, *Dictionnaire des antiquités*, s.v. *Kōneion*; cf. Plat., *Laws*, IX.873C. We continue to employ the traditional word "hemlock."

only that after execution the *corpses* of the victims were thrown unburied into a place that could be located outside the city, between the gate of the Piraeus and the Long Walls (pp. 36 f.).[25] There really would remain, then, only one proper form of capital punishment, *apotumpanismos*.

The problem we just posed, then, would be eliminated; and at the same time, *apotumpanismos* would take on a significance greater than it seemed to have at first. Even where it is not explicitly mentioned, Keramopoullos says that *apotumpanismos* is certainly what is meant. For example, he argues that in the trial of the generals of the Battle of Arginusae, when Euryptolemus proposes to the people a choice between the law affecting traitors and those guilty of sacrilege and the decree of Kannonos (Xen., *Hell.*, I.7. 20–22), the penalty that is prescribed, though not mentioned explicitly in the legislation, would in both cases be the fixing of the condemned to a pole (pp. 97 ff.).[26]

We disagree with the author and think that there were different forms of capital punishment; and such diverse forms make sense. But let us first consider two points. First – on the question of the *barathron* – it appears that Keramopoullos' thesis leads directly to criticism. Second – on the question of the burial permitted or denied to the condemned – the difficulty that Keramopoullos experiences in one respect could provide us with an argument.

One might say, with a brevity that is almost flippant, that the author "does not believe" in the *barathron*. He is not the first unbeliever: Thonissen[27] has already indulged in the luxury of a radical skepticism. But Thonissen is not exactly an authority and is hardly cited anymore. The question of the *barathron* is undertaken anew; it is currently acknowledged that in Athens some of the condemned were thrown off the Tarpeian Rock, and it was precisely this act that was their *supplicium* [punishment]. There may be some uncertainty as to whether this procedure survived after the fifth century B.C.,

---

[25] According to Plat., *Rep.*, 439E. It is here that one ordinarily situates the *barathron*.

[26] Keramopoullos seems to give too much importance to the decree of Kannonos; he is prepared to place it far back into the past, and sees it as the dominant law even in the fourth century B.C. In fact, it was a legislative action analogous to the decree of Diopeithes. Like that decree, it was designed to implement in certain instances the procedure of *eisangelia* ["impeachment", a procedure for major offences against the state]. It is difficult to see why it would be compared with the *arkhaios nomos* ["ancient law"] of which Demosthenes speaks in reference to the *apatē tou dēmou* "[deceiving the people"] (XX.135).

[27] J. J. Thonissen, *Le Droit pénal de la république athénienne*, pp. 94, 98 f. For a criticism, see G. Glotz, *L'Ordalie dans la Grèce primitive* (1904), pp. 91 f.; cf. H. Hager, *JHS*, VIII (1877), pp. 6 ff.

and there may be some topographical obscurities;²⁸ but these, for the moment, are not of primary importance. What is important is the existence of the practice. Is it traditional opinion – traditional, at least, from the period of the ancient scholiasts (not in itself a reason to reject it) – that Keramopoullos opposes? He opposes it with an argument that is sufficiently dispersive and very indirect. He begins by dismissing the question of the existence of the *barathron*, content to justify himself later, but having in mind a negative thesis (p. 20). First, because we find several sources that testify to a *barathron*, Keramopoullos represents it as the place where corpses of executed criminals were thrown (pp. 36 f.). He then believes he has grounds²⁹ for saying that *apotumpanismos* was the only method of execution employed before the practice of taking hemlock. And he argues this by presupposing the thesis, to be demonstrated later, that hurling someone into the *barathron* was not a way of putting a person to death (p. 47). But his anticipated demonstration fails to materialize. By fixing his attention solely on *apotumpanismos*, and by seeing its importance gradually increase at the expense of everything else, Keramopoullos is led unwittingly but with the best of intentions to a *petitio principii* [begging the question]. When considering expressions like *eis korakas* ["to the crows"] or *eis Kunosarges* ["to Cynosarges"],³⁰ he connects them with *apotumpanismos*. The corpses of the *apotetumpanismenoi* were, as he admits, discarded without burial; they therefore became the prey of beasts (the condemned were already such prey during their agony). It is precisely this *ataphia* [lack of burial] that he recognizes in the "hurling into the *barathron*." This additional penalty, then, was added to that of

---

²⁸ According to Bekker, *Anecdota*, I, p. 219, the *barathron* was located in the deme of Keiriadai; Plutarch (*Them.*, 22) seems to locate it in the deme of Melite; elsewhere, the scholiast of Aristophanes (*Plut.*, 431) mentions an *orugma* [ditch] that was filled in perhaps in the fifth century B.C. Thalheim (in *RE*, s.v. *barathron*) and W. Judeich (*Topographie von Athen*, p. 375, [2nd edition, 1931, p. 140]) extricate themselves from the difficulty, each in his own fashion. If pressed, we would admit that the new *orugma* of the fourth century B.C., as distinct from the older, fifth-century one, served only as a place in which to throw the corpses of the condemned. Throwing people in is no longer mentioned expressly after 406, and a grammatical interpretation of Dinarchus (I.62: τεθνᾶσι ... παραδοθέντες τῷ ἐπὶ τῷ ὀρύγματι ["there have been put to death, handed over to the man in charge of the ditch"]) does not necessarily presuppose this practice (for a contrary view, see Glotz, *L'Ordalie*, p. 92, n. 2); however, see Lyc., *Leocr.*, 121, which corresponds to the year 410 B.C., but in which the expression, παραδοῦναι τῷ ἐπὶ τοῦ ὀρύγματος ["hand over to the man in charge of the ditch"], if it is to be intelligible, must mean that the practice of tossing in had persisted into the orator's own age.

²⁹ An affirmation that relies on the scholiast of Aristophanes, *Ran.*, 541, which clearly is not a very valuable text.

³⁰ This last expression would be a popular burlesque and a corruption of εἰς κύνας ["to the dogs"].

apotumpanismos, and was practiced in conjunction with it (p. 83). This is what he should have proved.

One would perhaps like something else – the more so as the employment of a type of execution such as is admitted up to now is almost expected. There is not only the Roman analogue, but we know for a fact that in Sparta, Delphi, Corinth, and perhaps Elis and Thessaly,[31] the condemned were hurled to their deaths from a high rock. There would have to be some compelling reasons to doubt that the *barathron* had the same function as the Keadas or the Hyampeian Rock [in Sparta (n. 35) and Delphi (Plut., *De Sera*, 557A) respectively]. Now even if it is correct that the lexicographers have embroidered the historical facts, that we do not have to believe some of their horrifying tales,[32] and that contemporary texts are not always open to a single interpretation,[33] the hurling of the condemned into the *barathron* still remains a fact that is formally attested. It is certainly true in the case of enemies.[34] Will we say that in this instance it is a matter of vengeance and not internal law? This does not seem to be the answer.[35] In any case, how are we to understand the repeated references to it in Aristophanes?[36] What interpretation –

[31] For Sparta, see Thuc., I.134.4; Paus., IV.18.4. For Delphi, see Paus., X.42, and Plut., *De Sera*, XII.557A; cf. Aeschin., II.142. For Corinth, see Steph. Byz., 402 (where we note that the *kōs* has become *desmōtērion* [prison], like the quarries in Syracuse and the Keadas in Sparta; cf. Strab., VIII.7.367). For Elis, see Paus., V.6.7 f., a text that assumes the ancient practice of hurling in. For Thessaly, see Zen., 87 (ἐν Θεσσαλίᾳ τόπος ἐστὶ Κόρακες, ὅπου τοὺς κακούργους ἐνέβαλλον ["In Thessaly there is a place called Crows, into which they threw the criminals"]).

[32] Schol. Ar., *Plut.*, 431, in which there is a distortion of reality rather than an invention or fantasy (the *onkinoi* [hooks] are relics of harshness such as is found in the Keadas; see M. O. Rayet, in A. H. Couat, *La Poésie alexandrine sous les trois premiers Ptolémées (324–222 av. J.-C.)*, p. 344, n. 2).

[33] This is the case for some of Aristophanes' texts; for Dinarchus' text, which is mentioned in n. 28 above; and for Thucydides, II.67 (see n. 34).

[34] This seems to be proved by Herodotus, VIII.133: the envoys of Darius are thrown into a pit and a well in Athens and in Sparta (ἐσβαλόντες ἐκέλευον γῆν τε καὶ ὕδωρ ἐκ τούτων φέρειν παρὰ βασιλέα ["They threw them in and told them to take earth and water from there (from the pit and the well) to the King"]). This act can be understood only if the emissaries were thrown down while alive. On the other hand, Thucydides, II.67.4, on which people readily base arguments, is less clear: he speaks of nonbelligerent enemies of Greece who were killed by the Lacedaemonians and (in reprisal) by the Athenians (ἀπέκτειναν ... καὶ ἐς φάραγγας ἐσέβαλον ["they killed them and threw them into pits"]; ἀποκτείναντες καὶ ἐς φάραγγας ἐσβαλόντες ["killing them and throwing them into pits"]).

[35] See Thuc., I.134.4: τὸν Καιάδαν οὗπερ τοὺς κακούργους ἐμβάλλειν ["the Kaiadas, where they threw in the criminals"]. This can be no other place than the one from which the Persians were thrown (Her., VIII.133). As for the *barathron*, in addition to the passages already mentioned, see Plut., *Arist.*, 3, which presents an "apophthegm" of the hero: there would be no more safety for the Athenians εἰ μὴ καὶ Θεμιστοκλέα καὶ αὐτὸν εἰς τὸ βάραθρον ἐμβάλοιεν ["unless they threw Themistocles and himself into the pit"].

[36] The number of these allusions is already contested; and if, in a strict sense, texts like Ar., *Ran.*, 574, and *Plut.*, 431, are subject to misconstruction, there is all the clarity possible in *Eq.*, 1362–3 (εἰς τὸ βάραθρον ἐμβαλῶ, ἐκ τοῦ λάρυγγος ἐκκρεμάσας Ὑπέρβολον ["I shall

other than the obvious one – do we give to Plato's *Gorgias*, 516D? "It was determined by vote that Miltiades be thrown into the *barathron*; and had it not been for the prytanis [man presiding], he would have been." Whatever importance deprival of burial might have (which, whenever it has to be mentioned, is done so in explicit terms), it is simply incredible that one would have described only an accessory punishment while understanding the essential one. Finally, how are we to interpret the well-known passage in Xenophon, *Hellenica*, I.7.20, where the very terms of the decree of Kannonos are cited: "if someone is found to be guilty, he is to die by being thrown into the *barathron*"? Here equivocation is possible only if we allow Keramopoullos' emendation (p. 97) *apothanonta eis to barathron emblēthēnai*, that is, "after his death he is to be thrown into the *barathron*." But there is nothing to justify this arbitrary emendation,[37] and it produces a phrase that is less than satisfying.

The second question is closely connected with the first. Keramopoullos had to be impressed with something that the discovery at Phaleron made immediately clear. After being executed by *apotumpanismos* the condemned were buried. True, there were no offerings, no honors; but dead *were* buried. It is a well-known fact that deprival of burial in Attic soil was a penalty added to that of death in a good many cases. And Keramopoullos is forced to admit that in these instances this prohibition of burial is added to *apotumpanismos* regularly, since it is, according to author, the only mode of execution used until the end of the fifth century B.C. He also admits that corpses of those condemned to die by hemlock were as a rule returned to their families.[38] And herein lies a twofold difficulty. Keramopoullos must establish the direct relationship between *apotumpanismos* and the denial of burial; he must also recognize the exceptional character of the case of Phaleron and then justify the exception. It seems to us that the author does neither. No doubt he is forced to establish – and here, he is for the most part successful – that the prohibition *mē taphēnai en tēi Attikēi* ["not to be buried in Attica"] does not necessarily mean the removal of corpses beyond the boundaries. He shows that in addition to a *huperorismos* [removal beyond the boundaries] in the strict sense, there exist other methods

---

throw him into the *barathron*, hanging Hyperbolus from his windpipe"]), where the last few words hearken perhaps indirectly to one feature of the execution), *Nub.*, 1450, and *Plut.*, 1109.
[37] On this subject, Keramopoullos refers to Ar., *Eccl.*, 1089–90, which is an allusion to the decree of Kannonos; but the word διαλελημμένον ["bound"] is connected not with the punishment *apotumpanismos* but, as the scholiast sees it, with the procedure of hurling in.
[38] Lys., XII.18, and Plat., *Phaed.*, 115D; cf. Lys., XIX.7.

with the same function and effect, and that the annihilation of the
criminal as well as the purification of the group can be achieved
through water, fire, or air. Practically speaking, then, the abandonment of the corpse and the scattering of the bones (a result of its
abandonment) can satisfy the religious need that the rule in question
conveys. Let us – and quite correctly – concede this point to the
author. What use will he make of it? We can guess. He wants to see
in the examples of "hurling," evidence for the kind of treatment
inflicted on the corpse of the *apotetumpanismenos*. With these
examples, he wants to link those instances in which there is an
explicit prohibition against burial. Here his logic is quite arbitrary,
and once again he begs the question. He does not cite a single text
in which there is a question of actual *apotumpanismos*; and there
is only one instance – and it is a very special one[39] – where the
denial of burial is actually linked with the punishment. It is simply
gratuitous to say that outside of this singular case, denial of burial is
"understood" in the others. As far as we are concerned it would be
no less arbitrary to claim – and this would already contradict one text
– that the two elements are always separate. We can understand why
they could be lumped together; but Keramopoullos wants to see an
essential association between the two. It is easy to see why. According
to him, *apotumpanismos* is normally and by definition applied
to crimes the gods or the state, crimes specifically punished by
"hurling," or – and this could amount to the same thing – crimes
punished by the denial of burial. We would say that the questions are
connected.

     Whatever the case, there still remains the matter of those executed
at Phaleron.[40] The explanations offered by the author (pp. 99 and
102) are rather embarrassing. For him it is a question of date, locale,
or type of punishment. But if this is a question of "type," then we
are engaged in a new approach, and it seems quite likely that there
is a contradiction here, since in the same period, but elsewhere, a
separation of the two punishments is explicitly acknowledged as a
general principle. If it is simply a question of locale, one will say that
in a period when the law was not yet systematized, the condemned
who underwent *apotumpanismos* were buried in Phaleron but not in
Athens. This is not a very satisfying hypothesis, for it involves an
additional punishment that is so characteristic of a religious outlook.

---

[39] It is the case of the Samians whom Pericles had executed (Plut., *Per.*, 28: εἶτα προβαλεῖν
τὰ σώματα ἀκήδευτα ["then to cast forth their bodies unburied"]).
[40] It is true that they were buried apart from the rest of the dead, near a crossroads
(Keramopoullos refers to a prescription in Plato's *Laws*, IX.873A); still, burial was permitted.

If Phaleron is simply a matter of a date, as the author is inclined to believe, the same objection can be raised with even greater force. It is precisely the antiquity of this supposed exception which provides us with the strongest argument. How can we say that it was only at a relatively recent date that corpses of the condemned were denied burial?[41] How, then, can we understand that a short time before – or in any event, before the period in which *huperorismos* responded to a need that in some instances was so pressing that it was applied to the ancient dead of a *genos* ["clan"; actual or imagined kinship group], and even necessitated their exhumation (the story of the Alcmaeonids is well known) – seventeen individuals whose bodies were found in a common grave would be spared *huperorismos*? There exist here – and we say it immediately – two systems of practice and representation that are in principle incompatible. Keramopoullos has reason to recall the general obligation of burial, the purpose of which was the elimination of religious pollution from the community. Should one say that the deprival of burial is best understood as a weakening of a religious scruple? Apparently not. If, for reasons that remain to be seen, the community violates the obligation in the case of certain criminals, surely the situation must be such that the criminals in whose case it respects the obligation would be of a different order. Such a conclusion is made more necessary if we admit with Keramopoullos (whose deductions seem acceptable [pp. 47 ff.]) that the criminals punished at Phaleron were buried by authority of the state.

III

We end up finding in the types of capital punishment a diversity, and more especially a dualism, that must be accounted for, but we have to admit that the problem is a subtle one, and perhaps even insoluble.

Does this diversity correspond to an ethnic one? Such a hypothesis can hardly be held in the case of Athens. It is impossible to see how one could prove it; thus it remains nebulous. In addition, earlier observations take us in another direction; they suggest that the different treatments meted out to the condemned correspond to different

---

[41] But this could not be later than the beginning of the sixth century B.C., when because of the *katharmos* [purification] ordered by Epimenides the corpses of the Alcmaeonids were disinterred (Keramopoullos, *op. cit.*, p. 104, n. 2). There is even some reason to believe that this exhumation occurred in the seventh century B.C. (see Glotz, *Solidarité*, p. 461, n. 2). Concerning the antiquity of denial of burial, see ibid., pp. 29 f.

kinds of punishment. But this view at first appears deceptive; and it may be that Keramopoullos is conscious of this. He underlines the multiplicity of instances in which *apotumpanismos* seems to be attested. There is the question of quite different crimes: treachery, impiety, extortion, aggravated theft. On the other hand, we admittedly have the impression that this penalty would be applied principally to offenses against the state and crimes against religion. And these are the types of crimes where one finds mention of the penalty of being hurled into the *barathron*. We are, so it seems, caught in a dilemma. We must either admit with Keramopoullos that these two punishments are added to each other so as to be really equivalent to one, or we must be resigned to not understanding this duality.

But a closer study is less discouraging. Let us make one obvious observation: *apotumpanismos* is certainly a very ancient practice. If we want to define its proper domain and original function, we must not forget that from the moment when the state was endowed with a complete penal code, certain close associations and contaminations must have occurred. It is even the nature of this organization and centralization of law to create a syncretism between elements that were originally distinct. In the interpretation of events there is a principle that one could employ. Naturally it should not be abused. It is used correctly if one can recognize in the very attestations of the classical age the persistent mark of the specifically primitive.

As for death by hurling the condemned from a precipice, this seems to have been reserved for crimes against religion and the state.[42] The denial of burial also applies to these offenses (whether or not it is necessarily connected with death by hurling).[43] We should add that when it began to be used, death by poisoning was the penalty for crimes of the same category.[44] In connection with the links between these, certain questions may arise, but what we wish to emphasize here is the fact that there were specific penalties for impiety, treason, and other related crimes.

As far as *apotumpanismos* is concerned, analysis of the historical testimony about it offers us evidence that can correct our first im-

[42] Plat., *Gorg.*, 516D (cf. Her., VI.186); Ar., *Eq.*, 1362, and *Plut.*, 1109; Xen., *Hell.*, I.7.20; schol. Ar., *Plut.*, 431; Lyc., *Leocr.*, 121. In Delphi the *katakrēmnismos* [throwing from a cliff] was the punishment for sacrilege and for religious crimes in general (Paus., X.4.2; Eur., *Ion*, 1102, etc.; Aeschin., II.142).

[43] In Greece, denial of burial was a general rule for tyrants, traitors, and those guilty of sacrilege (Diod. Sic., XVI.25.2). In Athens, it was anticipated by the law concerning traitors and those who committed crimes of sacrilege (Xen., *Hell.*, 1.7.22) and by the law concerning *eisangelia* (Hyp., *Eux.*, 18). Cf. Plat., *Laws*, IX.855A.

[44] The political crimes under the Thirty Tyrants (Lys., XII.17, XVIII.24); the cases of Socrates and Phokion.

pressions. Among the sources dealing with crimes against the state, three references in Demosthenes must be set aside. Demosthenes does not say that the criminals about whom he is talking were executed by *apotumpanismos*; he says that they *should* have been executed in such a fashion. An orator's passion – and an Athenian's at that – is not restrained. He proposes for his enemies the most terrifying and ignominious punishments. It would certainly be incorrect to see here a valid testimony about the actual law or its normal practice. In fact, it would contradict what we know from other sources. In the fourth century B.C., criminals of this sort were executed by the administration of hemlock.[45] Again, this makes us see that as a rule, *apotumpanismos* is applied in the case of other kinds of crimes. This is exactly the impression one gets from reading Lysias, and a number of particulars justify it. To begin with, although it is usual practice merely to mention the condemnation to death, there is an insistence on giving a detailed account of the method of execution. These details are for the benefit of the orator's enemies. He evidently takes delight in recalling how they have been treated: they endured the lot of vile criminals. For one of them the situation is at once clear; he was a *lōpodutēs*, a "highway robber" (Lys., XIII.68). Another case (Lys., XIII.67) involves a traitor who was arrested while corresponding with the enemy. But the fact that the execution took place within the army, as well as the character of the criminal – he was a brother of the highway robber and was probably a slave[46] – must be taken into account. The individual himself belongs to the category of petty criminals.[47] The case of Cleon in the *Equites* and that of Mnesilokhos in the *Thesmophoriazousai* are somewhat different. Cleon is depicted as having robbed the public treasury.[48] This kind of *klopē* [theft] is easily associated with the image of a common thief.[49] Mnesilokhos, guilty of impiety, is the object of an *ephēgēsis* ["bringing" an official to the offender],[50] a procedure that during the classical period could replace the *apagōgē* (the "arrest"), to the degree that

[45] In Demosthenes' texts it is a question of popular justice (see especially IX.61); Demosthenes really enjoys bringing this up (cf. Aeschin., III.150; Dem., XXIV.208).

[46] Both are brothers of Agoratos, who was born a slave.

[47] The third case (Lys., XIII.56) does not lend itself to interpretation. Under the Thirty Tyrants, the individual in question had caused a man's death by his denunciations, but he was evidently not convicted as a murderer (see P. Cloché, *La Restauration démocratique à Athènes en 403 avant J.-C.*, pp. 341 ff.), and we do not know what crime set the judicial process in motion. At the most, we could suspect that the process was initiated by means of *apagōgē* [literally, "leading away" the offender to an official].

[48] Ar., *Eq.*, 79, 205, 248, 296, etc.

[49] Plat., *Laws*, IX.857A f.

[50] Someone goes to find the chief of the prytany, who then comes and catches Mnesilokhos *in flagrante delicto* [in the act] (Ar., *Thesm.*, 930 f.).

it was considered a kind of *apagōgē*⁵¹ and was equally suitable for the flagrant offense. Here, then, are two cases, both imaginary, that have some link to what seems to us to be the decidedly typical case: Lysias' *lōpodutēs*, who was himself the object of an *apagōgē*. And we could emphasize (if we agreed with Keramopoullos' suggestion) the myth of Prometheus, who is punished as a *kleptēs* [thief] and is subjected to *apotumpanismos*. In addition, we cannot overlook the fact that for the condemned figures of myth, the depiction of their punishment came before that of their crime.⁵² It would not be at all surprising to learn that it was precisely the image of a characteristic punishment which gave rise to the idea of a corresponding crime.⁵³

Finally, there is the case of the punishments in Phaleron.⁵⁴ On this subject Keramopoullos develops a hypothesis that he supports with arguments that are believable and that seem highly probable. He believes that corpses in Phaleron may be those of pirates captured in battle. Pirates qualify precisely as *kakourgoi*,⁵⁵ and they belong to that category of "criminals" which includes thieves of all sorts. We can well believe that pirates would have to undergo the kind of execution reserved for this category of criminals.

We now have several clues. On the one hand, *apotumpanismos* seems to have been employed for the punishment of "criminals." But it is also connected with *apagōgē*.⁵⁶ We still must define its real domain. We already have some idea that it has a domain or sphere; or to put it another way, we ought to be able to extrapolate from the Athenian penal system a design that would be more satisfactory and more coherent than the one we have in a theory that makes *apotumpanismos* the only method of execution. It is already clear

---

⁵¹ Dem., XXII.26.

⁵² See U. von Wilamowitz-Moellendorff, *Homerische Untersuchungen* (*Philologische Untersuchungen*) (VII [1884]), pp. 200 f.

⁵³ See S. Reinach, *Cultes, mythes et religions*, II, pp. 159 ff.

⁵⁴ We do not know for what crime Lysimachus had to undergo *apotumpanismos*, according to Aristotle's version (*Ath. Pol.*, 45.1). It must have been a public crime, since the accused was handed over before the Council; but this public crime could have been sacrilegious theft or the stealing of city property, the flagrancy of which justified the *apagōgē* (see Libanius; the *hupothesis* [ancient scholar's "argument"] of Demosthenes' *Aristogeiton*. The instances quoted by Herodotus and Plutarch (citing Douris of Samos) have to do with external enemies. The execution of Antiphon the poet (Arist., *Rhet.*, II.5) is the act of a tyrant.

⁵⁵ This use of the term is fairly well defined: Thuc., I.8.2, II.22; [Dem.], LVIII.53, etc. It is possible to admit with Lipsius (*op. cit.*, p. 79, n. 105) that in the classical era this term did not have a technical meaning. But it can also be said that in an earlier period the *apagōgē* was employed in a similar way, as it happened later, *outside* Athens (Lucian, *Navigium*, 14), and even *in* Athens in some instances in the fifth century B.C. (Lys., XIII.78).

⁵⁶ On the first point, see Dem., IV.47. On the second, see Sext. Emp., *Math.*, XXX.295: τινῶν μὲν εἰς τὸ δεσμωτήριον, τινῶν δ' ἐπὶ τύμπανον ἀπαγομένων ["some being led away to the prison, others to the *tumpanon*"].

that this horrid punishment was used in Athens; but its use must have been rather specialized, since it is so seldom mentioned and it remained a puzzlement for so long a time. We need to answer two questions: (1) Is there a class of criminals which is both definite and comprehensive, and which originally constituted the proper domain of *apotumpanismos*? (2) Are the procedure that characterizes *apotumpanismos* and the ideas attached to it capable of an extension that justifies the less well defined use of the method in the classical period? The answer to the first question is beyond doubt. The very concept of the *kakourgoi*, the subjects *par excellence* [above all others] of *apotumpanismos*, remains strictly and technically defined even in Aristotle's period. We should recall the list in the *Ath. pol.* (52.1), a list that is confirmed in other sources:[57] *kleptai* (thieves), *andrapodistai* (kidnappers), *lōpodutai* (highway robbers); we could add to these *toikhōrukhoi* ("wall-piercers") and *balantiotomoi* ("purse-snatchers"). All these individuals can be arrested if they are caught *in flagrante delicto* (*ep' autophōrōi*, ["in the act"]). Without any other process – that is, without a summons (*proklēsis*) – one drags them off to the competent authority, which at least since Solon's time[58] is the Committee of the Eleven. If the criminals plead guilty, they are immediately executed.

What we must keep in mind in all of this is the process of *apagōgē* or *manus iniectio* [seizing with one's hands]; there is no need to insist on the importance of the procedure within the law, especially in terms of its origins. The procedure is a principle of unity for the specific cases and a principle of organization for juridical theory. We define *apagōgē* as an improvised and hasty process, the aim of which is immediate execution. It applies to a category of criminals which is determined each time by the type of crime committed and the flagrancy of the offense. A primitive nucleus can be observed all the more readily in this instance since evolution has for the most part respected it. It is enough to abstract from what is more properly "judicial" and has been imposed on the process of *apagōgē*. Thus there is the possibility that a lawsuit (in the modern sense) could be grafted onto the *manus iniectio*.[59] This is indicated by the need for this legal action in a number of cases where it is certainly the result

---

[57] Isoc., XV.90; Ant., V.9 f.; Lys., X.10. Cf Dem., XXXV.47; Xen., *Mem.*, I.2.61; Plat., *Rep.*, IX.575B, VIII.552D.
[58] See Arist., *Ath. Pol.*, 7.3.
[59] Here the noun *apagōgē* applies more specifically; see H. Meuss, *De Apagoges Actione apud Atheniensis*, p. 3, 14, 22.

of later developments,[60] as well as by the option of resorting to other
legal means, means that are regarded as complementary to *apagōgē*,
but that could lead us into error regarding its fundamental nature
since they signify essentially a direct and immediate recourse to
public authority.[61] Finally, there is the intervention of a city magistrate, which however early it may have been instituted would not as
such have any connection with the most primitive form of *apagōgē*.
Apagōgē, then, appears to be a private process that can function only
at the hands of a victim and for the sake of vengeance. The specific
use of the verb *agein/apagein* ["lead"/"lead away"] leaves no room
for doubt; it is connected with the private seizure of a person.[62]
The aggrieved party seizes his thief for the purpose of summarily
executing him.

   Are we, then, strictly in the realm of private vengeance? No.
Instead we are in a complex domain, or in any event a different one.
To begin with, the use of *apagōgē* must be distinguished from what
we might call "self-defense"; a victim can kill the nighttime thief
or the daytime thief who puts up resistance. But one can also use
apagōgē against these criminal types,[63] and as such it appears to
be a social institution, a device that seems above all to put the solidarity of a territorial group into operation.[64] It is very different from
the blood feud, or repression of crimes like homicide or adultery.[65]

---

   [60] Cases in which the guilty party denies the crime. It is clear, however, that in principle a
denial has little effect if an instance of flagrant action is involved. It was allowed only when
flagrancy, which continued to be demanded, ceased to belong to the very definition of the
crime. See P. Huvelin, *Etudes sur le furtum dans le très ancien droit romain*, I, p. 148.
   [61] It seems that the *dikē* [private suit] takes place in cases of general or unspecified theft;
that is to say, when the crime is not a *flagrans delictum* [flagrant offence]. The *graphē* [public
suit] doubtless applies to a specific form of thievery (Lipsius, *op. cit.*, p. 438), but it came into
being late in the classical era. Two other procedures are closely related to the *apagōgē*: *endeixis*
["pointing out" the offender to an official] and *ephēgēsis* ["bringing" an official to the
offender: cf. p. 145]. But there is some doubt that the first was applied to *kakourgoi* (ibid.,
p. 331; for another viewpoint, see Huvelin, *op. cit.*, p. 146; but cf. Dem., XXII.26). As for
ephēgēsis, it appears that its primitive domain was crimes of a public and religious nature (Lys.,
VII.22), and in any case it seems that it could not coexist with the *apagōgē* at first.
   [62] On the essential nature of this procedure, see Huvelin, *op. cit.*, p. 145, n. 4. Even when
apagein and *agein* are distinguished from each other, the compound form applies to *apagōgē*
no less than does the simple form, which is sometimes used in its place. We know the meaning
of *agein* ["lead" to justice]; it is enough to recall its use with regard to the *iudicati* and the *nexi*
[the condemned and the enslaved] in the law of Gortyn and elsewhere. It applies to a summary
and private execution in Ant., V.34.
   [63] Dem., XXIV.113.
   [64] See Glotz, *Solidarité*, pp. 198 ff.
   [65] The *moikhos* [adulterer] does not belong to the category of *kakourgoi*; there is no way
to make allowances for the information in Aeschines (I.90), who includes murderers (see
Lipsius, *op. cit.*, p. 79, n. 105) when using the verb *kakourgein* in a general sense. This does
not imply – for naturally there are links between these two types of penalties – that the *flagrans
delictum* [manifest offence] was not established according to more or less solemn methods (see

Apagōgē is a private affair in terms of its effect. The word itself is not unimportant in this regard; the make-up of the verb *apagein* seems to exclude the idea of a vengeance exercised solely by the victim, who "would drag along" the guilty person to the victim's place.[66] On the contrary the verb seems to indicate an act directed to the outside, toward the public. It could be that it evokes that ignominious promenade inflicted on some criminals.[67] In any case, it suggests that the individual's vengeance is reinforced by the community's collaboration and assistance. This is surely what appears in a striking way in the very operation of *apagōgē*. Given the development of the procedure, public collaboration is already apparent in situations where the tradition has been established for such a long time that the execution, which is the very raison d'être [reason for the existence] of *apagōgē* – actually its first act – must from the very beginning have had a public character. It is possible to concede that from an early period local authorities could have presided over it; but such a hypothesis is not essential, for the social group can serve in a retributive capacity and at least endorse the vengeance. In addition, not only does the private repression of *kakourgēmata* [criminal acts] presuppose the cooperation of the "group," since in a rural milieu the primitive varieties of theft provoke a strong sympathy for vengeance,[68] and not only has the thief been regarded as the most ancient criminal in the precise sense of the term,[69] but *apagōgē* of necessity requires publicity, for such publicity suits the glaring quality of the crime. In a developed legal system, flagrancy no longer has much significance except that it provides more proof.[70] However, in a primitive stage of legal development it seems that the flagrant quality of the crime must be regarded as relevant to its very defi-

---

Lys., I.23 ff; cf. especially 25 and Ar., *Ran.*, 1361 ff.); but the flagrancy resulted in a purely private execution.

[66] Note the opposition set up by Demosthenes (XXIII.32) between *apagein* and *hōs hauton agein* [leading to one's own home].

[67] See Glotz, *Solidarité*, pp. 26 ff.

[68] According to Plutarch (*Sol.*, 17), this is the origin of the structure of Draconian law. Even much later, the law of revenge with regard to the thief is more widespread in the countryside than in the city; see the text of Harmenopoulos, VI.5.3–4 (fourteenth century), cited by Huvelin, *op. cit.*, p. 39. For solidarity in revenge, see Hom., *Od.*, XVI.424 ff. and *Il.*, XXIV.264; see also the texts cited by Glotz, *Solidarité*, pp. 202 ff.

[69] See O. Schrader, *Reallexikon der indogermanischen Altertumskunde* (Strassburg, 1901), pp. 137 ff. Notably, theft comes before homicide in the table of crimes.

[70] But it no longer exempts one from judicial action in the classical period (see n. 57 above). Moreover, the solemn investigation of the *phōra* [search], which was at first intimately connected with the idea of *ep' autophōrōi*, no longer has the power to determine the *flagrans delictum* or its consequent punishments (see Glotz, *Solidarité*, p. 206, following Plat., *Laws*, XII.954A–B).

nition, at least in the category we have been discussing.[71] In most cases, if not in all, a flagrant criminal act will result in an investigation under public control; this is therefore the necessary antecedent to the execution the traditional act of *apagōgē* initiates. In this typical case the punishment of the criminal and the very affirmation of the offense are subject to society's rules; that is to say, they are subject to certain rites in which the offended party is no doubt the principal actor. But all this is done with the obligatory assistance of a "chorus":[72] the participation of "neighbors"[73] who both oversee the procedure and guarantee its regularity. We all know about the *phōra*, that is, the *quaestio lance licioque* [investigation with the accused carrying a dish and wearing a girdle], which is designed to prove the defendant guilty of flagrant crime.[74]

Apagōgē, then, involves popular justice. Even for an occasional and ephemeral society, one of the first needs is to mark the place where the *kakourgoi*, objects of the *apagōgē*, have to be executed.[75] By definition and origin, *apagōgē* has two aspects. First, it originates from private vengeance. Second, it is connected with societal discipline. In this second aspect, *apagōgē* in the classical period is related to the suppression of public crimes. Thus we can explain the evident extension of the *apagōgē*, but we need not make this an issue at present. Let us limit ourselves to emphasizing the two facts that interest us.

To begin with, the instances of *apagōgē* that are foreign to the domain we have come to recognize depend on a more recent body of law and, if we can call it that, a second layer. These cases may involve an *apagōgē* used against *atimoi* [men deprived of rights] who are caught in forbidden areas or acts;[76] or they may be directed against certain crimes that do not fit into the primitive category of

---

[71] See Huvelin, *op. cit.*, pp. 142–43. There is little need to mention the obvious etymology of *ep' autophōrōi*, which allows us to define the primitive domain of the concept of flagrancy.

[72] This is more than a simple metaphor, since the ritual procedures furnished themes for the dance and drama (see Xen., *An.*,VI.1.7 [Sophocles' *Ikhneutai*]; Ar., *Ran.*, 1343 ff.).

[73] For the social importance and function of this category, see L. Radermacher, *Beiträge zur Volkskunde aus dem Gebiet der Antike*, pp. 3 f. (*Sitzungsberichte Wien, Philosophisch-Historische Klasse*, CLXXXVII.3).

[74] On the juridical scope of the *phōra* or *quaestio*, there is now some information in Huvelin, *op. cit.*, p. 143 ff. and 299 ff. (he is inclined to find in the *phōra* the unique source of flagrancy). On its ritual character, see Glotz, *Solidarité*, pp. 203 ff.

[75] Lys., XIII.78: ἄγουσιν ... ὡς ἀποκτενοῦντες οὖπερ καὶ τοὺς ἄλλους ἀπέσφαττον, εἴ τινα λῃστὴν ἢ κακοῦργον συλλάβοιεν ["they took him to kill him in the place where they executed the others, if they caught any pirate or criminal"].

[76] This is the second main application of the *apagōgē* in the classical period; see Lipsius, *op. cit.*, pp. 327 f. On the priority of the other, see ibid., p. 320. It is evident, moreover, that the former presupposes the mitigation of the primitive concept of *atimia* [deprivation of rights].

kakourgoi.[77] Or it could be a question of the *manus iniectio*, which in certain circumstances can legitimately be deployed against specific public enemies.[78]

Second, there are still visible points of agreement between the primitive *apagōgē* and its later applications. The latter are explained by the necessity of giving arms for private vengeance;[79] or by the legitimacy of summary procedures against a foreigner;[80] or by the concept of *actio popularis* ["popular prosecution," available to any prosecutor] exercised in situations that amount to *kakourgēma.*[81]

The extension of *apagōgē* is an indication of the artificial state of penal law. It is created out of regard for the polis, where there has been so much equalization between various types of crime that the religious dimensions – and certain conspicuous ones at that – have already begun to disappear.[82] The result of this process is a softening

[77] This is especially the case for murderers who are not citizens (Ant., V; Lys., XIII); further-more, it is quite clear from these two speeches what the opposition of the juridical conscience to this extension could be.

[78] Thus, in a decree proclaimed after the overthrow of the Four Hundred (Lyc., *Leocr.*, 121), *apagōgē* is used regarding traitors, who are not placed beyond the protection of law, as prescribed in the decree of Demophantos. Indeed, the end result is the assimilation of the two punishments; but the extension of the idea of *apagōgē* in a similar fashion is a recent pheno-menon: *agōgimos* ["arrestable"] becomes the term designating the *atimos*, "one without recourse to law," but not before the fourth century B.C. (P. Usteri, *Ächtung und Verbannung im griechischen Recht*, p. 57). On the purely private, primitive significance of the word *apagōgē*, see Dem., LIII.11; Arist., *Ath. Pol.*, 2.2. Cf. Diod. Sic., I.79; Dion. Hal., *Ant. Rom.*,V.69, VI.37.

[79] This is so in regard to murderers, but only to murderers who have violated the terms of their exile; that is, the *apagōgē* is subordinated to a social judgment, to an affirmation of joint liability. However, it belongs only to the parents of the victim (Dem., XXIII.28 ff.). We are not referring to another kind of *apagōgē*, which has an exceptional character (Goltz, *Solidarité*, pp. 428 ff.) and is merely a special case of the *apagōgē atimōn* [arrest of those deprived of rights] (Dem., XXIV.60, XXXIII.80).

[80] See n. 71 above. The case is the same for a certain kind of impiety: Plato (*Men.*, 80B) alludes to the *apagōgē* practiced against magicians, but ostensibly against foreigners (who are often the *goētes* [sorcerers]: see H. Hubert, *Dictionnaire des antiquités*, s.v. *Magia*); this caution serves to dispel the doubt of Lipsius (*op. cit.*, p. 322, n. 20). Let us note that impiety, which can be handled by way of *apagōgē* (Dem., XXII.27), is applied only in particular cases (Lipsius, *op. cit.*, p. 328; see, in this context, Lys., VII.22).

[81] Understood in the precise of the term, the *actio popularis* is sometimes attested in the form of the *apagōgē*: E. Ziebarth, *Hermes*, XXXII (1987), 618 ff. One of the two cases mentioned by Ziebarth is instructive; it concerns the procedure carried out according to the rules of the Andanian Mysteries (Michel, no. 694 [= *LSCG* 65], ll.78 f.) against the man who [κόπτει ἐκ τοῦ ἱεροῦ, "cuts wood from trees in the sanctuary"]. As for the ordinary *apagōgē*, which by means of a late extension of the idea of *kakourgoi* seems to be understood as a method used against the *hierosuloi* [temple-robbers] (Plat., *Rep.*, I.344B, VIII.552D, IX.575B; Xen., *Mem.*, I.2, and *Ap.*, 25), it really should be interpreted as applying to the flagrant theft of sacred treasures.

[82] In the "natural history of morality" this syncretism is of consequence; we can ask ourselves if the idea of *shame*, so familiar to us, was not at first limited to a special area of crime. We would have to bear in mind certain types of punishment, such as that exemplified precisely by *apotumpanismos*; "the crime produces the shame, and not the scaffold" is not really a historically accurate assessment.

of the penalty (e.g., permission to commit suicide by hemlock). However, as the idea of *kakourgia* tends to exceed its provenance,[83] something else can occur as well the application of a special punishment such as *apotumpanismos* for crimes that in primitive times did not incur this punishment.[84]

Therefore, what in primitive times called for *apotumpanismos* was, in our view, a *kakourgēma* in the strict sense of the term. This hypothesis seems to be confirmed by the treatment of certain thieves in the classical era. Legislation regarding the thief gives the impression of incoherence, as happens whenever layers of law of different ages find themselves in chance contact with one another. After being subjected to the *apagōgē*, the perpetrators of qualified theft – and flagrancy remains a necessary element[85] – are executed by *apotumpanismos*. But what of other thieves, against whom there has been no resort to *apagōgē* or in whose cases it would not be allowed – for want of the act being *flagrans delictum*. Those unaffected by primitive law have to be the concern of legislation: they are dealt with in a different way and their penalty is generally milder.[86] Still, some relic of the ancient penalty survives even in their case; when the penalty is monetary the tribunal can, in addition to imposing the fine, order that the condemned man be kept in chains for five days and nights.[87] How should this *prostimion* [additional assessment] be understood? The law cited by Demosthenes and Lysias – the law of Solon – says of the guilty party: δεδέσθαι δ' ἐν τῇ ποδοκάκῃ ["to be bound in the foot-bane"].[88] But Lysias informs us that even in his time the term *podokakē* had fallen into disuse, and that in a parallel case one ordinarily used the term *xulon* ["wood"]. *Xulon*, however,

---

[83] Common usage is sufficient evidence; see especially Ant., V.10.

[84] In this way we can explain the relative extension of this punishment. Besides the texts of Demosthenes in which *apotumpanismos* is treated, we could cite the allusion we think we have found in Aeschin., II.181 ff., and above all the punishment of Kinadon (Xen., *Hell.*, III.3.11), which bears some relationship to *apotumpanismos*. We know that the latter was inflicted upon the murderers of Philip of Macedon (from an anonymous historian in *P. Oxy.*, XV, no. 1798).

[85] Another condition is added in such a case: it is necessary that the sum total of the theft surpass a specific amount, at least in ordinary circumstances. But it is essentially the old practice that persists. See Dem., XXIV.114.

[86] In such a case the ordinary course is that of the *dikē* [private suit], the penalty for which is restitution and a fine double the value of what was stolen (Dem., XXIV.105); that is to say, while the crime, as far as we are concerned, is basically the same, the punishment is very unequal depending on whether or not the crime was a *flagrans delictum*. The *graphē* [public suit] could have the sanction of death (Dem., XXIV.103); but we have seen that death is probably directed at a specific kind of theft (n. 61), where it is a substitute for the *apagōgē*.

[87] Lys., X.16; Dem., XXIV.105 (cf. XXIV.103).

[88] The text of Demosthenes (differing from that of Lysias) adds τὸν πόδα ["with his foot"], which has the effect of a gloss; whether it is an echo of the classical age or reflects a later period, it confirms what we find in Lysias: the term *podokakē* ["foot-bane"] should, in principle, say more than what the composition of the world tells us at first glance.

is a possible equivalent of *tumpanon*;[89] yet it is also used as a synonym for *kuphōn*, "iron collar."[90] We cannot determine the precise nature of the thief's punishment – whether several parts of his body were chained by turns – or affirm that the *podokakē* had to be a *kuphōn* as well. But it is still possible to say that these terms evoke a weakened image of *apotumpanismos*. We should picture a wooden instrument on which the victim was restrained with iron clamps.[91] There is something else: the use of the *kuphōn*. Even though it is independent of the *podokakē*, it evidently resembles it and is especially well attested in the case of certain criminals like the *kleptai*;[92] it also shows that the guilty man was *exposed*.[93] In admitting that the *prostimion* in question consists of this form of ignominious exposure, one can better understand the raison d'être of a punishment whose methods and succinct quality attract our attention immediately. For thieves who do not undergo *apotumpanismos*, *prostimion* appears as its mitigated form.

Finally, let us note that among legal systems that were at first more or less isolated or independent but were eventually integrated into the penal code of the polis, there exists – in this group – one system in which *apotumpanismos* was a specific form of execution. It is characterized by all these specific ideas, which suggest one another: *kakourgos, ep' autophōrōi, apagein*. It is the system that concerns itself with the primitive varieties of theft. And since this system deals with a very ancient punishment, whose origins could go back to the earliest Mediterranean civilizations, it is our opinion that the punishment itself is the equivalent of the crucifixion inflicted according

---

[89] Ar., *Eq.*, 1049 (cf. 1040, 367, 705); Alexis, cited by Athen., IV.134.

[90] Ar., *Lys.*, 680.

[91] Aristophanes (*Lys.*, 680 f.) gives us a valuable piece of information: ἀλλὰ τούτων χρῆν ἁπασῶν ἐς τετρημένον ξύλον ἐγκαθαρμόσαι λαβόντας τουτονὶ τὸν αὐχένα ["But we must fit all of these into the perforated wood – seizing this neck"]. The *podokakē*, which Lysias calls *xulon*, cannot be understood as a wooden fetter; it is a plank to which *hēloi* [nails] are fastened (the *pedai* [fetters] also are something different: see Plat., *Phaed.*, 59E, 60B).

[92] Poll., VIII.107 (after Kratinos); Patmos Lexicon, in *BCH*, I (1877), pp. 143 f. (cf. Dem., XVIII.209); Arist. *Pol.*, VIII.6.1306b; Plut., *Nic.*, 11 (cf. Ar., *Plut.*, 476, 606). The punishment of the *kuphōn* (Pollux and Patmos Lexicon) is particularly applied to crimes committed in the marketplace; one automatically thinks of the *apagōgē* in these cases (Alexis, cited by Athen., II.226A–B); and a law of the first century B.C. expressly subjects to the law of *kakourgoi* the individual who is caught κακουργῶν ἐπὶ τὰ μέτρα καὶ τὰ σταθμά ["acting criminally with regard to the measures and weights"] (*IG* II², 1013, 56–62).

[93] The punishment is carried out in the agora. (Ar., *Plut.*, 476, 606; cf Poll., VIII.107, and Patmos Lexicon, in *BCH*, I [1877], pp. 143 f.). Plato (*Laws*, IX.855C) includes in the category of punishments the ἀμόρφους ἕδρας ἢ στάσεις ["unseemly postures of sitting or standing"] (cf., a little earlier, δεσμοῖς τε χρονίοις καὶ ἐμφάνεσι καί τισι προπηλακισμοῖς ["lengthy imprisonment and pillorying and various humiliations"]). This is the same kind of thinking that governs the use of the pillory for certain kinds of delinquents.

to the Twelve Tables. This was prescribed for the category of
fures ["robbers"],[94] who by night either harvested the farmland of
others or grazed their own livestock there.[95] Since it confirms our
hypothesis, this fact should be taken into account.

Even so, the link between *apotumpanismos* and its proper area of
application could still seem only extrinsic. Is there a more profound
nexus, and one that is more intelligible?

I V

We have already alluded to the diversity of origins in the development of penal law It is a point we cannot overemphasize. *Sacratio*
(["cursing"] or "a placing outside the law"), blood vengeance,
manus iniectio, summary execution in the case of a thief (not to
mention the disciplinary law and a kind of collective policing in the
religious assemblies)[96] – there are at least three types of penal law
here, the individuality of which tends to disappear under the unifying regimen of the state. But given their distinct origins, they still put
into play specific sentiments and reactions. This diversity manifests
itself even in the execution of criminals. If the act of putting a
criminal to death were only a practical solution to the problem of
legal responsibility, and nothing more than the brutal manifestation
of a quasi-instinctive passion, then our tour through the garden of
punishments would hardly merit any interest, even the interest of the
curious. But such is not the case; and now it is quite legitimate for us
to emphasize a contrast between two types of capital punishment.

One of these might be best represented by typical procedures, two
of which are especially well known to us from Greece:[97] stoning[98]
and hurling. Here the death penalty is a means employed to eliminate
a *miasma*, a "pollution." In essence, this type of execution belongs
to domestic law and in itself has a religious character. This is because
it is applied specifically to crimes that are religious in nature, an area
of criminality that from early on was a vast one. The most significant
term for a crime of this kind is *agos*.[99] No doubt an act of passion,

  [94] See Huvelin, *op. cit.*, pp. 61 f.
  [95] Pliny, *HN*, XVIII.3–12 (see P. F. Girard, *Textes de droit romain* [Twelve Tables, VIII.9]).
  [96] See S. Reinach, *REG*, XIX (1906), pp. 356 ff.
  [97] See also Glotz, *L'Ordalie*, pp. 30 ff., on the *katapontismos* [throwing into the sea].
  [98] R. Hirzel, *Die Strafe der Steinigung* (*Abhandlungen der königlichen Sächsischen
Gesellschaft der Wissenschaften, Philologisch-Historische Klasse*, XXVII.7), has established
not only that stoning in Greece was a manifestation of "lynch law" but that it also functioned
in ancient times as a true penal institution.
  [99] See Schrader, *Reallexikon*, pp. 905–6, for some characteristic examples, the list of which

capital punishment in this case is still far from being an act of pure passion. It is precisely because a religious concept regulates it that we miss its true significance when we define it as the psychological tendency whose object is simply the elimination of the guilty party. First, capital punishment seeks to remove an element that exists on the religious level; and it manifests itself primarily as an *aphosiōsis*,[100] or as a purificatory "freeing" of the group among whom the responsibility for shedding new blood is at times diluted or even disappears.[101] Second, the violent expulsion by death of a worthless and accursed member of a society goes hand in hand with the concept of *devotio* [consecration].[102] In effect, the putting of the accursed to death appears to be an act of piety, especially when we recall those dispositions of ancient law in which it is made quite specific that the murder of an outlaw does not incur impurity;[103] or when we recall that prescription of Germanic law which makes a similar type of murder an obligation[104] – a striking antithesis to the sentiments elicited by the executioner, who is forever an object of horror.[105]

But there is also a genuine religious function that the victim himself fulfills in such a case, and it is not without some analogy to the function of the priest-kings who were similarly executed.[106] This is testified to sufficiently by such designations of criminals as *homo*

we could lengthen. *Agos* concerns crimes against a divinity, incest, treachery, attacks on the sacred person of the chief, etc. For the grouping of types, see Tac., *Germ.*, 12, concerning Germanic law. Cf. Livy, I.51; C. Ferrini, *Diritto penale romano*, p. 244.

[100] See Plat., *Laws*, IX.873B. The drama of the punishment is played out on a religious plane – e.g., Bouphonia, pursuit of *pharmakoi* [scapegoats] at the Ionian Thargelia, etc.

[101] This could at least be the case with stoning.

[102] This entire category of punishments has links with the curse (see R. Vallois, *BCH*, XXXVII [1914], pp. 250 f.) and the ordeal (for the *devotio*, see Glotz, *L'Ordalie*, pp. 7, 33, etc.). Hence the designation of the guilty party is *eparatos* ["accursed"], and *hamartōlos* ["sinner"], followed by the god's name in the genitive. Cf. the use of the term *anathema* in modern Greek as explained by Keramopoullos, *op. cit.*, pp. 53 ff. (the connection with stoning). In extreme cases the *devotio* can take place without the active intervention of society – without there being any punishment (e.g., in cases of perjury).

[103] Andoc., I.96; Dem., IX.44; Lyc., *Leocr.*, 125. The idea is already slightly weakened in Festus's definition of *sacer* ["impious"].

[104] For the necessity of killing the *friedlos* [outlaw], see H. Brunner, *Deutsche Rechtsgeschichte*, II, p. 472.

[105] The *dēmios* [executioner] is termed an impure *alitērios* [accursed]: Athen., X.420B; Eust., on Hom., *Od.*, XVIII. 1.1833.54. The institution of executioner does not go back to very ancient times (see Keramopoullos, *op. cit.*, p. 107). We recall that among the Germans the pagan priests were responsible for this task.

[106] This is suggested by the institution of the *pharmakoi* in Athens (at least in the classical period), Asia Minor, and Marseilles. It is also suggested by the human sacrifices on Rhodes. The subjects of the rituals are selected from among criminals and are sometimes treated with special honor.

sacer ["sacred, i.e. impious, man"] in Rome[107] and *pharmakos* in Greece.[108] It is the same idea of *devotio* that explains how – through a paradox that is at first disconcerting – in some extreme cases (which were nonetheless foreseen) the act of execution result in death;[109] how in particular the condemned who had not died after being thrown from the Tarpeian Rock was spared.[110] If the divine powers release the person who has been delivered up to them, no one has the right to recapture what was theirs. The same thing applies to the corpse: there is still life in it, some evil or "sacred" power. It is then a possible object of *devotio*. By expelling the corpse beyond the city's borders and by destroying it completely (through exposure to the elements of wind, water, and fire), one strives to bring about its annihilation. This is not the product of rage, nor does it have anything to do with a precaution taken out of fear that the dead man's ghost will return;[111] it is done as a *piaculum* [propitiation].[112] Thus it is possible to explain the prohibition of burial, which within a religious concept of crime and the criminal is not unusual. The ordinary attitude toward the corpse, which would necessitate the ritual measures of enshroudment, does not apply in this instance, for this religious view is in some way blocked out by the other.

The case of the *kakourgos* is another matter altogether. Here we are dealing with a penal response that of itself and at least in the beginning[113] does not involve religious elements: it involves them no

---

[107] For the primitive meaning of the institution, see R. von Jhering, *Geist des römischen Rechts* (7th/8th edn, Leipzig, 1924), I, pp. 279–81. In the same sense we recall the use of the term *supplicium* ["kneeling," for supplication or punishment]. Some doubts have been raised concerning the currently accepted etymology of the word, but they do not seem justified in our opinion; nevertheless, see E. A. Juret, *Dominance et résistance dans la phonétique latine*, pp. 41 ff.

[108] [Lys.], VI.53 (with the very clear relic of the Thargelian *pharmakos*); Ar., *Eq.*, 1045; [Dem.], XXV.80. See the analogous use of *katharma* ["outcast"] in Dem., XXI, etc. On the concept of the *pharmakos* among the Romans, see Dion. Hal., *Ant. Rom.*, II.68.

[109] See Glotz, *L'Ordalie*, pp. 50 f., 90 f. We know the Germanic analogues: in particular, J. Grimm, *Deutsche Rechtsaltertümer*, p. 701. For ethnographical comparisons, see A. H. Post, *Grundriss der ethnologischen Jurisprudenz*, II, pp. 268, 269, 273.

[110] For the meaning of the action and character of the punishment itself, see A. Piganiol, *Essai sur les origines de Rome*, p. 149, which has the merit of presenting with clarity the problem of different kinds of execution.

[111] According to Keramopoullos, *op. cit.*, p. 105.

[112] The function of the *huperorismos* is clearly present in the institution of the Prytaneion, where it is applied to animals and inanimate objects. The same psychology is found in the ritual of tearing down a house.

[113] In Rome, a religious element was introduced into the punishment of crucifixion: the tree used for the punishment was consecrated to Ceres. But the primitive idea of execution still appears in the obligation of either abandoning the condemned at night (this can be applied to the corpse [the citation of Gaius in the *Autun Gaius*, 82]) or paying a settlement (see Huvelin, *op. cit.*, p. 63, n. 3). It is true, of course, that practices of an essentially analogous nature could have been used in a completely different spirit in different cultures: the punishment of the *arbor*

more than does the criminal notion to which it corresponds.[114] In a rural society such as the one we must depict here, the thief and those of his ilk – and among the Romans, the individuals who harvest the crops of others – provoke an angry response. But it is in no way the same reaction that we find in instances of impiety or incest. We catch a glimpse of how this reaction takes place in Greece: it has as its prototype the form of a strictly private vengeance, memories of which come alive again in some well-known scenes from Homer and Sophocles.[115] *Apotumpanismos* has retained some element of this penal reaction.

We are not saying that this penal reaction had no organization or that it did not conform to an obligatory schema; the demands relating to a flagrant offense and the necessity for judicial rites amply demonstrate that it did. But if the penal reaction leads to the death of the guilty party, it is a death that is different from that of the *homo sacer*; it is a death that, though equally predetermined, has a different significance. In this case the need to make someone suffer is fulfilled because the need is a pure one; legitimate acts of cruelty are given free rein. It is thus possible to understand that the method of execution, since it is, properly speaking, social and defined in advance, implies a particular kind of thinking that goes beyond individual reaction to the exasperated wrath of the victim. But this is a *profane* way of thinking. The victim of *apotumpanismos* is *exposed* as an object of public indignation and cruel laughter. The victim is

infelix [unlucky tree] in Livy, I.26, is specifically religious, as is hanging for the Germans. For these, see K. von Amira, *Die germanischen Todesstrafen* (*Abhandlungen der Bayerischen Akademie der Wissenschaften, Philosophisch-Historische Klasse*, XXXI.3 [1922]), where all the methods of execution are understood as different forms of the *sacratio* (pp. 198–235) – especially that of the thief (pp. 201 ff.; cf. pp. 182 ff.). It is impossible here to engage in a discussion of comparative law. Let us simply say that it is natural for a penal method, at first foreign to any religious representation, eventually to assume a formal religious quality through the participation of society. We do not find this development in Greece, and are thus persuaded that it was only secondary. In the same work by von Amira, one should note (pp. 170 ff.) his discussion of the torture of the wheel, the way it works and its antiquity; it is not without parallels to *apotumpanismos* (see p. 109). The author, in fact, makes some direct connections between the two punishments.

[114] For the essentially secular quality of the punishment of *kakourgēma* [criminal activity], see the significant reflections of Antiphon, V.10. Within the juridical and religious system of the classical period, the murder of the *kakourgos* required no purification – in contrast to other equally unpunished murders (Plat., *Laws*, IX.874C, 865A). This does not mean that there could not have been some magical element in the "prosecution of the thief"; but that is another question.

[115] According to Hom., *Od.*, XXII.173 ff., 187 ff., Melanthios is fixed to a column of the *thalamos* [store-room] (note l. 177: ὥς κεν δηθὰ ζωὸς ἐὼν χαλέπ' ἄλγεα πάσχῃ ["that he may stay alive and suffer grievous torments"]). Cf. Soph., *Aj.*, 105 ff., which describes the punishment that Ajax believes he inflicts on Odysseus: δεθεὶς πρὸς κίον' ἑρκείου στέγης ["bound to a pillar of the courtyard roof"].

also an *exemplum* [example],[116] since agony is more telling than a dead body. But the agony is eventually ended; what will be done with the corpse? We will not exactly say that the victim has a right to burial; the victim's enemies may not have been satisfied. Their anger may well go beyond the death of the criminal. But here the ordinary attitude interposes itself, for we are not in the area of *sacratio*; the minimal rites for the dead are required. So strange at first glance, the burial of the condemned in Phaleron merely conforms to the normal mechanics regarding the dead body.

The feeling of social vindictiveness is in principle complex: it confounds a superficial psychology that treats it as a brutal and base response. There is in it something institutional; and following the direction in which this sentiment of society leads us, we find that it corresponds to some associations of ideas which are essential but also diverse.

---

[116] This kind of penal practice is at the basis of the concept of punishment's "exemplary quality" – a concept often found in Greece; see Keramopoullos, *op. cit.*, p. 41, n. 2.

PART II

Political Activity

Introduction to Part II

The formal institutions are important as providing the framework of the Athenian democracy, but it is also important to discover how active politicians and ordinary citizens in Athens pursued their objectives within that framework; and again a variety of approaches can be helpful. This Part contains a re-evaluation of the position of demagogues in the Athenian democracy, a detailed investigation of how Athenian politicians made friends and influenced people, an examination of the part played by competitive festivals in the *polis*, and a study of the unusual extent to which the Athenian *polis* tried to separate public life from private life.

M. I. Finley (1912–86) was an American who in the McCarthy era of the 1950s became politically suspect and migrated to Britain, where eventually he was appointed Professor of Ancient History at Cambridge; a man whose first studies were not in classics but in psychology and law.[1] His academic interests included the Greek *poleis* and their politics; he believed strongly in the relevance of the ancient world to the modern, though not in any simplistic drawing of lessons from the ancient world; he was happier attacking large issues than disentangling intricate details. In Chapter 6 he rejects the scorn for upstart demagogues which academics have taken over from Thucydides and Aristophanes, to argue that in the direct, assembly-based democracy of Athens leaders who made proposals, and who could not count on a majority but again and again had to win support for their proposals, were a structural necessity, and should be judged on what they actually achieved.

I am Professor of Ancient History at Durham, have interested myself in political institutions and political activity in Athens and in the Greek world generally, and am happy disentangling intricate

---

[1] See C. R. Whittaker, *Proceedings of the British Academy* xciv '1996 Lectures and Memoirs', 459–72.

details. In Chapter 7 I work through the evidence for the different kinds of opportunities which were available and were used within the structure of the Athenian democracy for established politicians to gain and to mobilise supporters, and for aspiring politicians to find themselves influential mentors.

Chapter 8 provides another kind of approach to political activity. R. Osborne, Professor of Ancient History at Cambridge, starts from the study of Athenian drama in its institutional setting which has become fashionable, to set the dramatic festivals in the wider context of the competitive festivals of which democratic Athens had an exceptionally large number, and to show how competition between ambitious men presented both benefits and dangers for the *polis*, while noting that the need to reap those benefits and cope with those dangers was not limited to the democracy.

S. C. Humphreys has been one of the most anthropologically aware of Greek historians writing in English: she taught in the Department of Anthropology as well as the Department of History at University College, London, before moving to the USA to be professor in the University of Michigan, and is now a professor of the Central European University. Chapter 9 is a paper of hers which is particularly relevant to the theme of Athenian democracy: she argues that in the second half of the fifth century Athens at *polis* level went much further than Greek societies in other times and places (and even than Athens at subsidiary levels) in the direction of distinguishing a public realm in which matters were settled through public institutions, and private patronage was kept on the sidelines or channelled through public institutions, from a private realm in which connections through the family and through private institutions remained important.

6 Athenian Demagogues*

M. I. FINLEY

When the news of their defeat in Sicily in 413 B.C. reached the Athenians, they received it with disbelief. Then came the realization of the full scale of the disaster, and the people, writes Thucydides (8.1.1), "were indignant with the orators who had joined in promoting the expedition, as if they [the people] had not themselves decreed it [in assembly]." To this George Grote made the following rejoinder: "From these latter words, it would seem that Thucydides considered the Athenians, after having adopted the expedition by their votes, to have debarred themselves from the right of complaining of those speakers who had stood forward prominently to advise the step. I do not at all concur in his opinion. The adviser of any important measure always makes himself morally responsible for its justice, usefulness, and practicability, and he very properly incurs disgrace, more or less according to the case, if it turns out to present results totally contrary to those which he had predicted."[1]

These two opposing quotations raise all the fundamental problems inherent in the Athenian democracy: the problems of policy-making and leadership, of decisions and the responsibility for them. Unfortunately Thucydides (6.1–25) tells us very little about the orators who successfully urged on the Assembly the decision to mount the great invasion of Sicily. In fact, he tells us nothing concrete about the meeting, other than that the people were given misinformation by a delegation from the Sicilian city of Segesta and by their own envoys just returned from Sicily, and that most of those who voted were so ignorant of the relevant facts that they did not even know the size of the island or of its population.

* Originally published in *Past and Present* xxi 1962, 3–24; this revised version published in M. I. Finley, *Democracy Ancient and Modern*, 2nd edition (Hogarth Press/Rutgers University Press, 1985), 38–75 with 177–9 ch. ii. Reprinted with the permission of The Past and Present Society, the Random House Group and Rutgers University Press.
[1] *A History of Greece*, [12-vol. ed. (1869/84) VII 201 n. 2 = 10-vol. ed. (1888) VI 193 n. 2].

Five days later a second Assembly was held to authorize the necessary armament. The general Nicias took the opportunity to seek a reversal of the whole programme. He was opposed by a number of speakers, Athenian and Sicilian, who are neither named by the historian nor described in any way, and by Alcibiades, who is given a speech which throws much light on Thucydides himself and on his judgment of Alcibiades, but scarcely any on the issues, neither the immediate ones being debated nor the broader ones of democratic procedure and leadership. The result was a complete defeat for Nicias. Everyone, Thucydides admits, was then more eager than before to go ahead with the plan – the old and the young, the hoplite soldiers (who were drawn from the wealthier half of the citizenry) and the common people alike. The few who remained opposed, he concludes, refrained from voting lest they appear unpatriotic.

The wisdom of the Sicilian expedition is a very difficult matter. Thucydides himself had more than one view at different times in his life. However, he seems not to have changed his mind about the orators: they promoted the expedition for the wrong reasons and they gained the day by playing on the ignorance and emotions of the Assembly. Alcibiades, he says, pressed hardest of all, because he wished to thwart Nicias, because he was personally ambitious and hoped to gain fame and wealth from his generalship in the campaign, and because his extravagant and licentious tastes were more expensive than he could really afford. Elsewhere, writing in more general terms, Thucydides says this (2.65.9–11): under Pericles "the government was a democracy in name but in reality ruled by the first citizen. His successors were more equal to each other, and each seeking to become the first man they even offered the conduct of affairs to the whims of the people. This, as was to be expected in a great state ruling an empire, produced many blunders."

In short, after the death of Pericles Athens fell into the hands of demagogues and was ruined. Thucydides does not use the word "demagogue" in any of the passages I have been discussing. It is an uncommon word with him[2] as it is in Greek literature generally, and that fact may come as a surprise, for there is no more familiar theme in the Athenian picture (despite the rarity of the word) than the demagogue and his adjutant, the sycophant. The demagogue is a bad thing: to "lead the people" is to mislead – above all, to mislead by failing to lead. The demagogue is driven by self-interest, by the desire to advance himself in power, and through power, in wealth. To

---

[2] Used only in 4.21.3, and "demagogy" in 8.65.2.

achieve this, he surrenders all principles, all genuine leadership, and he panders to the people in every way – in Thucydides' words, "even offering the conduct of affairs to the whims of the people." This picture is drawn not only directly, but also in reverse. Here, for example, is Thucydides' image of the right kind of leader (2.65.8): "Because of his prestige, intelligence and known incorruptibility with respect to money, Pericles was able to lead the people as a free man should. He led them instead of being led by them. He did not have to humour them in the pursuit of power; on the contrary, his repute was such that he could contradict them and provoke their anger."

This was not everyone's judgment. Aristotle puts the breakdown earlier: it was after Ephialtes took away the power of the Council of the Areopagus that the passion for demagogy set in. Pericles, he continues, first acquired political influence by prosecuting Cimon for malfeasance in office; he energetically pursued a policy of naval power, "which gave the lower classes the audacity to take over the leadership in politics more and more"; and he introduced pay for jury service, thus bribing the people with their own money. These were demagogic practices and they brought Pericles to power, which, Aristotle agrees, he then used well and properly.[3]

But my interest is neither in evaluating Pericles as an individual nor in examining the lexicography of demagogy. The Greek political vocabulary was normally vague and imprecise, apart from formal titles for individual offices or bodies (and often enough even then). All writers accepted the need for political leadership as axiomatic; their problem was to distinguish between good and bad types. With respect to Athens and its democracy, the word "demagogue" understandably became the simplest way of identifying the bad type, and it does not matter in the least whether the word appears in any given text or not. I suppose it was Aristophanes who established the model in his portrayal of Cleon, yet he never directly applied the noun "demagogue" to him or anyone else.[4] Similarly, Thucydides surely thought that Cleophon, Hyperbolus, and some, if not all, of the orators responsible for the Sicilian disaster were demagogues, but he never attached the word to any of these men.

It is important to stress the word "type," for the issue raised by

[3] *Constitution of Athens* 27–28; cf. *Politics* 2. 1274a3–10. A. W. Gomme, *A Historical Commentary on Thucydides* II (Oxford 1956) 193, points out that "Plutarch divided Perikles' political career sharply into two halves, the first when he did use base demagogic arts to gain power, the second when he had gained it and used it nobly."

[4] Aristophanes uses "demagogy" and "demagogic" once each in the *Knights*, lines 191 and 217, respectively. Otherwise in his surviving plays there is only the verb "to be a demagogue," also used once (*Frogs* 419).

Greek writers is one of the essential *qualities* of the leader, not (except
very secondarily) his techniques or technical competence, nor even
(except in a very generalized way) his programme and policies. The
crucial distinction is between the man who gives leadership with
nothing else in mind but the good of the state, and the man whose
self-interest makes his own position paramount and urges him to
pander to the people. The former may make a mistake and adopt the
wrong policy in any given situation; the latter may at times make
sound proposals, as when Alcibiades dissuaded the fleet at Samos
from jeopardizing the naval position by rushing back to Athens in
411 B.C. to overthrow the oligarchs who had seized power there, an
action to which Thucydides (8.86) gave explicit approval. But these
are not fundamental distinctions. Nor are other traits attributed to
individual demagogues: Cleon's habit of shouting when addressing
the Assembly, personal dishonesty in money matters, and so on. Such
things merely sharpen the picture. From Aristophanes to Aristotle,
the attack on the demagogues always falls back on the one central
question: in whose interest does the leader lead?

Behind this formulation of the question lay three propositions.
The first is that men are unequal, both in their moral worth and capa-
bility and in their social and economic status. The second is that any
community tends to divide into factions, the most fundamental of
which are the rich and well-born on one side, the poor on the other,
each with its own qualities, potentialities, and interests. The third
proposition is that the well-ordered and well-run state is one which
overrides faction and serves as an instrument for the good life.

Faction is the greatest evil and the most common danger.
"Faction" is a conventional English translation of the Greek *stasis*,
one of the most remarkable words to be found in any language. Its
root-sense is "placing," "setting" or "stature," "station." Its range
of political meanings can best be illustrated by merely stringing out
the definitions to be found in the lexicon: "party," "party formed for
seditious purposes," "faction," "sedition," "discord," "division,"
"dissent," and, finally, a well-attested meaning which the lexicon
incomprehensibly omits, namely, "civil war" or "revolution." Unlike
"demagogue," *stasis* is a very common word in the literature, and
its connotation is regularly pejorative. Oddly enough, it has been a
relatively neglected concept in modern study of Greek history.[5] The

---

[5] A. W. Lintott, *Violence, Civil Strife and Revolution in the Classical City* (London 1982),
is unsatisfactory. One must still return to the inaugural lecture of D. Loenen, *Stasis* (Amsterdam
1953). He saw, contrary to the view most common among modern writers, that "illegality is
precisely not the *constant* element in *stasis*" (p. 5).

implication has not been drawn often enough or sharply enough, I believe, that there must be deep significance in the fact that a word which has the original sense of "station" or "position," and which, in abstract logic, could have an equally neutral sense when used in a political context, in practice does nothing of the kind, but immediately takes on the nastiest overtones. A political position, a partisan position – that is the inescapable implication – is a bad thing, leading to sedition, civil war, and the disruption of the social fabric. And this same tendency is repeated throughout the language. There is no eternal law, after all, why "demagogue," a "leader of the people," must become "mis-leader of the people." Or why *hetairia*, an old Greek word which means, among other things, "club" or "society," should in fifth-century Athens have come simultaneously to mean "conspiracy" and "seditious organization." Whatever the explanation, it lies not in philology but in Greek society itself.

No one who has read the Greek political writers can have failed to notice the unanimity of approach in this respect. Whatever the disagreements among them, they all insist that the state must stand outside class or other factional interests. Its aims and objectives are moral, timeless, and universal, and they can be achieved – more correctly, approached or approximated – only by education, moral conduct (especially on the part of those in authority), morally correct legislation, and the choice of the right governors. The existence of classes and interests as an empirical fact is, of course, not denied. What is denied is that the choice of political goals can legitimately be linked with these classes and interests, or that the good of the state can be advanced except by ignoring (if not suppressing) private interests.

It was Plato who pursued this line of its reasoning to its most radical solutions. In the *Gorgias* (502E–519D) he had argued that not even the great Athenian political figures of the past – Miltiades, Themistocles, Cimon and Pericles – were true statesmen. They had merely been more accomplished than their successors in gratifying the desires of the *demos* with ships and walls and dockyards. They had failed to make the citizens better men, and to call them "statesmen" was therefore to confuse the pastrycook with the doctor. Then, in the *Republic*, Plato proposed to concentrate all power in the hands of a small, select, appropriately educated class, who were to be freed from all special interests by the most radical measures: denying them both private property and the family. Only under these conditions would they behave as perfect moral agents, leading the state to its proper goals without the possibility that any self-interest might intrude.

Plato, to be sure, was the most untypical of men. One cannot safely generalize from Plato to all Greeks, nor even to any other single Greek. Who else shared his passionate conviction that qualified experts – philosophers – could make (and should therefore be empowered to enforce) universally correct and authoritative decisions about the good life, the life of virtue, which was the sole end of the state?[6] Yet regarding the one problem with which I am immediately concerned – private interests and the state – Plato stood on common ground with many Greek writers (much as they disagreed with him on the solutions). In the great final scene of Aeschylus' *Eumenides* the chorus expresses the doctrine explicitly: the welfare of the state can rest only on harmony and freedom from faction. Thucydides implies this more than once.[7] And it underlies the theory of the mixed constitution as we already find it in Aristotle's *Politics*.

The most empirical of Greek philosophers, Aristotle collected vast quantities of data about the actual workings of Greek states, including facts about *stasis*. The *Politics* includes an elaborate taxonomy of *stasis*, and even advice on how *stasis* can be avoided under a variety of conditions. But Aristotle's canons and goals were ethical, his work a branch of moral philosophy. He viewed political behaviour teleologically, according to the moral ends which are man's by his nature, and he believed that those ends are subverted if the governors make their decisions out of personal or class interest. That was the test by which he distinguished between the three "right" forms of government ("according to absolute justice") and their degenerate forms: monarchy becomes tyranny when an individual rules in his own interest rather than in the interest of the whole state, aristocracy similarly becomes oligarchy, and polity becomes democracy (or, in the language of Polybius, democracy becomes mobrule).[8] Among democracies, furthermore, those in rural communities will be superior because farmers are too occupied to bother with meetings, whereas urban craftsmen and shopkeepers find it easy to attend, and such people "are generally a bad lot."[9]

The great difference between political analysis and moral judgment could not be better exemplified than in the passage by the "Old Oligarch" I quoted in chapter 1 [of *Democracy Ancient and*

---

[6] See R. Bambrough, "Plato's Political Analogies," in *Philosophy, Politics and Society*, ed. Peter Laslett (Oxford 1956), pp. 98–115.

[7] It is developed most fully in his long account (3.69–85) of the *stasis* in Corcyra in 427 B.C.

[8] *Politics* 3. 1278b–79b; 4. 1293b–94b; cf. Polybius 6.3–9.

[9] Aristotle, *Politics* 6. 1319a19–32; cf. Xenophon, *Hellenica* 5.2.5–7.

Modern]: "As for the Athenian system of government, I do not like it. However, since they decided to become a democracy, it seems to me that they are preserving the democracy well."[10] Do not be misled, says the author in effect: I and some of you dislike democracy, but a reasoned consideration of the facts shows that what we condemn on moral grounds is very strong as a practical force, and its strength lies in its immorality. This is a very promising line of investigation, but it was not pursued in antiquity. Instead, those thinkers whose orientation was anti-democratic persisted in their concentration on political philosophy. And those who sided with the democracy? A. H. M. Jones tried to formulate the democratic theory from the fragmentary evidence available in the surviving literature, most of it from the fourth century.[11] Then Eric Havelock made a massive attempt to discover what he called the "liberal temper" in fifth-century Athenian politics, chiefly from the fragments of the pre-Socratic philosophers. In reviewing his book, Momigliano suggested that the effort was foredoomed because "it is not absolutely certain that a well-articulated democratic idea existed in the fifth-century."[12]

I have already indicated in the previous chapter [of *Democracy Ancient and Modern*] that I do not believe that an articulated democratic theory ever existed in Athens. There were notions, maxims, generalities – which Jones has assembled – but they do not add up to a systematic theory. And why indeed should they? It is a curious fallacy to suppose that every social or governmental system in history must necessarily have been accompanied by an elaborate theoretical system. Where that does occur it is often the work of lawyers, and Athens had no jurists in the proper sense. Or it may be the work of philosophers, but the systematic philosophers of this period had a set of concepts and values incompatible with democracy. We must attempt on our own to make the analysis the Athenians failed to make for themselves.

No account of the Athenian democracy can have any validity if it overlooks four points, each obvious in itself. The first is that this was a direct democracy, and however much such a system may have in common with representative democracy, the two differ in certain fundamental respects, and particularly on the very issues with which I am here concerned. The second point is what Ehrenberg calls the

[10] Pseudo-Xenophon, *Constitution of Athens* 3.1; see A. Fuks, "The 'Old Oligarch,'" *Scripta Hierosolymitana*, 1 (1954) 21–35.
[11] *Athenian Democracy* (Oxford 1957), ch. 3.
[12] E. A. Havelock, *The Liberal Temper in Greek Politics* (London 1957), reviewed by A. Momigliano in *Rivista storica italiana*, 72 (1960) 534–41.

"narrowness of space" of the Greek city-state, an appreciation of which, he has rightly stressed, is crucial to an understanding of its political life.[13] The implications were summed up by Aristotle in a famous passage: "A state composed of too many ... will not be a true state, for the simple reason that it can hardly have a true constitution. Who can be the general of a mass so excessively large? And who can be herald, except Stentor?" (*Politics* 7. 1326b3–7).

The third point is that the Assembly was the crown of the system, possessing the right and the power to make all the policy decisions, in actual practice with few limitations, either of precedent or of scope. (Strictly speaking there was appeal from the Assembly to the popular courts with their large lay membership. Nevertheless, I ignore the courts in much, though not all, of what follows, because I believe, as the Athenians did themselves, that although the courts complicated the practical mechanism of politics, they were an expression, not a reduction, of the absolute power of the people functioning directly, and because I believe that the operational analysis I am trying to make would not be significantly altered and would perhaps be obscured if in this brief compass I did not concentrate on the Assembly.) The Assembly, finally, was nothing other than an open-air mass meeting on the hill called the Pnyx, and the fourth point therefore is that we are dealing with problems of crowd behavior; the psychology and laws of behavior at work in the Assembly could not have been identical with those at work in the small group, or even in the larger kind of body of which a modern parliament is an example (though, it must be admitted, we can do little more today than acknowledge the existence of these influences).

Who were the Assembly? That is a question we cannot answer satisfactorily. Every male citizen automatically became eligible to attend when he reached his eighteenth birthday, and he retained that privilege to his death (except for the small number who lost their civic rights for one reason or another). In Pericles' time the number eligible was of the order of 35,000 or 40,000.* Women were excluded; so were the fairly numerous non-citizens who were free men, nearly all of them Greeks, but outsiders in the political sphere; and so were the far more numerous slaves. All figures are a guess, but it would not be wildly inaccurate to suggest that the adult male citizens

[13] *Aspects of the Ancient World* (Oxford 1946), pp. 40–45.
* Recent work suggests that there may have been as many as 60,000 adult male citizens at the beginning of the Peloponnesian War: M. H. Hansen, *Three Studies in Athenian Demography* (Copenhagen 1988) ch. 3; P. J. Rhodes, *Thucydides; History, II* (Warminster 1988) 271–7.

comprised about one sixth of the total population (taking town and countryside together). But the critical question to be determined is how many of the 40,000 actually went to meetings. It is reasonable to imagine that under normal conditions the attendance came chiefly from the urban residents. Fewer peasants would have taken the journey in order to attend a meeting of the Assembly.[14] Therefore one large section of the eligible population was, with respect to direct participation, excluded. That is something to know, but it does not get us far enough. We can guess for example, with the aid of a few hints in the sources, that the composition was normally weighted on the side of the more aged and the more well-to-do men – but that is only a guess, and the degree of weighting is beyond even guessing.

Still, one important fact can be fixed, namely, that each meeting of the Assembly was unique in its composition. There was no membership in the Assembly as such, only membership in a given Assembly on a given day. Perhaps the shifts were not significant from meeting to meeting in quiet, peaceful times when no vital issues were being debated. Yet even then an important element of predictability was lacking. When he entered the Assembly, no policy-maker could be quite sure that a change in the composition of the audience had not occurred, whether through accident or through more or less organised mobilization of some particular sector of the population, which could tip the balance of the votes against a decision made at a previous meeting. And times were often neither peaceful nor normal. In the final decade of the Peloponnesian War, to take an extreme example, the whole rural population was compelled to abandon the countryside and live within the city walls. It is beyond reasonable belief that during this period there was not a larger proportion of countrymen at meetings than was normal. A similar situation prevailed for briefer periods at other times, when an enemy army was operating in Attica. We need not interpret Aristophanes literally when he opens the *Acharnians* with a soliloquy by a farmer who is sitting in the Pnyx waiting for the Assembly to begin and saying to himself how he hates the city and everyone in it and how he intends to shout down any speaker who proposes anything except peace. But Cleon could not have afforded the luxury of ignoring this strange element seated on the hillside before him. They might upset a policy line which he had been able to carry while the Assembly had a majority of city-dwellers.

[14] On attendance at Athenian Assembly meetings, see two articles by M. H. Hansen in *Greek, Roman and Byzantine Studies*, 17 (1976) 115–34 and 23 (1982) 241–49, reprinted with addenda in his *The Athenian Ecclesia* (Copenhagen 1983), chs 1–2.

The one clearcut instance came in the year 411. Then the Assembly was terrorized into voting the democracy out of existence, and it was surely no accident that this occurred at a time when the fleet was fully mobilized and stationed on the island of Samos. The citizens who served in the navy were drawn from the poor and they were known to be the staunchest supporters of the democratic system in its late fifth-century form. Being in Samos, they could not be in Athens, thus enabling the oligarchs to win the day through a majority in the Assembly which was not only a minority of the eligible members but an untypical minority. Our sources do not permit us to study the history of Athenian policy systematically with such knowledge at our disposal, but surely the men who led Athens were acutely aware of the possibility of a change in the composition of the Assembly, and included it in their tactical calculations.

Each meeting, furthermore, was complete in itself. Granted that much preparatory work was done by the Council (*boule*), that informal canvassing took place, and that there were certain devices to control and check frivolous or irresponsible motions, it is nevertheless true that the normal procedure was for a proposal to be introduced, debated, and either passed (with or without amendment) or rejected in a single continuous sitting. We must reckon, therefore, not only with narrowness of space but also with narrowness of time, and with the pressures that generated, especially on leaders (and would-be leaders). I have already mentioned the case of the Sicilian expedition, which was decided in principle on one day and then planned, so to speak, five days later when the scale and cost were discussed and voted.

Another kind of case is that of the well-known Mytilene debate. Early in the Peloponnesian War the city of Mytilene revolted from the Athenian Empire. The rebellion was crushed and the Athenian Assembly decided to make an example of the Mytileneans by putting the entire male population to death. Revulsion of feeling set in at once, the issue was reopened at another meeting the very next day, and the decision was reversed (Thucydides 3.27–50). Cleon, at that time the most important political figure in Athens, advocated the policy of frightfulness. The second Assembly was a personal defeat for him – he had participated in the debates on both days – though he seems not to have lost his status even temporarily as a result (as he well might have). But how does one measure the psychological effect on him of such a twenty-four hour reversal? How does one estimate not only its impact, but also his awareness all through his career as a leader that such a possibility was a constant factor in

Athenian politics? I cannot answer such questions concretely, but I submit that the weight could have been no light one. Cleon surely appreciated, as we cannot, what it promised for men like himself that in the second year of the Peloponnesian War, when morale was temporarily shattered by the plague, the people turned on Pericles, fined him heavily, and deposed him for a brief period from the office of general (Thucydides 2.65.1–4). If this could happen to Pericles, who was immune?

In the Mytilene case Thucydides' account suggests that Cleon's was a lost cause the second day, that he tried to persuade the Assembly to abandon a course of action which they intended to pursue from the moment the session opened, and that he failed. But the story of the meeting in 411, as Thucydides (8.53–54) tells it, is a different one. Pisander began the day with popular feeling against his proposal that the introduction of an oligarchical form of government should be considered, and he ended it with a victory. The actual debate had swung enough votes to give him a majority.

Debate designed to win votes among an outdoor audience numbering many thousands means oratory, in the strict sense of the word. It was therefore perfectly precise language to call political leaders "orators," as a synonym and not merely, as we might do, as a mark of the particular skill of a particular political figure.[15] Under Athenian conditions, however, much more is implied. The picture of the Assembly I have been trying to draw suggests not only oratory, but also a "spontaneity" of debate and decision which parliamentary democracy lacks, at least in our day.[16] Everyone, speakers and audience alike, knew that before night fell the issue must be decided, that each man present would vote "freely" (without fear of whips or other party controls) and purposefully, and therefore that every speech, every argument must seek to persuade the audience on the spot, that it was all a serious performance, as a whole and in each of its parts.

I place the word "freely" within quotation marks for the last thing I wish to imply is the activity of a free, disembodied rational faculty, that favourite illusion of so much political theory since the Enlightenment. Members of the Assembly were free from the controls

---

[15] See M. H. Hansen, "The Athenian 'Politicians,' 403–322 B.C.," *Greek, Roman and Byzantine Studies* 24 (1983) 33–55, and "*Rhetores* and *Strategoi* in Fourth-Century Athens," *ibid.*, 151–80 [reprinted with addenda in his *The Athenian Ecclesia II* (Copenhagen 1989) chs 1–2].

[16] See the valuable article by O. Reverdin, "Remarques sur la vie politique d'Athènes au Ve siècle," *Museum Helveticum* 2 (1945) 201–12; and generally my *Politics in the Ancient World* (Cambridge 1983), especially ch. 4.

which bind the members of a parliament: they held no office, they were not elected, and therefore they could neither be punished nor rewarded in subsequent elections for their voting records. But they were not free from the human condition, from habit and tradition, from the influences of family and friends, of class and status, of personal experiences, resentments, prejudices, values, aspirations, and fears, much of it in the subconscious. These they took with them when they went up on the Pnyx, and with these they listened to the debates and made up their minds, under conditions very different from the voting practices of our day. There is a vast difference between voting on infrequent occasions for a man or a party on the one hand, and on the other hand voting every few days directly on the issues themselves. In Aristotle's time the Assembly met at least four times in each thirty-six day period. Whether this was also the rule in the fifth century is not known, but there were occasions, as during the Peloponnesian War, when meetings took place even more frequently.

Then there were the two other factors I have already mentioned, the smallness of the Athenian world, in which every member of the Assembly knew personally many others sitting on the Pnyx, and the mass-meeting background of the voting – a situation virtually unrelated to the impersonal act of marking a voting paper in physical isolation from every other voter, an act we perform, furthermore, with the knowledge that millions of other men and women are simultaneously doing the same thing in many places, some of them hundreds of miles distant. When, for example, Alcibiades and Nicias rose in the Assembly in 415, the one to propose the expedition against Sicily, the other to argue against it, each knew that, should the motion be carried, one or both would be asked to command in the field. And in the audience there were many who were being asked to vote on whether they, personally, would march out in a few days, as officers, soldiers, or members of the fleet. Such examples can be duplicated in a number of other, scarcely less vital areas: taxation, food supply, pay for jury duty, extension of the franchise, laws of citizenship, and so on.

To be sure, much of the activity of the Assembly was in a lower key, largely occupied with technical measures (such as cult regulations) or ceremonial acts (such as honorary decrees for a great variety of individuals). It would be a mistake to imagine Athens as a city in which week in and week out great issues dividing the population were being debated and decided. But on the other hand, there were very few single years (and certainly no ten-year periods) in which some great issue did not arise: the two Persian invasions, the long series of measures which completed the process of democratization, the empire, the Peloponnesian War (which occupied twenty-seven years) and its two oligarchic interludes, the endless diplomatic manoeuvres and wars of the fourth century, with their attendant fiscal crises, all culminating in the decades of Philip and Alexander. It did not often happen, as it did to Cleon in the dispute over Mytilene, that a politician was faced with a repeat performance the following day; but the Assembly did meet constantly, without long periods of holiday or recess. The week-by-week conduct of a war, for example, had to go before the Assembly week by week, as if Winston Churchill were to have been compelled to take a referendum before each move in World War II, and then to face another vote after the move was made, in the Assembly or the law-courts, to determine not merely what the next step should be but also whether he was to be dismissed and his plans abandoned, or even whether he was to be held criminally culpable, subject to a fine or exile, or, conceivably, given the death penalty either for the proposal itself or for the way the previous move had been carried out. It was part of the Athenian governmental system that, in addition to the endless challenge in the Assembly, a politician was faced, equally without respite, with the threat of politically inspired lawsuits.

If I insist on the psychological aspect, it is not to ignore the considerable political experience of many men who voted in the Assembly – experience gained in the Council, the law-courts, the demes, and the Assembly itself – nor is it merely to counter what I have called the disembodied-rationalism conception. I want to stress something very positive, namely, the intense degree of involvement which attendance at the Athenian Assembly entailed. And this intensity was equally (or even more strongly) the case among the orators, for each vote judged them as well as the issue to be decided on. If I had to choose one word which best characterized the condition of being a political leader in Athens, the word would be "tension."

In some measure that is true of all politicians who are subject to a vote. "The desperateness of politics and government" is R. B. McCallum's telling phrase, which he then developed in this way: "Certainly a note of cynicism and weariness with the manoeuvres and posturings of party politicians is natural and to an extent proper to discerning dons and civil servants, who can reflect independently and at leisure on the doings of their harried masters in government. But this seems to arise from a deliberate rejection ... of the aims and ideals of party statesmen and their followers and the continual responsibility for the security and well-being in the state. For one thing party leaders are in some sense apostles, although all may not be Gladstones; there are policies to which they dedicate themselves and policies which alarm and terrify them." [17]

I believe this to be a fair description of Athenian leaders, too, despite the absence of political parties, equally applicable to Themistocles as to Aristides, to Pericles as to Cimon, to Cleon as to Nicias; for, it should be obvious, this kind of judgment is independent of any judgment about the merits or weaknesses of a particular programme or policy. More accurately, I should have said that this understates the case for the Athenians. Their leaders had *no* respite. Because their influence had to be earned and exerted directly and immediately – this was a necessary consequence of a direct, as distinct from a representative, democracy – they had to lead in person, and they had also to bear, in person, the brunt of the opposition's attacks. More than that, they walked alone. They had their lieutenants, of course, and politicians made alliances with each other. But these were fundamentally personal links, shifting frequently, useful in helping to carry through a particular measure or even a group of measures, but lacking that quality of support, that buttressing or cushioning effect, which is provided by a bureaucracy or a political party, in another way by an institutionalized establishment like the Roman Senate. The critical point is that there was no "government" in the modern sense. There were posts and offices, but none had any standing in the Assembly. A man was a leader solely as a function of his personal, and in the literal sense, unofficial status within the Assembly itself. The test of whether or not he held that status was simply whether the Assembly did or did not vote as he wished, and therefore the test was repeated with each proposal.

These were the conditions which faced all leaders in Athens, not merely those whom Thucydides and Plato dismissed as "demagogues," not merely those whom some modern historians mis-call "radical democrats," but everyone, aristocrat or commoner, altruist or self-seeker, able or incompetent, who, in George Grote's phrase, "stood forward prominently to advise" the Athenians. No doubt the motives which moved men to stand forward varied greatly. But that does not matter in this context, for each one of them, without exception, *chose* to aspire to, and actively to work and contest for, leadership, knowing just what that entailed, including the risks.

---

[17] A review in *The Listener* (2 Feb. 1961), p. 233.

Within narrow limits, they all had to use the same techniques, too. Cleon's platform manner may have been inelegant and boisterous, but how serious is Aristotle's remark (*Constitution of Athens* 28.3) that he was the first man to "shout and rail"? Are we to imagine that Thucydides the son of Melesias (and kinsman of the historian) and Nicias whispered when they addressed the Assembly in opposition to Pericles and Cleon, respectively? Or Thucydides, who brought his upperclass backers into the Assembly and seated them together to form a claque?[18]

This is obviously a frivolous approach. As Aristotle noted (*Constitution of Athens* 28.1), the death of Pericles marked a turning-point in the social history of Athenian leadership. Until then they seem to have been drawn from the old aristocratic landed families, including the men who were responsible for carrying out the reforms which completed the democracy. After Pericles a new class of leaders emerged. Despite the familiar prejudicial references to Cleon the tanner or Cleophon the lyre-maker, these were in fact not poor men, not craftsmen and labourers turned politician, but men of means who differed from their predecessors in their ancestry and their outlook, and who provoked resentment and hostility for their presumption in breaking the old monopoly of leadership.[19] When such attitudes are under discussion, one can always turn to Xenophon to find the lowest level of explanation (which is not therefore necessarily the wrong one). One of the most important of the new leaders was a man called Anytus, who, like Cleon before him, drew his wealth from a slave tannery. Anytus had a long and distinguished career, but he was also the chief actor in the prosecution of Socrates. What is Xenophon's explanation? Simply that Socrates had publicly berated Anytus for bringing up his son to follow in his trade instead of educating him as a proper gentleman, and that Anytus, in revenge for this personal insult, had Socrates tried and executed (*Apology* 30–32).

None of this is to deny that there were very fundamental issues behind the thick façade of prejudice and abuse. Throughout the fifth century there were the twin issues of democracy (or oligarchy) and empire, brought to a climax in the Peloponnesian War. Defeat in the war ended the empire and it soon also ended the debate about the

---

[18] Plutarch, *Pericles* 11.2. It was against such tactics that the restored democracy in 410 required members of the Council to swear to take their seats by lot: Philochorus *FGrH* 328 F 140.
[19] See W. R. Connor, *The New Politicians of Fifth-Century Athens* (Princeton 1971), with the review by C. Ampolo in *Archeologia Classica*, 27 (1975) 95–100.

kind of government Athens was to have. Oligarchy ceased to be a serious issue in practical politics. Only the persistence of the philosophers creates an illusion about it; they continued to argue fifth-century issues in the fourth century, but politically in a vacuum. Down to the middle of the fourth century, the actual policy questions were perhaps less dramatic than before, though not necessarily less vital to the participants: such matters as navy, finance, foreign relations both with Persia and with other Greek states, and the ever-present problem of corn supply. Then came the final great conflict, over the rising power of Macedon. That debate went on for some three decades, and it ended only in the year following the death of Alexander the Great when the Macedonian army put an end to democracy itself in Athens.

All these were questions about which men could legitimately disagree, and with passion. On the issues, the arguments of, for example, Plato require earnest consideration, but only in so far as he addressed himself to the issues. The injection of the charge of demagogy into the polemic amounts to a resort to the very same unacceptable debating tricks for which the so-called demagogues are condemned. Suppose, for example, that Thucydides was right in attributing Alcibiades' advocacy of the Sicilian expedition to his personal extravagance and to various discreditable private motives. What relevance has that to the merits of the proposal itself? Would the Sicilian expedition, as a war measure, have been a better idea if Alcibiades had been an angelic youth? To ask the question is to dismiss it, and all other such arguments with it. One must dismiss as summarily the objections to oratory: by definition, to wish to lead Athens implies the burden of trying to persuade Athens, and an essential part of that effort consisted in public oratory.

One can draw distinctions, of course. I should concede the label "demagogue" in its most pejorative sense, for example, if a campaign were built around promises which a clique of orators neither intended to honour nor were capable of honouring. But, significantly enough, this accusation is rarely levelled against the so-called demagogues, and the one definite instance we know of comes from the other camp. The oligarchy of 411 was sold to the Athenians on the appeal that this was now the only way to obtain Persian support and thus to win the otherwise lost war. Even on the most favourable view, as Thucydides makes quite clear (8.68–91), Pisander and some of his associates may have meant this originally but they quickly abandoned all pretence of trying to win the war while they concentrated on preserving the newly won oligarchy on as narrow a base as possible. That is what I should call "demagogy," if the word is to merit its pejorative flavour. That is "misleading the people" in the literal sense.

But what then of the interest question, of the supposed clash between the interests of the whole state and the interests of a section or faction within the state? Is that not a valid distinction? It is a pity that we have no direct evidence (and no indirect evidence of any value) about the way the long debate was conducted between 508 B.C., when Clisthenes established the democracy in its primitive form, and the later years of Pericles' dominance. Those were the years when class interests would most likely have been expounded openly and bluntly. Actual speeches survive only from the end of the fifth century on, and they reveal what anyone could have guessed who had not been blinded by Plato and others, namely, that the appeal was customarily a national one, not a factional one. There is little open pandering to the poor against the rich, to the farmers against the town or to the town against the farmers. Why indeed should there have been?

At the same time a politician cannot ignore class or sectional interests or the conflicts among them, whether in a constituency today or in the Assembly in ancient Athens. The evidence for Athens suggests that on many issues – the empire and the Peloponnesian War, for example, or relations with Philip of Macedon – the divisions over policy did not closely follow class or sectional lines. But other questions, such as that of opening the archonship and other offices to men of the lower property censuses or that of pay for jury service, or, in the fourth century, the financing of the fleet or the theoric fund [the fund for festival grants], were by their nature class issues. Advocates on both sides knew this and knew how and when (and when not) to make their appeals accordingly, at the same time that they each argued, and believed, that only their respective points of view would advance Athens as a whole. To plead against Ephialtes and Pericles that *eunomia*, the well-ordered state ruled by law, had the higher moral claim, was merely a plea for the status quo dressed up in fancy language.[20]

In his little book on the Athenian constitution, Aristotle wrote the following (27.3–4): "Pericles was the first to give pay for jury service, as a demagogic measure to counter the wealth of Cimon. The latter, who possessed the fortune of a tyrant ... supported many

[20] "Eunomia ... the ideal of the past and even of Solon ... now meant the best constitution, based on inequality. It was now the ideal of oligarchy": Ehrenberg, *Aspects*, p. 92.

of his fellow-demesmen, every one of whom was free to come daily and receive from him enough for his sustenance. Besides, none of his estates was enclosed, so that anyone who wished could take from its fruits. Pericles' property did not permit such largesse, and on the advice of Damonides ... he distributed among the people from what was their own ... and so he introduced pay for the jurors."

Aristotle himself, as I indicated earlier, praised Pericles' regime and he refused responsibility for this explanation, but others who repeated it, both before and after him, thought it was a telling instance of demagogy pandering to the common people. The obvious retort is to ask whether what Cimon did was not pandering in equal measure, or whether opposition to pay for jury service was not pandering, too, but in that case to the men of property. No useful analysis is possible in such terms, for they serve only to conceal the real grounds for disagreement. If one is opposed to full democracy as a form of government, then it is wrong to encourage popular participation in the juries by offering pay; but it is wrong because the objective is wrong, not because Pericles obtained leadership status by proposing and carrying the measure. And vice versa, if one favours a democratic system.

What emerges from all this is a very simple proposition, namely, that demagogues – I use the word in a neutral sense – were a structural element in the Athenian political system. By this I mean, first, that the system could not function at all without them; secondly, that the term is equally applicable to all leaders, regardless of class or point of view; and thirdly, that within rather broad limits they are to be judged individually not by their manners or their methods, but by their performance. (And that, I need hardly add, is precisely how they *were* judged in life, if not in books.) Up to a point one can easily parallel the Athenian demagogue with the modern politician, but there soon comes a point when distinctions must be drawn, not merely because the work of government has become so much more complex, but more basically because of the differences between a direct and a representative democracy. I have already discussed the mass-meeting (with its uncertain composition), the lack of a bureaucracy and a party system, and the resulting state of continuous tension in which an Athenian demagogue lived and worked. But there is one consequence which needs a little examination, for these conditions make up an important part (if not the whole) of the explanation of an apparently negative feature of Athenian politics, and of Greek politics generally. David Hume put it this way: "To exclude faction from a free government, is very difficult, if not altogether impracticable; but such inveterate rage between the factions, and such bloody maxims are found, in modern times, amongst religious parties alone. In ancient history we may always observe, where one party prevailed, whether the nobles or people (for I can observe no difference in this respect), that they immediately butchered ... and banished ... No form of process, no law, no trial, no pardon. ... These people were extremely fond of liberty, but seem not to have understood it very well."[21]

The remarkable thing about Athens is how near she came to being the complete exception to this correct observation of Hume's, to being free, in other words, from *stasis* in its ultimate meaning. The democracy was established in 508 B.C. following a brief civil war. Thereafter, in its history of nearly two centuries, armed terror, butchery without process or law, was employed on only two occasions, in 411 and 404, both times by oligarchic factions which seized control of the state for brief periods. And the second time, in particular, the democratic faction, when it regained power, was generous and law-abiding in its treatment of the oligarchs, so much so that praise has been attributed even from Plato. Writing about the restoration of 403, he is supposed to have said that "no one should be surprised that some men took savage personal revenge against their enemies in this revolution, but in general the returning party behaved equitably."[22] This is not to suggest that the two centuries were totally free from individual acts of injustice and brutality. Hume – speaking of Greece generally and not of Athens in particular – observed "no difference in this respect" between the factions. We seem to have a less clear vision of Athens, reflected in the distorting mirror of men like Thucydides, Xenophon and Plato, which mag-nifies the exceptional incidents of extreme democratic intolerance – such as the trial and execution of the generals who won the battle of Arginusae and the trial and execution of Socrates – while it minimizes and often obliterates altogether the behaviour on the other side, for example, the political assassination of Ephialtes in 462 or 461 and of Androcles in 411, each in his time the most influential of the popular leaders.

If Athens largely escaped the extreme forms of *stasis* so common elsewhere, she could not escape its lesser manifestations. Athenian politics had an all-or-nothing quality. The objective on each side was

---

[21] "Of the Populousness of Ancient Nations," in *Essays* (World's Classics ed., London 1903), pp. 405–6. Cf. Jacob Burckhardt, *Grichische Kulturgeschichte* (reprint Darmstadt 1956) II 80–81.
[22] *Epistles* VII 325B; cf. Xenophon, *Hellenica* 2.4.43; Aristotle, *Constitution of Athens* 40.

not merely to defeat the opposition but to crush it, to behead it by destroying its leaders. And often enough this game was played within the sides, as a number of men manoeuvred for leadership. The chief technique was the political trial, and the chief instrumentalities were the dining-clubs and the sycophants [those who undertook prosecutions in the hope of reward]. These, too, I would argue, were structurally a part of the system, not an accidental or avoidable excrescence. Ostracism, the so-called *graphe paranomon* [prosecution for making an illegal proposal], and the formal popular scrutiny of archons, generals and other officials, were all deliberately introduced as safety devices, either against excessive individual power (and potential tyranny) or against corruption and malfeasance or unthinking haste and passion in the Assembly itself. Abstractly it may be easy enough to demonstrate that, however praiseworthy in intention, these devices inevitably invited abuse. The trouble is that they were the only kind of device available, again because the democracy was a direct one, lacking a party machinery and so forth. Leaders and would-be leaders had no alternative but to make use of them, and to seek out still other ways of harassing and breaking competitors and opponents.

Hard as this all-out warfare no doubt was on the participants, even unfair and vicious on occasion, it does not follow that it was altogether an evil for the community as a whole. Substantial inequalities, serious conflicts of interest, and legitimate divergences of opinion were real and intense. Under such conditions, conflict is not only inevitable, it is a virtue in democratic politics, for it is conflict combined with consent, not consent alone, which preserves democracy from eroding into oligarchy. On the constitutional issue which dominated so much of the fifth century it was the advocates of popular democracy who triumphed, and they did so precisely because they fought for it and fought hard. They fought a partisan fight, and the Old Oligarch made the correct diagnosis in attributing Athenian strength to just that. Of course, his insight, or perhaps his honesty, did not extend so far as to note the fact that in his day the democracy's leaders were still men of substance, and often of aristocratic background: not only Pericles, but Cleon and Cleophon, and then Thrasybulus and Anytus. The two latter led the democratic faction in overthrowing the Thirty Tyrants in 403, and in following their victory with the much praised amnesty. The partisan fight was not a straight class fight; it also drew support from among the rich and the well-born. Nor was it a fight without rules or legitimacy. The democratic counterslogan to *eunomia* [a good state of law] was *isonomia* [equality of law], and, as Vlastos has said, the Athenians pursued "the goal of political equality ... not in defiance, but in support of the rule of law." The Athenian poor, he noted, did not once raise the standard Greek revolutionary demand – redistribution of the land – throughout the fifth and fourth centuries.[23]

In those two centuries Athens was, by all pragmatic tests, the greatest Greek state, with a powerful feeling of community, with a toughness and resilience tempered, even granted its imperial ambitions, by a humanity and sense of equity and responsibility quite extraordinary for its day (and for many another day as well). Lord Acton was one of the few historians to have grasped the historic significance of the amnesty of 403. "The hostile parties," he wrote, "were reconciled, and proclaimed an amnesty, the first in history."[24] *The first in history*, despite all the familiar weaknesses, despite the crowd psychology, the slaves, the personal ambition of many leaders, the impatience of the majority with opposition. Nor was this the only Athenian innovation: the structure and mechanism of the democracy were all their own invention, as they groped for something without precedent, having nothing to go on but their own notion of freedom, their community solidarity, their willingness to inquire (or at least to accept the consequences of inquiry), and their widely shared political experience.

Much of the credit for the Athenian achievement must go to the political leadership of the state. That, it seems to me, is beyond dispute. It certainly would not have been disputed by the average Athenian. Despite all the tension and uncertainties, the occasional snap judgment and unreasonable shift in opinion, the people supported Pericles for more than two decades, as they eventually supported a very different kind of man, Demosthenes, under very different conditions a century later. These men, and others like them (less well-known now), were able to carry through a more or less consistent and successful programme over long stretches of time. It is altogether perverse to ignore this fact, or to ignore the structure of political life by which Athens became what she was, while one follows the lead of Aristophanes or Plato and looks only at the

---

[23] G. Vlastos, "*Isonomia*," *American Journal of Philology*, 74 (1953) 337–66. Cf. Jones, *Democracy*, p. 52: "In general ... democrats tended like Aristotle to regard the laws as a code laid down once and for all by a wise legislator ... which, immutable in principle, might occasionally require to be clarified or supplemented." The "rule of law" is a complicated subject on its own, but it is not the subject of this chapter. Nor is the evaluation of individual demagogues.

[24] "The History of Freedom in Antiquity," in *Essays on Freedom and Power*, ed. G. Himmelfarb (London 1956), p. 64.

personalities of the politicians, or at the crooks and failures among them, or at some ethical norms of an ideal existence.

In the end Athens lost her freedom and independence, brought down by a superior external power. She went down fighting, with an understanding of what was at stake clearer than that possessed by many critics in later ages. That final struggle was led by Demosthenes, a demagogue. We cannot have it both ways: we cannot praise and admire the achievement of two centuries, and at the same time dismiss the demagogues who were the architects of the political framework and the makers of policy, or the Assembly in and through which they did their work.

7 Political Activity in Classical Athens*[1]

P. J. RHODES

'Only the naïve or innocent observer', says Sir Moses Finley in his book *Politics in the ancient world*, 'can believe that Pericles came to a vital Assembly meeting armed with nothing but his intelligence, his knowledge, his charisma and his oratorical skill, essential as all four attributes were.'[2] Historians of the Roman Republic have been assiduous in studying *clientelae* [groups of clients], *factiones* ['factions'] and 'delivering the vote',[3] but much less work has been done on the ways in which Athenian politicians sought to mobilise

* Originally published in *Journal of Hellenic Studies* cvi 1986, 132–44; reprinted with the permission of the Council of the Society for the Promotion of Hellenic Studies.

[1] This paper was read to the Hellenic Society in London and to the University of Göttingen in January 1985, and an earlier version was read to the Oxford Philological Society in October 1982 and to the northern universities' ancient historians at Leeds in December 1982: I am grateful to those who discussed it with me on those occasions, and to the University of Durham for grants from its Travel and Research Fund and to the British Council and the Deutsche Akademische Austauschdienst, under whose auspices I visited Göttingen.

I cite the following books by abbreviated titles: W. R. Connor, *New Pol.* = *The new politicians of fifth century Athens* (Princeton 1971); J. K. Davies, *A.P.F.* = *Athenian propertied families, 600–300 B.C.* (Oxford 1971); id., *Wealth* = *Wealth and the power of wealth in classical Athens* (New York 1981); M. I. Finley, *Politics* = *Politics in the ancient world* (Cambridge 1983); S. C. Humphreys, *Family* = *The family, women and death* (London 1983); P. J. Rhodes, *Boule* = *The Athenian Boule* (Oxford 1972); id., *Comm.* = *A commentary on the Aristotelian Athenaion Politeia* (Oxford 1981); P. Siewert, *Trittyen* = *Die Trittyen Attikas und die Heeresreform des Kleisthenes* (*Vestigia* xxxiii, Munich 1982). H. Montgomery, *The way to Chaeronea* (Bergen etc. 1983), is good in the questions which he asks but disappointing in the answers which he supplies.

Not all the sayings and anecdotes which I cite are likely to be authentic, but they will have seemed plausible to those who retailed them, and those known to us from Plutarch and others who wrote under the Roman Empire may have originated in or closer to the society to which they refer. Caution is in order, but I shall not pause to discuss the likelihood of each item.

[2] Finley, *Politics*, 76(–84). Dem. xiii 19 complains that men who are eager to be elected to office go around as δοῦλοι τῆς ἐπὶ τῷ χειροτονεῖσθαι χάριτος, 'slaves to the need to win support for election'; Plut. *Nic.* 3.1 leaves Pericles on the pedestal on which Thucydides placed him when he says that he led the city as a result of his true *aretē* and the power of his speech, and needed no *schematismos*, 'put-on-act', towards the masses or *pithanotes*, 'means of persuasion'.

[3] This phrase is the title of ch. iii of L. R. Taylor, *Party politics in the age of Caesar* (Berkeley and Los Angeles 1949). Excessive reliance on *clientelae* as a master key seems now to be going out of fashion: see F. G. B. Millar, *JRS* lxxiv (1984) 1–19.

support. There have been studies of family connections and of links between individual politicians;[4] there have been studies of the associations known as *hetaireiai* [groups of companions];[5] but many questions remain unanswered. W. R. Connor in *The new politicians of fifth-century Athens* contrasted an old style of politics, based on ties of *philia* ['friendship'] within the upper classes, with a new style, which spurned *philia* and appealed directly to the people. Even in his old style, the votes of the ordinary, middling-to-poor citizens counted for more in the straightforward Athenian assembly than in the Roman *comitia* [assemblies] with their complex systems of block votes. Connor limits political friendship to the upper classes;[6] he pours cold water on Sealey's suggestion that rich families might have brought pressure to bear on their tenants and other dependants (saying, 'The proud and independent Athenian might be expected to resist intimidation');[7] but apart from general references to largesse he does not really explain how an old-style Cimon or a new-style Cleon would ensure that the assembly was full of voters willing to elect him as general or approve a motion which he proposed.[8] J. K. Davies has tried to take the matter further in *Wealth and the power of wealth in classical Athens*. He suggests that essentially there were three phases in Athenian political history: the first, in which aristocratic families with a hereditary control of particular cults exercised power through those cults; the second, in which aristocrats and their cults lost influence, and politics were dominated by rich men who used their wealth in various ways to acquire favour (*charis*) and so win the support of citizens; the third, where the power of wealth in turn declined and what counted was rhetorical and administrative skill.[9] Here I should like to continue this investigation.

For the seventh and sixth centuries I imagine most people would accept some version of what W. G. Forrest has described as a system of pyramids:[10] serious political activity was the preserve of a limited

---

[4] E.g. B. R. I. Sealey, *Essays in Greek politics* (New York 1967); P. J. Bicknell, *Studies in Athenian politics and genealogy* (*Historia* Einz. xix [1972]); Davies, *A.P.F.*

[5] See n. 69.

[6] *New Pol.* 75–9; *cf.* the view of M. H. Hansen, *The Athenian Ecclesia* (*Opuscula Graecolatina* xxvi [Copenhagen 1983]) 220–2, and at greater length *The Athenian Assembly in the Age of Demosthenes* (Oxford 1987) 72–86 that in the fifth and fourth centuries there were groups of leaders but not parties of their supporters.

[7] *New Pol.* 18–19, contr. Sealey, *Hermes* lxxxiv (1956) 241 = *Essays* (n. 4) 65–6.

[8] *New Pol.* 18–22 on largesse; 134 suggests that groups of friends could mobilise a majority in the assembly or council.

[9] *Wealth*, esp. 88–131 (ch. vi).

[10] *The emergence of Greek Democracy* (London 1966) 48–50.

number of nobles at the tops of the pyramids; underneath were the lesser citizens, each of whom tended to be linked by ties of various kinds to one of the nobles, and would normally give that noble his political support. Attacks on the old orthodoxy[11] have made it harder than was once imagined to give a detailed account of how this will have worked in Athens, but the attempt should be made.

Some citizens, but not all, belonged to the nobility of the *eupatridai* ['well-fathered'], the families which had emerged most successfully from the upheavals of the dark age and which had closed their ranks against the others as the upheavals came to an end: they acquired a monopoly of public offices (probably filled without much competition when Buggins's turn came round), and they will have been the active participants at occasional assemblies of the citizen body. Some citizens, but not all, belonged to a *genos* ['clan': actual or imagined kinship group]. The view that the *genē* formed a wider aristocracy than the *eupatridai*, but still an aristocracy, has been challenged: the new emphasis on the religious function of the *genē* is probably right; but the suggestion of the iconoclasts that the *genē* and their members were not otherwise important is no less hypothetical than the old orthodoxy.[12] We simply do not know what proportion of the *eupatridai* were also *gennētai* [members of a *genos*]. Every citizen belonged to one of the four tribes, and also to one of an unknown number of phratries: it is reasonable to assume that the *eupatridai*, who will have been leading members of the tribe and the phratry to which they belonged, were able through these organisations to influence their lowlier fellow-members. The *genē*, even if we regard them primarily as families in which certain priesthoods were hereditary, may yet have had political influence: those who participated in a certain cult will naturally have looked up to the *genē* which provided the officials of that cult; and cults which attracted a wide circle of participants, like the Eleusinian cult of Demeter and Core, will have brought a large number of men within reach of the influence of the *genē* concerned.

Before the reforms of Solon, one other kind of dependence is attested in Athens. Many men were *hektēmoroi* ['sixth-parters'], not absolute owners of the land which they farmed but bound to

---

[11] A. Andrewes, *JHS* lxxxi (1961) 1–15, *Hermes* lxxxix (1961) 129–40; more drastically, F. Bourriot, *Recherches sur la nature du génos* (Paris 1976), D. Roussel, *Tribu et cité* (Paris 1976).

[12] I cannot share the belief of Bourriot 460–91 and Roussel 79–87, 146 that there also existed *genē* of another kind, the 360 of *Ath. Pol. fr.* 3 Kenyon.

surrender part of its produce to an overlord;[13] and probably other men were dependent on the major landowners in other ways, for instance by dividing their working time between their own plot and the land of the great family. Like Sealey,[14] I should guess that this economic dependence could easily have repercussions in other areas of life. We do not know how far overlords were *eupatridai* and *gennētai*, and *hektēmoroi* were not, though we should expect the *eupatridai* and *gennētai* to be among the richer members of the community. We do not know how often the overlord of a *hektēmoros* was a leading member of the *hektēmoros'* phratry or had a vested interest in a cult in which the *hektēmoros* participated; but I should guess that, in a society in which social and geographical mobility were rare, it often happened that the different forms of dependence did not compete but reinforced each other.

Forrest's picture of pyramids will, then, be generally correct. Various kinds of link will have held a pyramid together: cult power, which Davies regards as characteristic of his earliest phase; power exercised through the tribes and phratries, which we may call social power; and power exercised by the great landowners over men economically dependent on them, the power of wealth.

Beyond this, for early Athens, we can look only at the well-known moments of crisis. In the seventh century Cylon failed to make himself tyrant. He was a distinguished man, an aristocrat and an Olympic victor; he had useful connections, the tyrant of Megara as his father-in-law and an encouraging oracle from Delphi. He must have thought he could win the support of a sufficient number of Athenians, but whatever the basis for his confidence it was unjustified: the citizens rallied behind the authorities 'in full force'.[15]

In 594 Solon was appointed archon, and was given a special commission to solve Athens' problems. He was a eupatrid; probably he was not responsible for the 'purification' of Athens from the killing of Cylon's supporters, but probably he had encouraged the Athenians to embark on the war in which they captured Salamis from Megara. Also he was a poet, and in some of his poems he had written of Athens' troubles and had blamed the rich for them: poems recited on occasions when many could hear them would reach far beyond the range of Solon's own family connections, and this may have helped him to win the widespread support which Cylon had

---

[13] *Ath. Pol.* 2. 2–3, Plut. *Sol.* 13. 4–5.
[14] P. 186 with n. 7, above.
[15] These points are all in the account of Thuc. i 126. 3–7.

failed to win. Probably there was nothing remarkable in his being appointed archon; but his special commission made him more than just another archon, and to achieve that he must have won the confidence not only of the poor and unprivileged but also of his fellow aristocrats. Connections will not have been enough: in poems written after the event he complains that both sides felt he had let them down; no poems survive which would have gained the confidence of the aristocrats, but he must have put it to them that there was a crisis (a crisis which his appeal to the poor had in fact helped to crystallise), and that he could be trusted to handle it so as to protect the aristocrats' interests. Nevertheless, what he did significantly weakened aristocratic kinds of influence. The institutionalised dependence of the *hektēmoroi* was abolished; it became possible for some men who were rich but not eupatrid to hold office, and the new council of four hundred will have drawn new men into political activity and have given the citizen assembly a new freedom; the judicial reforms gave a better chance of obtaining justice to men who were afraid to prosecute on their own account, or who when they did prosecute or were prosecuted came up against a hostile magistrate.[16]

I have nothing new to say on the three factions (*staseis*), of the plain, the coast and beyond the hills, which provide the background to Pisistratus' rise to power. All three leaders were eupatrids; the regional names should characterise not only the three leaders but a substantial part of their followings, though Pisistratus' support cannot have been limited to men remote from Athens; the ideological labels of *Ath. Pol.* and Plutarch are clearly anachronistic, but Pisistratus did appeal to those who were still poor and unprivileged, and Megacles did sometimes support him but sometimes oppose him.[17] Pisistratus had his natural family and local following, and his appeal to the poor; he also had prestige from his success in the latest war against Megara. In his rise to power we see various *motifs*: the bodyguard granted to a leading citizen unjustly attacked; a religious charade, naïve but evidently successful; marriage alliances, successively with Megacles and with a family from Argos; further support from outside Athens, including the mercenaries whom his wealth enabled him to hire.[18] The effect of the tyranny was to continue the undermining of the old influences: a tyrant monopolising power is bad for the aristocratic families who want a share in power; taxation

---

[16] *Ath. Pol.* 5–12, Plut. *Sol. passim.*
[17] Her. i 59.3, *Ath. Pol.* 13.3–5, Plut. *Sol.* 13.1–3 (before Solon's archonship), 29.1.
[18] Her. i 59–64, *Ath. Pol.* 14–15.

of the rich, and perhaps confiscation from some of them, and loans and perhaps grants of land to the poor, will have dealt a further blow to the economic dependence of the peasants on the great families; the encouragement of national cults and festivals will have lessened the importance of the local ones. In the background were the tyrants' mercenaries and the threat of force, but more directly the tyrants' power was exercised through patronage: state loans to small peasants, and state judges to give impartial decisions in their disputes;[19] honour and office for nobles who cooperated, and exile or worse for those who did not.[20]

The fall of the tyrants was followed by the resumption of aristocratic rivalry, until Cleisthenes 'attached the *dēmos* to his following', a *dēmos* in which allegedly he had shown no interest before.[21] Argument continues about how Cleisthenes combined demes to form thirty trittyes and ten tribes, but if there is truth in the suggestion that he wanted to produce units of equal size, on which the organisation of the army could be based,[22] that does not rule out the possibility that he had other objectives too. To arrive at his trittyes [thirds] and tribes, Cleisthenes produced a number of extremely unnatural groupings: he at least did not mind if Probalinthus was separated from its neighbours both in the Marathonian tetrapolis and to the south, if Hecale north-east of Mount Pentelicon was isolated from the other demes of its tribe; and it is hardly accidental that the Alcmaeonids were to find themselves surrounded by familiar faces in the assemblies of the new tribes.[23] Old associations, like the old tribes and the phratries, were not abolished; but the new units proved highly successful, and it soon mattered more to a man of Plotheia or Marathon that he belonged to Aegeis or Aiantis and the men of Hecale did not than that he was given a warm welcome when he attended the festivals of Zeus *Hekalēsios*, it mattered more to a man of Decelea that he belonged to the deme of Decelea than that he belonged to the phratry of the Deceleans. The influence of the aristocracy, social and religious, continued to decline.

Cleisthenes had devised a system in which the Alcmaeonids were going to be advantageously placed: we should expect men ambitious for success to seek ways of exercising their influence through this new

[19] Cf. *Ath. Pol.* 16.
[20] Cf. Meiggs and Lewis 6, *c*, Andoc. ii 26.
[21] Her. v 66.2, 69.1, cf. *Ath. Pol.* 20.1.
[22] J. S. Traill, *Hesperia* xlvii (1978) 109; Siewert, *Trittyen*.
[23] This is admitted even by Siewert, *Trittyen*, 137.

system.[24] Cimon provides a good example: in the better versions of the story of his lavish hospitality he kept open house not to all Athenians but to his fellow demesmen,[25] and there are more modest examples in Lysias of men giving financial support to members of their own demes.[26] Men would support members of their deme or their tribe in the lawcourts: Andocides ends his speech *On the Mysteries* with an invitation to the members of his tribe chosen to speak for him;[27] in Plato's *Apology* the witnesses who will testify that Socrates is not an evil influence are headed by Crito, *emos hēlikiōtēs kai dēmotēs*, 'my contemporary and fellow demesman';[28] Hyperides reports that when Polyeuctus was prosecuted he asked for ten advocates from his tribe (and supporters from the rest of the citizen body as well).[29] A particular barber's shop in Athens was frequented by the demesmen of Decelea.[30] At the beginning of the *Theages* Demodocus complains that his son has been excited by reports brought from the city by 'some of his contemporaries and fellow-demesmen';[31] and there are many passages where words such as *hēlikiōtēs*, 'contemporary', or *philos*, 'friend', are combined with *dēmotēs*, 'demesman', or *phyletēs*, 'fellow tribesman'.[32] Classical Athens did not have the same elaborate series of age-classes as classical Sparta, but even before a programme of compulsory national service was instituted in the 330s[33] young men of eighteen and nineteen were classed as *ephēboi* ['those on the verge of adulthood', undergoing a period of training], distinct from fully-fledged adults, and were given opportunities for military service.[34] There were other contexts, such as the gymnasium, in which young Athenians could associate with their contemporaries in the gap between childhood restrictions and adult responsibilities.[35]

---

[24] 'Community patronage had to be at least partially integrated into the new institutional framework if it were not to be a disruptive factor': Finley, *Politics* 35(-49). The interaction of demes and the Athenian state is explored by R. G. Osborne, *Demos: the discovery of classical Attika* (Cambridge 1985).

[25] E.g. *Ath. Pol.* 27.3.

[26] Lys. xvi 14, xxxi 15–16, cf. xx 2.

[27] Andoc. i 150.

[28] Plat. *Ap.* 33d8–e1.

[29] Hyp. iv 12; cf. also Lys. xxvii 12, Dem. xxiii 206, also Dem. xxix 23. The importance of the deme is stressed by Finley, *Politics* 46.

[30] Lys. xxvi 3, cf. *IG* ii² 1237. 63–4 (I am among those who believe that the Deceleans in this inscription are a phratry).

[31] [Plat.] *Theag.* 121d1–3.

[32] Ar. *Ach.* 568, *Eq.* 320, *Nub.* 1209–10, 1322, *Eccl.* 1023–4, *Pl.* 254.

[33] *Ath. Pol.* 42.2–5, with Rhodes, *Comm. ad loc.*

[34] Rhodes, *Comm.* 494–5: notice especially Aeschin. ii 167.

[35] Cf. Humphreys, *CJ* lxxiii (1977/8) 101–2 = *Family*, 28 [= pp. 229–30, below]. Other passages mentioning *hēlikiōtai* are Her. v 71. 1 (Cylon assembled a '*hetaireia* of his contem-

These links inevitably have their sinister side. It was an argument against Polystratus, implicated in the oligarchy of the Four Hundred, that he was a demesman and alleged kinsman of Phrynichus.[36] In 404 the oligarchic leaders who took the title 'ephors' appointed *phylarchoi*, tribal agents, to tell men how to vote.[37] If we can believe the allegations in Demosthenes lvii; Eubulides when demarch of Halimus controlled the votes of many members in the deme assembly,[38] and his father had been a crooked deme-boss before him.[39]

In Davies' account a period characterised by cult power is followed by one characterised by wealth power: he notices various kinds of expenditure by leading politicians which contributed to their *lamprotēs*, which made them distinguished men. F. J. Frost in a study of Athenian politics in the sixth and early fifth centuries has argued that such *lamprotēs* should be seen as a political end in itself, not merely as a means of acquiring support in the pursuit of further ends;[40] but it should not be overlooked that generosity to one's fellow demesmen, like that of Cimon, could be expected to bring a grateful *clientela* as well as *lamprotēs*.[41] The same can be said of some other kinds of expenditure. The liturgies [public duties to be performed by a man at his own expense] in connection with Athenian festivals involved paying for,[42] and taking responsibility for a chorus, a relay team for a torch race, or the like; in many cases this was for an inter-tribal competition, and in many cases the tribe appointed its choregus:[43] the choregus who devoted his money and attention enthusiastically to his team could expect to win not only glory for himself but also glory for, and gratitude from, the performers and their families, and the whole tribe. The choregus of Antiphon vi draws attention to the way in which he recruited a chorus without

---

poraries': evidence for the fifth century if not for the seventh); Ar. *Vesp.* 728, *Nub.* 1006; Lys. xx 36; Plat. *Clit.* 408c6, *Soph.* 218b3, *Symp.* 183c7 *Ep.* vii 332d4; [Dem.] xl 59, liii 4, Dem. liv 7; Aeschin. i 42, 49 (and *synephēbos*), ii 168 (*synephēboi* 167), 184.

[36] Lys. xx 11–12.

[37] Lys. xii 43–4.

[38] Dem. lvii 8–16.

[39] Dem. lvii 60 cf. 26. B. Haussoullier, *La vie municipale en Attique* (Paris 1883/4) 59–62, claimed that deme officials came from a limited range of families: I do not know how far the evidence now available supports this.

[40] *Classical Contributions ... M. F. McGregor* (Locust Valley 1981) 33–9.

[41] Lys. mentions expenditure in the pursuit of glory, xix 18, but expenditure to gain appointment to office (and opportunities for enrichment), xix 57. Humphreys, *CJ* lxxiii (1977/8) 102 = *Family* 28–9 [= p. 232, below], remarks that in Athens 'clients' tended to be collective (demes, phratries and so on) rather than individual.

[42] [Xen.] *Ath. Pol.* 1.13 claims that the people benefit from such payments.

[43] Cf. Dem. xxi 13, xxxix 7, *Ath. Pol.* 56.3.

making enemies;[44] a client of Isaeus says that his fellow tribesmen know how ambitiously (*philotimōs*) he discharged his duties as gymnasiarch [man responsible for athletic team].[45] In addition to the state liturgies there were deme liturgies: these provided further opportunities for patronage, and if here there was not the stimulus of direct competition it would no doubt be remembered that the man who had given this year's party for the demesmen's wives at the Thesmophoria had been keen and generous but the man who had given last year's party had not.[46]

Not all the men who rowed the navy's ships were Athenian citizens, but many were, and a trierarch [man responsible for a ship in the navy] who was energetic and willing to spend more than the minimum would not only provide the navy with a good ship but would earn the gratitude of his crew. On occasions when oarsmen had to be conscripted, this was done (as we should expect) through the tribes and their subdivisions:[47] there are fifth-century boundary markers (*horoi*) from the Piraeus which served to indicate areas reserved for particular trittyes;[48] Xenophon twice mentions the taxiarchs, normally the commanders of tribal infantry regiments, in his account of the naval battle of Arginusae;[49] and Demosthenes in his speech *On the Symmories* says that to man the fleet the generals should divide the dockyards into ten tribal areas and the taxiarchs should subdivide their tribal areas into sections for the separate trittyes.[50] In 362 it was ordered that the bouleutae [councillors] and demarchs [chief officials of the demes] should make out lists of demesmen and supply sailors – but the men produced by this method failed to appear or were incompetent, so Apollodorus recruited his own crew by offering financial incentives.[51]

Gratitude and influence could be bought in other ways too. One could stand as guarantor for a man who was prosecuted or took a public contract; one could join with others in making a loan to a man

---

[44] Ant. vi 11.
[45] Isae. vii 36.
[46] Cf Isae. iii 80, viii 18–20.
[47] B. Jordan, *U. Cal. Publ. Cl. Stud.* xiii (1975) 101–2, 225–30; Siewert, *Trittyen* 10–13.
[48] *IG* i² 897–901.
[49] Xen. *Hell.* i 6.29, 35.
[50] Dem. xiv 22–3.
[51] Dem. i. 6–7. In the same year the bouleutae were made to report those men whose ownership of property in their deme rendered them liable for *proseisphora* [advance payment on behalf of members of their *eisphora* group] (*ibid.* 8–9), I believe because it was suspected that rich men were failing to declare all their own property and this method would produce a more comprehensive register: see Davies, *Wealth* 143–6; Rhodes, *AJAH* vii (1982: published 1985) 1–19.

in need: in Antiphon's *First Tetralogy engyai* and *eranoi* [acting as guarantor and making loans] are mentioned after liturgies as proofs of the defendant's virtue.[52] Not all disputes were taken to court: another way to acquire influence was to gain a reputation for fair dealing as a private arbitrator, and the cunning Themistocles as well as the upright Aristides is said to have done this.[53] Simply knowing people was important: Themistocles is said to have known every one by name;[54] in 421 Nicias canvassed men individually to urge them to support his peace with Sparta,[55] and we have other references to individual canvassing.[56]

Other forms of conspicuous expenditure would not win the support of particular citizens, but they would indicate that the spender was a patriotic Athenian, who made good use of his wealth and deserved the gratitude of the citizen body as a whole.[57] Prompt payment of *eisphora*, the property tax, and generous *epidoseis*, voluntary contributions in response to a special appeal, come into this category; and so do private payments for public buildings. In lawsuits men list these along with their liturgies as evidence that they are public-spirited citizens;[58] Themistocles and Cimon were rivals as builders as well as in other respects;[59] while we find Demosthenes alleging that Midias avoided his obligations as far as he could, and when unable to avoid them exploited them for his private profit, that Aeschines never spent his money for patriotic purposes.[60]

A form of display to which Davies attaches much importance is victory in the great games, especially in the contest which called for the heaviest expenditure, the chariot race. Now certainly horse-breeding was an acknowledged way of displaying great wealth;[61]

---

[52] Ant. ii *Tetr*. i β. 12.

[53] Plut. *Them*. 5.6, *Arist*. 4.2, 7.1.

[54] Plut. *Them*. 5.6.

[55] Plut. *Nic*. 9.5.

[56] Thuc. viii 53.2, 93.2, Xen. *Hell*. ii 3.23; cf. lobbying before the allotment of jurors Dem. xix 1, xxi 4, Aeschin. iii 1.

[57] On men's reasons for expenditure of this kind see Lys. xix (n. 41), xxv 12–13 (to enhance one's reputation and so have a better chance in the courts if disaster strikes). R. J. Seager in F. C. Jaher (ed.), *The rich, the well born and the powerful* (Illinois 1973) 7–26, and D. White-head, *ClMed* xxxiv (1983) 55–74, discuss the democratic ethos requiring those with wealth and talent to use them for the good of the state, so that *philotimia* [ambition for honour] found an outlet in public service: notice especially Dem. xviii 257, xxi 159, [Dem.] xlii 25.

[58] Lys. xxi, esp. 1–11, cf. vii 31–2, xii 20, xviii 7, 21, xix 9, 29, 42–3, 57, xxv 12, xxx 26.

[59] Cf. Rhodes, *CAH* v² (1992) 63–4.

[60] Dem. xxi 151–74; xix 281–2, xviii 312–13; cf. also Lys. xxi 12, Xen. *Oec*. 2.6. Lys. xxvi 3–5 casts aspersions on a man who has spent his money in the approved way.

[61] Arist. *Pol*. iv 1289b33–40; Lys. xxiv 10–12, [Dem.] xlii 24; cf. Ar. *Nub*. 14–16, 25–32, etc.

certainly cities did bask in reflected glory when a victory was won in their name (Athenians who won victories at the principal festivals were given dinner in the prytaneum [town hall][62]), and the career of Cimon *Koalemos* under the Pisistratids shows that victories could have political consequences.[63] Naturally, those who had won victories tried to make the most of them (Alcibiades, after his extravagance in entering seven teams at the Olympics of 416, is made by Thucydides to say that this gave a corresponding impression of the city's strength[64]); and, naturally, their enemies claimed that to win such victories did not make a man a desirable citizen in other respects (Lycurgus objects that horse-breeding, and indeed festival liturgies, bring glory only to the individual and are not to be compared with useful expenditure such as trierarchies and public building projects[65]). If one looks at Davies' list of Athenian competitors in chariot races[66] one finds for the fifth century various Alcmaeonids, Callias and Alcibiades (all men from socially and politically great families), and then Pronapes, Lysis and his son Democrates, and Tisias (of whom the last was of some account in politics but the others, as far as we know, were not at all important[67]). Davies notes a sharp drop in Athenian chariot-racers in the fourth century, and suggests that this form of expenditure was abandoned because it no longer paid political dividends. I suspect that we are dealing here with a social phenomenon rather than a political, and that chariot-racing had never paid political dividends, but was a part of the lifestyle of the rich aristocracy which simply did not appeal so much to the richest Athenians of the fourth century.[68]

Hetaireiai, upper-class clubs, have been fairly thoroughly studied.[69] Andocides claims that the mutilation of the Hermae in 415 was the work of a *hetaireia* to which he belonged;[70] in 411 Pisander when he

---

[62] *IG* i³ 131, 11 ff., Plat. *Ap.* 36d5–9.

[63] Her. vi 103.1–3.

[64] Thuc. vi 16.2, cf. Isoc. xvi 32–4.

[65] Lyc. *Leocr.* 139–40.

[66] *Wealth* 167–8 (appendix iii).

[67] See *PA* 12250 = 12251 = 12253, 9567 = 9573, 3519, 13470 = 13479, and the relevant entries in Davies, *A.P.F.*

[68] On Demades see p. 202, below.

[69] G. M. Calhoun, *Athenian clubs in politics and litigation* (*Bull. U. Texas* cclxii, Humanistic Series xiv [1913]); F. Sartori, *Le eterie nella vita politica ateniese del VI e V secolo a.C.* (Rome 1957); A. E. Raubitschek, review of Sartori, *AJP* lxxx (1959) 81–8; F. Ghinatti, *I gruppi politici ateniesi fino alle guerre persiane* (Rome 1970); C. Pecorella Longo, *'Eterie' e gruppi politici nell' Atene del IV sec. a.C.* (Florence 1971).

[70] Andoc. i 61–4, cf. 49, 54.

came from Samos to Athens encouraged the *xynōmosiai* ('groups bound by oath') or *hetaireiai* 'which already existed in the city with a view to lawsuits and offices' to join forces and work against the democracy,[71] in 404 the so-called ephors were appointed by the *hetaireiai*,[72] and in reaction to this link between *hetaireiai* and oligarchy the fourth century law of impeachment (*nomos eisangeltikos*) threatened any one who 'combined for the dissolution of the democracy or organised a *hetairikon* [group of companions: equivalent to *hetaireia*]'.[73] Plato in his *Seventh Letter* says that he did not pursue a political career because nothing could be done without *philoi* and *hetairoi* ['friends' and 'companions'], and he could not find suitable associates;[74] and elsewhere he mentions 'the efforts of *hetaireiai* for offices' among things which the non-political philosopher avoids.[75]

Leading politicians seem to have been surrounded by a circle of lesser men who worked on their behalf, holding offices, appearing in the courts and proposing measures in the assembly.[76] According to Plutarch, Pericles saved himself for the great occasions and otherwise had various men acting for him[77] (there is probably some truth in this, even if the example of Pericles' using Ephialtes to attack the Areopagus[78] makes Pericles a dominant figure too early); by contrast Metiochus, a *hetairos* of Pericles who rose to the generalship but dabbled in everything, fell into disrepute.[79] Aristides is said to have used others to propose his decrees (so as not to incur the hostility of Themistocles);[80] likewise Demosthenes after Chaeronea (afraid that his name would lead to their rejection).[81] Friends of Lycurgus were appointed 'in charge of administration' (*epi tēi dioikēsei*) to control Athens' finances, after he had completed the four years' tenure which was the maximum allowed.[82] Chares was alleged to have spent part of the money voted for his campaigns on 'speakers, proposers of

[71] Thuc. viii 54. 4 cf. 65.2.

[72] Lys. xii 43–4.

[73] Hyp. iv 8.

[74] Plat. *Ep.* vii 325c5–d5.

[75] Plat. *Theaet.* 173d4. For allegations of corrupt appointments see [Dem.] lviii 29, Aeschin. iii 62, 73.

[76] In addition to what follows, see the references to Cimon's *hetairoi*, Plut. *Cim.* 5.2, 17.6–7, *Per.* 10.3; to Pericles' friends, Plut. *Per.* 10.1; to Crito and Archedemus, Xen. *Mem.* ii 9 [; also Ar. *Vesp.* 1033, [Dem.] lix 43].

[77] Plut. *Praec. Ger. Reip.* 811c–813a, *Per.* 7.7–8.

[78] Plut. *Praec. Ger. Reip.* 812d, *Per.* 7.8, 9.5.

[79] Plut. *Praec. Ger. Reip.* 811e–f (comic fragment *Adespota* 1325 Kock).

[80] Plut. *Arist.* 3.4.

[81] Plut. *Dem.* 21.3.

[82] [Plut.] *X Orat.* 841b–c.

decrees and private citizens sued in the courts';[83] Demosthenes refers
to the men who will speak on Midias' behalf as the 'mercenaries' who
surround him, and says that there is also the *hetaireia* of witnesses
which he has organised;[84] and various passages of Demosthenes
suggest that his opponents developed something approaching a party
organisation.[85]

Too much energy has been devoted to arguments about whether a
particular set of men was or was not a *hetaireia*. We can identify two
relevant uses of the word which are fairly common: of the small sets
of upper-class men, like the one to which Andocides belonged, and
through which Pisander worked in 411, who met for drink, talk,
amusement and political jobbery; and of groups of men, commonly
on the fringe of the leisured class, whom a leading politician could
employ as his agents. Individual politicians will have had their lower-
class supporters as well, men often in their own deme or tribe, whose
allegiance they had secured by a good *chorēgia* [service as *chorēgos*,
with financial and general responsibility for a group of performers
at a festival] or by financial or judicial help at a critical time, and
they no doubt mobilised these supporters on important occasions.
Unfortunately we do not know what kind of organisation lies behind
the 191 ostraca [potsherds used for voting in ostracisms] prepared
by fourteen men for use against Themistocles.[86] For Athens' last
ostracism we should probably accept that Hyperbolus wanted the
Athenians to choose between Alcibiades and Nicias, but these
arranged that the supporters of each should vote not against the
other but against Hyperbolus, and Hyperbolus was ostracised:[87] even
if, as I believe, 6,000 votes was the quorum, not the number that had
to be cast against the victim,[88] this will have meant arranging for
2,000 or more votes to be cast against Hyperbolus.[89]

There may be much that is dubious in Plutarch's account of the
politics of Thucydides son of Melesias, his polarisation of the *oligoi*
['few': the oligarchs] and the *dēmos*, and his inducing his supporters
to sit together in the assembly.[90] However, Thucydides was active at

[83] Theopompus *FGrH* 115 F 213, cf. Aeschin. ii 71.
[84] Dem. xxi 139.
[85] Dem. xiii 20 ~ ii 29, xix 225–6, xviii 312–13.
[86] O. Broneer, *Hesperia* vii (1938) 228–43.
[87] Plut. *Arist.* 7.3–4, *Nic.* 11, *Alc.* 13, with the discussion of A. Andrewes in A. W. Gomme *et al.*, *Historical commentary on Thucydides* v (Oxford 1981) 258–64.
[88] Plut. *Arist.* 7.6, with Rhodes, *Comm.* 270.
[89] Hansen (n. 6) is not prepared to believe in political organisation on this scale. Large-scale bribery of ordinary citizens is alleged by Lys. xxix 12.
[90] Plut. *Per.* 11.1–3: see the doubts expressed by A. Andrewes, *JHS* xcviii (1978) 1–8, esp. 2, Hansen, *loc. cit.*; K. J. Dover in A. W. Gomme *et al.*, *Historical commentary on Thucydides*

the time when the Greeks started to think of themselves as oligarchs or democrats. Moreover, from 410/09 members of the boule were required to sit there in the places assigned to them;[91] the idea that political allies could be more effective if they sat together recurs in the *Ecclesiazusae*;[92] and it may well have been intentional that the elaborate system of allotting juries described in *Ath. Pol.* ensured not only that no one could predict which jurors would try which case but also that the same men would not sit together on the same panel day after day[93] (and the token mentioned in *Ath. Pol.* 65.2, whose function is not explained, may have been used to assign jurors to seats[94]). Although scholars have rightly grown afraid of the analogy of modern political parties, we should not be too reluctant to believe that political leaders might mobilise large numbers of supporters.[95]

As fourth-century writers were aware, a change in the style of politics gathered momentum towards the end of the fifth century.[96] For Connor, the new style is characterised by the abandonment of working through friends and by appealing directly to the people *en masse* [as a body].[97] Pericles and Nicias both avoided social occasions and devoted themselves entirely to public affairs;[98] Cleon on entering politics formally renounced his friends,[99] and advertised himself as a lover of the *dēmos*;[100] while Cimon had used his own wealth to win *clientes*, Pericles used the state's wealth to pay stipends to jurors and officials,[101] and to have public buildings erected under public supervision;[102] Xenophon remarks in his *Memorabilia* that a man

iv (Oxford 1970) 238 on vi 13.1, concludes that 'it was not customary for the supporters of a particular speaker to sit all together', but that does not rule out the possibility that it was sometimes done.

[91] Philochorus *FGrH* 328 F 140.

[92] Ar. *Eccl.* 296–9.

[93] *Ath. Pol.* 63–5.

[94] A. L. Boegehold, *Hesperia* xxix (1960) 400–1.

[95] Cf. the references to packed assemblies Thuc. vi 13.1, Xen. *Hell.* i 7.8 (but Diod Sic. xiii 101.6 does not imply the same degree of organisation), Dem. xviii 143; also Thuc. viii 66.1, Lys. xii. 44, 75–6. Dem. xxii 38 refers to the men who 'together with him [i.e. Androtion] had the council-house in their hands' in ?356/5.

[96] E.g. Isoc. viii 75, 124–8, xv 230–6, 306–9, Theopompus *ap.* schol. Ar. *Pax* 681, *Ath. Pol.* 28.

[97] *New Pol.* 87–198, esp. 117–18.

[98] Plut. *Per.* 7.5, *Praec. Ger. Reip.* 800c, *Nic.* 5 (but contr. *Nic.* 7.7, *Praec. Ger. Reip.* 799d). For Pericles see also Plut. *Alc.* 7.3; Lycurgus is said by [Plut.] *X Orat.* 841c always to have been occupied with public business. But what is attributed to Themistocles is ambition and the abandonment of a dissolute life: Plut. *Them.* 3.4, *Reg. Imp. Ap.* 184f–185a, *Praec. Ger. Reip.* 800b.

[99] Plut. *Praec. Ger. Reip.* 806f–807b.

[100] Ar. *Eq.* 732, 1340–4, cf. (Pericles) Thuc. ii 43.2.

[101] *Ath. Pol.* 27.3–4, Plut. *Per.* 9.2–3.

[102] Plut. *Per.* 12–14.

who dares to use violence needs many allies but one who is able to persuade needs none.[103]

For Davies, power exercised through wealth was supplanted by power exercised through skill – skill in making speeches to the assembly and other bodies, and skill in coping with the increasing complexity of Athenian administration:[104] while Cimon put his wealth to political use, Pericles was uninterested in his estate, sold all his produce together, and bought in the market for his own needs;[105] while Nicias was a great performer of liturgies,[106] Cleon is not known to have performed any liturgies, but he is described by Thucydides as 'by far the greatest persuader of the *dēmos* at that time',[107] and seems to have been the first to adopt a new style of oratory, extravagant both in manner and in content;[108] in the fourth century elective financial offices were devised for men of administrative ability, the control of the theoric fund in its original form as held by Eubulus, and later when that office had been weakened the post 'in charge of administration' held by Lycurgus;[109] men from poor backgrounds, such as Demades, began to make a name for themselves in politics.[110]

The deliberate appeal to the *dēmos* as such, which Connor places at the centre of his picture, is amply attested for the late fifth century, but it was, I think, a passing phase. I believe that the democracy of which fifth-century Athenians were proudly conscious did not come into existence accidentally, as a by-product of factional manoeuvring or foreign policies, but was brought to completion in the middle of the fifth century by men who seriously believed that the state ought to be run on democratic lines.[111] The appeal to the *dēmos*, by Pericles and by Cleon in their different styles, reflects this attitude; without it I doubt if the Old Oligarch would have described the Athenian democracy as rule by the lower classes in their own interests.[112] In the fourth century this *motif* disappears: after two experiences of oligarchy based not on patronage but on violence, every one accepted democracy, but we no longer find the old enthusiasm for it; Isocrates and others talked of the Good Old Days, Plato and Aristotle pointed

---

[103] Xen. *Mem.* i 2.11.
[104] *Wealth* 114–15.
[105] Plut. *Per.* 16.3–4.
[106] Plut. *Nic.* 3–4.1.
[107] Thuc. iii 36.6 cf. iv 21.3.
[108] *Ath. Pol.* 28.3 with Rhodes, *Comm.* 352–4; cf. Eupolis fr. 207 Kock on Syracosius.
[109] Rhodes, *Boule* 105–8, 235–40, *CJ* lxxv (1979/80) 312–14.
[110] *Wealth* 117.
[111] Cf. Rhodes, *CAH* v² (1992), 67–77.
[112] [Xen.] *Ath. Pol.*, esp. 1.1–9.

out the weaknesses of democracy, Demosthenes' opponents accused him of being undemocratic while he accused them of being unpatriotic;[113] but no one found it necessary to parade his devotion to the *dēmos* as Pericles and Cleon had done.

The importance of oratory is undeniable. The sophists taught the arts of argument and rhetoric as those which were needed for political success (Plato's Gorgias defines rhetoric as 'the art of using words to persuade jurors in a lawcourt and councillors in a council-chamber and members in an assembly, and in every other meeting which is of a political nature'[114]); and the Athenians became connoisseurs of political speeches (Thucydides' Cleon describes them as 'spectators of words, hearers of deeds, judging the possibility of future acts from those who make good speeches to recommend them, and past acts from those who appraise them well, not regarding facts they have seen for themselves as more reliable than facts they have merely heard of'[115]). Presentation may have counted for too much and substance for too little, but the Athenian citizen is more likely than the modern MP to have gone to a meeting intending to make up his mind as a result of the debate. Pericles left no written works,[116] but he is said to have been the first man to write out a lawcourt speech in advance;[117] and we have ample evidence of the importance of oratory, in the assembly and in the lawcourts, for the century after his death. The word *rhētōr* ['speaker'], indeed, comes almost to mean 'politician'.

The sophists also introduced theoretical discussion of various political topics: whether states ought to be ruled by one man, a select few or the many; whether one needs particular skills to know what is best for one's state (discussed, for instance, in Plato's *Protagoras*;[118] Book iii of Xenophon's *Memorabilia* begins with five chapters on what is required of good military officers followed by two on what is required of good politicians). This, I think, is the origin of the idea of the politician and the soldier as specialists, like the doctor and the cobbler. The administration of the Delian League required a grasp of detail, which must have been possessed by the political leaders who interested themselves in the subject but can hardly have been

[113] Cf. Rhodes, *LCM* iii (1978) 208–9.
[114] Plat. *Gorg.* 452e1–4.
[115] Thuc. iii 38.4.
[116] Plut. *Per.* 8.7.
[117] Suid. 'Perikles' (Π 1180). On Pericles as a persuasive speaker see Eupolis *fr.* 94 Kock.
[118] Plat. *Prot.* 318e5–320c1, 322c1–328d2, cf. Thuc. vi 39.1 (Athenagoras), [Xen.] *Ath. Pol.* 1.6–7, Arist. *Pol.* iii 1281a39–b15.

possessed by every citizen who attended the assembly to vote on the subject;[119] but there is no evidence that in the fifth century the Athenians departed from the principle that civilian jobs could be done by any public-spirited citizen. When Pericles and Nicias avoid dinner parties to concentrate on affairs of state,[120] they are cultivating their reputation as full-time politicians, but they are not claiming the possession of any special expertise.[121] It is only when we come to the middle of the fourth century, to such works as Demosthenes' speech *On the Symmories* and Xenophon's *Revenues*, to such administrators as Eubulus and Lycurgus, that we find men displaying financial expertise (we know hardly anything about the *poristai*, providers [i.e. of revenue], of the late fifth century,[122] but there is no reason to suppose that they were of a different nature from other fifth-century officials). Expertise of another kind is to be found in Aeschines, who held various secretarial posts[123] (and learned the art of public speaking as an actor[124]) before he entered politics, and the statement that Lycurgus employed the services of an Olynthian who was 'most capable with regard to decrees'[125] is so strange that I am prepared to believe it.

Apart from the appearance of experts, there is a change in the kind of man who rises to the top in politics: no longer usually the well-born,[126] after a while no longer necessarily the rich; and with a premium on rhetorical skill we find in Demosthenes and Hyperides an anticipation of what was to become common in the late Roman Republic, the man who comes to politics from writing speeches for the lawcourts. Davies shows, interestingly, that the new-style politicians were not always from rich families, did not make political marriages, and failed to transmit their skill and their political standing to their sons and grandsons, but the specialist generals of the

[119] This need for administrative skill is stressed by A. Andrewes, *Phoenix* xvi (1962) 83–4, S. Hornblower, *The Greek world, 479–323 B.C.* (London 1983), 123–6 [revised 3rd ed. (2002), 145–8]; but W. E. Thompson, *Classical contributions ... M. F. McGregor* (n. 40) 153–9, argues that a political leader needed charisma more than skill. Finley, *Politics* 77–82, writes in terms of a division of labour among the 'expert-lieutenants' of the leading politicians.

[120] Cf. p. 198 with n. 98, above.

[121] According to Plut. *Nic.* 6.2 Nicias attributed his successes not to his ability but to fortune. Thuc. viii 68.1 writes of Antiphon that he avoided public appearances, was suspected by the masses because of his reputation for *deinotēs* ('cleverness', still not expertise), and was a powerful supporter of contestants in the lawcourts and the assembly.

[122] See Rhodes, *Comm.* 356, citing Ant. vi 49, Ar. *Ran.* 1505.

[123] Dem. xix 200, 237, 249, xviii 261, 265.

[124] Dem. xix 200, 246, 337, xviii 129, 180, 265.

[125] [Plut.] *X Orat.* 842c.

[126] Cf. *Ath. Pol.* 28.1.

fourth century were still from rich families and did still tend to belong to or to found dynasties.[127]

Those who could afford to do so continued to use their wealth in ways that would advertise their public-spiritedness and win them supporters: with Demosthenes' contrast of himself with Midias and Aeschines,[128] with Lycurgus' attack on Leocrates,[129] we are in the same atmosphere as with the speeches of Antiphon and Lysias; the allusions to the supporters hired by Chares and Midias[130] suggest that little has changed; the conspicuous upstart[131] Demades is found not only as choregus[132] and trierarch but even as a chariot-racer[133] (which I think is a piece of social ostentation, not a political investiment[134]). But a politician who, like Aeschines or Demades, is worth substantial bribes and so can enrich himself by his political activity has already become a man of influence and importance.

How could a man rise to that level? How, particularly, could a man with no inherited advantages, with no family distinction to give him a start, with no money to build up a *clientela* or advertise himself as a public-spirited citizen?

Athens, unlike Rome, did not have a political career structure with many men at the lower levels and some of them climbing to the top. There were many offices which a man might hold; archons, even in the fifth and fourth centuries, were more important than inspectors of weights and measures, and they had the advantage that their term of office was followed by life membership of the Areopagus; but the archonships and most other civilian offices were filled by lot and could be held only for one year in a man's life; most could not be ranked in any order of importance; and for nearly all one became eligible at the age of thirty. Life might be short, and an ambitious man would not want to wait until he was thirty to start attracting public attention: Xenophon in the *Memorabilia* writes of Glaucon attempting to be a public speaker (*dēmēgorein*) and eager to become a politi-

---

[127] *Wealth* 117–30. Humphreys, *CJ* lxxiii (1977/8) 99–100 = *Family* 24–6 [= pp. 277–30, below], discusses the circumstances in which marriage could be politically significant in Athens. Private wealth was an advantage to fourth-century generals because they might have to dip into their own pockets when public provision for their campaigns was inadequate.

[128] Cf. p. 194 with n. 60, above.

[129] Cf. p. 195 with n. 65, above.

[130] Cf. pp. 196–7 with nn. 83–4, above.

[131] *Pace* E. Badian, *JHS* lxxxi (1961) 34 n. 134.

[132] He was particularly ostentatious as choregus: Plut. *Phoc.* 30.5–6.

[133] Davies, *A.P.F* 100–1.

[134] Cf. pp. 194–5 above.

cal leader when he was not yet twenty.[135] What could he do? The answer given by Socrates is that he needs to acquire knowledge – of Athens' revenue and expenditure, her own and her enemies' strength, the defence of the country, the corn supply.[136]

Other answers can be given too. He could attach himself to some one already active in politics, to learn from him and to be supported by his supporters (this is not invalidated by the fact that Plutarch's examples begin with the chronologically unlikely attachment of Aristides to Cleisthenes).[137] Such a course was easier for those who already had connections, but possible for all: Aeschines seems to have entered politics as a supporter of Aristophon.[138] From the age of twenty (probably)[139] he could attend the assembly, vote and even try to make speeches (though the oldest citizens were invited to speak first, in theory if not in classical fact[140]). A rich man could learn rhetoric from a professional teacher, but a poor man might discover a natural gift for speaking, in his deme assembly and then in the city assembly: we have noticed Aeschines' career as an actor;[141] and Demades was an extempore speaker[142] who left no written works.[143] He could attend the lawcourts, as a spectator, and indeed as a witness, speaker or even litigant (though he could not serve as a magistrate or on a jury until he was thirty[144]). A man who was rich and whose father had died (so that he was in control of his own property) could perform liturgies: we first encounter Pericles at the age of about twenty-two,[145] as choregus for Aeschylus when the *Persae* was produced.[146] Apollodorus, son of the former slave Pasion, spent large sums on an extravagant style of life and on liturgies.[147] Once the age of thirty was reached, a man could start holding the various civilian offices which were filled by lot, and a man without other advantages might be particularly likely to do this: Aeschines,

[135] Xen. *Mem.* iii 6.1.
[136] Xen. *Mem.* iii 6.2–18.
[137] Plut. *An Seni* 790e–791a *Praec. Ger. Reip.* 805e–f (cf. *An Seni* 795c–d), also *Arist.* 2.1.
[138] Dem. xix 291, xviii 162. Similarly Polyaenus became known as a friend of Sostratus: Lys. ix 13–14.
[139] Rhodes, *Boule* 173, from Xen. *Mem.* iii 6.1.
[140] Rhodes, *Boule* 37–8, citing Aeschin. i 23, iii 2, Plut. *An Seni* 784c–d. Lys. xvi 20 replies to those who disapprove of young speakers. F. Bourriot, *Hist.* xxxi (1982) 417 with n. 63, suggests that only an exceptional man would propose a decree before he was thirty.
[141] Cf. p. 201 with n. 124, above.
[142] Plut. *Dem.* 8.7, 10.1.
[143] Cic. *Brut.* 36, Quint. ii 17.13, xii 10.49.
[144] Magistrates: Rhodes, *Comm.* 510; jurors: *Ath. Pol.* 63.3, oath *ap.* Dem. xxiv 151.
[145] Davies, *A.P.F.* 457.
[146] *IG* ii² 2318. 9–11.
[147] Davies, *A.P.F.* 440–2.

we have noticed, held various secretarial posts;[148] Eubulus, we
happen to know from an inscription, was one of the nine archons in
370/69.[149]

Further opportunities were provided by the army: Aeschines had
a good military record.[150] Training was available for young men
of eighteen and nineteen until the mid 330s, and was then made
compulsory.[151] Otherwise Spartan training is regularly contrasted
with Athenian lack of it,[152] but it is hard to believe that Athenian
soldiers never joined their regiments except to confront the enemy:
Andrewes has suggested that the Athenian army drilled not as a
whole but in small units, perhaps trittys-based.[153] Though in the
fourth century there was tendency for the generalship to become a
separate profession,[154] a military reputation was an important part
of the reputation of a leading citizen, and inspiring confidence as a
military officer was one more way in which a man could gain the
support of the citizens as a whole, and particularly those of his own
tribe.

Military offices were filled by election, re-election was possible
without limit, and there was a hierarchy of offices.[155] The young
ephēboi, at any rate after the mid 330s, had their own officers).[156]
It has normally been assumed that for the regular offices, as for the
civilian posts, one had to be over thirty.[157] The only career which has

[148] Cf. p. 201 with n. 123, above.
[149] *SEG* xix 133, 4.
[150] Aeschin. ii 167–9.
[151] Cf. p. 191 with nn. 33–4, above.
[152] Thuc. ii 39.1, 4 (Pericles), Xen. *Mem.* iii 5.15, 12.5.
[153] *The Greeks* (London 1967), 150: cf. Xen. *Lak. Pol.* 11.7, Plut. *Pel.* 23.4; see also P. J.
Bicknell (n. 4) 21 with n. 67, Siewert, *Trittyen*, 141–5.
   R. T. Ridley, *AC* xlviii (1979) 508–48, esp. 530–47, looks for evidence that Athenian
hoplites trained; W. K. Pritchett, *The Greek state at war* ii (Berkeley and Los Angeles 1974)
208–31, studies military training and on p. 217 concludes that there was no compulsory training for Athenian hoplites. E. L. Wheeler in *GRBS* xxiii (1982) 223–33 follows Pritchett on the
lack of training at Athens (esp. 229–30 with n. 37) and argues that pyrrhic dances were of little
relevance to military training, and in *Chiron* xiii (1983) 1–20 discusses *hoplomachoi* [experts
in hoplite-fighting] as 'military sophists' in the late fifth and early fourth centuries and argues
that they originated in Arcadia (cf. Hermippus fr. 83 Wehrli and Ephorus *FGrH* 70 F 54, *ap.*
Athen. iv 154d–e). Plat. *Lach.* 178a–184c and the other texts cited by Wheeler indicate that
experts in hoplite-fighting existed but were not highly thought of; Arist. *Pol.* viii 1338b24–9
says that once only the Spartans trained but now all do; there must have been some training
for the contest in *euandria* ['manliness'] at the Panathenaea, a competition in military prowess
between tribal teams (*Ath. Pol.* 60.3 with Rhodes, *Comm.* 676). [See also G. L. Cawkwell,
*CQ*² xxii (1972) 262 n. 4. The cavalry trained: Xen. *Hipparch.* i 3–7, 13.]
[154] Cf. Isoc. viii 54–5, Plut. *Phoc.* 7.5–6.
[155] *Ath. Pol.* 43.1, 61, 62.3; for the hierarchy cf. Ar. *An.* 798–800.
[156] F. W. Mitchel, *TAPA* xcii (1961) 347–57: e.g. *Hesperia* ix no. 8 = O. W. Reinmuth, *The
Ephebic inscriptions of the fourth century* B.C. (*Mnem.* Supp. xiv [1971]), no. 9, i 20–31.
[157] E.g. C. Hignett, *History of the Athenian constitution* (Oxford 1952), 224. It is doubted
by Pritchett, *The Greek state at war* ii (n. 153) 63 n. 17.

been seen as an obstacle is that of Iphicrates: an entry in Harpocration, derived from the *Atthides* [histories of Athens], uses the verb *strategein* [to be a *strategos*, 'general'] of him in 391/0,[158] when according to other sources he was little over twenty;[159] but the troops he was commanding were mercenaries, so he may not have been an Athenian general then. It is implied in the oligarchic constitution of summer 411 in *Ath. Pol.* that the age requirement does not exist for generals (but that could be a matter of careless drafting or summarising);[160] the requirement does exist for all military officers in the 'future' constitution in chapter 30.[161] In the present state of our evidence I am prepared to keep to the normal assumption for generals; but I am not so sure that it is correct for the other offices. The officers had to be men who could be trusted as commanders, as the Athenians recognised in their method of appointment. In Xenophon's *Memorabilia* Nicomachides is disappointed when he is not elected general after serving as *lochagos* [commander of a *lochos*, squadron] and taxiarch but an inexperienced man is elected:[162] I should like to think that normally experience was rewarded, and that if a man was elected general when barely thirty it was because he had already been able to prove himself in one or more of the lower offices. Phocion was entrusted by Chabrias with the command of the fleet's left wing at Naxos in 376, when he was twenty-six,[163] and it appears in Menander's *Samia* that Moschion had been phylarch [commander of a tribal regiment] while still young.[164]

We might expect a political career to be more difficult for a man without inherited wealth and connections,[165] and the attainment of a position of importance therefore to come rather later in life: on the whole the evidence for the politicians of the Demosthenic period confirms this. Of men from a rich background Aristophon, born in the 430's, earned *ateleia* [immunity from obligations] by his conduct in 404/3,[166] and was responsible for the re-enactment of Pericles' citizenship law in the following year;[167] Androtion born about 410,

---

[158] Harpocration, ξενικὸν ἐν Κορίνθῳ (Androtion *FGrH* 324 F 48, Philochorus *FGrH* 328 F 150).

[159] Just. vi 5.2, Oros. iii 1.21.

[160] *Ath. Pol.* 31.2 (31.3 on other officers is too brief to justify conclusions).

[161] *Ath. Pol.* 30.2.

[162] Xen. *Mem.* iii 4.1.

[163] Plut. *Phoc.* 6.5 with 24.5.

[164] Men. *Sam.* 15. According to l.13 he had been a choregus while his adoptive father was still alive: had he volunteered with his father's support?

[165] Dem. xviii 257–62 contrasts his own respectable with Aeschines' disreputable upbringing and career.

[166] Dem. xx 148.

[167] Carystius fr. 11 Müller *ap.* Athen. xiii 577b–c.

had a political career of thirty years or more behind him in the mid 350s;[168] Phocion born in 402/1, was given a subordinate command at the age of twenty-six,[169] and when he died at the age of eighty-three had been general forty-three times;[170] Hyperides, born in 390/89,[171] prosecuted Aristophon in 362;[172] Demosthenes, born in 384,[173] was active in politics from about 354; but Lycurgus, born about 390, is not heard of until 343.[174] Contrast with these some men from humbler backgrounds: Eubulus, born not later than 400 and one of the nine archons in 370/69,[175] is not heard of in politics until the mid 350s. Aeschines, born in the 390s,[176] likewise entered politics about the mid 350s. Demades and his son Demeas present an effective contrast: the upstart father was born about 390,[177] as one of the guarantors of the ships which Athens lent to Chalcis in 341/0[178] he must have become rich by then, but otherwise we know nothing of his public career until 338; the son, born perhaps in the 350s, was the author of a decree of the assembly[179] and was prosecuted by Hyperides[180] before 321.

More work is needed, but I hope that in this paper I have shed some light on political activity in classical Athenes.

---

[168] Dem xxii 66, xxiv 173.

[169] Cf. p. 205 with n. 163, above.

[170] Plut. *Phoc.* 8.2.

[171] This is the correct inference from the fact that he was a *diaitētēs* [arbitrator; duty imposed on fifty-nine-year-olds] in 330/29 (*IG* ii² 1924 11), *pace* Davies, *A.P.F.* 518.

[172] Schol. Aeschin i 64, Hyp. iv 28.

[173] Davies, *A.P.F.* 123–6, Rhodes, *Comm.* 497–8.

[174] Davies, *A.P.F.* 350–1; first appearance [Plut.] *X Orat.* 841e cf. some manuscripts of Dem. ix 72.

[175] Cf. p. 204 with n. 149, above.

[176] C. 398 D. M. Lewis, *CR²* viii (1958) 108; but E. M. Harris, *CP* lxxxiii (1988) 211–14, argues for the date which used to be accepted, *c*.390.

[177] His and his son's birth dates: Davies, *A.P.F.* 100.

[178] *IG* ii² 1623 188–9.

[179] *Hesperia* xiii no. 5 (non-probouleumetic, *pace* Davies, *A.P.F.* 101).

[180] Hyp. frs. 87–91, 92–3, Kenyon = 26B, 33B Burtt.

8 *Competitive Festivals and the Polis: A Context for Dramatic Festivals at Athens**

ROBIN OSBORNE

At festivals throughout the year Athenians repeatedly competed and observed competitions. This paper surveys the Athenian competitive year and its development, and attempts to assess the place of competition in the Athenian political order. It suggests that the critical relationship of drama to the city may be engendered by its competitive context as well as by a peculiarly Dionysiac alterity.

The year started, in Hekatombaion, with the Panathenaia. In every fourth year this was the big contest, with competitions in *mousikē* [poetry/music] and athletics both for individuals and for teams drawn from the ten Kleisthenic tribes. The prizes were not simply the Panathenaic amphorae of wine and oil with which we are so familiar, but also sums of cash of up to 600 dr., and gold crowns to the value of 1000 dr. for the winners in certain events. This was a serious competition on which the city spent, in the early fourth century, well over a talent in prizes; contrary to the claim often made that in Greek athletic and other competitions, apart from chariot races, it was only being first that counted, here there were prizes for those second, third, fourth and fifth in certain events, and regularly prizes for the runner-up.[1]

In the same month as the Panathenaia, and apparently in the same

* Originally published in A. H. Sommerstein *et al.* (edd.), *Tragedy, Comedy and the Polis* ('Le Rane', xi. Bari: Levante, 1993), 21–38; reprinted with the permission of the author and of Levante Editore.

[1] The best evidence on the Greater Panathenaia derives from *IG* ii² 2311, which dates from the early fourth century and from which the figures for prize money are derived. See Johnston 1987. Note also [Aristotle] *Ath. Pol.* 60, [Andokides] 4.42, and on all festivals with an athletic element, Kyle 1987. For competitions at the lesser Panathenaia see Lysias 21.2,4, [Xenophon] *Ath. Pol.* 3.4, and J. K. Davies 1967: 37. Note that there are already prizes for all in the funeral games for Patroklos in the *Iliad*.

year of each Olympiad (the third), the Herakleia were celebrated at Marathon. Already by the time of Pindar these games had both men's and boys' divisions, and the prizes included silver phialai [bowls].[2]

In the following month Eleusis was the focus of competitive attention. Games were held in the second and fourth years of each Olympiad, and in the late fourth century those in charge allowed 70 medimnoi [measures, equivalent to about 52.5 litres or 1½ bushels] of grain (*sitos*) for the trieteric [every two years: three by inclusive counting] festival, and for the penteteric [every four years: five by inclusive counting] 70 medimnoi were specially allocated for prizes for the horse race, and an uncertain figure, which must be at least 260 medimnoi, for the rest of the competition. The same contests are listed for both trieteric and penteteric celebrations: athletics (*gumnikos*), *mousikē*, and horse racing, along with 'the ancestral' contest.[3]

Two months later came a competition of a different sort: the race at the Oskhophoria during the month of Pyanepsion. Twenty ephebes [eighteen- and nineteen-year-olds, undergoing a period of training], two individuals or a pair from each tribe, raced from the temple of Dionysos to Phaleron, and the winner drank the 'fivefold cup' of oil, wine, honey, cheese and flour. Victory in this race was evidently so worth celebrating that one victor commissioned an epinician [victory] ode from Pindar to mark his success – something surely quite remarkable in a competition limited to ephebes.[4] Games seem to have been added to the Theseia in the same month to celebrate Kimon's bringing back the bones of the hero from Skyros in the 470s. The festival is mentioned by Aristophanes, but the only details we have come from the second century, when there was a torch race, equestrian events, and an athletic contest, and when at least some of the events saw competition in tribes.[5] If we can believe the rather confused statement of Proclus (*Commentary on Plato Timaios* 21b) there was also a competition at the Apatouria: 'The

----

[2] For the Herakleia see *IG* i[3] 3, [Aristotle] *Ath. Pol.* 54.7 (with Rhodes 1981 ad loc.), and Pindar *Olympian* 9.88–90 with Scholia (134d Drachmann). The ascription of the Herakleia at Marathon to Hekatombaion depends on the assumption that it is these Herakleia that are at issue in Demosthenes 19.125. See also Vanderpool 1942.

[3] [Aristotle] *Ath. Pol.* 54.7 (and Rhodes 1981 ad loc.). On trieteric and penteteric celebrations of the Eleusinia see *IG* ii[2] 1672 and Clinton 1979: 9–12. Clinton shows that *IG* i[2] 5 (*IG* i[3] 5) does not refer to the Eleusinia.

[4] Our evidence derives mainly from Proclus, *Chrestomathia* 91–2. For Pindaric celebration see Rutherford and Irvine 1988 on *P. Oxy.* 2451 B fr. 17 (Pindar fr. 6c Snell/Maehler). Note also Vidal-Naquet 1981: 156 and n. 31.

[5] Modern scholars derive the institution of the games from Plutarch *Kimon* 8.6 and *Theseus* 36.4: see Deubner 1932: 225. For the second century see *IG* ii[2] 956.65. Pélékidis 1962: 229 ff.

third day of the Apatouria is called Koureotis. On this day they inscribed the kouroi [young males] who were three and four years old into the phrateres [members of the phratry, i.e. 'brotherhood', an actual or imagined kinship group]. On this day also the more skilful of the boys sing certain poems, and those who have the better memory beat the rest. For they sang rhapsodically the poems of the ancients.'

At some stage during the winter there were the games associated with the public burial of the dead. According to Diodoros the *agōn* [contest] at the public burial was introduced in 479 B.C. (Diodoros 11.33.3), and the fact that the festival was administered by the Polemarkh [one of the nine archons] and closely associated with the sacrifice to Artemis Agrotera marking the anniversary of the battle of Marathon and with the commemoration of Harmodios and Aristogeiton might be held to support this date. Three bronze vessels inscribed 'Athenians: prizes [[in the games]] over those who died in the war' have been found, one at Marathon, one at Ambelokepoi, and one at Karabournaki outside Thessaloniki, and on grounds of script all can be ascribed to the fifth century, two to not long after the Persian Wars. By the second century one of the main features of the games was an armed display by ephebes and a race in arms from the polyandreion ['place of many men', the cemetery for state burials].[6]

The first four months of the second half of the year, Poseideon, Gamelion, Anthesterion and Elaphebolion, saw the festival calendar dominated by competitions in cultural rather than physical prowess as the Athenians celebrated the Rural Dionysia, the Lenaia, the Anthesteria and the City Dionysia.[7] The competition at the Rural Dionysia may have extended beyond drama, and the competition at the Anthesteria certainly did. The comedy of the *agōnes khytrinoi* ['contests of the pitchers'] of the third day of the festival, and the possible dithyrambic performances, were just two competitions among many: not only was the festival kicked off by the drinking competition of the Khoes ['pitchers'] on its second day, memorably celebrated by Aristophanes in the *Akharnians*, but, to judge by the iconography of the miniature khoes, there was a wide variety of other competitions, particularly athletic.[8] In this festival dramatic

[6] [Aristotle] *Ath. Pol.* 58.1 with Rhodes 1981 ad loc.; Stupperich 1977: I. 54–6, II.41 n. 5; *IG* ii² 1006. 22.
   [7] It is possible that there was also a literary competition at the Diasia in Anthesterion: [Lucian] *Kharidemos* 1.
   [8] [Plutarch] *Lives of the Ten Orators* 841f; Pickard-Cambridge 1968/1988: 16–17; Hoorn 1951.

competitions were just one among many forms of competitive entertainment for the Athenians.

Further athletic and further poetic competition came in the
eleventh month of the Athenian year with the mounted torch race at
the Bendideia and the dithyrambic competition at the Thargelia, in
which the tribes competed in pairs and with both men's and boys'
divisions. At the Bendideia the torch race seems to have been a relay
race, but we have no indication of how the teams were made up. A
mounted torch race was evidently a novelty in the late fifth century.[9]

In addition to those festivals which we can place in a particular
month of the year there were also a number of competitive festivals
which we cannot date. Both the Prometheia and the Hephaisteia
featured torch races organised by tribe, and there was also a torch
race for Pan about which we know nothing.[10] Regulations made in
332/1 B.C. and enacted from 329/8 B.C. established extensive agonistic events at the Amphiareia – athletics, equestrian events – perhaps
on both annual and penteteric basis. There is some evidence suggesting that there had been agonistic events at the Amphiaraion even
when the sanctuary was not in Athenian control earlier in the fourth
century, and it is possible that a competitive Amphiareia was of some
antiquity.[11] Second-century evidence indicates a festival for Aias on
Salamis with competitive athletics, a torch race, a boat race, and a
long distance race. Deubner suggested that this festival may have
been established in the wake of the battle of Salamis in which Aias
and Telamon gave aid to the Athenians.[12] On the cultural side there
seems to have been a festival to the Muses, presumably competitive,
held in schools![13]

Numerous local festivals also included competitive elements.
Information is in short supply, but from a local commemoration and
from Pausanias we know of a festival of Artemis at Amarousia
at Athmonon with an *agōn*, and ancient lexica and local com-

[9] Plato *Rep.* 328 a, *IG* i³ 136 for Bendis; *IG* ii² 1138, Antiphon 6.11–13 for Thargelia competitions; Pickard-Cambridge 1968/1988.
[10] Tribal events at the Prometheia and Hephaisteia: *IG* ii² 1138.10–11, [Xenophon] *Ath. Pol.* 3.4. Torch race: Harpokration *s.v. Lampas.* Herodotos 8.98.2 attests to the Hephaisteia, and *IG* i³ 82 indicates its fifth-century expansion. Torch race for Pan: Herodotos 8.98.2. There were competitive events at the Hermaia too (Plato *Lysis* 206d, Aiskhines 1.10, *IG* ii² 1227.7) but I know no evidence for the torch race at the Hermaia alleged by How and Wells 1912 on Herodotos 8.98.2.
[11] *SIG*³ 287, 298; cf. 973 and *IG* ii² 338, Petrakos 1968: 194–8. Walbank 1982 published a new inscription which he suggested related to the Amphiaraia, but Humphreys 1985 suggests that it relates to the Epitaphia.
[12] *IG* ii² 1227. 32 of 131 B.C., 1011. 16f., 53ff., of 106 B.C. for the festival; Herodotos 8.64 for the Heroes' rôle at Salamis; Deubner 1932: 228.
[13] Aiskhines 1.10, Theophrastos *Characters* 22.6.

memorations combine to indicate a festival of the Tetrakomoi at its Herakleion, featuring competitive athletic events and either a competitive or a celebratory song and dance routine.[14] These festivals were in addition to the very considerable local investment of energy and resources in the Rural Dionysia.[15]

Two features of this activity need to be noted: the quantity, and the date of inception. Competitive elements appear in about half the festivals about which we have sufficient knowledge for them to merit an entry in Deubner's *Attische Feste*. Given the state of our evidence it may well be that other festivals too had competitions not noted in our sources. It seems fair to conclude that by the end of the fifth century, at least, competition was a basic element in the worship of the gods at Athens, and that the more grand the worship offered the more likely it was to include something competitive.

Claims about the development of competitive elements in festivals over time are bound to be, given the state of the evidence, tentative and tendentious. We rarely have secure knowledge of the date at which the competitive element was introduced to a festival, and even more rarely can we be sure that our first knowledge of a festival or of a competitive element within it indicates the inauguration of that festival or of the competition. Nevertheless the accumulated list of possible or probable dates of inauguration of agonistic elements in Athenian festivals is of some interest.

It is very likely that some competitive festivals had a long history. The drinking competition is so basic to the Anthesteria as surely to have its origins in the mists of time; the other competitive events at the Anthesteria may well be later accretions. Similarly the race at the Oskhophoria might be regarded as having its antiquity guaranteed by the nature of the prize, but the organisation of the race may well have altered over time. Some form of competition in association with the other main Dionysiac festivals, the Lenaia and Dionysia, may also be posited earlier than the sixth century, but the nature of the competition on those occasions certainly changes in the second half of the sixth century, and continues to be modified from time to time later.

Other festivals are most probably either themselves invented in historic time (after Solon) or else have agonistic elements added at a historic date. The Panathenaic competitions are pretty firmly estab-

[14] Artemis Amarousia: *IG* ii² 1203.17, Pausanias 1.31.4–5 and cf. *IG* i² 865. Tetrakomoi: Pollux 4.105, Steph. Byz. *s.v. Ekhelidai*, *IG* ii² 3103–4.
[15] Whitehead 1986a: 212–22.

lished as of sixth-century inception, and the competitions at the Eleusinia seem likely to belong to the sixth century also.[16] Given that victory monuments celebrating success in the Thargelia were dedicated at the Pythion, and given the Peisistratid interest in the sanctuary of Apollo Pythios, a Peisistratid date for the agonistic element at the Thargelia is attractive.[17] That the festival of Pan instituted after Marathon featured a torch race might be taken as showing that the torch race at the Hephaisteia and/or the Prometheia was already established by 490, but it does not give a firm date. Torch races first appear on painted pottery in the early classical period.[18]

The games at the Aianteia may have been introduced following the victory at Salamis, the games at the Epitaphia may be dated to 479 B.C., and the games at the Theseia seem reasonably reliably instituted after the return of Theseus' bones from Skyros in the 470s. Competition at the Herakleia at Marathon, open to the city as a whole and organised by thirty *athlothetai* ['prize-setters', competition organisers], three from each of the ten tribes, goes back to c.490 B.C. The race at the Bendideia is firmly an institution of the second half of the fifth century, and the games at the Amphiareia may be a fourth-century innovation. In other cases we have no knowledge – as with the Hermaia, although their close association with the kleroukhs [Athenian settlers] of Salamis might be held to be suggestive.

This chronological pattern looks interestingly skewed. The festivals where competition most plausibly goes back a long way are the various Dionysiac festivals (most certainly the Anthesteria and Oskhophoria). Of the rest, the vast majority plausibly date to the century after the rejuvenation of the Panathenaia in 566 B.C., with perhaps a particularly high frequency of competitive innovations in the fifty years after 510 (Herakleia at Marathon, Pan race, Aianteia, Epitaphia, Theseia, perhaps Hephaisteia and Prometheia). Subsequent major festivals seem to get competitions at their inception (Bendideia, Amphiareia), but the frequency of innovation seems less after say 460 B.C.

---

[16] Panathenaia: J. A. Davison 1958: 25–33, Corbett 1960: 57–8. The earliest Panathenaic amphora commemorates victory in a two horse chariot race. Scenes on pots not implausibly interpreted as showing *apobatai* [men leaping from a horse] rather than any act of war go back to the eighth century, but not necessarily in association with this particular festival: Tölle 1963: 224–5 on a late Geometric neck amphora in the Volkwang-Museum, Essen, Inv. No. 969. See also more generally C. A. Morgan 1990: 205–12.

[17] Souda *s.v. Pythion*. For Peisistratid connections with Apollo Pythios see Meiggs and Lewis 11, Thucydides 6.54.7, and D. M. Lewis' comments in *CAH* IV[2] 294–5.

[18] For torch races on vases see Webster 1972: 131–2, 200–1. For torch races generally see Kyle 1987: 190–3.

How are we to explain this pattern? Where do the dramatic competitions at the Great Dionysia fit in? Recent contributions have emphasised the fragility of the evidence generally taken to indicate that dramatic competitions at the Dionysia date to the 530s B.C.[19] Were *IG* ii² 2318 to have survived complete we would know what the Athenians later considered to be the date of the first *kōmoi* ['revels'] and the date of the first tragedies at the Dionysia. The tradition that tells of Pegasus bringing Dionysos from Eleutherai to Athens need not be directly connected with the decision of the people of Eleutherai to join the Athenians, and could almost equally plausibly be earlier or later than that event, whose date is in any case totally uncertain. The Marmor Parium (*FGrH* 239A46) gives 509/8 as the date of the first men's choruses, presumed dithyrambic, but this might have been in association with some festival other than the Dionysia. Thus it appears that none of the evidence which might be regarded as having a direct bearing on the inception of the Dionysia as a dramatic competition is strong enough on its own to establish the date. But to make a judgement on the basis of indirect evidence precisely requires inserting the Dionysia into the context of the competitive festivals.[20]

It is often argued that the origin and continuing *raison d'être* [reason for the existence] of athletic competitions lay in the desire for glory of an aristocratic society. So, recently, C. A. Morgan (1990: 208): 'It is clear that athletics, and ritualised competition of all kinds, did not form an integral part of community or state consciousness during the eighth and seventh centuries, but instead remained the preserve of the aristocracy.' There is certainly no doubt that athletic success could be turned to political advantage: Kylon tried to do so in the seventh century and in fifth century Alkibiades and Theagenes of Thasos both succeeded in doing so.[21] The decline in the numbers of monumental commemorations by individual victors in athletic events after *c.*460 B.C., which is particularly marked at Athens but seems to be a phenomenon found all over Greece, might seem to offer further support to this hypothesis.[22] Yet athletic events

---

[19] West 1989, Connor 1990.

[20] Connor's emphasis on the political context and on the liberating effects of Dionysiac ritual ignores the considerable amount that different competitive festivals have in common, just as it fails to account for the quasi-dramatic activity which vase paintings show to have gone on in mid-sixth-century Athens.

[21] Kylon: Herodotos 5.71; Alkibiades: Thucydides 6.16; Theagenes: Pausanias 6.11, Dio Chrysostom 31.95, Athenaios 412 d–e, Pouilloux 1954: 52–105.

[22] C. A. Morgan 1990: 211–12, Thomas 1981. But the amount of epigraphic evidence suggests that the argument from sculpture should not be overplayed.

continue to be included in and added to festivals after 460 B.C. Thus even if we suggest a strong correlation between the blossoming of competitive festivals in the period 560–460 B.C. and the high degree of publicity given to athletic success in those years, as marked by the corpus of Pindaric Epinicians, the commemorative dedications, and the frequency of athletic statues, we are faced with the need to explain the *continued* importance of competitive festivals during a period when such publicity was more uncommon and generally muted.

The model event from the point of view of competitive festivals as struggles for brownie points among the élite is the chariot race, the one event in which money could be made to yield victory in a pretty direct, if not entirely reliable, way, and an event with clear heroic overtones. But chariot racing was a comparatively late arrival at the Olympic festival: four-horse chariots seem first to have been involved at the end of the seventh century, and two-horse chariots only come in in the late fifth century.[23] Far from athletic competitions as a whole being modelled upon aristocratic athletic competition, the signs are that at Athens, at least, non-athletic competitive elements receive public recognition at least as early, if not earlier than athletic ones, in the basically nonathletic competitions at the various Dionysiac festivals. Pictorial evidence does suggest that some sorts of games may have been familiar to Athenians already in the eighth century B.C., but nothing indicates that these games took place in the context of a festival (as opposed to e.g. a funeral). Hard evidence for games associated with a festival is available at an earlier date for Olympia and, for boxing and dancing, Delos, than for any city, and this is surely the reverse of what would be expected were aristocratic competition for political position within the city at the heart of such heroic athletic activity at festivals, and certainly in contrast to the apparent privileging of victories in an Athenian competition in commemorative dedications from the Athenian Akropolis in the sixth century (C. A. Morgan 1990: 211).

Since, even for athletic competition, the ambition of the individual aristocrat seems an inadequate explanation for the competitive practices of the classical city, it is worth looking at the collective interest of the city as well as at the divisive interests of individuals. For most competitive events at festivals there are obvious practical equivalents to the ritualised contest. Footraces, short and long, not only encour-

---

[23] For the chariot as heroic see most recently Lissarrague 1990: 98–101. For chariots at the Olympics, C. A. Morgan 1990: 90–2. See also above n. 16.

age general physical fitness but promote excellence in an area actually crucial to effective hoplite warfare, and the hoplite race in armour does this even more directly (it seems, however to be a late development); similarly wrestling, boxing and the pankration not only encouraged a general toughness, but could be fairly directly converted into desirable qualities in the hoplite front line. The field events that had less direct relevance to warfare, the discus and javelin throwing, seem at Athens to have been promoted only as part of the all-round athletic excellence tested in the pentathlon-running, jumping, wrestling, discus and javelin throwing (Kyle 1987: 178–84). Significant also, in this context, are the events of a less purely athletic nature – the *apobatai*, who apparently jumped on and off a racing chariot, and the *pyrrichistai*, who engaged in an armed dance. Success in the contest of the *pyrrichistai* was very clearly highly valued: the fourth-century prize for the victor in each of the three categories of competition (men, youths, and boys) was an ox (*IG* ii² 2311.72–4). In the case of equestrian events too, the relation to the skills desirable in knights in war was direct – speed, skill with a javelin, and disciplined group control were the qualities tested.[24]

The practical advantage of these contests was to some extent balanced by the disadvantage that all these competitions produced *winners*. Winning can be turned to political advantage precisely since winning matters, but open competition also means that winning cannot be guaranteed. Whatever the régime, the political promotion of that, effectively arbitrary, set of individuals who win in festivals is unlikely to be welcome: races and the like may encourage certain desired civic virtues, but they may equally subvert the existing order. The story of Kimon son of Stesagoras (Herodotos 6.103) illustrates this nicely.

Democratic Athens (we simply do not know about earlier practice) minimised the dangers of competitions in two ways: prizes were given to second, third and fourth place men as well as to winners; and competition was organised in more or less arbitrary groups. At the Great Panathenaia the armed dance, the *anthippasia* [fight on horseback], the torch race, the boat race, and the contest in *euandria* ['manliness'] were all tribal events.[25] Athenians competed in these events in the same artificial units in which they fought and in which they served together as *prytaneis* [tribal contingents in the council of five hundred]. These competitions were thus not only

24 *IG* ii² 2311.53–71 and Kyle 1987: 186–90. For Sparta see Hönle 1968: 136–42.
25 *IG* ii² 2311.72–81; Xenophon *Hipparkhikos* 3.10–13; *IG* ii² 3130.

relevant to the training of current and future citizens in their encouragement of activities which would promote military competence,
they also built up an *esprit de corps* [spirit of solidarity] within, and
a rivalry between, the basic political and military building blocks
of the Athenian state. We cannot tell whether the Ionian tribes had
been used as competitive units in Athens before Kleisthenes, but it is
notable that the events that are later tribal at the Great Panathenaia
are events which seem in several cases to have no long history.

Events under the patronage of the Muses might have practical
advantages too. Dithyramb, which involved both song and dance,
promoted desirable skills of co-ordination of physical action.
Competitive dancing goes back in Athens as far as literacy, for the
earliest of all Attic inscriptions is a graffito offering a reward for the
most frisky dancing.[26] Plato in the *Laws* (815) assumes the formative
importance of the dance in discussing the promotion and restriction
of desirable and undesirable dancing, and Athenaios (628 d–f)
quotes Sokrates on those who dance best being the best in war.
Dithyramb was organised on a tribal basis in classical Athens,
although if the *Marmor Parium* is right in dating the first choruses
to 509/8 and if by choruses it means dithyramb, the use of the
Kleisthenic tribes in the competition must have been a later addition.
It is not clear whether the context in which Hipparkhos had earlier
promoted the dithyramb was festival competition or not.[27]

For a city which had decided that competition was desirable song
might also play an important role in promoting that competition.
The Homeric Hymn to Delian Apollo not only celebrates the dancing and boxing at Apollo's festival but itself vies for the praise of the
chorus of girls which it itself praises – for what sounds like a dramatic
performance (lines 147–76). This combination of evocation of competition between dancers and a sense of the song itself being in
competition is a feature plain to behold in Alkman's *Partheneia*. Such
encouragement of competitive choral activity was encouragement of
competition among the young: as more generally in the *agōgē* [train-
ing programme] at Sparta, so in festal dances everywhere the young
were educated in competition, and in competition not on an individual basis but as to how best to serve the city and its gods as a
group.[28]

In the light of all this, we might suggest that from the city's point

[26] *CEG* I 432, B. B. Powell 1988.
[27] Pickard-Cambridge 1962: 13–15; Herington 1985: 93–4.
[28] On Sparta see Finley 1975: 161–77, Hodkinson 1983, Calame 1977.

of view the decision to promote competitive festivals in general is a decision that the advantages of the competitions to the city outweigh the disadvantages. In Sparta it is relatively easy to see that the promotion of competition, especially but not solely among the young, could be undertaken safely because of the strength of the social and political constraints on converting competitive success into social dominance or political influence. In Athens such constraints were relatively weak throughout the archaic period and both before and while Athens was under tyrannical control competitive success was a destabilising factor in Athenian political life. Kleisthenic democracy certainly did not prevent competitive success being cashed out in political ways, but its diffusion of political power meant that competitive success could not be a route to official or long-lasting political control.

Whereabouts should we place the dramatic competitions in this context? Tragedy and comedy clearly shared with dithyramb the singing and dancing chorus, but unlike dithyramb they were never organised on a tribal basis. Even more than with dithyramb, however, the responsibility for a successful play or set of plays was clearly divided: author and individual actors as well as choregos [the man with financial and general responsibility for a group of performers at a festival] and his choros could reckon to take some of the credit. The city rewarded success in dithyrambic competition with a tripod, and in the fourth century, at least, victorious choregoi dedicated these tripods in expensive and very visible monuments.[29] Just what the choregoi of tragedy received is unclear, and there is little sign of any more lasting celebration of victory than a party. Plutarch (*Themistokles* 5.5) records Themistokles setting up a tablet (*pinax*) to celebrate a successful turn as tragic choregos, but no such monuments survive, and the only epigraphic records of victories occur either in the context of monuments celebrating a variety of victories in various competitions or in the official records, in the case of the Lenaia the responsibility of the *basileus* ['king', one of the nine archons]. It is worth noting that responsibility for selecting the comic choregoi was transferred from the *basileus* to the tribes, giving an aspect of tribal competition to competitive comedy. In the case of tragedy the judging of the competition, at least, was tribal, with one

---

[29] Monument of Lysikrates: *IG* ii² 3042; of Thrasyllos: *IG* ii² 3056; of Nikias: *IG* ii² 3055. See more generally Pausanias 1.20.2 and Pickard-Cambridge 1968/1988: 77–9. More monuments have recently been discovered: *Archaeological Reports* 1988–9: 9. It is notable that the monuments of Thrasyllos and Nikias were put up under oligarchy (in 319 B.C.) – clear cases of showing off among the élite?

man selected by lot from each tribe to serve as a panel and five of their written verdicts being selected by lot to decide the competition. Although, as the evidence we have from the orators shows, this could not entirely eliminate attempts to win the competition by influencing the judges, it clearly is an attempt to minimise the possibility that such manipulation could be successful.[30]

In athletic competition and even in rhapsodic competition it was the way in which one performed, by comparison with other competitors, that was measured and rewarded. In dramatic competition it was not simply the way the play was executed but what the play was that was important. We cannot tell how 'political' the contents of the earliest tragedies was, but it is clear that by the time of Phrynikhos' *Capture of Miletos* the contents of a play might be very overtly of political interest. Given the implicit political claims that lie behind the competing genealogies and myths in the lyric poets it seems highly likely that the politicisation of tragedy could have been foreseen from the beginning.[31] It is precisely on the grounds that they will offer competing 'representations' of the city that Plato in the *Laws* (817) proposes to censor tragedies before allowing them to be produced. In Athens the archon decided who should be granted choruses but we have no evidence about how he came to a decision and no reason to think that the archon's decisions were, or were even suspected to be, political. Dramatic competition at Athens must surely be seen to invite, rather than preclude, competing visions of the city.

While other festival competitions had a *potential* political effect, by offering publicity to the victor which he could turn to political account, dramatic competitions not only offered similar potential political effects, but actually and necessarily made politics one of the axes around which the competition revolved. Where the other competitions could thrust men into political prominence dramatic competition thrust issues into prominence. And just as the city's promotion of other forms of competition implies a confidence that the political effects of promoting particular individuals can be

[30] Monument recording various victories including dramatic: Poursat 1967 (David Lewis suggests to me that Amumo[nē] should be read as a play title). Official records set up by *basileus* at Lenaia: cf. *SEG* 32.239 with Pickard-Cambridge [1968/1988]: 360. Transfer of responsibility for choosing comic choregoi: [Aristotle] *Ath. Pol.* 56.3. Judging: Pickard-Cambridge 1968/1988: 95–8. Victors at the rural Dionysia did celebrate the success of their choregia: *IG* ii² 3090, 3092–100. See also Whitehead 1986b. It must be said that *IG* ii² 3091 and 3101 may commemorate victories at the City Dionysia rather than at the Rural Dionysia, but advertised in the home deme.

[31] Cf. e.g. the different names given to minor mythic figures (*PMG* 218, 308); Stesichoros and Helen (*PMG* 192–3).

controlled, so the city's promotion of dramatic competition implies a confidence that the political effects of promoting certain issues can be controlled.

All festival competitions threaten to overturn the values of the city which promotes them. The competitive drinking at the feast of the Khoes at the Anthesteria reinforced the norm of strictly regulated drinking in a group by its stress on unregulated individual drinking of large quantities in a short time. All competition encouraged individual ambition which the city normally battled to regulate and control. But as the Khoes competition was a competition in a quality, ability to take one's drink, highly valued and indeed vital to the life of the community (as the aitiological myth of Erigone which 'explained' that other Anthesteria ritual, the Aiora, stresses), so the ambitious individual was also vital to the city.[32] Ambition had to be cultivated both in order to ensure that the city was strong in the face of ambitious cities elsewhere, and in order to prevent the odd ambitious individual or group from coming to dominate civic life unchallenged. It is the recognition of the fact that the ambitious individual was both politically vital to the city and also its greatest threat that is seen clearly in the love–hate relationship which the city has with the notion of *philotimia* [love of honour].[33]

The encouragement of ambition becomes especially important at times when there is a desire to widen political access, whether because it has been previously restricted by law or because it has previously been restricted by custom. Solon's widening of access to political office in Athens had to be accompanied by the stimulation of larger numbers to civic activity. Whether or not Solon moved the Law on Stasis attributed to him, which obliges people to take sides in political disputes, it accurately identifies the crucial area of concern (Manville 1980). It is in this context that Solon's granting of civic rewards to Athenians successful in the Olympic games should perhaps be understood: bringing such people to prominence was a way of creating another route, at least in part independent of birth and wealth, to political influence, and hence another way of widening access to political power. The story of Athenian politics after Solon, for which we are all too reliant on the Aristotelian *Athenaion Politeia* (13–14), suggests that, if anything, Solon was too successful in stimulating some individuals to political ambition, and not

[32] For Erigone see Servius on Vergil *Georgics* 2.385–9, and Hyginus *Fabulae* 130, *Poet. Astr.* 2.4.5.
[33] J. K. Davies 1978: 126–8; Whitehead 1983: 55–74.

successful enough in ensuring that political ambition was widely
enough distributed to be self-regulating (compare, perhaps, Figueira
1984: 466–9).

For all the determination of some modern scholars to put
Peisistratos' name to the reform of the Panathenaia in 566 B.C., there
is no good evidence for the link, and it may be better to see the reform
more as a product of the competition between rival political leaders
(including Peisistratos) for supremacy: increasing the number of
competitions and their prominence offered more people a chance to
promote themselves and their supporters, and so this was a reform
from which any, and all, might hope to gain, and from which no long
term domination should result. Such diffusion of competition, and
hence of the glory to be won by victory, was further in the interests
of a tyranny which, far from attempting to quell routine political
life at Athens, promoted it, filling the traditional magistracies with
undoubtedly ambitious men and increasing the numbers of city
officials. The interests of the tyrants were not in fact very divergent
from those of the freed city after 510. It is unsurprising that tragic
competitions should begin under the tyranny (at whatever precise
date) and dithyrambic competitions immediately after the liberation.
Herington has stressed that the birth of the tragic festival is to be
understood in the context of Peisistratid encouragement of song
culture, and wants to treat the fact that tragedy is put on in competition as simply an inevitable result of its being in the tradition of
agōnes mousikoi [contests in poetry/music]; without ignoring the
first insight we need to acknowledge that the competitive context is
more than just an accidental by-product of it.[34]

Democracy needed an ambitious demos but feared ambitious individuals – that indeed is one of the issues which competing tragedies,
and comedies, thrust into prominence. Achieving the one without the
other was assisted by reorganising old competitions, and organising
new ones, on a tribal basis, thus encouraging corporate competition
while diffusing the resulting glory, and ensuring that there were
always enough losers to prevent the discomfiture of loss being more
politically unsettling than the boost of victory was politically advan-
tageous. By 460 most of the competitions I listed at the beginning
were in existence, and even a people proud of having more festivals
than other cities might put a lower value on inventing yet more.
The turn of political events meant that there were plenty of external
stimuli to ambition (e.g. the empire) and that straightforwardly

[34] Herington 1985: 9 and chapter 4.

political means of quelling the too ambitious individual were available (compare the declining use of ostracism). But the high value put on continuing critical openness towards government meant that competitive festivals continued to have an important role in the city even in these changed circumstances. As the tale of Kleon's relations with Aristophanes may show, there were threats to openness even from the heart of democratic political debate, and the competitive festivals had an active role to play in ensuring that the city did not succumb to those threats.

There are many lenses through which the Dionysia may be viewed. Connor has recently stressed the liberation associated with Dionysos, Goldhill the subversive qualities peculiarly associated with Dionysos.[35] In this paper I have chosen to emphasise the competitive nature of the dramatic festival, an aspect of which Connor takes no and Goldhill little account, and in doing so I hope to have offered a framework for understanding the relationship of drama to the city as a whole and for understanding why it was in the second half of the sixth century that tragedy, and during the first half of the fifth century that comedy, became part of the packed calendar of Athenian competitive festivals.[36]

THE COMPETITIVE CALENDAR

Month	Competitive festival	Events	Date of first competition
Hekatombaion	Panathenaia	Athletics, *Mousike*	Major reorganisation 566
	Herakleia	Athletics	*c.*490
Metageitnion	Eleusinia	Athletics, *Mousike*	Sixth century?
Boedromion			
Pyanepsion	Oskhophoria	Race	before sixth century?
	Theseia	Athletics	*c.*470?
		Torch race	
	Apatouria	Rhapsodic singing?	
Maimakterion			
Poseideon	Rural Dionysia	Drama	?
Gamelion	Lenaia	Drama	440
Anthesterion	Anthesteria	Drinking	
		Athletics	before sixth century with
		Drama	later additions?
		Mousike	

continued on next page

[35] Connor 1990; Goldhill 1990.
[36] I am grateful to the audience at Nottingham for their comments, to David Wiles who convinced me that carnivals were irrelevant, and to Ewen Bowie, David Lewis, Robert Parker and Oliver Taplin who read and commented on an earlier draft and much improved the material base on which this paper is built.

THE COMPETITIVE CALENDAR – *continued*

Month	Competitive festival	Events	Date of first competition
Elaphebolion	City/Great Dionysia	Drama	late sixth century
		Mousike	
Mounikhion			
Thargelion	Thargelia	Dithyramb	Peisistratids?
	Bendideia	Torch race	429/8
Skirophorion	Skira	Race?	?
Uncertain	Prometheia	Torch race	*c.*500?
	Hephaisteia	Torch race	*c.*500?
	Pan	Torch race	489?
	Amphiareia	Athletics	reorganised 332/1
	Aianteia	Athletics	
		Torch race	470s?
	Epitaphia	Athletics	479?

REFERENCES

Calame, C. (1977), *Les Choeurs de jeunes filles en Grèce archaïque*, Rome: Ed. dell' Ateneo.

Clinton, K. (1979), '*IG* i² 5, the Eleusinia and the Eleusinians', *AJP* 100, 1–12.

Connor, W. R. (1990), 'City Dionysia and Athenian Democracy', in W. R. Connor *et al.*, *Aspects of Athenian Democracy* (*ClMed* Diss. 11, Copenhagen), 7–32; these papers published also in *ClMed* 40 (1989) [publ. 1993], same pagination.

Corbett, P. E. (1960), 'The Burgon and Blacas Tombs', *JHS* 80, 52–60.

Davies, J. K. (1967), 'Demosthenes on Liturgies: A Note', *JHS* 87, 33–40.

—— (1978), *Democracy and Classical Greece*, London: Fontana (2nd edn 1993).

Davison, J. A. (1958), 'Notes on the Panathenaea', *JHS* 78, 23–42.

Deubner, L. (1932), *Attische Feste*, Berlin: Keller.

Figueira, T. J. (1984), 'The 10 *Archontes* of 579/8 at Athens', *Hesperia* 53, 447–73.

Finley, M. I. (1975), *The Use and Abuse of History*, London: Chatto & Windus.

Goldhill, S. D. (1990), 'The Great Dionysia and Civic Ideology', in J. J. Winkler and F. I. Zeitlin (eds), *Nothing to Do with Dionysos?* Princeton, NJ: Princeton University Press.

Herington, C. J. (1985), *Poetry into Drama: Early Tragedy and the Greek Poetic Tradition*, Berkeley and Los Angeles, CA: University of California Press.

Hodkinson, S. (1983), 'Social Order and the Conflict of Values in Classical Sparta', *Chiron* 13, 239–81.

Hönle, A. (1968), *Olympia in der Politik der griechischen Staatenwelt (von 776 bis zum Ende des 5. Jahrhunderts)*, Tübingen dissertation.

Hoorn, G. van (1951), *Choes and Anthesteria*, Leiden: Brill.

How, W. W., and Wells, J. (1912), *A Commentary on Herodotus*, Oxford: Oxford University Press.

Humphreys, S. C. (1985), 'Lycurgus of Butadae: An Athenian Aristocrat', in J. W. Eadie and J. Ober (eds), *The Craft of the Ancient Historian: Essays in Honor of Chester G. Starr* (Lanham, MD: University Press of America), 199–252.

Johnston, A. W. (1987), '*IG* ii² 2311 and the Number of Panathenaic Amphorae', *BSA* 82, 125–30.

Kyle, D. G. (1987), *Athletics in Ancient Athens*, Leiden: Brill.

Lissarrague, F. (1990), *L'Autre Guerrier: Archers, peltastes, cavaliers dans l'imagerie attique*, Paris: La Découverte, and Rome: École Française de Rome.

Manville, P. B. (1980), 'Solon's Law of Stasis and Atimia in Archaic Athens', *TAPA* 110, 213–21.

Morgan, C. A. (1990), *Athletes and Oracles: The Transformation of Olympia and Delphi in the Eighth Century* B.C., Cambridge: Cambridge University Press.

Pélékidis, Ch. (1962), *Histoire de l' éphébie attique, des origines à 31 av. J.-C.*, Paris: De Boccard.

Petrakos, B. Ch. (1968), ὁ Ὠρωπὸς καὶ τὸ ἱερὸν τοῦ Ἀμφιαράου, Athens: Archaeological Society.

Pickard-Cambridge, A. W. (1962), *Dithyramb, Tragedy and Comedy*. 2nd edn, Oxford: Oxford University Press.

—— (1968/1988), *The Dramatic Festivals of Athens*, 2nd edn, with addenda 1988, Oxford: Oxford University Press.

Pouilloux, J. (1954), *Recherches sur l'histoire et les cultes de Thasos*, i. *De la fondation de la cité à 196 avant J.-C.* (Etudes thasiennes, 3), Paris: De Boccard.

Poursat, J.-C. (1967), 'Une Base signée du Musée National d' Athènes', *BCH* 91, 102–10.

Powell, B. B. (1988), 'The Dipylon Oinochoe and the Spread of Literacy in Eighth-Century Athens', *Kadmos* 27, 65–86.

Rhodes, P. J. (1981), *A Commentary on the Aristotelian Athenaion Politeia*, Oxford: Oxford University Press.

Rutherford, I., and Irvine, J. (1988), 'The Race at the Athenian Oskhophoria and an Oskhophorion by Pindar', *ZPE* 72, 43–51.

Stupperich, R. (1977), *Staatsbegräbnis und Privatgrabmal im klassischen Athen*, Münster dissertation.

Thomas, R. (1981), *Athletenstatuetten der Spätarchaik und des strengen Stils*, Rome: L'Erma di Bretschneider.

Tölle, R. (1963), 'Eine geometrische Amphora in Essen', *Archäologischer Anzeiger* (1963), 210–25.

Vanderpool, E. (1942), 'An Archaic Inscribed Stele from Marathon', *Hesperia* 11, 329–37.

Vidal-Naquet, P. (1981), 'The Black Hunter and the Origin of the Athenian Ephebeia', in R. L. Gordon (ed.), *Myth, Religion and Society* (Cambridge: Cambridge University Press), 147–62.

Walbank, M. (1982), 'Regulations for an Athenian Festival', in *Studies in Attic Epigraphy, History and Topography Presented to Eugene Vanderpool* (*Hesperia* Supp. 19), 173–82.

Webster, T. B. L. (1972), *Potter and Patron in Classical Athens*, London: Methuen.

West, M. L. (1989), 'The Early Chronology of Attic Tragedy', CQ^2 39, 251–4.

Whitehead, D. (1983), 'Competitive Outlay and Community Profit: *Philotimia* in Democratic Athens', *ClMed* 34, 55–74.

—— (1986a), *The Demes of Attica, 508/7 to ca. 250 B.C.*, Princeton, NJ: Princeton University Press.

—— (1986b), 'Festival Liturgies at Thorikos', *ZPE* 62, 213–20.

9 Public and Private Interests in Classical Athens[*]

S. C. HUMPHREYS

The fifth century saw a double development in the relation between public finance and private resources. On the one hand, the dependence of the state on the generosity of ambitious rich men was limited; conspicuous spending was channelled, routinised and above all overshadowed by the disbursal of state funds in the spheres once dominated by the Athenian nobility: religious festivals, public building, war. This separation of the activity of the state from the activities of its leading citizens helped to prepare the ground for the debate on the rival claims of private and public loyalties analysed in W. R. Connor's *The New Politicians of Fifth-Century Athens* (1971). On the other hand, the concentration of the decision-making process in council and assembly and the central position of war and the profits of empire in the Athenian economy meant that decisions taken in the public sphere affected the private life of Attic families as never before – especially during the Peloponnesian war, when far larger numbers became wholly dependent upon the urban economy. Hence the tensions over the introduction of Demos' private interests into assembly debates reflected in Aristophanes, Thucydides and above all Plato.

In other words, the Athenians in the fifth century discovered two of the major problems of western political theory: the relation between public and private interests, and the relation between politics and the economy. It seems worth trying to take a closer look at the institutional roots of these pervasive and entangling ideological growths.

* Originally published in *Classical Journal* lxxiii 1977/8, 97–104; republished in S. C. Humphreys, *The Family, Women and Death* (Routledge, 1983; 2nd edition University of Michigan Press, 1993), 22–32 ch. ii. Reprinted with the permission of the author and of the Classical Association of the Middle West and South.

[Additional note written by Prof. Humphreys for this book.] For sequels to this article see Humphreys, *The Family, Women and Death*, 2nd edition, pp. xi–xxii, and 'From a Grin to a Death: The Body in the Greek Discovery of Politics', in J. J. Porter (ed.), *Constructions of the Classical Body* (University of Michigan Press, 1999), 126–46.

I start with three situations which can usefully be contrasted with that of democratic Athens.

1 In Homeric Ithaca important political decisions were taken in the *oikos* [household] of Odysseus or some other *basileus* [leading man]. The struggle for the succession was carried on in Odysseus' *oikos* in the form of competition for his wife and exhaustion of his estate by persistent demands for hospitality. Telemachus' attempt to transfer the scene of action from his *oikos* to the assembly was unsuccessful. Ithaca's contribution to the war against Troy was sought by Agamemnon and Menelaus, who stayed in the *oikos* of their guest-friend Amphimedon (*Odyssey* xxiv 115–19), and tradition represented the decision as taken by Odysseus alone. In Phaeacia, Alkinoos and his fellow-*basileis* make gifts from their own stores to Odysseus (while announcing their intention to recoup their outlay later by collections from the *demos*); there is, of course, no public store-chest in the Homeric state. Only the public sacrifice which Nestor and his sons are conducting by the shore in Pylos when Telemachus arrives, for which each of the nine segments (*hedrai*) of Pylian society had contributed nine bulls, hints at the development of the finances of the state which was to come in later centuries.

2 A glance at any collection of Hellenistic inscriptions will show the dependence of the ordinary Greek city on its rich men, both for the routine expenses of city life and, more particularly, in facing any emergency. In many cities the concepts of political office and of liturgy [public duty to be performed by a man at his own expense] – which in Athens were perfectly distinct even if ostentatious performance of liturgies increased one's chances of election to office – had completely merged. In crisis years it was difficult to find anyone to stand for office. The mechanisms of the economic grip which these oligarchs had on their cities need further investigation (one suspects that many of the commodities which they gave were produced on their own estates, cf. Van Bremen, 1983), but we are clearly in a different world to that of Athens in the second half of the fifth century.

3 The subordinate segments of Athenian society, demes [local units] and phratries ['brotherhoods', actual or imagined kinship groups] though they borrowed all the forms of public procedure in the assembly, lacked its revenues and remained often under the sway of private resources and private interests. Private loyalties and, on occasion, conflicts were bound to be sharp in small patrilineally recruited groups. A rich and powerful man could successfully oppose the admission to his phratry of a boy presented by a father as his

son by a second marriage, on the grounds that the boy was of slave descent, and could subsequently have the decision reversed after he and his father had come to a private compromise (Isaeus vi).

Demosthenes lvii presents the story of a conflict between two rival deme notables one of whom, Euxitheos, is appealing against the decision of the deme taken in the term of office of the other, Euboulides, as deme representative on the council of 500 (and perhaps also as *demarchos* [principal officer of the deme]), to remove his name from the list of deme members and so deprive him of citizenship. Euxitheos himself has served as *demarchos* fairly recently and has made himself unpopular during his term of office by trying to exact arrears of rent from members of the deme who held sacred land on lease (§ 63). He and Euboulides had competed for the deme priesthood of Heracles (§ 48). Euxitheos had dedicated armour in a local shrine of Athena and had an honorary decree passed by the deme on his behalf (§ 64). His father had held office in the deme; Euboulides' father had been demarch. A hereditary family rivalry for the honours of a group of only about eighty members. Note that it was a commonplace of Athenian politics – ably deployed in § 57 ff. here – that small demes were easy to bribe and irregular in their conduct of affairs.

Compared to these three sketches of the interlocking of public and private affairs in more archaic, poorer or smaller communities, there is no doubt that Athenian democracy in the fifth century achieved quite a substantial disengagement. Nevertheless, in studying Athenian kinship I have had to ask whether Athenians manipulated ties of kinship and marriage in political contexts, and what importance the *oikos* still had as a power-base. J. K. Davies' *Athenian Propertied Families* (1971) has made it very much easier to ask such questions; but the harvest for the later part of the fifth century is meagre. Connor's attribution of a decisive hardening of the public/private boundary to Perikles seems to me to be confirmed by Perikles' repudiation of his citizen wife in order to set up what was evidently a widely known and stable relationship with a foreign woman, just in the years when his own law had made marriage with foreign women impossible. The dogmatic separation of public and private life which led to Perikles' citizenship law* (to prevent families based on international dynastic marriages from using their private relationships to manipulate foreign policy) led also, taken to extremes in Perikles'

---

* This law prescribed as qualifications for citizenship an Athenian mother as well as an Athenian father.

own private life, to a repudiation of all personal relationships to which a political significance might be attached, and therefore to the choice of metics [resident non-citizens] as his personal associates. The reverse implication of the drive to eliminate private ties from public life was freer association between citizens and metics in the private sphere; this was especially marked in the philosophical circles to which Perikles, Aspasia and Perikles' friend and adviser, Anaxagoras, belonged. (Attacks in comedy and courts showed, however, that the Athenians saw that Perikles had merely exchanged one kind of private life for another, in which the possibility of determining political decisions in extra-political contexts remained.)

Marriage and divorce have their inconveniences as modes of political manipulation. The conditions in which one would expect to find marriage playing an important part in political alliance seem to be as follows: (1) where political power rests largely on inherited patrimony and control over persons of a feudal or patrimonial type, and these can be owned or transmitted by women. This possibility was for the most part precluded in Athens by the law of inheritance and epiclerate.* (2) As a means of making alliances outside one's own state. The marriage of Agariste** is the classic example of the import-ance attached to such alliances in sixth-century Greece; Iphikrates' Thracian marriage in the 380s is an interesting fourth-century case. But in general such marriages were excluded after 451 by Perikles' citizenship law. Hereditary guest-friendship [*xenia*] had always existed as an alternative to marriage in forming foreign alliances, and persisted right through the fifth century. Archidamos of Sparta tried to play on his *xenia* with Perikles to damage the latter politically (the negative side of personal ties, as usual, comes uppermost where Perikles is concerned), while Alkibiades in Sparta exploited his family's hereditary friendship with that of the ephor Endios. Heredi-tary *xenia* was often also transformed into a relation to the whole state of the personal *xenos*, as proxeny (consulship). (3) Marriage was also a useful mechanism for public proclamations of political alliance within one's own state, as in the case of Peisistratos' marriage to the daughter of Megakles. The ordinary network of political ties between men in a small city-state scarcely ever divided itself neatly into distinct opposing groups. Everyone had connections in different camps (for Rome, see Brunt, 1965). But marriage provided a means

---

* Arrangements made for an *epikleros*, daughter of a deceased man who left no sons.
** Daughter of Kleisthenes, tyrant of Sikyon; married to the Athenian Megakles, of the Alkmaeonid family, after a competition among suitors from different places.

of making a dramatic ritual gesture of alliance which was lacking in the wholly male sphere (though Solon had restricted the display of wealth in marriage-processions, he had not placed any limits on attendance). (4) Finally, politically conditioned marriages occur when those who occupy an isolated political status marry close kin because they can find no equals to marry. The paradigmatic Athenian case is the marriage of Themistokles' children Archeptolis and Mnesiptolema (patrilateral half-siblings) after their father's disgrace. If Kimon married his half sister Elpinike he did so for the same reason. These marriages which occur when a leading political family has suffered disgrace are formally the same as the sister marriages of Ptolemaic kings (and royal families in other societies).

It is not quite clear to me whether the dynastic marriages of Kimon and Isodike and Kallias and Elpinike in the 480s should be placed in category 3 or category 4. The three families involved all seem to have been under attack at this time. Kimon and Elpinike had been brought to disgrace and financial ruin by the condemnation of their father, Miltiades, in 489. Isodike belonged to the Alkmaeonid family who were suspected of trying to betray Athens to Persia in 490; repeated attacks were made on the group and their associates (such as Perikles' father Xanthippos, married to an Alkmaeonid wife) in the 480s. (It is normally rash to deduce political affiliations from kinship, but where a concerted campaign is waged against a whole lineage, they have little choice but to act in concert.) Kallias was the victim of gossip and at least one attack, in the courts, for having acquired a great deal of wealth about the time of the battle of Marathon (490) in suspicious circumstances. The marriage of Kimon and Isodike can be seen as a dramatic political gesture only if it took place after the battle of Salamis when both families were again on the rise. Kallias' use of his wealth to save Kimon and Elpinike from debt must belong to the 480s and was at best a somewhat ambiguous gesture in the circumstances.

Inside Athens, although marriage could be used as a means of making public statements about alliance, it presupposed alliance rather than creating it. Appeals to ties of kinship through marriage had no special status distinguishing them from appeals to ties of friendship. When we find that men associated with each other as *hetairoi* ['comrades'] are also connected by marriage – as in the case of Andocides, Kallias, son of Telokles, and Eukrates, the brother of Nikias, in the affair of the Mysteries – there is no way of telling which of the two relationships came first. For political alliance inside Athens it was not necessary to penetrate into the inmost private sector of the *oikos*, the women's quarters: the companionship of gymnasium and symposium [drinking-party] was enough. It was therefore in relations with other states, which inevitably implied hospitality and used a concept of friendship which went back to the Homeric days when the *oikos* was a political centre, that personal ties acquired their greatest weight.

The procedure by which ambassadors were nominated in Athens is not well known, but it is clear that 'private' qualifications often determined their selection. Ambassadors were expected to be rich (and to supplement the official travel allowance from their own pockets in order to travel in fitting state); their political sympathy with the policy they were asked to negotiate often had to be considered; they might be chosen for their ties of hereditary proxeny or other personal links with the state to which the embassy was despatched. Xenophon (*Hellenica* VI. iii. 4ff.) has given us a brilliant parody of an ambassadorial speech at Sparta by Kallias III, *daidouchos* ['torchbearer'] of Eleusis and hereditary *proxenos* of the Spartans in Athens. The combination as ambassadors to Dionysios I of Syracuse in 393 of Konon's associate Aristophanes, Eunomos, 'friend and *xenos*' of Dionysius, and the rich Eurippides of Myrrhinous excellently illustrates the qualifications required of ambassadors – in a period when private means and private relationships were more than usually important, owing to the low state of Athens' finances. (Aristophanes' marriage, which is exceptional in being explicitly ascribed by our sources to political patronage, belongs to the same years.) The re-entry of Persia into Greek affairs also brought with it a new twist to the concept of hereditary guest-friendship, the 'token' of friendship which could be passed, presumably, from father to son. (It would not be surprising if something of this kind lay behind the choice of Hagnias of the Bouselidai as ambassador to Persia in 396 at an early age – if the identification is correct.) One of the reasons for the continued importance of personal relationships in foreign affairs was the personal style of politics in many of the states with which Athens was involved. The more patrimonial and personal power relations were in a foreign state, the greater the importance of the private resources and connections of the ambassadors sent to it.

Within Athens, personal ties could be forged in the semi-private, semi-public masculine world of the symposium and gymnasium without recourse to marriage. The culture and the traditions of the *hetaireia* [group of comrades] are more important than dynastic marriages. The cries of 'Conspirators, conspirators!' which Kleon voices in Aristophanes' *Knights* whenever he sees the chorus – typical members of the upper-class gymnasium/symposium set – were justified in 411 and 404. What made the *hetaireia* a revolutionary element in Athenian politics?

It is remarkable that Kleisthenes, who is generally credited with the creation of the institutional basis for fifth-century democracy, should also be credited with the introduction of ostracism [annual vote on whether to exile a man for ten years]. I am not concerned here to discuss whether Kleisthenes' contribution would have developed as it did if the financial resources of the Athenian state and consequently the numbers and importance of the decisions taken by council and assembly had not grown so dramatically at the time of the Persian wars. Nor am I concerned with the precise date of the introduction of ostracism. What I want to underline is that in the 480s and for the rest of the first half of the fifth century the major political issues in Athens were still very largely settled outside the assembly, without speeches, by votes mobilised, in all probability, on personal as much as ideological grounds with the help of canvassing by the supporters and enemies of the principals. The problem of sixth-century politics had been that the support built up for use in elections by political leaders had grown too powerful for the peaceful working of a system of rotation of office. Ostracism harnessed this machinery developed for winning elections to the fear of tyranny by providing for its use in anti-elections designed to rid the city of potential tyrants.

Two elements seem to be involved here: the *hetairoi* who actually canvassed for their friend and the members of the demos persuaded to vote on his side. Both were recruited through the private sphere. The links between *hetairoi* were forged in the young men's world of the gymnasium and symposium – a prepolitical world, in the sense that its members were not expected yet to take an active part in politics, yet one which had its own traditions of political opposition (the tyrannicides in Athens, Alkaios in Lesbos, Damon and Phintias in Syracuse ...). The gymnasium was a scene of play war, and its homosexual loyalties were celebrated as the basis of solidarity on the battle-field and in internal political conflicts; the symposium by the late fifth century had become a place of play oratory, where the conventions of the assembly were both practised and mocked. Whatever Kleon might say, symposia were not meetings of political parties. But the world of the symposium and gymnasium provided a network of friends whose support could be drawn on in later years, a set of values which stressed daring and loyalty, and a social milieu in which political business could be transacted outside the official contexts without attracting attention.

So much for the *hetairoi* – friends who would lend you money if you were short of liquid funds for political expenses, speak for you in courts, drum up feeling against your opponent if you were threatened with ostracism. It was a fairly egalitarian relationship. There were few opportunities for patronage in Athenian politics. The three chief archons each had two *parhedroi* [assistants], whom they appointed themselves, to accompany them (*Athenaion Politeia* 56); but the post was powerless. There were rather more openings in the military and diplomatic spheres. A naval commander selected the trierarch* whose vessel he would use as flagship, and chances of singling out individuals for favour must presumably have arisen whenever small detachments were sent off to operate independently (a study of Greek warfare from this point of view would be useful). But the frequency of collegiate commands gave the Athenian general less scope than the Roman proconsul.

In so far as patron–client relationships, or something analogous to them, existed in Attica, the 'clients' were collective rather than individual. The support of demes, phratries, *genē*, tribes,** neighbours, could be won by generous spending. In Plutarch's story of the contrast between Kimon's use of his own wealth to build political support and Perikles' use of the funds of the city and empire, there is a difference not only of quality but of range. Perikles spends the city's money for the city as a whole, whereas Kimon's gestures tend only to reach a limited group: fellow demesmen and neighbours, gymnasium-users. Although when rich men in law-courts boast of their liturgies they speak of their generosity to 'the city', the principal beneficiary in the case of the older liturgies (choregia and trierarchy as against eisphorai, proeisphorai, epidoseis, etc.***) was always a smaller group. A generous man could do a great deal for the well-being of the crew of his trireme, the poorer hoplites from his deme, a tribal team or chorus.

The presupposition of the use of private resources in politics was that the *demos* voted for people rather than policies. At its best,

---

* The man given financial responsibility for a ship, who, at any rate originally, was expected to act as its commander.
** *Genē* ('clans') and tribes were actual or imagined kinship groups.
*** Choregia was responsibility for a chorus or other group of performers at a festival; for trierarchy see above; eisphora was a tax on property, proeisphora the obligation imposed on a rich man to advance the eisphora due from a symmory (contribution group) of payers, epidosis a voluntary donation.

Athenian democracy in the second half of the fifth century was a political system in which it was more exciting to be one of the judges in a debating contest on which two orators were staking their prestige than to vote in an election or ostracism. Thucydides' reports of the Mytilenean debate and the debate in which Kleon was given the mandate to take charge of operations at Pylos show how exciting confrontations in the assembly could be. At its worst, it was a struggle over the level of public expenditure and employment in which the least scrupulous could easily get the advantage. Conditions in the Peloponnesian war increased the need for state employment in military service, since many Athenians were cut off from their land, and made it easy for Kleon to play openly on the *demos*' economic interest in assembly decisions.

The sanctions his tactics aroused were sharp. By the 420s, evidently a considerable proportion of the upper class had internalised the Periklean boundary between public and private spheres, although it had originally been directed against their own use of private resources. The long supremacy of Perikles gave him ample opportunity to develop the dignified and didactic style of political oratory which Thucydides admired. Financial affairs – and the greater part of the assembly's business had some financial aspect – were handled in a sophisticated, efficient and impersonal fashion. The hereditary ties of Kimon's family with Sparta, and the name of his eldest son, Lakedaimonios, gave plenty of opportunity for reminders that private loyalties should not be allowed to interfere with public interests. It was easy enough thereafter to turn the accusation of importing private interests into public business against Kleon, by accusing him of appealing to the (metaphorical) pockets of the *demos*. This became a stock accusation against demagogues and, in time, the basis of the oligarchic political theory that *banausoi* [low-grade workers] could not be trusted with political power.

It might be thought that the impersonality of the public sphere as experienced in the assembly and council would be contradicted by experience in the law-courts, where private interests were emphasised rather than concealed. But our sources suggest that in the later fifth century attention was concentrated on the figure of the sycophant ['fig-exposer', a man who undertook prosecutions for the sake of the rewards offered to successful prosecutors] as scapegoat for the sufferings of the rich and prominent in the courts. Prosecutions undertaken for purely financial motives were much more feared than prosecutions undertaken for political motives; and the typical victim of the sycophant was thought to be the rich quietist or ally rather

than an active member of the political elite. Sycophants were classed
as another manifestation of the monetary greed of the *banausos*
rather than as an example of the use of friendship in politics (cf.
the very idealistic and apolitical picture of Krito's 'friendship' with
Archedemos in Xenophon *Memorabilia* ii. 9). Personal friendship or
enmity was stressed as a motive for appearance in court in defence
against the accusation that the speaker's motives were economic, that
he made a living either as a sycophant or as a professional speech-
writer. It was acknowledged that *hetairoi* played an important part
in court cases, but their role was thought of as purely defensive and
not in any way programmatic. In the fourth century matters were
different. Private alliances both inside Attica and with foreign powers
were of great importance, as were private resources. A successful
general had to be able when necessary to pay his own troops, make
his own alliances with foreign rulers and maintain good relations
with leading politicians at home in Athens. When the difficulties of
the immediate postwar period were over, the *demos'* enthusiasm for
military service began to be damped by the frequent irregularities of
pay, and their economic interests in the assembly were increasingly
focused on the Theoric fund from which payments for attendance at
festivals were made – a ritual symbol rather than a key element in the
Athenian economy. For Demosthenes, those who put private before
public interests are those who prefer peace to war: the tax-dodgers.
Whereas fifth-century radical democrats had striven to limit the
excessive use of private wealth in liturgies and similar expenses as
a way of acquiring political power, Demosthenes contrasts the
good citizen who spends his money in this way with the egotist who
avoids all forms of political activity and spends his money on private
pleasure.

My interest in the development of the distinction between public
and private realms in classical Athens has been two-fold. On the one
hand I wanted to know how Plato had managed to persuade himself
and his public that the economy of Athens had in principle nothing
to do with politics, why he remained blind to the economic implications of imperialism. It seemed inadequate to say simply either that
his view of economic matters was that of a conservative trying vainly
to put the clock back in an age of economic development (the empire
had been in existence for 50 years by the time he was born!), or that
it reflected the view of the oligarchic opposition in the later stages
of the Peloponnesian war, who felt that they were being bled dry by
taxation in order to pay for policy mistakes made by irresponsible
demagogues and a greedy *demos*. The latter view is correct as far as

it goes, but does not explain the appeal of Plato's analysis among both Greek and modern readers. It is only when we have taken into account the historical reality of the process of defining the boundary between the public and private realms in fifth-century Athens (bearing in mind that some of the external trappings of Athenian democracy were spread throughout the empire and beyond, and handed down to the Greek cities of later ages even when the real distribution of political power was very different) that we can see how easy and persuasive it was to turn the weapons of radical democracy against itself.

My second concern with the relation of public and private spheres comes from work on kinship and is more difficult to define, let alone to satisfy. Anthropologists have developed great skill in analysing kinship systems as maps of social relationships. The phratry, tribe, deme, *genos*, *anchisteis* [those within defined limits of kinship] and wider kindred all fit easily into this framework. The unit which I find really problematic is the *oikos*. Part of the difficulty comes from the highly tendentious statements made about the sacred duty of continuing the *oikos* by fourth-century orators. But this is a superficial problem. The real trouble is the difficulty of discovering from ancient sources the meaning of family life to an ancient Athenian. Tragedy and comedy seem to show an increasing concern with the personal relationships of the *oikos* during the course of the classical period (it is difficult to date the change in comedy, but *Ploutos* already has a domestic atmosphere, though we have to wait for Menander to find the full development). Orators' speeches are full of lively domestic detail; the professionalisation of speech writing led to concentration on *ethos* [character] and the dramatic aspects of case presentation, and not to interest in technical points of law. Philosophers' discussions of friendship stress the pleasure of the company of a like-minded friend rather than the need for friends to help in political or financial difficulties – friendship is seen as an essential complement to the contemplative part of the personality, part of the *theoretikos bios* ['life of contemplation'] as well as being an ingredient of action and the *bios praktikos* ['life of action']. We see to be approaching something like the modern western notion of private life. But there are dangers of ethnocentrism in this view. I should like to throw open to general discussion the question of the effects on private life of the claim that in a democracy politics must be concentrated in specifically political and public contexts, from which private interests and loyalties must be excluded.

REFERENCES

Brunt, P. A. (1965), '"Amicitia" in the Late Roman Republic', *Proceedings of the Cambridge Philological Society* 191 = ^{2}11, pp. 1–20; revised in Brunt, *The Fall of the Roman Republic and Related Essays* (Oxford: Oxford University Press, 1988), pp. 351–81, ch. vii, with some material transferred to another chapter.

Connor, W. R. (1971), *The New Politicians of Fifth-Century Athens*, Princeton, NJ: Princeton University Press.

Davies, J. K. (1971), *Athenian Propertied Families*, 600–300 B.C., Oxford: Oxford University Press.

Van Bremen, R. (1983), 'Women and Wealth', in A. Cameron and A. Kuhrt (eds), *Images of Women in Antiquity* (London: Croom Helm; revised edition London: Routledge, 1993), pp. 223–42.

PART III

Moments in History

Introduction to Part III

Parts I and II have presented synchronic studies of various aspects of the classical Athenian democracy of the fifth and fourth centuries B.C. It is important also to study the stages by which Athens arrived at that democracy. Three of the major steps in the development towards the classical democracy (nos. 3, 5 and 7 in the numbered list of advances and setbacks in *Ath. Pol.* 41. ii) are the reforms of Solon, in 594/3, of Cleisthenes, in 508/7, and of Ephialtes, in 462/1; and this Part contains studies of them from different points of view.

Fashion in the study of Solon has swung from investigations of what he did and the significance of it to doubts about how far we can believe what he is said by our non-contemporary sources to have done – a swing which has been encouraged by the insistence of the 'postmodernists' that history is what is constructed by those who write about it. In Chapter 10 C. Mossé, who was professor in the École des Hautes Études en Sciences Sociales at the Université de Paris VIII, and who has written extensively on Greek political and on Greek social history, asks how the Athenians of the late fifth and fourth centuries constructed the image of Solon as the founder of a respectable kind of democracy, and ends with her own construction of property classes not introduced by Solon but first used for Pisistratus' produce tax, and of judicial appeals directed by Solon not to popular law-courts but to the Areopagus.[1]

After the downfall of the Pisistratid tyranny, political rivalry between Cleisthenes and Isagoras led to the advancing of proposals for reform by Cleisthenes, to the involvement of the Spartan Cleomenes and the exile of Cleisthenes and his supporters, and

---

[1] M. H. Hansen, 'Solonian Democracy in Fourth-Century Athens', *ClMed* xl 1989, 71–99 = W. R. Connor *et al.*, *Aspects of Athenian Democracy*, 71–99, proceeds from the fact of fourth-century reconstruction to agnosticism rather than to new constructions. P. J. Rhodes, 'The Reforms and Laws of Solon: An Optimistic View', forthcoming, is more willing to believe that the account given in *Ath. Pol.* is essentially reliable.

finally to the return of Cleisthenes and the enactment of his proposals. J. Ober is Professor of Ancient History at Princeton, and is
particularly interested in the Athenian democratic ethos and in the
relevance of the Athenian democracy to today's world. In Chapter 11
he notes that Herodotus names no leaders when the council resisted
Cleomenes and Isagoras and the Athenians besieged them on the
acropolis, and he argues that in their resistance the Athenians were
not directed by leaders but joined in a spontaneous popular movement. D. M. Lewis (1928–94) held a special lectureship in Greek
epigraphy at Oxford before he was promoted to be a Professor of
Ancient History. In Chapter 12 he studies Cleisthenes' complicated
new articulation of the Athenian citizen body in ten tribes, thirty
trittyes ('thirds') and 139 demes, by exploiting the evidence (much of
it epigraphic) for the way in which demes were combined to form
trittyes and tribes, and for the effects of this new system on older
associations, to suggest that Cleisthenes was engaging in electoral
geography to undermine an old order in which his own family, the
Alcmaeonids, was at a disadvantage. This implies a less democratic
view of the whole episode than that championed by Ober.

We are frustratingly ill informed on what powers Ephialtes took
away from the Areopagus, the council of all living former archons.
I have argued that Ephialtes made a major and significant change,
taking from the Areopagus the trial of *eisangeliai* (often translated
'impeachments'), charges of major offences against the state, and
the procedures for the control of officials, including the *dokimasia*
(validation) before they entered office and the *euthynai* (accounting)
when they retired from office.[2] R. Sealey, who migrated from Britain
to become Professor of History at the University of California,
Berkeley, has always been suspicious of claims that particular states
and people within them were committed to democracy or to any
particular ideology: in his earlier writings he was one of those who
investigated personal connections between politicans;[3] and more
recently he has taken a particular interest in the development of law
and legal procedures. In Chapter 13, in reply to me, he argues that
the development of and changes in procedures such as *eisangelia*
are likely to have occurred through changing practice rather than by
deliberate enactment, and that if Ephialtes was concerned simply
with the *dokimasia* and *euthynai* of the archons his aim will have

[2] P. J. Rhodes, *The Athenian Boule*, 144–207, esp. 203–5; cf. recently Rhodes, 'The
Athenian Revolution', in *CAH*, v[2] (1992), 67–75.
[3] Cf. pp. 6–7, above.

been to remedy a particular abuse rather than to achieve a fundamental reform.[4]

---

[4] A similar view of Ephialtes is taken by J. K. Davies, 'Democracy Without Theory', in P. Derow and R. Parker (eds), *Herodotus and his World*, 319–35; but C. Meier in Chapter 14 offers an account which implies a greater significance for Ephialtes' reform.

10 How a Political Myth Takes Shape: Solon, 'Founding Father' of the Athenian Democracy[*][†]

CLAUDE MOSSÉ

translated by Rosh Ireland

Today's historians, while nevertheless not neglecting the *realia* [concrete facts], give more and more scope in their research to the image which past societies have presented of themselves, to the way they have remade their histories, and to the workings of this imagined structure. Ancient historians cannot fail to be aware of this direction in research, the more so since the greater part of the sources they use, by their very nature (historical accounts, political speeches, the meditations of philosophers, etc.), present them with particularly rich material. Others have already begun to investigate it.[1] For my part, I should like to try to show how the image of Solon as founder of Athenian democracy took shape from the end of the fifth century onwards.

Solon is one of the great figures of the history of Athens. Becoming

[*] Originally published in French, as 'Comment s'élabore un mythe politique: Solon, "père fondateur" de la démocratie athénienne', in *Annales (Économies, Sociétés, Civilisations)* 34. iii (1979), 425–37, © EHESS, Paris; reprinted with the permission of the author and of the Rédaction of *Annales*.

The translator has used the following translations of Greek texts: for the Aristotelian *Constitution of Athens*, K. von Fritz and E. Kapp, *Aristotle's Constitution of Athens and Related Texts* (New York: Hafner, 1950); for Aristotle's *Politics*, T. A. Sinclair rev. T. J. Saunders, *Aristotle: The Politics* (Harmondsworth: Penguin, 1981).

[†] This article owes much to Moses I. Finley's study published under the title of *The Ancestral Constitution* (Cambridge, 1971; revised in M. I. Finley, *The Use and Abuse of History* [London, 1975], 34–59 ch. ii), in which the great English historian pondered the working of that historical 'mythology' of 'great ancestors' which he found both in seventeenth-century England and in the twentieth-century United States. I devoted part of my seminar in 1976/7 on the Greek citizen to an analysis of the myth of the *patrios politeia*, the ancestral constitution, in fourth-century Athens. This article presents a first draft of that reflection, centred on the figure of Solon.

[1] I have in mind above all the thesis of Nicole Loraux, *L'Invention d'Athènes: Histoire de l'oration funèbre dans la 'cité classique'* [(Paris, 1981); trans. A. Sheridan as *The Invention of Athens: The Funeral Oration in the Classical City* (Cambridge, MA, 1986)].

archon in the early years of the sixth century, he faced a grave crisis. This he resolved by proclaiming a series of laws, which were constantly invoked by the political orators of the fourth century, when democracy was in full flower. The circumstances of this crisis and Solon's performance are known to us in part through the legislator's own evidence. He is in fact the author of poems in which he describes his action, the dangers menacing the city, and how he came to overcome them. We possess fragments of these poems, quoted by later commentators. There are, however, many unclear points which modern scholars have attempted to clarify, proceeding essentially from two accounts providing additional information related to these fragments: chapters 2 and 5–7 of Aristotle's *Constitution of Athens* and the *Life of Solon* written by Plutarch. The latter relies quite substantially on Aristotle for everything beyond the province of anecdote. It is therefore the *Constitution of Athens* which is the starting point for most historians attempting to establish what the legislator accomplished, even if some have justifiably emphasised the systematic nature of the historical reconstruction undertaken by the philosopher.[2] It is specifically this text which I intend to re-read, not to submit it to a critical examination, which others have already undertaken, but to attempt to reconstruct the process by which the Athenians of the end of the fifth and of the fourth centuries recreated the image of Solon to make of him the founding father of the democracy, a democracy which was not the radical and excessive regime denounced by the philosophers, but a wise and stable regime, which, while respecting the sovereignty of the *demos*, ensured that it was contained within strict limits, by means of a skilful blending which made it the prototype of that *mikte politeia*, that mixed constitution which was to be one of the favourite subjects of political discourse in the Hellenistic age. Hence I should wish to attempt to shed light on the ways in which the imagined memory of a society is formed, in the case of democratic Athens, and to try to understand how it works.

The starting point must be Solon's evidence: in the fragments of his poems, he evokes the conflict which he had to settle, a conflict which set the *demos*, the people, in the city against those 'who possessed power and wealth'. The conflict arose from a serious social situation: the land, or at least a part of the land of Attica, was 'enslaved'.

---

[2] This applies particularly to the book by J. Day and M. Chambers, *Aristotle's History of Athenian Democracy* (Berkeley and Los Angeles, 1962).

Marker stones gave substance to this servitude. Those who worked this 'enslaved' land were themselves personally under threat, and a number of them had already fallen into servitude or been forced into exile to escape it. In the face of this situation and this threat, some were demanding an equal redistribution of the land. Solon, elected archon, arbitrated the conflict in accord with justice and impartiality: 'Firmly I stood, holding out my strong shield over both of them, and I did not allow either party to triumph over the other in violation of justice' [fr. 5 West, quoted in *Constitution of Athens*, 12. 1].

In the name of *dike*, justice, Solon 'freed' the land from servitude, removing the marker stones, *horoi*, which signalled it. In the same way, he freed the people, returning to Attica those who, forced into exile, had come to lose even the use of their mother tongue. He drew up laws applying to all equally so that his work would not be open to challenge, thus granting to the *demos* its proper share of *geras*, honour. He was, however, firmly opposed to an egalitarian redistribution of the land, having no wish to follow the example of the tyrants who were his contemporaries, or that of the Spartan legislator Lycurgus, to whom tradition (had it already taken shape in Solon's time?) attributed such a redistribution.[3]

This conflict and the resolution applied by Solon could not fail to give rise to exegeses from ancient times onwards. Aristotle recalls it at length in the *Constitution of Athens*, but in order to mould it into a conflict between poor (*penetes*) and rich (*plousioi*), employing those terms which in the fourth century are applied to the opposing social groups in the city.[4] Certainly Aristotle preserved the recollection of a particular status, that of *hektemoroi*, i.e sixth-parters, which vanished following Solon, in other words dependent peasants obliged to pay rent.[5] When, however, he comes to deal with the problem of the *seisachtheia*, the shaking-off of the burden which Solon brought about, he makes it into an abolition of debts (*chreon*

[3] In fact the image of Lycurgus as author of an egalitarian agrarian reform was very slow to take shape. It is known, however, from a fragment of Tyrtaeus that a demand for an egalitarian land redistribution had been made in Sparta at the time of the second Messenian war. Cf. C. Mossé, 'Sparte archaïque', *La Parola del Passato* xxvii (1973), 7–20.

[4] Cf. for the problems relevant to this period of the history of Athens my account in E. Will, C. Mossé and P. Goukowsky (eds), *Le Monde grec et l'Orient*, vol. ii, *Le IVe Siècle et l'époque hellénistique* (Paris, 1975), 97 ff.

[5] On this aspect of Solon's reforms, refer to the paper of E. Will, 'La Grèce archaïque. B: Autour de l'oeuvre de Solon', *Deuxième Conférence internationale d'histoire économique*, vol. i, *Commerce et politique dans l'Antiquité* (Paris, 1965), 74–94. Cf. also G. Ferrara, *La politica di Solone* (Naples, 1964); V. Ehrenberg, *From Solon to Socrates* (London, 1968 [2nd edn 1973]), 48ff.; M. I. Finley, *Early Greece: The Bronze and Archaic Ages* (London, 1970 [2nd edn 1981]); E. Will, 'Soloniana: Notes critiques sur les analyses récentes', *REG* 52 (1969), 112.

apokope), thus calling to mind one of the demands which, together with the distribution of the land, constituted the 'programme' of the revolutionary elements in the Greek world of the fourth century, so much so that Philip of Macedon, following his victory, was to forbid cities entering his alliance to enact such measures.[6] Aristotle's contemporary, the orator Androtion, the author of a chronicle of Athens, was to go even further in 'modernising' Solon's measure: on the pretext that tradition attributed to Solon a reform of weights and measures, he made the *seisachtheia* into a kind of 'devaluation', thus alleviating the debts of the poor and ultimately furthering the speculations of the rich.[7] Plutarch, writing his *Life of Solon* close to eight centuries after the events he relates, is somewhat disturbed by Androtion's interpretation, finding nothing of the sort in Solon's poems, yet he too speaks of the abolition of debts and mortgaged lands.

The measure most authentically attributed to Solon,[*] since he himself took pride in it, was no longer fully understood by the men of the fourth century and their successors. The disappearance of the status of dependant became either an abolition or a remission of debts, or a devaluation, and the credit given to Solon was for having refused to append to this *chreon apokope* its usual corollary, land redistribution.

Solon had, however, not only put an end to the *stasis*, to the threat of civil war; he had also promulgated laws. It is striking here too to note the discrepancy between the language of the legislator and that of his later 'biographers'. In his poems, Solon says that he has 'composed' laws alike for the 'good' and the 'bad'. Naturally, one should not attach to these terms a moral sense which they do not have. They refer primarily to two different statuses, noble and non-noble. It is to make the *dike* equal for all that Solon laid down a code of laws in writing. It must, however, be noted that, speaking of laws, Solon uses the term *thesmoi* [ordinances], whereas Aristotle in the *Constitution of Athens* [7. 1] says that Solon established laws (*nomoi*) and a constitution (*politeia*) to replace the *thesmoi* of Draco, henceforth abandoned.

In the fourth century, the terms *nomoi* and *politeia* acquired a

---

[6] Cf. Ps.-Demosthenes, [XVII] *On the Treaty with Alexander*, 15.

[7] Cf. Plutarch, *Life of Solon*, 15. 3.

[*] The interpretation accepted here by Mossé is still almost universally accepted; but for a recent reinterpretation of the *hektemoroi* and of the removal of the *horoi* see E. M. Harris, 'A New Solution to the Riddle of the *Seisachtheia*', in L. G. Mitchell and P. J. Rhodes (eds), *The Development of the Polis in Archaic Greece* (London, 1997), 103–12, ch. ix.

Moments in History

quite specific meaning. The *nomos* is the law, a legal rule which cannot be infringed without exposure to the heaviest sanctions. The *politeia* is at once the body of laws and also the constitution which regulates the life of the city, the organisation of powers within it, and ultimately the citizenship which implies submission to the laws and the constitution. These terms came into use relatively recently, linked to the assertion of the structures of the city.[8] In contrast, the term *thesmos* is much older, since it is found in Homer. Admittedly it implies the existence of a law, but a law which may not be 'written' and which always bears a sacred connotation. Solon, a poet inspired by the Muses, employs this term, not merely as a literary device, but since it is the only term then in use and since it conveys well the 'divine' nature of his work.

What was there that was actually Solonian in the *nomoi* attributed to Solon by the writers of the fourth and succeeding centuries? It is very difficult to say. Aristotle, who remains our principal source, recognises that Solon composed his laws in an 'obscure', unclear manner, with which his detractors were quick to reproach him, perceiving here a device intended to make the courts all-powerful. In reality, this 'obscurity' is highly significant, reflecting a pre-legal situation in which the categories of law were not yet fixed. This legal arsenal developed during the fifth century, though not forming a consistent whole, prompting the leaders of the democracy, immediately following the oligarchic attempt of 411, to set up a commission of legislators (*nomothetai*) charged with harmonising the laws. Interrupted by the second oligarchic revolution of 404, the commission resumed its work upon the restoration of democracy. This restoration was brought about by the common people in its great majority and by all those who refused to accept the tyranny of the Thirty, established following the defeat of Athens. Once masters of Athens, however, the leading democrats, and the most renowned of them, Thrasybulus, signalled firmly to the *demos* that there was to be no revenge taken on the defeated opponents, as was the practice elsewhere. On the contrary, an amnesty was announced, and an opponent of democracy like Plato did not fail to pay tribute to the victorious democrats for their moderation. In fact those who now controlled the city and whose names have been passed down to us by the orators of the time, Archinus, Euclides and Anytus, the future accuser of Socrates, were moderates impelled towards democracy only by the excesses of the Thirty. They opposed any 'revolutionary'

[8] Cf. M. Ostwald, *Nomos and the Beginnings of the Athenian Democracy* (Oxford, 1969).

measure; hence Archinus attacked as illegal a decree proposed by Thrasybulus which would have awarded citizenship to some metics [free non-citizen residents] or slaves who had fought on his side. It is not surprising then that the restoration should have been placed under the aegis of Solon, one who prided himself on having kept an equal balance between his opponents. It is also significant that Aristotle, asserting that the Athenians had then taken the finest and most civic attitude, particularly by reimbursing the Lacedaemonians for the debts of the Thirty, adds: 'in other cities the democrats, if they come to power, do not even think of making any contributions out of their own money, but, on the contrary, seize the land for redistribution' [40. 3]. Refusing to distribute the assets of the defeated oligarchs, the Athenians quite naturally were to take the course which had been Solon's two centuries earlier.[9]

In these circumstances, it might be thought permissible to examine the Solonian source of the laws revised early in the fourth century. Significantly, Aristotle in the *Constitution of Athens* contents himself with a brief allusion to what might be called the legislation regarding private law established by Solon, referring to inheritance and to daughters known as *epikleroi*, i.e. heirs to property. On the contrary, in the *Life of Solon*, Plutarch, having available the whole arsenal of 'Solonian' laws invoked in their law-court speeches by the orators of the fourth century, draws a full picture of this legislation, regarding not only *epikleroi* and inheritance, as Aristotle says, but also marriage in general, funeral ceremonies, and games, and looking forward, in the case of the rich and especially of women, to sumptuary measures to limit private extravagance. These laws, which contain many obscurities, have been analysed at length by jurists.[10] Our question here, however, is to discover which of these laws are actually Solon's. The answer is not straightforward. It is important to draw a distinction on the one hand between the substance and the form, and on the other among the laws themselves. It is likely that those laws which sought to regulate problems arising within the family had their origin in Solon, even if the form in which they have come down to us reflects the revision of the early fourth century. It might be conceded that, in this respect, the *nomothetai* did no more than adapt them to the realities of their time. The laws of inheritance and wills present more problems, to the extent that they involve the

    [9] On the events of 404–403 and the conditions of the democratic restoration cf. E. Will, *Le Monde grec et l'Orient*, vol. i, *Le Ve Siècle* (Paris, 1972), 393 ff.
    [10] I refer to the book by A. R. W. Harrison, *The Law of Athens*, vol. i, *The Family and Property* (Oxford, 1968); vol. ii, *Procedure* (Oxford, 1971).

status of the land, about which we confess we know nothing, at least to the end of the archaic period, if not to the end of the fifth century.[11] The sumptuary laws recall measures taken at Athens at the end of the fourth century under the government of the pro-Macedonian philosopher Demetrius of Phalerum, a disciple of Aristotle.[12] So it can be seen that, if some of the laws presented to us as Solon's might apply to Athenian society of the archaic period, others reflect rather the realities of Athens of the end of the fifth and of the fourth centuries.

This is still truer of the economic measures traditionally attributed to Solon. The latest research in the field of numismatics has proved that the first Athenian coin issues post-date Solon. His supposed monetary reform, which some in the fourth century, as we have seen, connected with the *seisachtheia*, could not then be interpreted in an 'economic' sense, as has too often been done. An attempt has recently been made to shed light on this difficult problem by suggesting that Solon, within the framework of a body of work essentially pursuing justice in social relations, established the Attic system of weights.[13] It is evident in particular that, if one wished to establish a certain justice among members of a community, without nevertheless undertaking an egalitarian division of the land, one had to 'have available a system of quantitative evaluation (i.e. a system of weights and measures) and a system of qualitative evaluation (i.e. an instrument to correlate the value of goods, or, if one prefers, prices)' (E. Will). One must probably be equally prudent before accepting the notion of a new direction given by Solon to the Athenian economy by favouring the artisans, prohibiting the export of agricultural produce with the exception of oil, and developing arboriculture at the expense of cereals. Such an initiative stands as one of the preoccupations more of the fourth century, when the city regulated the grain trade to ensure the *trophe* [sustenance] of the *demos*, than of the archaic period. That does not mean that the economic life of Athens did not at that time undergo great changes. Undoubtedly the great develop-

---

[11] Cf. M. I. Finley, *Studies in Land and Credit in Ancient Athens* (New Brunswick, NJ, 1952), and M. I. Finley (ed.), *Problèmes de la terre en Grèce ancienne* (Paris, 1971).

[12] Cf. C. Mossé, *La Tyrannie dans la Grèce antique* (Paris, 1969), 163.

[13] E. Will, 'Autour de l'oeuvre de Solon' [n. 5, above], 79 ff. [For the current orthodoxy on the introduction of coinage see C. M. Kraay, *Archaic and Classical Greek Coins* (London, 1976), 55–6; on Solon and weights, measures and coinage see, for the greatest scepticism, M. H. Crawford, 'Solon's Alleged Reform of Weights and Measures', *Eirene* 10 (1972), 5–8; for the suggestion that Solon legislated for the use of standard measures and weights but did not change Athens' standards, P. J. Rhodes, 'Solon and the Numismatists / Postscript', *Numismatic Chronicle*[7] 15 (1975), 1–11 / 17 (1977), 152.]

ment of the Athenian artisanate took place in the second quarter of the sixth century, and it could be connected with the reforms of Solon, who, freeing the people while refusing to divide the land, made his contribution to the growth of the class of *thetes*, landless freemen who supplied an important labour force to the artisanate.[14] Equally the law attributed to Solon by Plutarch, authorising the granting of citizenship to any foreigner settling in Athens to pursue a trade, may recognise a reality: the settlement in Athens of foreign skilled tradesmen (potters in particular) who eventually became integrated into the community at the time of the Cleisthenic revolution. If, however, there is no doubt that Athenian society underwent profound changes in the course of the sixth century, and if moreover it is possible to connect certain of these changes with Solon's work in the social sphere, in contrast it seems more difficult to fit them into a coherent system developed by the legislator. No such coherent vision of economic necessities is put forward even by the most lucid authors of the fourth century, at a time when nevertheless the realities of exchange, if not of production, were clearly perceived.[15] It is then significant that this 'economic' work of Solon does not appear in the exposition of the *Constitution of Athens*, with the exception of the supposed monetary reform – but monetary problems fall within the political more than the economic province. It is only Plutarch who raises them, moreover in a moralising perspective proper to the Roman world of the second century. For the Athenians of the fourth century, Solon appeared first and foremost as a legislator, the legislation presenting a double aspect. On the one hand, it established norms in relation to private law: family, marriage, dowry, inheritance. In this respect, it was relatively simple to adapt to the realities of the fourth century measures in effect intended to establish basic social relations in a structure still based essentially on kinship. On the other hand, it modified the *politeia*, the organisation of the powers at the heart of the city. Now, if Solon in his poems recalled his action in freeing the *demos* on one hand, and the composition of laws on the other, there was no indication that these laws had any other intention than to restore to the *demos* its share of *geras*. It is easiest then to follow the formation of the myth of Solon in the fourth century in connection with political and constitutional reforms.

[14] E. Will, *op. cit.*, 77.
[15] Cf. on Aristotle the article by M. I. Finley, 'Aristotle and Economic Analysis', *Past and Present* 47 (1970), 1–25; and my article, 'Xenophon the Economist', *Hommages à Claire Préaux* (Brussels, 1975), 169–76.

The starting point must be Aristotle's text. In fact Plutarch essentially copies it, departing from it only to bring up the problem of Solon's creation of the Areopagus, not even raised by Aristotle. As presented by Aristotle, Solon's political work boils down to three points: the division of the population into classes; the organisation of judicial power in the city; and the creation of the *boule* [council] of the Four Hundred.

Of all the reforms attributed to Solon, the division into classes is the one most generally accepted by modern critics.* It is taken that Solon divided the body civic of Athens into four classes: *pentakosiomedimnoi, hippeis, zeugitai* and *thetes*. This division was made in accordance with the *timema*, which the translator of the most recent French edition translates as 'revenu imposable' [taxable revenue]. Without entering into all the problems raised by this term, it must nevertheless be remembered that its meaning is not always so straightforward and it can also denote total assets, the essential notion being of assessment.[16] The translation of *timema* by 'revenue' is in some way implied by the text which follows. Aristotle in fact specifies that those drawing from their estate five hundred measures [*medimnoi*] of dry or liquid produce were allocated to the *pentakosiomedimnoi*, those drawing three hundred to the *hippeis*, those drawing two hundred to the *zeugitai*, and those whose income was less than two hundred measures were *thetes*. This evaluation of income in measures of grain or liquids lends Aristotle's information an archaising tone which can only authenticate its source. Nevertheless, I believe that things are not so simple, since the names borne by the four classes raise many problems. Why, in fact, if it was in the nature of a system, was the classification not based on the revenue obtained? Of the four names, one only possesses this character, that of the *pentakosiomedimnoi* [five-hundred-measure men]. The *hippeis* are cavalry. Aristotle certainly felt that there was a difficulty here, since he mentions in this context an interpretation somewhat different from his own (one which has every chance of being true): the *hippeis* would have been those able to raise a horse. The term

* Some suppose that the three lower classes already existed and that Solon filtered out the *pentakosiomedimnoi* from the *hippeis* (e.g. P. J. Rhodes, *A Commentary on the Aristotelian Athenaion Politeia* [Oxford, 1981], 137–8); recently it has been suggested that the qualifications given for the *hippeis* and *zeugitai* would make the three higher classes an elite minority (L. Foxhall, 'A View from the Top: Evaluating the Solonian Property Classes', in Mitchell and Rhodes [above], 113–36, ch. x), or that these qualifications are simply the product of later speculation (V. J. Rosivach, 'The Requirements for the Solonic Classes in Aristotle, A.P. 7. 4', *Hermes* 130 [2002], 36–47).

[16] Cf. R. Thomsen, *Eisphora* (Copenhagen, 1964), 49 ff.

zeugitai is still more ambiguous. *Zeugos* is yoke; it comes naturally to mind that the term could have applied to the owner of a team of oxen, relatively well-off peasants. Aristotle, remarkably, gives no explanation for the name. Certain modern commentators have suggested that the yoke referred to in the name of the *zeugitai* could be the bond which held together hoplites in battle.[17] Hence two at least of the four names given to the classes might refer to military categories, to the two essential groups which made up the army of a Greek city in the archaic period, the cavalry and the hoplites.[18] As for the term *thetes*, it had been much longer in use, since it occurs in Homer: it refers to those who have nothing, who must seek service on another's land to obtain subsistence.

It might be asked why Solon, dividing the Athenians into classes according to revenue, nevertheless took terms with military connotations for two of the four classes. Moreover, at least on the surface, this division was not consistent with a definition of the service that each must provide, but (we shall return to this) was intended to establish conditions for access to magistracies. Here one is reminded of what certain modern commentators have called the 'hoplite revolution'. The equipment of a hoplite is known to have become fixed towards the middle of the seventh century, when the rules of hoplite combat were set. The changed techniques of warfare contributed to increasing the numbers engaged in combat, perhaps also to creating amongst those who formed the phalanx a sense of equality which played its part in undermining aristocratic society.* The example of Sparta shows just how far this equality of *homoioi* [those who are alike] can go. Yet for all that the aristocratic privilege of the cavalry continued, as is once more proved at the end of the fifth century in democratic Athens by the celebrated comedy of Aristophanes. So it can be conceded that cavalry and hoplites covered the two categories which Solon in his poems calls 'those possessed of power and outstanding through wealth' [fr. 5 West, quoted in *Constitution of*

---

[17] Cf. M. Détienne, 'La Phalange: Problèmes et controverses', in J.-P. Vernant (ed.), *Problèmes de la guerre en Grèce ancienne* (Paris, 1968), 119–42; P. Vidal-Naquet, 'La Tradition de l'hoplite athénien', ibid., 161–81.

[18] Nevertheless the absence of cavalry has been noted in certain engagements in the archaic period or early in the classical period. The 'cavalrymen' would have been mounted hoplites. That does not at all detract, however, from the value of the distinction between those who were able to raise a horse and plain hoplites. On these questions, as on the 'hoplite revolution' referred to below, see the articles cited above, n. 17.

* For a recent discussion of the so-called hoplite revolution see K. A. Raaflaub, 'Soldiers, Citizens and the Evolution of the Early Greek *Polis*', in Mitchell and Rhodes [above], 49–59, ch. v.

Athens, 12. 1] on one hand and the *demos* on the other. It can clearly be seen, however, that the problem is not to understand why two of the classes took their names from things military, but why the wealthiest were distinguished from the cavalry by a name which manifestly implied income from land. For the *thetes*, the problem is really relatively simple: these were Athenians who did not have the capacity to be hoplites. The only difficulty is that, if one follows Aristotle, the classification was based on revenue from land alone. Should it then be supposed that those who supported themselves by other activities, artisans or merchants, fell automatically into this class? Modern commentators, disturbed by this problem, have taken it, on the basis of a hint by Plutarch, that shortly after Solon the rating in kind was replaced by a rating in coin, a measure of grain or liquids being equivalent to a drachma.[19] Apart from Plutarch, however, who moreover attributes this change to Solon himself, no trace of such a provision is to be found. Besides, and this brings us back to the essential question, there is no doubt that the name *pentakosiomedimnoi* can be connected very well with a valuation in kind. Perhaps a detour is needed to escape this difficulty.

The detour is by way of this question: why does Aristotle consider the classification one of the essential aspects of Solon's work? He says so specifically: the conditions for access to the *archai*, magistracies, had to be set. Aristotle tries to prove this by the fact that in his time the treasurers could in principle still be chosen by lot only from among the *pentakosiomedimnoi*. If that, however, was the law, it was frequently evaded. In that very passage of the *Constitution of Athens*, the philosopher cites the case of poor treasurers, and it is known that one of the criticisms most often levelled at the Athenian democracy was that public office was a way to enrichment. In the moderate programmes of the end of the fifth and of the fourth centuries, signalled as a return to the *patrios politeia*, to the ancestral constitution, the conditions for access to magistracies appear as an essential provision, together with their corollary, the suppression of *misthophoria*, the payment of a salary for public office, which had characterised Athenian democracy since Pericles. To reserve the *archai* for the well-off is a provision found as much among the measures taken by the oligarchs at the time of the two revolutions of 411 and 404 as in the 'programme' set out by Isocrates in the *Areopagiticus*. It is, however, without doubt Aristotle himself who most clearly formulated this obligation, which he saw as being the

[19] So P. Lévêque, *L'Aventure grecque* (Paris, 1964), 188.

aristocratic aspect of the 'mixed' constitution which he regarded as best.[20]

Hence it can be better understood why the source of such a practice had to be Solonian. In fourth-century Athens, however, social structures were no longer what they had been in Solon's time. The wealthy formed a relatively narrow group, the group of those subject to liturgies, contributions which, though invested with honour, were nonetheless highly burdensome. In contemporary speeches and inscriptions, the members of this group are frequently designated as the Twelve Hundred, and the richest of them as the Three Hundred. These *plousioi* were, however, far from all great landowners. Among them were wealthy owners of workshops worked by slave labour, like the father of the orator Demosthenes, holders of silver-mining concessions at Laurium, and shipping financiers. It was this minority for which the opponents of radical democracy wished to reserve access to public office, and they saw the 'Solonian' classification as justifying their claims.

Which brings us back to the problem of the *pentakosiomedimnoi*. These wealthy Athenians liable to liturgies were effectively part of the *pentakosiomedimnoi* group, even though their income was only distantly related to income from land. In a speech by Demosthenes, one of those which he delivered against his guardians, whom he accused of having misappropriated his patrimony, there is an indication which remains disturbing: the wealthiest Athenians are designated as those who pay a contribution of five *minai*, i.e. five hundred drachmas.[21] Accepting for the archaic period that a drachma is equivalent to a *medimnos*, might it not be supposed that the term *pentakosiomedimnoi* designated at first, not those who had five hundred measures of produce, but those who, at a given time, had been liable to a contribution of five hundred measures? It appears to me that a contribution of this kind could be the tithe established by Pisistratus when he seized power after the disturbances which had followed the departure of Solon. It must not be forgotten that taxation is, and remains until the fourth century, an exceptional measure resorted to only on occasions of extreme necessity. Moreover a tithe on harvests is a particularly unpopular measure, regarded as characteristic of the policy of a tyrant. Solon, who, in his poems, prides himself on resisting the solicitations of those who saw in him

---

[20] Cf. *Politics*, II. 12, 1273 b 35 ff. (on Solon); VI. 4, 1318 b 27 ff. On the theme of the mixed constitution, see K. von Fritz, *The Theory of the Mixed Constitution in Antiquity* (New York, 1954).

[21] Demosthenes, [XXVII] *Against Aphobus*, i, 7; cf. also *Constitution of Athens*, 21. 2.

a tyrant, would clearly not have had recourse to such a practice. Besides, there is no allusion to it made anywhere. Hence one may wonder whether the heterogeneous nature of the names applied to these four classes, far from relating to a systematic redistribution brought about by Solon, did not in fact transmit a reality which was quite different: superimposing, in the course of the sixth century, on factual distinctions linked to military roles a new redistribution based on wealth, and leading to setting apart amongst the 'cavalry' those who were liable to the tithe of five hundred measures. Let us be clear that this tithe may have been levied only once. As for the systematic codification of this redistribution, one is tempted to attribute it to Cleisthenes, inasmuch as he, creating new territorial divisions and establishing among the Athenians *isonomia*, i.e. equality before the law, also set down the conditions of a classification in which only income – or wealth – was counted.

In the fourth century, however, the image of Cleisthenes as founder of Athenian democracy faded. For Isocrates, he did no more than restore the system founded by Solon.[22] As for Aristotle, if he attributes a significant role to him, that role is far from being a beneficial one, and Cleisthenes, having not hesitated to increase the number of citizens, has the primary responsibility for the degradation of the ancestral democracy.[23] Hence it can be seen clearly why Solon had to be the author of the classification. It was a way of securing the authority of the 'father of democracy' for a system which implied the exclusion from magistracies of all those who did not meet the requisite rating, but who nevertheless, sitting in the assembly and on the jury courts, would retain sovereignty.

In Aristotle's analysis, the classification had its counterbalance in the organisation of the jury courts. According to all the political writers of the fourth century and, even earlier, to Aristophanes, these were the democratic institution above all, but also the most criticised. Concluding the historical part of the *Constitution of Athens*, Aristotle noted: 'The people have made themselves masters of everything, and administer everything through decrees of the Assembly and decisions of the jury courts, in which they hold the power' [41. 2]. This popular justice was in fact a formidable weapon in the hands of the *demos*. We know through Aristotle the organisation of the courts which formed the Heliaea.[24] Any citizen of Athens more than thirty years old could take part in a jury court. A finely controlled allotment

---

[22] Cf. particularly *Areopagiticus*, 16.
[23] *Politics*, III. 2, 1275 b 35 ff.; see also *Constitution of Athens*, 21. 2.
[24] Cf. *Constitution of Athens*, 63–9.

governed the appointment of judges. The many speeches which have come down to us are a striking illustration of how this popular justice worked. Furthermore we know the importance which trials assumed in Athenian political life. It was Solon who was by tradition responsible for this popular justice, and Aristotle in his *Politics* notes the reproaches which some levelled at the legislator who had given 'supreme power over all matters to the courts, appointed by lot' [II. 12, 1274 a 4–5]. It is fair to wonder, however, whether we are facing another aspect of the Solonian myth. Solon's actual judicial work is no more easily grasped than the rest. In the *Constitution of Athens*, Aristotle attributes to Solon two essential measures: first 'the rule that anyone who wished to could claim redress on behalf of a person who had been wronged' and second 'the right of appeal to a jury court', both of these rights assuming laws known to all [9. 1]. Clearly, the compilation of a code of laws is, with the *seisachtheia*, a measure incontestably to be attributed to Solon, since he claims it in his poems. Hence it could be conceded that the right to intervene on behalf of a person wronged, together with the right of appeal to the jury courts against the decision of a magistrate, derived directly from that. Nevertheless, this does not imply that the courts were actually popular. In other words, there is no proof that Solon instituted the jury court of the Heliaea or the system of allotment described by Aristotle. There is no proof either that the citizens' assembly, regarding which we do not know its composition, or even whether it had an institutional reality – the *demos* was assembled when circumstances demanded, but the *ecclesia*, the people's assembly, became a reality only from the time when the regularity of its meetings was set and when it had to make decisions on the agenda of a specific day – that this assembly possessed the powers it has in the fourth century. Let us for the moment leave aside the problem of the *boule* [council], itself capable in the fourth century of setting itself up as a high court of justice, to recall the existence of the jury courts which still operated in Aristotle's time, the most important of which was that formed by the Areopagites. We know from Plutarch that there was a tradition which made Solon the founder of the Areopagus. As for Aristotle, he takes the Areopagus for an institution pre-dating Solon; it is in fact the aristocratic council which is found in all the cities of the archaic period. Neverthless he accords it a privileged place in Solon's legislation: Solon 'made it the task of the Aeropagus to watch over the laws, just as in the preceding period it had been the guardian of the political order; and this Council still supervised the greater and more important part of public life and, in particular, chastised offenders, with full power to impose punishment and fines. It deposited money exacted through fines in the Acropolis without having to indicate the reasons for the imposition of the fine. It also tried those who had conspired to deprive the people of their political rights, Solon having enacted a law of impeachment for such cases' [8. 4]. These are precisely the majority of the functions fulfilled by the jury courts in the fourth century. The tradition echoed by Aristotle attributed to a democrat, Ephialtes, a series of measures taken seventeen years after the end of the Persian Wars (i.e. in 462/1), depriving the Areopagus of its powers as guardian of the laws and the constitution, and handing them over to the *boule* of the Five Hundred, to the people and the jury courts. Quite clearly these were the powers which made the *demos*, the master of the jury courts, master of the *politeia*. Hence this 'happy blend', which, according to Aristotle, was the virtue of the supposed Solonian *politeia*, was merely a delusion: since, if judicial sovereignty really resided in the Areopagus in respect of the defence of the constitution and the laws, it is hard to see what might have been the functions of any jury court. Whereas the removal by Ephialtes of the judicial powers of the Areopagus, followed several years later by the institution of a salary for judges of the jury courts, is a better indication of a radical change in the balance of powers.

   This is, however, another instance in which we can see how the myth of Solon, founder of popular justice, was able to take shape. Placing the laws within the reach of all, Solon in effect created the conditions for popular justice. In order for this actually to function, however, the *demos*, or those who spoke in its name, had to have the means to deprive the Areopagus of its traditional privileges. This took place in the late sixties of the fifth century. In the fourth century, there could be no question of going back, of taking from the people its power to judge: the failure of the two oligarchic revolutions was the proof of that. Hence Solon had to be the inventor of the jury courts in order to justify their retention, yet at the same time it was important to recall that he had entrusted the Areopagus with the defence of the constitution, the only means of counterbalancing the excesses of popular power. It is known, besides, that propaganda in favour of the Areopagus develops in the second half of the fourth century, to the point that an increase in its powers has even been supposed in the years which follow the defeat at Chaeronea in 338.[25]

----

[25] Cf. G. Colin, 'Démosthène et l'affaire d'Harpale', *REG* 39 (1926), 31–89 at 31–3. [For recent discussions of the powers of the Areopagus in the third quarter of the fourth century see

Once again we can measure how much contemporary preoccupations were reflected in the image of the legislator.

This remains true, although modern commentators still disagree, of the last institution attributed by Aristotle to Solon: the *boule* of the Four Hundred. The author of the *Constitution of Athens* says only that Solon created a council of four hundred members, one hundred from each tribe, referring to the four 'Ionian' tribes into which the Athenians were divided until Cleisthenes instituted the ten territorial tribes. No evidence exists of the activity of this council, which disappeared after the Cleisthenic revolution. There are at least two grounds for doubting its existence. The first is that one cannot see what would have been the role of this council in the absence of a regular democratic mechanism. According to tradition, Solon had established his laws for one hundred years. Hence there was no question of modifying them. Now, the preparation of draft laws was to be one of the essential functions of the Cleisthenic *boule*. Moreover, since the Areopagus was guardian of the laws and the constitution, and also had the task of supervising the political administration, it is hard to see what the council of the Four Hundred could have done. There is, however, another ground for doubting the existence of the Solonian *boule*, which is that it was precisely a *boule* of four hundred members which the oligarchs set up when they took control of Athens in 411. This *boule* may perhaps have been inspired by a Boeotian model, since, like the *boule* of the Boeotian confederation, it was to be made up of four sections of one hundred members which would act in turn.[26] The rule of the Four Hundred lasted only some months, but it contributed to forming the image of a Solonian *boule*, the more so since it coincided admirably with the pre-Cleisthenic tribal organisation. If to that is added the obvious concern of the oligarchs of 411 to appear to adhere to tradition and the constitution of their ancestors, to the *patrios politeia* which is to be one of the themes of political propaganda in the fourth century, it

---

P. J. Rhodes, 'Judicial Procedures in Fourth-Century Athens: Improvement or Simply Change?', in W. Eder (ed.), *Die athenische Demokratie im 4. Jahrhundert v. Chr. ... 3–7. viii. 1992* (Stuttgart, 1995), 303–19; R. W. Wallace, ' "Investigations and Reports" by the Areopagos Council and Demosthenes' Areopagos Decree', in P. Flensted-Jensen *et al.* (eds), *Polis and Politics ... M. H. Hansen* (Copenhagen, 2000), 581–95; J. Sullivan, 'Demosthenes' Areopagus Legislation – Yet Again', *CQ²* 53 (2003), 130–4.]

[26] Cf. J. A. O. Larsen, 'The Boeotian Confederacy and Fifth-Century Oligarchic Theory', *TAPA* 86 (1955), 40–50. [Mossé here applies to the Four Hundred the 'future' constitution of *Constitution of Athens*, 30. It is now more commonly thought that that constitution was never put into effect: see Rhodes, *Commentary* (above), 385–9, discussing various views of the constitutional documents of chs 30–1.]

is conceivable that Aristotle, and Plutarch after him, could accept the reality of this phantom *boule* of the Four Hundred.

At the end of this rapid analysis of the formation of a historical and political myth, the historian may be permitted to wonder what Solon's real role was in the history of Athens. Dispossessed through a critical reading of Aristotle's text of his 'economic' policy and his constitutional reform, Solon takes his place among those legislators whose image has been passed down to us in many forms: Hammurabi, Moses, Servius Tullius, and in Greece itself Lycurgus, Zaleucus, Charondas ... It is clear that, once a society reaches a certain stage of its development, when structures based on kinship are replaced by a political and territorial organisation, a written code becomes necessary in order that all may share in knowledge of the law. In the world of the Greek cities, however, since, to repeat an expression of Herodotus, power lies at the centre, not above the community, this knowledge of the law assumes a certain equality among its members. This equality before the law, this *isonomia*, has specific implications: that dependent relations among members of the community should be suppressed. This was the work of Solon. After him, there are no longer in Athens, at the heart of the community, people who are dependent on others, even if there persist what we should call in modern terms social inequalities. In suppressing the condition of *hektemoros*, removing the markers, Solon created conditions which would permit the Athenian *demos* to become master of its own destiny. Thereby, in relation to the other legislators, he acquires a significant dimension, the more significant in the eyes of the historian since it is his own evidence which illuminates for us its meaning.

What we find striking, however, appeared to the Athenians of the fourth century to be only an aspect – one which was questionable to say the least, since it was no longer fully understood and could be seen as 'revolutionary' (the abolition of debts, if not land redistribution) – of a body of work which, in the context of Athenian democracy, was properly first of all political. Today's historian knows that Athenian democracy could be what it was – an egalitarian political system in which the only dependence possible was that of those utter outsiders, the slaves – only because Solon suppressed the institution of the *hektemoroi* and also because a long evolution was needed, an evolution of more than a century, for the effects to be felt. The men of the fourth century were not unaware of this evolution, but, since they feared the ultimate consequences, they had in a way to demonstrate that a return to the past would not entail abandoning the democracy to which – as the events of 411 and 404 had proved – the majority of Athenians remained faithful. Hence the image which becomes established in the fourth century of Solon as founding father of Athenian democracy, but a wise and moderate democracy in which the power of the *demos* was tempered by the recruitment of magistrates on a basis of assessment of wealth and by the control of the Areopagus.

A final problem would remain: to what extent was this myth of Solon as father of democracy effective? This is a problem difficult to resolve, to the extent that we know almost nothing of what might be called Athenian public opinion. It would be false nevertheless, on the pretext that we know Athenian opinion only through the writings of a small elite, to conclude that such a political mythology was ineffective. The *Constitution of Athens* certainly was addressed to a limited public only, made up of the pupils of the Peripatetic school. The ideas which it conveyed, however, were the same as those invoked by popular orators before the assembly or the jury courts. If the Solonian myth could nourish imagination to the time of Plutarch and beyond, it was because it was rich in all that the Athenians had added to it during the two centuries when they were masters of their own destiny.

11 *The Athenian Revolution of 508/7 B.C.: Violence, Authority, and the Origins of Democracy*[*]

JOSIAH OBER

The first draft of this essay was written for a conference on cultural poetics in archaic Greece, held at Wellesley College in October 1990; it was substantially revised in the summer of 1991, when I was Visiting Fellow at the University of New England in Armidale, New South Wales. I owe thanks for help in the process of revision to the conference's organizers (Carol Dougherty and Leslie Kurke), and to many colleagues at UNE, especially to Minor M. Markle, and to G. R. Stanton, whose erudite and insightful comments much improved a paper with whose fundamental tenets he disagreed.

Methodologically, this chapter attempts to put into practice the premises developed in Ober 1989b and thereby to advance the larger project and defend some of the main ideas sketched out in Ober 1993. By reading scanty sources for a particular event closely and sympathetically – that is, without assuming a priori [as a starting point] that Greek writers were misled by their ignorance of sociological "Iron Laws" – I try to break away from two increasingly ossified "Great Man" models, employed by Greek historians since the early 1960s to explain the behavior of Cleisthenes the Alcmaeonid, the figure often credited with "founding" Athenian democracy in 510–506 B.C. In terms of the politics of historiography, the essay cuts two ways: it rejects the Great Man as the motor driving Athenian history, but it also urges the genuine importance of certain historical events as turning points, as moments of rupture that can result in fundamental changes in both ideologies and institutions. The relative importance of discrete events vis-à-vis the *longue durée* [long duration] of established social structure and

[*] Originally published in C. Dougherty and L. Kurke (eds), *Cultural Poetics in Ancient Greece* (Cambridge University Press, 1993), 215–32, © Cambridge University Press; this revised version with introduction published in J. Ober, *The Athenian Revolution* (Princeton University Press, 1996), 32–52 ch. iv, © 1996 Princeton University Press. Reprinted with the permission of the author, Cambridge University Press and Princeton University Press.

the potential of human societies to change rapidly have been much debated by twentieth-century historians. Although there is an increasing interest among some historians in events and narrative, within the area of Greek democracy studies the superiority of the *longue durée* approach is vigorously defended, notably by Ian Morris (1996 and 1999).

Among other key questions at issue here are: How important to the history of democracy were the various events of 510–506 B.C., relative to prior and subsequent events and relative to one another? What are the proximate causes and the eventual results of the events at issue? And who (individual or collectivity) is to be assigned credit or blame for the several developments? Arguing that the sources raise serious problems for the two most commonly applied explanatory models, I offer an alternative that seems to fit the evidence better. I suggest that the signal event in the history of democracy was the Athenian uprising against the Spartans in 508/7, that this event defined the nature of Athens' subsequent democratic reforms, and that the primary historical agent was the Athenian demos, acting on its own initiative and without aristocratic leadership. This reading demotes Cleisthenes from his accustomed central position as "leader" of the progressive movement and new government, although it allows him to play an innovative and indeed essential role as an interpreter of mass action and designer of institutions capable of framing and stabilizing a new ideology.

My explanation for the Athenian Revolution requires not only (as with Ober 1993) exposing and assessing the theoretical underpinnings of other scholars' arguments, but also (as Ober 1989b suggests will be necessary) importing concepts and ideas from outside archaic Greek history. In this case, the primary external "supplement" to the sources is the example of the French Revolution. Rather than attempting to argue that the Athenian and French revolutions offer a full set of historical parallels, however, I take a detour through the history of revolutionary France in order to demonstrate that focused and effective revolutionary activities can be carried out by masses of citizens in the absence of established leaders or traditional structures of leadership. The goal is not to show that sixth-century B.C. Athens was fundamentally similar to eighteenth-century France, but rather to show that the argument "a leaderless uprising could not have occurred because such things do not happen" is misinformed.

My reading of the French and Athenian revolutions is, in part, predicated on the speech-act theory developed by J. L. Austin; and speech-act theory remains a key methodological tool in several of the subsequent essays [in Ober's *The Athenian Revolution*]. Where I part company with some other recent work influenced by Austin is in my insistence that speech acts must be read together with other sorts of action: the proof of the revolutionary speech act must be sought in the rebellion. The analysis of revolutionary action and its radical implications for subsequent democratic regimes develop directly from the premises sketched in Ober 1993. Comparisons could be extended; it would be interesting to look, for example, at the

American Revolution (especially in light of G. S. Wood 1992) or the Russian revolutions of 1917 and 1989–91.

From the time of its first, oral, presentation, my Athenian Revolution thesis has generated controversy. I retain oddly fond memories of a distinguished classicist eloquently admonishing the Wellesley audience not to believe a word of it on the grounds that (sources be damned!) Cleisthenes simply must have been in Athens directing affairs throughout the revolution. My focus on the demos and my decentering of Cleisthenes as the key historical actor is discussed in critical detail by David Ames Curtis in the translator's foreword to a new English translation of the classic work on Cleisthenes by Lévêque and Vidal-Naquet (1996, xiii–xvii). Meanwhile, Vidal-Naquet, in his new author's introduction to the same work (xxiv–xxv), acknowledges that "our principal error [in the French original of 1964] seems to me to have given in to the temptation to gather everything under the name of Cleisthenes." In several new essays Kurt Raaflaub (1995, and 1996a, b, and c) attempts to demonstrate that my argument for the primary importance of the events of 510–516 is in error and that the true origin of Athenian democracy (should one desire a single date) is 462 B.C., with the constitutional reforms associated by later authors with the name Ephialtes. I offer a reply to Raaflaub in' "Revolution Matters" (Ober 1996). In that essay (published along with Raaflaub 1996b and c), I restate, and attempt to buttress and extend, some of the main arguments presented here.

The periodization of history is, of course, a product of hindsight, and most historians realize that any past era can accurately be described as an "age of transition." Fixing the end of the archaic period and the transition to the classical is thus a historiographic problem, one that reflects contemporary scholarly inclinations more than it does ancient realities. Nevertheless, since historians cannot work without periodization, and since English-language historiography seems to be entering a post-Annales phase characterized by a renewed interest in the significance – especially the symbolic and cultural significance – of events,[1] it may be worthwhile to look at a series of events that can be taken as the beginning of a new phase of Greek history. The events we choose to mark the transition will be different for any given region or polis, but for those interested in Athenian political history, the end of the archaic and the beginning of something new may reasonably be said to have come about in the period around 510 to 506 B.C., with the revolutionary events that established the form of government that would soon come to be called *dēmokratia*.[2]

[1] See the introduction to Hunt 1989.
[2] This is a traditional breaking point: Burn (1960, 324), for example, ends his narrative of archaic Athenian history with the expulsion of Hippias. Hansen (1986) argues that

If the "Athenian Revolution" is a historically important event (or series of events), it is often described in what seem to me to be misleading terms. Historians typically discuss the revolution in the antiseptic terminology of "constitutional development," and their narrative accounts tend to be narrowly centered on the person and intentions of Cleisthenes himself. Putting Cleisthenes at the center of the revolution as a whole entails slighting a significant part of the source tradition. And that tradition, which consists almost entirely of brief discussions in Herodotus (5.66, 69–78) and the *Athēnaiōn Politeia* (20–21), is scanty enough as it is. The reconstruction of the events of 508/7 offered here is simultaneously quite conservative in its approach and quite radical in its implications. I hope to show that by sticking very closely to the primary sources, it is possible to derive a plausible and internally coherent narrative that revolves around the Athenian people rather than their leaders. A close reading of the sources shows that the dominant role ascribed to elite leaders in modern accounts of a key point in the revolution is supplementary to the ancient evidence. All historians supplement their narratives with assumptions, models, and theories; supplementation of the source material, in order to fill in apparent gaps and silences, is an inevitable part of the process of even the most self-consciously narrative (rather than analytical) forms of historical writing. But such supplements (especially those that are widely accepted) must be challenged from time to time, lest they become so deeply entrenched as to block the development of alternative readings that may explain the source tradition as well or better.

Both of our two main sources state that during a key period of the revolution, Cleisthenes and his closest supporters were in exile. They imply that the main Athenian players in the revolt were corporate entities: the *boulē* [council] and the demos. The ascription of authoritative leadership in all phases of the revolution to Cleisthenes may, I think, be attributed to the uncritical (and indeed unconscious) acceptance of a view of history that supposes that all advance in human affairs comes through the consciously willed actions of individual members of an elite.[3] In the case of other historical figures,

---

dēmokratia was the name Cleisthenes used from the beginning. The relevant ancient sources are conveniently collected, translated, and annotated in Stanton 1990, 130–67.

[3] For representative statements of the centrality of Cleisthenes' role, see Zimmern 1931, 143–44: "Cleisthenes the Alcmaeonid, the leader of the popular party, ... made a bid for power. [After the Spartan intervention an the occupation of the Acropolis,] *Cleisthenes and the councillors* [my emphasis] called the people to arms and blockaded the rock ... [upon the surrender of the Spartans] Cleisthenes was now master of the situation." Murray 1980, 254: "Kleisthenes 'took the people into his party' ... proposed major reforms, *expelled Isagoras* [my

for example Solon, proponents of this elite-centered Great Man approach to history can at least claim support in the primary sources. But although he *is* regarded by the sources as the driving force behind important political reforms, Cleisthenes is not described in our sources as a Solon-style lawgiver (*nomothetēs*). The *Athēnaiōn Politeia* (20.4) calls him *tou dēmou prostatēs* (the leader who stands up before the people) and, though the label is anachronistic for the late sixth century, it seems to me a pretty reasonable description of Cleisthenes' historical role: like later Athenian politicians, Cleisthenes' leadership was not dependent on constitutional authority, but rather upon his ability to persuade the Athenian people to adopt and to act on the proposals he advocated. In sum, I will attempt to show that though Cleisthenes is indeed a very important player in Athens' revolutionary drama, the key role was played by the demos. And thus, *dēmokratia* was not a gift from a benevolent elite to a passive demos, but was the product of collective decision, action, and self-definition on the part of the demos itself.

Having advocated the study of historical events, and having simultaneously rejected the individual intentions of the elite leader as the motor that necessarily drives events, I shall go one step further out on the limb by suggesting that *the* moment of the revolution, the end of the archaic phase of Athenian political history, the point at which Athenian democracy was born, was a violent, leaderless event: a three-day riot in 508/7 that resulted in the removal of King Cleomenes I and his Spartan troops from the soil of Attica.

In order to explain the events of 508/7, we need to review the revolutionary period that began in 510 B.C. – a fascinating few years characterized by a remarkable series of expulsions from the territory of Attica and returns to it. The series opened with the ouster of Hippias, son of Peisistratos. In 510 the Spartans, urged on by multiple oracles from Deiphic Apollo, decided to liberate Athens from the rule of the Peisistratid tyrant. A preliminary seaborne invasion of Attica was repulsed by the tyrant's forces. King Cleomenes I then raised a second army, which he marched across the Isthmus into Athenian territory. This time Hippias' forces failed to stop the invasion. With the Spartans in control of Attica, the tyrant and his

emphasis], and in the next few years held off the attempts of the Spartans and their allies to intervene." Forrest 1966, 194: "Finally, with the *demos'* firm support, *he was able to rout Isagoras* [my emphasis] together with a Spartan force." Other textbooks do point out that Cleisthenes was in exile, e.g., Sealey 1976, 147; Bury and Meiggs 1975, 36; and especially M. Ostwald in *The Cambridge Ancient History*, 2nd ed. (1988), 4: 305–7. The modern account of the revolution closest in spirit to the one I offer here is perhaps Meier 1990, 64–66.

family were forced to retreat to their stronghold on the Acropolis. The Acropolis was a formidable obstacle, the defenders were well supplied with food and drink, and the Spartan besiegers were initially stymied. Indeed, it looked as if they might abandon the attempt after a few days (Her. 5.64–65). But then Hippias made the mistake of trying to smuggle his sons past the besiegers and out of Athens. They were caught by the Spartans and held hostage. Hippias then surrendered on terms, and was allowed to leave Athens with his family. Thus ended the tyranny.[4]

But the liberation raised more questions than it answered. Who would now rule Athens? One might suppose that the spoils of political authority would end up going to the victors. But as Thucydides (6.53.3; cf. Aristophanes *Lysistrata* 1150–56) pointed out, few Athenians had played much part in the expulsion. The victorious Spartans, for their part, had no interest in progressive political innovation. They surely intended Athens to become a client-state, with a status similar to that of their allies in the Peloponnesian League. This would presumably mean that Athens would be governed by a rather narrow oligarchy, the form of government that (at least in the mid-fifth century: Thuc. 1.19) Sparta mandated as standard for all members of the league.[5] Spartans did not permanently garrison Athens (this was not their style), but after withdrawing their forces they remained very interested in Athenian politics. In the aftermath of the "liberation," King Cleomenes, the dominant figure in late-sixth-century Sparta, encouraged attempts by Isagoras and other Athenian aristocrats to establish a government that would exclude most Athenians from active political participation.

In the period 510–507 the political battlefield of Athens was disputed not between men who called themselves or thought of themselves as oligarchs and democrats, but rather between rival aristocrats. We cannot say exactly what sort of government Isagoras envisioned, but in light of subsequent developments it seems safe to assume that he intended to place effective control of affairs into the hands of a small, pro-Spartan elite. Isagoras' main opponent was Cleisthenes the Alcmaeonid. Despite the fact that Cleisthenes himself had been willing to accept the high office of archon under the Tyranny, some elements of the Alcmaeonid family had probably been

---

[4] For the tyranny and its end, see D. M. Lewis in *The Cambridge Ancient History*, 2nd ed. (1988), 4: 287–302, with sources cited.
[5] The government would not have been called an oligarchy because the word had not yet been invented; for the history of the term, see Raaflaub 1983.

active in resistance to the Tyrants.[6] Cleisthenes, obviously a leading figure among the Alcmaeonids by 508/7, may have felt that his family's antityrannical activity had earned him a prominent position in the political order that would replace the Tyranny. But that position did not come automatically. Indeed, Isagoras, with his Spartan connections, was gaining in influence and was elected archon for 508/7 B.C.[7] Thus, as Herodotus (5.66.2) tells us, Cleisthenes was getting the worst of it. In response, Cleisthenes did a remarkable thing: *ton dēmon prosetairizetai*. I will leave this phrase untranslated for the time being, for reasons that will become clear later. At any rate, because he had in some way allied himself with the demos, Cleisthenes now began to overshadow his opponents in the contest for political influence in Athens (Her. 5.69.2).

It is worth pausing at this point in the narrative to ask what the social and institutional context of the struggle between Isagoras and Cleisthenes would have been. Herodotus and the author of the *Athēnaiōn Politeia* employ the political vocabularies of the mid-fifth and late fourth centuries, respectively. But we must not apply the model of politics in Periclean or Demosthenic Athens to the late sixth century. Isagoras and Cleisthenes had recourse to few if any of the weapons familiar to us from the political struggles of those later periods – ideologically motivated *hetaireiai* (aristocratic clubs), ostracism, the *graphē paranomōn* (a legal procedure for use against those proposing illegal decrees) and other public actions in people's courts, finely honed orations by orators trained in the art of rhetoric. What shall we imagine in their place?

Late-archaic Athens was surely more dominated by the great families than was Athens of the fifth and fourth centuries. On the other hand, it would be a serious mistake to suppose that the scion-of-a-great-family/ordinary-citizen relationship can be seen in

---

[6] Accommodation and resistance of Alcmaeonids to the tyranny: Lewis in *The Cambridge Ancient History*, 2nd ed. (1988), 4: 288, 299–301. But cf. the skepticism of Thomas (1989, 263–64), who argues that the Alcmaeonids may have made up the tradition of their antityrannical activity and the story of their exile under the Peisistratids from whole cloth.

[7] Isagoras as archon: *Ath. Pol.* 21.1. The attempt by McCargar (1974) to separate Isagoras, opponent-of-Cleisthenes, from the archon of 508/7 on the grounds that *some* archons in this period were evidently relatively young (perhaps not much over thirty) and Isagoras *may* have been relatively mature seems to me chimerical, especially in light of the extreme rarity of the name. *Ath. Pol.* 22.5 claims that after the institution of the tyranny, and until 487/6, all archons were elected (*hairetoi*). The Tyrants had manipulated the elections to ensure that their own supporters were in office (see Rhodes 1981, 272–73); exactly how the elections would have been carried out in 509/8 (and thus what Isagoras' support consisted of) is unclear. We need not, anyway, suppose that Isagoras' election was indicative of a broad base of popular support; more likely his support was centered in the (non-Alcmaeonid) nobility. On the power of the archaic archon, see *Ath. Pol.* 3.3, 13.2 with the comments of Rhodes 1981, ad locc.

fully developed patron/client terms – for late-archaic Athens, the model of Roman republican politics is as anachronistic as is that of democratic politics. The reforms of Solon had undercut the traditional authority associated with birth. The policies of the Tyrants themselves had gone a long way in breaking down the traditional ties of dependence and obedience between upper- and lower-class Athenians. Moreover, Solon's creation of the formal status of citizen – a result of prohibiting debt slavery and of legal reforms that made Athenians potentially responsible for one another's welfare – had initiated a process whereby the demos became conscious of itself in forthrightly political terms. The Tyrants had encouraged political self-consciousness on the part of the masses of ordinary citizens by the sponsorship of festivals and building programs. The upshot was that by 510–508 B.C. the ordinary Athenian male had come a long way from the status of politically client of a great house. He saw himself as a citizen rather than as a subject, and at least some part of his loyalty was owed to the abstraction "Athens."[8]

And yet, the political institutions in which an Athenian man could express his developing sense of citizenship were, in early 508, still quite rudimentary and were still dominated by the elite. We may suppose that the traditional "constitution," as revised by Solon, still pertained. Thus there were occasional meetings of a political Assembly that all citizens had the right to attend. But it is unlikely that those outside the elite had the right or power to speak in that Assembly; nor could they hope to serve on the probouleutic [preparing business for the assembly] council of 400, as a magistrate, or on the Areopagus council.[9] Cleisthenes, as a leading member of a prominent family and as an Areopagite, surely did have both the right and the power to address the Assembly. It seems a reasonable guess that it was in the Assembly (although not necessarily uniquely here) that he allied himself to the demos, by proposing (and perhaps actually passing) constitutional reforms. The masses saw that these reforms would provide them with the institutional means to express more fully their growing sense of themselves as citizens. By these propositions and/or enactments Cleisthenes gained political influence, and so Isagoras began to get the worst of it (Her. 5.69.2–70.1).[10]

---

[8] See Ober 1989a, 60–68; Manville 1990, 124–209; Meier 1990, 53–81. On the lack of formal patronage structures in classical Athens, see Millett 1989.

[9] Solonian constitution: Ober 1989a, 60–65, with references cited. For the Areopagus from the time of Solon to Cleisthenes, see Wallace 1989, 48–76.

[10] Cleisthenes' connection with the demos is underlined by Her. 5.69.2: ὡς γὰρ δὴ τὸν Ἀθηναίων δῆμον πρότερον ἀπωσμένον τότε πάντως πρὸς τὴν ἑωυτοῦ μοῖραν προσεθήκατο

But if Cleisthenes now had the people on his side, Isagoras was still archon, and moreover he could call in outside forces. No matter what measures Cleisthenes had managed to propose or pass in the Assembly, a new constitutional order could become a practical political reality only if the Assembly's will were allowed to decide the course of events. Isagoras, determined that this would not be allowed, sent word of the unsettling developments to Cleomenes in Sparta. Cleomenes responded by sending a herald to the Athenians, informing them that, ostensibly because of the old Cylonian curse, they were to expel (*exeballe*) Cleisthenes and many others from the city (Her. 5.70.2). Cleisthenes himself duly left (*autos upexesche*: Her. 5.72.1).

Even after Cleisthenes' departure, Isagoras and/or Cleomenes must still have felt uneasy about the Athenian situation. A smallish (*ou ... megalēi cheiri*) mixed-nationality military force, featuring a core of Spartans and led by Cleomenes, soon arrived in the city (*parēn es tas Athēnas*: Her. 5.72.1). Cleomenes now, on Isagoras' recommendation, ordered further expulsions; Herodotus (5.72.1) claims that a total of 700 families were driven out (*agēlateei*). The archon Isagoras and his Spartan allies were clearly in control of Athens. That could have been the end of what we might call the progressive movement in Athenian politics. Athens might well have become another Argos – an occasionally restive but ultimately impotent client-state of Sparta. After all, the Spartans were the dominant military power in late-sixth-century Greece, whereas Cleisthenes and the other leading Athenians who opposed Isagoras were now powerless exiles.

But, of course, that was not the end of it. What happened next is the moment of revolution I alluded to earlier. According to Herodotus, Isagoras and Cleomenes next (*deutera*)

> attempted to abolish the *boulē* (*tēn boulēn kataluein epeirato*),[11] and to transfer political authority to a body of 300 supporters of Isagoras. But when the *boulē* resisted and refused to obey (*antistatheisēs de tēs boulēs kai ou boulomenēs peithesthai*), Cleomenes, together with Isagoras and

["When the Athenian *demos*, which had formerly been held in contempt, he had then wholly attached to his own side"], and by *Ath. Pol.* 20.1: ὁ Κλεισθένης προσηγάγετο τὸν δῆμον, ἀποδιδοὺς τῷ πλήθει τὴν πολιτείαν ["Cleisthenes attached the *demos*, giving political power to the *plethos* (mass)"]. Since Wade-Gery's seminal article (1933, 19–25), it has been widely accepted that the Assembly was the arena in which Cleisthenes won the favor of the people; cf. discussion by Ostwald 1969, 149–60.

[11] The implied subject of the verb *epeirato* is either Cleomenes or Isagoras. The grammar seems to point to Cleomenes, although presumably it was Isagoras (as archon) who gave the official order to the *boulē*. The point is in any case merely procedural: Herodotus' narrative demonstrates that Cleomenes and Isagoras were working hand in glove throughout.

his supporters, occupied the Acropolis (*katalambanousi tēn akropolin*). However, the rest of the Athenians (*Athēnaiōn de hoi loipoi*), who were of one mind (*ta auta phronēsantes*) [regarding these affairs], besieged them [on the Acropolis] for two days. But on the third day a truce was struck and the Lacedaemonians among them were allowed to leave the territory [of Attica]. (Her. 5.72.1–2)

In the aftermath of the expulsion of the Spartans, at least some of the non-Spartan members of Cleomenes' army (perhaps including Athenian supporters of Isagoras, although not Isagoras himself), who had been detained in Athens, were summarily executed (Her. 5.72.4–73.1). After these events (*meta tauta*) the Athenians recalled (*metapempsamenoi*) Cleisthenes and the 700 families (Her. 5.73.1). A new constitutional order (presumably resembling the order proposed by Cleisthenes or enacted on his motion before he was expelled) was soon put into place.[12]

Meanwhile, Cleomenes felt that the Athenians had "outraged" him "with both words and deeds" (*periubristhai epesi kai ergoisi*: Her. 5.74.1). I would gloss Herodotus' statement as follows: Cleomenes had been outraged by "the words" (of the *bouleutai* when they refused the dissolution order) and "the deeds" (of the demos in its uprising against the Spartans and the Athenian quislings). The Spartan king wanted revenge. He still planned to put Isagoras into power in Athens, but his counterattack of 506 fizzled due to a lack of solidarity in the Peloponnesian ranks on the one side and Athenian unity and military discipline on the other (Her. 5.74–77). Within just a few years, Athens had moved from the position of Spartan client-to-be to that of a powerful, independent polis. Athens twice had been occupied by an outside power, and the Athenians had rejected the rule of a narrow elite in favor of a radical program of political reforms, risen up successfully against their occupiers when the reform program was threatened, institutionalized the reforms, defended the new political order against external aggression, and begun on the road that would soon lead to democracy. It is an amazing story, and Herodotus (5.78) points out to his readers just how remarkable was the Athenian achievement. This, then, was the Athenian Revolution.

---

[12] Herodotus (5.66.2) implies that at least some of the reforms were put into place before Cleomenes' arrival; *Ath. Pol.* (20–21) discusses the reforms after giving the history of the revolution proper. I think it is most likely that some reforms were proposed and perhaps actually enacted by the Assembly before Cleomenes' arrival, but presumably there would not have been time for all the details of the new constitution to have been put into place. See below for the question of when the Council of 500 was established. For a review of the chronological issue, see Hignett 1952, 331–36; Rhodes 1981, 244–45, 249; Chambers 1990, 221–22.

Herodotus' account is quite closely followed, and perhaps in a few places amplified, by the account of the Aristotelian *Athēnaiōn Politeia*. I will focus on three aspects of the story that seem to me particularly notable. Two are familiar topoi [conventional themes] of Cleisthenes scholarship; the third is not.

The first peculiarity is that Cleisthenes, an Areopagite and a leading member of a fine old family, was willing in the first place to turn to the demos – the ordinary people, who, as Herodotus points out, "formerly had been held in contempt" (*proteron apōsmenon*: Her. 5.69.2). The second striking thing is that after his recall from exile, Cleisthenes *fulfilled* the promises he had made to the demos (in the form of proposals or enactments of the Assembly). He fully earned the trust they placed in him by establishing a form of government that, at least in the long run, doomed aristocratic political dominance in Athens. Much ink has been spilled over Cleisthenes' apparently peculiar behavior. Since Cleisthenes' actions seem to fly in the face of the aristocratic ethos ("Thou shalt not mix with the lower sort") and to contradict a common assumption about human nature itself ("Thou shalt always act in self-interest"), sophisticated explanations have been devised to explain what he was up to. Among views of Cleisthenes in the scholarly literature, two dominate the field, at least in the English-speaking world. One, well represented by David M. Lewis' influential article in *Historia*, is what we might call the "cynical realist" view, which holds that Cleisthenes was no true friend of the Athenian demos, but instead he benefited (or at least intended to benefit) the Alcmaeonids by extraordinarily clever gerrymandering in his establishment of the demes.[13] Lewis' "realist" view was advanced to counter the other dominant view: the "idealist" view of an altruistic Cleisthenes. This second viewpoint is perhaps best exemplified by the work of Victor Ehrenberg, who saw Cleisthenes as a selfless democratic visionary.[14]

I would not want to deny that Cleisthenes embraced a vision of a new society (see below) or that he hoped for a privileged place for his own family in that society. Yet neither the "realist" view of Cleisthenes the diabolically clever factional politician, nor the

---

[13] Lewis 1963 [= pp. 287–309, below].

[14] Ehrenberg 1973, 89–103: In 510 Cleisthenes was "a man of new and radical ideas" (89); in 508 he gained support "by revealing plans of a new democratic order" (90); "his reforms were ... the first examples of democratic methods" (91). Cleisthenes was not primarily interested in personal power, rather "power was to him a means of creating the constitutional framework for a society on the verge of becoming democratic" (91). For Ehrenberg, then, Cleisthenes is both selfless and a strong leader whose place is "at the helm" (102). Cf. Ehrenberg 1950.

"idealist" view of Cleisthenes the self-consciously altruistic Father of Democracy, adequately accounts for the third peculiarity in Herodotus' story – the uprising that doomed Isagoras and his partisans by forcing the surrender and withdrawal from Attica of the Spartans. Although the sparing accounts of Herodotus and the *Athēnaiōn Politeia* do not give us a great deal to work with, it appears that a spontaneous insurrection against Isagoras and the Spartans followed in the wake of Cleomenes' attempt to abolish the *boulē* and his occupation of the Acropolis. Without the uprising, the Cleisthenic reforms would have remained empty words: proposals or enactments voided by the efficient use of force by an outside power.

We will probably never know the details of what actually happened between Cleomenes' attempt to dissolve the *boulē* and his surrender on terms, but we can at least say what did *not* happen, and this may be useful in itself. First, and perhaps foremost, we should not imagine the siege of the Spartans on the Acropolis as an organized military campaign. Whatever may have been the form of the pre-Cleisthenic Athenian military forces, there is no mention in Herodotus or the *Athēnaiōn Politeia* at the siege of military leaders, or of any other sort of formal leadership – no reference to a polemarch* or to *stratēgoi* [generals], no *naukraroi*** calling in their clients from the fields. Now, the silence of our sources is a notoriously slippery ground for argument, but (as demonstrated by their accounts of, e.g., Cylon and the *naukraroi*, Solon and the Eupatrids, and Peisistratos and the Alcmaeonids) both Herodotus and the author of the *Athēnaiōn Politeia* were very interested in aristocratic leadership – whether it was individual or collective and institutional. I find it hard to believe that the presence of aristocratic leaders at the insurrection could have been forgotten or their identity fully suppressed in the sixty years or so between the revolution and Herodotus' arrival in Athens. Surely this brave resistance to the Spartan occupiers of the Acropolis is just the sort of thing that aristocratic families would remember for several generations. And it was just this sort of family tradition that formed the basis of much of Herodotus' Athenian narrative. One cannot, of course, exclude the possibility that Herodotus intentionally covered up the role played by leaders. But why would he want to do so? To further glorify the Alcmaeonid Cleisthenes? Yet even if Herodotus did favor the Alcmaeonids (which is far from certain), the hypothetical leaders

* The member of the board of nine archons with military responsibilities.
** Officials of early Athens whose function and the meaning of whose title is disputed: perhaps "ship-chiefs."

would have been Alcmaeonid allies, since Cleisthenes was immediately recalled and his constitutional reforms enacted.[15] In the end, positing aristocratic leadership for the action that expelled the Spartans is an *ignotus per ignotum* argument [explaining the unknown by means of the unknown], a modern supplement that relies for its credibility entirely on the unprovable (and elitist) assumption that aristocratic leadership in such matters would have been *sine qua non* [without which it could not have happened]. It is preferable in this case to trust our only sources and suppose that Herodotus and the *Athēnaiōn Politeia* mention no leaders because Athenian tradition recorded none, and that Athenian tradition recorded none because there were none – or at least none from the ranks of the leading aristocratic families.

Moreover, there is no mention in Herodotus or the *Athēnaiōn Politeia* of Athenian hoplites at the siege of the Acropolis: according to Herodotus, it is *Athēnaiōn hoi loipoi* (the rest of the Athenians) who, united in their view of the situation, do the besieging. *Athēnaiōn Politeia* (20.3) mentions *to plēthos* ["the mass"] and *ho dēmos*. This does not, of course, mean that no men wearing hoplite armor took part in the siege – but it is noteworthy that there is no suggestion in either source that anything resembling a "regular" army formation was called up. This might best be explained by the hypothesis that no "national" army existed in the era before the carrying out of Cleisthenes' constitutional reforms. If there was no national army properly speaking, then archaic Athenian military actions were ordinarily carried out by aristocratic leaders (presumably often acting in cooperation with one another): men who were able to muster bodies of armed followers.[16] If this is right, the mass expulsion recommended by Isagoras and carried out by Cleomenes (which no doubt focused on aristocratic houses) would have completely disrupted the traditional means of mustering the Athenian army – and this may well have been among their motives for the expulsion. It is not modern scholars alone who doubt the ability of masses to act without orders from their superiors.

The action that forced the surrender of the Spartans was evidently carried out in the absence of traditional military leaders and without a regular army. How then are we to visualize this action? The Athenian siege of the Acropolis in 508/7 is best understood as a riot

– a violent and more or less spontaneous uprising by a large number of Athenian citizens. In order to explain Cleomenes' actions, we must assume that the riot broke out very suddenly and was of relatively great size, intensity, and duration.[17]

After their occupation of the Acropolis, Cleomenes and his warriors were barricaded on a natural fortress, one that had frustrated the regular Spartan army during the siege of Hippias only a couple of years earlier. Yet on the third day of the siege the royal Spartan commander agreed to a humiliating conditional surrender – a surrender that left his erstwhile non-Lacedaemonian comrades to the untender mercies of the rioters. Cleomenes' precipitous agreement to these harsh terms must mean that he regarded the forces arrayed against him as too numerous (throughout the period of the siege) to contemplate a sortie. Why could the Spartans not simply have waited out the siege, as Hippias had been prepared to do? Given the undeveloped state of archaic Greek siegecraft, it is unlikely that the Spartans feared a successful assault on the stronghold. It is much more likely that (unlike Hippias) they had not had time to lay in adequate supplies. This suggests that Cleomenes had occupied the Acropolis very quickly, which in turn probably means that he was caught off guard by the uprising. This inferential sequence supports a presumption that the uprising occurred quite suddenly. What, then, was the precipitating factor?

Herodotus' account, cited above, describes the action in the following stages:

1. Isagoras/Cleomenes attempts to dissolve the *boulē*.
2. The *boulē* resists.
3. Cleomenes and Isagoras occupy the Acropolis.
4. The rest of the Athenians are united in their views.
5. They besiege the Spartan force.
6. Cleomenes surrenders on the third day of the siege.

If we are to follow Herodotus, we must suppose that steps 1, 2, 3, 5, and 6 are chronologically discrete and sequential events. Step 4 cannot, on the other hand, be regarded as a chronological moment; word of events 1–3 would have spread around Athens through

---

[17] I am assuming throughout that Cleomenes was an experienced and sane military commander, and that his decisions were made accordingly. On the dubious tradition of the madness of Cleomenes, see Griffiths 1989. It is interesting to note how the demos' action simply disappears in some respectable scholarly accounts, e.g., Ehrenberg 1973, 90: "Cleomenes and Isagoras met, however, with the resistance of the council ... which they had tried to disband and which was most likely the Areopagus. ... The Spartans withdrew, Isagoras was powerless, and many of his followers were executed."

the piecemeal word-of-mouth operations typical of an oral society. Presumably those living in the city would have learned what was going on first, and the news would have spread (probably very quickly, but not instantaneously) to the rural citizenry.[18] Herodotus' language (*ta auta phronēsantes* – "all of one mind") supports the idea of a generalized and quite highly developed civic consciousness among the Athenian masses – an ability to form and act on strong and communal views on political affairs.

If we take our lead from Herodotus' account, two precipitating factors can be adduced to explain the crystallization of opinion and the outbreak of violent anti-Spartan action on the part of the Athenian demos. First, the riot may have been sparked by the Spartan attempt to dissolve the *boulē* and the *boulē*'s resistance (thus the demos' action would commence as a consequence of steps 1 and 2, but before step 3). According to this scenario, Cleomenes and Isagoras will have been frightened by the sudden uprising into a precipitous defensive retreat to the nearby stronghold of the Acropolis. Alternatively, the riot might have broken out only after the Spartan occupation of the Acropolis (thus after step 3). On this reading of the evidence, the riot would be precipitated by the Spartan's offensive (in both senses of the term) takeover of the sacred Acropolis. This second hypothesis would certainly fit in with Herodotus' (5.72.3–4, cf. 5.90.2) story of Cleomenes' sacrilegious behavior and disrespect to the priestess of Athena. Yet this scenario is not, to my mind, fully satisfactory. It does not explain why Cleomenes felt it necessary to bring his entire force up to the Acropolis. Why did Isagoras and his partisans (*ho te Kleomenēs kai ho Isagorēs kai hoi stasiōtai autou**: Her. 5.72.2) go up to the Acropolis with Cleomenes? And if the occupation of the Acropolis by Spartan forces was a deliberate and unhurried act of aggression, how are we to explain the failure to bring up enough supplies to last even three days?[19]

---

[18] On how information was disseminated in Athens, see Hunter 1990.

* "Cleomenes and Isagoras and his partisans"

[19] Herodotus' statement that Cleomenes seized the Acropolis and was subsequently thrown out along with the Lacedaemonians (ἐπεχείρησέ τε καὶ τότε πάλιν ἐξέπιπτε μετὰ τῶν Λακεδαιμονίων: 5.72.4) makes it appear likely that the whole force had gone up to the Acropolis together, had been besieged together, and had surrendered together. It is unlikely that a significant part of Cleomenes' forces joined him on the hill after the commencement of the siege, and Herodotus says nothing about any of his men being captured in the lower city before the surrender. It is worth noting that Cylon (Her. 5.71; Thuc. 1.126.5–11) and Peisistratos (twice: Her. 1.59.6, 60.5) had earlier seized the Acropolis, each time as the first stage in an attempt to establish a tyranny. Cleomenes' case is different in that his move came *after* he had established control of the city.

It is certain that *Athēnaiōn Politeia* (20.3) saw Cleomenes' move to the Acropolis as a defensive response to a riot: when "the *boulē* resisted (*tēs de boulēs antistasēs*) and the mob gathered itself together (*kai sunathroisthentos tou plēthous*), the supporters of Cleomenes and Isagoras fled for refuge (*katephugon*) to the Acropolis."[20] Here the move to the Acropolis is specifically described as a defensive reaction to the council's resistance and the gathering of the people. *Athēnaiōn Politeia*'s statement has independent evidentiary value only if its author had access to evidence (whether in the form of written or oral traditions) other than Herodotus' account – on which he obviously leaned heavily. This issue of Quellenforschung [source criticism] cannot be resolved in any definitive way here, but it is not de facto [in fact] unlikely that the author of *Athēnaiōn Politeia*, who certainly had independent information on Cleisthenes' actual reforms, could have read or heard that Cleomenes and Isagoras fled to the Acropolis when a mob formed subsequent to the unsuccessful attempt to dissolve the *boulē*. At the very least, we must suppose that *Athēnaiōn Politeia* interpreted Herodotus' account of the move to the Acropolis as describing a flight rather than a planned act of aggression.[21]

Finally, let us consider the only other classical source for these events: Aristophanes' *Lysistrata* (lines 273–82). Here the chorus of Old Athenian Men, girding themselves for an assault on the Acropolis (held by a mixed-nationality force of women), urge each other on "since when Cleomenes seized it previously, he did not get away unpunished, for despite his Laconian spirit he departed giving over to me his arms, wearing only a little cloak, hungry, dirty, hairy-faced ... that's how ferociously I besieged that man, keeping constant guard, drawn up seventeen ranks deep at the gates." This is not, of course, history, but a poetic and comic description. Cleomenes' surrender of arms and his hunger are plausible enough, but the overly precise reference to "seventeen ranks" is unlikely to reflect historical reality. Nevertheless, as Rosalind Thomas points out, the Aristophanes passage probably does represent a living popular tradition

---

[20] Stanton (1990, 142, 144 n. 6) translates *sunathroisthentos tou plēthous* as "the common people had been assembled," on the grounds that "the verb 'had been assembled' is definitely passive." But I take the (morphologically) passive participle *sunathroisthentos* as having a reflexive rather than a passive meaning; on the distinction, see Rijksbaron 1984, 126–48. For a reflexive meaning for the passive participle of *sunathroizō*: Xen. *Anabasis* 6.5.30; of *athroizō*: Thuc. 1.50.4, 6.70.4; and especially Aristotle *Pol.* 1304b33.

[21] For a discussion of the relationship between Herodotus' narrative and *Ath. Pol.* 20–21, see Wade-Gery 1933, 17–19; and Rhodes (1981, 240–41, 244), who argues that Herodotus was *Ath. Pol.*'s sole authority for 20.1–3. For general discussions of *Ath. Pol.*'s use of sources, see Chambers 1990, 84–91.

about the siege.[22] And that tradition evidently focused on the military action of the people rather than on any doings of their leaders.

Although certainty cannot be achieved in the face of our limited sources, I think it is easiest to suppose that a spontaneous riot broke out when the *boulē* resisted. Caught off guard, Cleomenes and Isagoras retreated with their forces to the Acropolis stronghold to regroup. Rapidly spreading news of the occupation of the Acropolis further inflamed the Athenians, and so the ranks of the rioters were continually augmented as rural residents took up arms and streamed into the city. From Cleomenes' perspective, the bad situation, which had begun with the resistance of the *boulē*, only got worse as time went on. Stranded on the barren hill without adequate food or water, and with the ranks of his opponents increasing hourly, Cleomenes saw that his position was hopeless and negotiated a surrender. This scenario has the virtue of incorporating all major elements of Herodotus' account and the two other classical sources for the events, explaining Cleomenes' behavior in rational terms, and accommodating the means of news transmittal in an oral society.

If, as I have argued above, the Athenian military action that led to the liberation of Athens from Spartan control was a riot, precipitated by the refusal of the *bouleutai* [councillors] to obey Isagoras' or Cleomenes' direct order that the *boulē* dissolve itself in favor of the 300 Isagoreans, how are we to explain the relationship between the *boulē*'s act of defiance and the uprising itself? In the absence of direct textual evidence for either the motives of the *bouleutai* or their relationship to the demos, I offer, for comparative purposes, the example of another famous revolutionary refusal by a political body to dissolve when confronted with authority backed by force. Although such comparisons are supplementary, and not evidentiary in a formal sense, they are useful if they expand common assumptions about the limits of the possible, in this case by showing that an act of disobedience could indeed precipitate a revolution.

On June 17, 1789, the representatives of the Third Estate of the Kingdom of France, a body originally called together by the king, declared themselves to be the National Assembly of France. This act of self-redefinition was not accepted as valid by the existing, and heretofore sovereign, authority of the kingdom. Six days later, on June 23, King Louis XVI surrounded the assembly hail with some 4,000 troops and read a royal proclamation to the self-proclaimed

---

[22] Thomas 1989, 245–47.

Assemblymen in which he stated that the Third Estate's act in taking the name "The National Assembly" was voided; all enactments of the so-called National Assembly were nullified. Louis concluded his speech with the words, "I order you, gentlemen, to disperse at once." But the National Assembly refused either to disperse or to renounce its act of self-naming.[23]

According to the brilliant interpretation of these events by Sandy Petrey, the Third Estate's renaming of itself, and Louis' declaration that the renaming was void, set up a confrontation between speech acts – both the Third Estate and Louis made statements that were intended to have material effects in the real world of French society; both sides were attempting to *enact* a political reality through the speech act of naming (or, in Louis' case, "unnaming"). In the normal environment of prerevolutionary France, the king's statement would have been (in the terminology of J. L. Austin's speech-act theory, on which Petrey's interpretation is based) "felicitous" or efficacious – the Assembly would *be* dissolved because a sovereign authority had stated that it was dissolved. Yet, as Petrey points out, in a revolutionary situation, speech acts are not, at the moment of their enunciation, either felicitous or infelicitous *ipso facto* [by the actual fact (of being enunciated)]. Rather, their felicity or efficacy is demonstrated only in retrospect. In this case, the National Assembly did not dissolve when so ordered. By refusing to acknowledge the power of the king's speech to create real effects in the world, the Assembly contested the legitimacy of the king's authority.[24]

The confrontation of speech acts was not the end of the story. Louis subsequently attempted to enforce his will through the deployment of military force. This attempt was frustrated by the outbreak of riots in the streets of Paris. In the words of W. Doyle, in the weeks after the confrontation of June 23, "nobody doubted that the King was still prepared to use force to bring the Revolution to an end. The only thing that could prevent him was counterforce, and as yet the Assembly had none at its disposal. It was saved only by the people of Paris."[25] And thus the French Revolution was launched. Because the revolution succeeded, it turned out that the Third Estate's act of

---

[23] "Je vous ordonne, Messieurs, de vous séparer toute de suite." For the resolution of the Abbé de Sieyès renaming the Assembly, and the response of Louis at the "Royal Session" of June 23, see Wickham Legg 1905, 18–20, 22–33. For a narrative account of this stage of the revolution, see Doyle 1980, 172–77.

[24] Petrey 1988, esp. 17–51. Petrey's work is based on the ground-breaking linguistic theory of Austin 1975.

[25] Doyle 1980, 177.

renaming had been felicitous and Louis' proclamation of nullifica-
tion infelicitous; if the proof of the pudding is in the eating, the proof
of the revolutionary speech act is in the rebellion.

Although the efficacy of its speech acts was as yet undemon-
strated, the self-redefinition of the Third Estate as the National
Assembly on June 17 and the refusal of the Assemblymen of France
to acknowledge the force of the king's proclamation of dissolution
on June 23 helped to precipitate a revolution because they contested
the "inevitability" or "naturalness" of the power of the king's speech
to create political realities. Once the king's official proclamations
were no longer regarded as expressions of sovereign authority, political discourse ceased to be a realm of orderly enactment and became
a realm of contested interpretations. The success of any given interpretation was no longer based on its grounding in eternal and universally accepted truths about power and legitimacy; rather, success in
interpretation was now contingent upon the subsequent actions
of the French people acting en masse [as a body] – in this case, by
rioting and besieging the Bastille.

The parallels between the early stages of the French and the
Athenian revolutions are certainly not exact, but both similarities
and differences may be instructive. First, it is much less clear in the
Athenian case where, at any point in the story, sovereign authority
lay – or indeed, if we should be talking about sovereignty at all.
Isagoras was archon in 508/7, and so the dissolution order issued to
the *boulē* could be seen as carrying the weight of legitimately sanc-
tioned authority. But the archon of Athens did not (I suppose)
command the absolute sovereignty claimed by Louis XVI, and
the perceived legitimacy of Isagoras' authority was probably not
enhanced by his employment of foreign military support. What of the
comparison of the Athenian *boulē* to the National Assembly? This
will depend on what body Herodotus meant by the word *boulē*.
There are three choices (and all have had supporters among modern
scholars) – the Areopagus Council, the Solonian Council of 400, or
a newly established Council of 500. The parallel to the National
Assembly is closest if we follow the hypothesis, recently revived by
Mortimer Chambers, that the *boulē* in question was (perhaps a pro
tem [temporary] version of) the Council of 500, set up according
to Cleisthenes' proposals and the Assembly's enactment before the
arrival of the Spartans. This hypothesis would go far in explaining
both Cleomenes' interest in eliminating the council and the brave
determination of the councilmen to resist. But Chambers' argument,
based in part on his rejection of the existence of a Solonian Council

of 400, must remain for the time being an attractive speculation.[26] In any event, we cannot be sure exactly what powers the *boulē* claimed or its constitutional relationship to the archon.

Yet despite these caveats and uncertainties, several relevant factors in the French and Athenian cases seem quite similar. Herodotus' revealing comment that a king was "outraged by both words and deeds" (5.74.1) fits the French Revolution as well as the Athenian. In both cases, because of a verbal act of defiance by a political body, "official" political discourse – previously regarded by all concerned as authoritative and stable, as productive of acts of establishment, as a *thesmos* [ordinance] – became a battleground contested by two mutually exclusive interpretations regarding the source of legitimate public authority. Isagoras (or Cleomenes) said the *boulē* was dissolved. The *bouleutai* denied, by their resistance, the validity of this statement. As in the case of the French Revolution, it would be the actions of the ordinary people in the streets that would determine which of the opposed interpretations was felicitous and efficacious – rapidly evolving realities would decide whether the statement of Isagoras or of the *bouleutai* conformed to reality. In both revolutions, the official authority's recourse to military force was stymied by superior unofficial force in the form of mass riots. Both revolutions featured short but decisive sieges (the Acropolis and the Bastille) by leaderless crowds of citizens; both sieges ended in a negotiated surrender by the besieged leaders of organized military forces.[27] Furthermore, both uprisings featured summary (and, I would add, morally reprehensible) killings of individuals identified as enemies of the revolution. The Athenian Revolution, no less than the French, was baptized in the blood of "counter-revolutionaries."[28] Yet the difference between Athens and France in this regard is also salient:

[26] Chambers 1990, 222–23.

[27] For the siege of the Bastille, see Godechot 1970, 218–46. The Bastille was a formidable, if dilapidated, fortress, guarded by a small force of eighty-four pensioners and thirty-two Swiss mercenaries. For the week before the assault of July 14, its commander, Governor de Launey, had refurbished the defenses to withstand an assault. Yet "he had only one day's supply of meat and two days' supply of bread, and moreover there was no drinking water inside the fortress. … de Launey may … have thought that if he were attacked by an unarmed or ill-armed crowd the assault would not last longer than one day and that at nightfall the rioters would disperse" (219). It is tempting to suppose that Cleomenes thought along similar lines.

[28] On the killing of Governor de Launey and seven other defenders of the Bastille on July 14, and of other agents of the Old Regime in the days thereafter, see Godechot 1970, 243–46. The Athenian killings have been questioned on the grounds of the wording of *Ath. Pol.* 20.3 (Κλεομένην μὲν καὶ τοὺς μετ᾽ αὐτοῦ πάντας ἀφεῖσαν ὑποσπόνδους ["they released Cleomenes and all those with him under a truce"]), but as Ostwald (1969, 144 with n. 6) points out, this need only refer to the Lacedaemonian troops; cf. Rhodes 1981, 246–47.

the decade after 507 saw no equivalent to either Jacobinite Terror or Thermidorian reaction.

In terms of assigning credit (or blame) for the uprising and its aftermath, it is important to note that though the brave action of the bourgeois gentlemen of the Third Estate in naming themselves the National Assembly helped to foment the French Revolution, those gentlemen did not take the lead in storming the Bastille,[29] and they were not able subsequently to control the direction of the revolution. Nor were the *bouleutai* in control of the Athenian Revolution. Neither Herodotus nor *Athēnaiōn Politeia* assigns the *boulē* a leadership role in the insurrection after its refusal to disperse: according to Herodotus, after the *boulē* refused to obey the dissolution order, Cleomenes and Isagoras occupied the Acropolis, and *ta auta phronēsantes, Athēnaiōn hoi loipoi* besieged the Acropolis – taken literally, this comment would seem to exclude the *bouleutai* from any role at all. For *Athēnaiōn Politeia* (20.3), it was when "the *boulē* resisted and the mob gathered itself together" that "the supporters of Cleomenes and Isagoras fled to the Acropolis," and subsequently it was *ho dēmos* that besieged them. Both authors seem to agree on the importance of the *boulē*'s act of defiance, but both also agree in seeing the key event as the uprising of the Athenian masses.[30]

Finally, how are we to interpret the political implications of this riotous uprising and its relationship to the subsequent Athenian political order – to the "constitution of Cleisthenes"? Once again, a comparative approach may offer some clues. The highly influential work of E. P. Thompson on food riots in eighteenth-century England, and that of Natalie Z. Davis on religious riots in sixteenth-century

[29] For the composition of the crowd (mostly artisans from Paris) that stormed the Bastille, and the absence of Assemblymen or any other formal leaders, see Godechot 1970, 211, 221–26, 230, 237–39.

[30] Cf., for example, Hammond 1959, 185–86: "The Council resisted. It raised the people against Cleomenes and Isagoras, who seized the Acropolis and found themselves besieged"; Ostwald 1969, 144; "The Council refused to be intimidated and, with the support of the common people, besieged the acropolis"; Stanton 1990, 144 n. 6: the council in question must have been the Areopagus, since unlike the councils of 400 or 500, it "would have been sufficiently permanent and would have contained a sufficient accumulation of politically experienced men to organize resistance to a military forte. A major thrust was the assembling of the common people ... and this could have been achieved by the influence which ex-arkhon clan leaders in the Areopagos held over their retainers." The Areopagus leadership theory would need to explain how Cleomenes' force could be strong and decisive enough to "drive out" 700 families dispersed through Attica (cf. Stanton [1990, 141 n. 14], who questions the number 700), but too weak to stop at most 100–200 men (numbers of Areopagites: Wallace 1989, 97 with n. 23; Hansen 1990 – from which we must deduct those expelled with the 700), who were presumably gathered in one place to hear the dissolution order, from organizing a resistance.

France, has led to the development of a useful approach to the historical assessment of rioting. This model is discussed in some detail
in a recent article by Suzanne Desan, who points out that, according
to Thompson and Davis, violent collective actions in early-modern
England and France were not merely random outbreaks indicative of
generalized popular dissatisfaction. Rather, these riots are best read
as acts of collective self-definition, or redefinition. The English
peasants were, for example, rioting in support of the reenactment of
what Thompson described as a "moral economy" – a view of the
world that was actually quite conservative in that it assumed the
legitimacy of paternalistic (or at least clientistic) relations between
peasantry and local aristocracy.[31]

The riot of 508/7 can thus be read as a collective act of political
self-definition in which the demos rejected the archon Isagoras as the
legitimate public authority. As Herodotus' account suggests, the riot
was the physical, active manifestation of the Athenians having come
to be "of one mind" about civic affairs. This reading clarifies the
general role of Cleisthenes in the Athenian Revolution and the
scope of his accomplishments. More specifically, it helps to explain
the relationship between Cleisthenes and the demos in the months
before and after the definitive moment of the riot.

Let us return to the problems of the context and meaning
of Herodotus' famous and problematic comment (5.66.2) that
Kleisthenēs ton dēmon prosetairizetai. This phrase is often taken to
be a description of a straightforward event with a straightforward
subject and object. A. de Sélincourt's Penguin translation is typical:
"Cleisthenes ... took the people into his party." But we need not give
the middle form *prosetairizetai* quite such a clearly active force, nor
need we imagine it as describing an event that occurred in a single
moment. I would suggest as an alternate (if inelegant) translation:
"Cleisthenes embarked on the process of becoming the demos'
trusted comrade."[32] Herodotus' account certainly implies that
Cleisthenes had developed a special relationship with the demos
before his expulsion from Athens. That relationship, which I have
suggested above was characterized by proposals or enactments in the
Assembly, was evidently the proximate cause of Isagoras' calling in
of Cleomenes. But there is no reason to suppose that the process
referred to by the verb *prosetairizetai* was completed before

---

[31] Desan 1989.

[32] It is important to keep in mind that the terminology is in any event Herodotus', not
Cleisthenes'. It was probably not in use in Cleisthenes' day, and reflects rather the political
vocabulary of the mid-fifth century: Chambers 1990, 221.

Cleisthenes was expelled. In short, I would suggest that Cleisthenes
did not so much absorb the demos into his *hetaireia* [group of
comrades], as he *himself* was absorbed into an evolving, and no
doubt somewhat inchoate, demotic vision of a new society, a society
in which distinctions between social statuses would remain but in
which there would be no narrow clique of rulers.

The sea change in Athenian political practice implied by
Cleisthenes' new relationship with the demos was not signaled by an
act of noblesse oblige – opening the doors of the exclusive, aristocratic *hetaireia* to the masses. Rather, it was a revolution in the
demos' perception of itself and in an aristocrat's perceptions regarding his own relationship, and that of all men of his class, to the
demos. Cleisthenes acknowledged the citizens of Athens as equal
sharers in regard to the *nomoi* (laws), and under the banner of
isonomia [legal equality] the men of the demos became, in effect
if not in contemporary nomenclature, Cleisthenes' *hetairoi*
[comrades].[33] We must remember that Herodotus' terminology is
that of the mid-fifth rather than the late sixth century. But in the fifth
century, when Herodotus was writing his *Histories*, Athenian
hetairoi were expected to help one another, and to seek to harm their
common enemies. The demos looked out for Cleisthenes' interests by
attacking the Spartans and by recalling him immediately upon their
departure. Political friendship is a two-way street, and Cleisthenes
had no real option other than to look after the interests of the demos
by devising and working to implement (through enactments of the
Assembly) an institutional framework that would consolidate and
stabilize the new demotic vision of politics. That vision had grown
up among the Athenian citizen masses in the course of the sixth
century and had found an active, physical manifestation in the riot
that occurred during Cleisthenes' enforced absence from the scene.
The "constitution of Cleisthenes" channeled the energy of the demos'
self-defining riot into a stable and workable form of government.

In sum, Cleisthenes was not so much the authoritative leader of
the revolution as he was a highly skilled interpreter of statements
made in a revolutionary context and of revolutionary action itself.
This is not to deny any of his brilliance, or even his genius. But it is
to see his genius *not* in an ability to formulate a prescient vision of a
future democratic utopia, *nor* in an ability to hide a selfish dynastic
scheme behind a constitutional façade, but rather in his ability to
"read" – in a sensitive and perceptive way – the text of Athenian

---

[33] On *isonomia* and its meaning, see Ober 1989a, 74–75, with literature cited.

discourse in a revolutionary age, and to recognize that Athenian mass action had created new political facts. Cleisthenes saw that the revolutionary action of the Athenian demos had permanently changed the environment of politics and political discourse. After the revolution there could be no secure recourse to extra-demotic authority. If Athens were to survive as a polis, there would have to be a new basis for politically authoritative speech, but that basis must find its ground in the will of the demos itself. Having read and understood his complex text, Cleisthenes knew that there could be no turning back to rule by aristocratic faction – or at least he saw that any attempt to turn back the clock would bring on a bloodbath and make effective resistance to Sparta impossible. And so, acting as a good *hetairos*, well deserving of the *pistis* (good faith) placed in him (*Athēnaiōn Politeia* 21.1) by his mass *hetaireia*, Cleisthenes came up with a constitutional order that both framed and built upon the revolution that had started without him.

REFERENCES

Austin, J. L. (1975), *How to Do Things with Words*, eds J. O. Urmson and M. Sbisà, 2nd edn, Oxford: Oxford University Press/Cambridge, MA: Harvard University Press.

Burn, A. R. (1960), *The Lyric Age of Greece*, London: Arnold.

Bury, J. B., and Meiggs, R. (1975), *A History of Greece to the Death of Alexander the Great*, 4th ed., London: Macmillan.

Chambers, M. (ed. and comm.) (1990), *Aristoteles, Staat der Athener* (Aristoteles Werke in deutscher Übersetzung, x. i), Berlin: Akademie-Verlag.

Desan, S. (1989), "Crowds, Community and Ritual in the work of E. P. Thompson and Natalie Davis," in L. Hunt (ed.), *The New Cultural History* (Berkeley and Los Angeles: University of California Press), 47–71.

Doyle, W. (1980), *Origins of the French Revolution*, New York: Oxford University Press.

Ehrenberg, V. (1950), "Origins of Democracy," *Historia* 1, 515–48 = Ehrenberg, *Polis und Imperium: Beiträge zur alten Geschichte*, eds K. F. Stroheker and A. J. Graham (Zurich: Artemis, 1965), 264–97.

—— (1973), *From Solon to Socrates*, 2nd ed., London: Methuen.

Forrest, W. G. (1966), *The Emergence of Greek Democracy: The Character of Greek Politics, 800–400 B.C.*, London: Weidenfeld and Nicolson.

Frost, F. J. (1984), "The Athenian Military Before Cleisthenes," *Historia* 33, 283–94.

Godechot, J. (1970), *The Taking of the Bastille, July 14, 1789*, trans. J. Stewart, London: Faber.

Griffiths, A. (1989), "Was Kleomenes Mad?," in A. Powell (ed.), *Classical Sparta: Techniques Behind Her Success* (London: Routledge), 51–78.

Hammond, N. G. L. (1959), *A History of Greece to 322 B.C.*, Oxford: Oxford University Press (3rd edn 1986).

Hansen, M. H. (1986), "The Origin of the Term *Demokratia*," *Liverpool Classical Monthly* 11, 35–6.

—— (1990), "The Size of the Council of the Areopagos and its Social Composition in the Fourth Century B.C.," *Classica et Mediaevalia* 41, 55–61.

Hignett, C. (1952), *A History of the Athenian Constitution to the End of the Fifth Century B.C.*, Oxford: Oxford University Press.

Hunt, L. (ed.) (1989), *The New Cultural History*, Berkeley and Los Angeles: University of California Press.

Hunter, V. (1990), "Gossip and the Politics of Reputation in Classical Athens," *Phoenix* 44, 299–325.

Lévêque P., and Vidal-Naquet, P. (1996), *Cleisthenes the Athenian: An Essay on the Representation of Space and Time in Greek Political Thought from the End of the Sixth Century to the Death of Plato*, trans. D. A. Curtis, Atlantic Highlands, NJ: Humanities Press.

Lewis, D. M. (1963), "Cleisthenes and Attica," *Historia* 12, 22–40 = Lewis, *Selected Papers in Greek and Near Eastern History* (Cambridge: Cambridge University Press, 1997), 77–98, ch. x = this book, ch. 12.

McCargar, D. J. (1974), "Isagoras, Son of Teisandros, and Isagoras, Eponymous Archon of 508/7: A Case of Mistaken Identity," *Phoenix* 28, 275–81.

Manville, P. B. (1990), *The Origins of Citizenship in Ancient Athens*, Princeton, NJ: Princeton University Press.

Meier, C. (1990), *The Greek Discovery of Politics*, trans. D. McLintock, Cambridge, MA: Harvard University Press.

Millett, P. (1989), "Patronage and its Avoidance in Classical Athens," in A. Wallace-Hadrill (ed.), *Patronage in Ancient Society* (London: Routledge), 15–47.

Morris, I. (1996), "The Strong Principle of Equality and the Archaic Origins of Greek Democracy," in J. Ober and C. Hedrick (eds), *Demokratia: A Conversation on Democracies, Ancient and Modern* (Princeton, NJ: Princeton University Press), 19–48.

—— (1999), *Archaeology as Cultural History: Words and Things in Iron Age Greece*, Oxford: Blackwell.

Murray, O. (1980), *Early Greece*, London: Fontana (2nd ed. 1993).

Ober, J. (1989a), *Mass and Elite in Democratic Athens: Rhetoric, Ideology and the Power of the People*, Princeton, NJ: Princeton University Press.

—— (1989b), "Models and Paradigms in Ancient History," *Ancient History Bulletin* 3, 134–7 = Ober, *The Athenian Revolution* (Princeton, NJ: Princeton University Press, 1996), 13–17, ch. ii.

—— (1993), "Public Speech and the Power of the People in Democratic

Athens," *PS: Political Science and Politics* (September 1993), 481–5 = Ober, *The Athenian Revolution* (Princeton, NJ: Princeton University Press, 1996), 18–31, ch. iii.

—— (1996), "Revolution Matters: Democracy as Demotic Action (Response to Kurt A. Raaflaub)," in I. Morris and K. A. Raaflaub (eds), *Democracy 2500? Questions and Challenges* (Dubuque, IA: Kendall–Hunt, for Archaeological Institute of America), 67–85, ch. iv.

Ostwald, M. (1969), *Nomos and the Beginnings of the Athenian Democracy*, Oxford: Oxford University Press.

Petrey, S. (1988), *Realism and Revolution. Balzac, Stendahl, Zola and the Performances of History*, Ithaca, NY: Cornell University Press.

Raaflaub, K. A. (1983), "Democracy, Oligarchy and the Concept of the 'Free Citizen' in Late Fifth-Century Athens," *Political Theory* 11, 517–44.

—— (1995), "Einleitung und Bilanz: Kleisthenes, Ephialtes und die Begründung der Demokratie," in K. H. Kinzl (ed.), *Demokratia: Der Weg der Griechen zur Demokratie*, Wege der Forschung (Darmstadt: Wissenschaftliche Buchgesellschaft), 1–54.

—— (1996a), "Equality and Inequalities in the Athenian Democracy," in J. Ober and C. Hedrick (eds), *Demokratia: A Conversation on Democracies, Ancient and Modern* (Princeton, NJ: Princeton University Press), 139–74.

—— (1996b), "Power in the Hands of the People: Foundations of Athenian Democracy," in I. Morris and K. A. Raaflaub (eds), *Democracy 2500? Questions and Challenges* (Dubuque, IA: Kendall–Hunt, for Archaeological Institute of America), 31–66, ch. iii.

—— (1996c), "The Thetes and Democracy (Response to Josiah Ober)," in I. Morris and K. A. Raaflaub (eds), *Democracy 2500? Questions and Challenges* (Dubuque, IA: Kendall–Hunt, for Archaeological Institute of America), 87–103, ch. v.

Rhodes, P. J. (1981), *A Commentary on the Aristotelian Athenaion Politeia*, Oxford: Oxford University Press.

Rijksbaron, A. (1984), *The Syntax and Semantics of the Verb in Classical Greek*, Amsterdam: Gieben.

Sealey, R. (1976), *A History of the Greek City States, ca.700–338 B.C.*, Berkeley and Los Angeles: University of California Press.

Stanton, G. R. (1990), *Athenian Politics, c.800–500 B.C.: A Sourcebook*, London: Routledge.

Thomas, R. (1989), *Oral Tradition and Written Record in Classical Athens*, Cambridge: Cambridge University Press.

Wade-Gery, H. T. (1933), "Studies in the Structure of Athenian Society, II: The Laws of Kleisthenes," *Classical Quarterly* 27, 17–29 = Wade-Gery, *Essays in Greek History* (Oxford: Blackwell, 1958), 135–54.

Wallace, R. W. (1989), *The Areopagos Council, to 307 B.C.*, Baltimore: Johns Hopkins University Press.

Wickham Legg, L. G. (ed.) (1905), *Select Documents Illustrative of the French Revolution*, Oxford: Oxford University Press.

Wood, G. S. (1992), *The Radicalism of the American Revolution*, New York: Knopf.

Zimmern, A. E. (1931), *The Greek Commonwealth: Politics and Economics in Fifth-Century Athens*, 5th ed., Oxford: Oxford University Press.

12 *Cleisthenes and Attica**

DAVID M. LEWIS

There has been much recent work on Cleisthenes.[1] The justification for yet another article lies, I hope, in its different approach, from the land of Attica itself and the framework which Cleisthenes gave it. I hope also that this difference of approach will excuse what may seem a somewhat cavalier attitude to my immediate predecessors, whose arguments will seldom appear, although I have read them with attention and profit. The argument of this article proceeds largely from survivals, and leads to the paradox that we can understand Cleisthenes' work best in the places where he failed. These failures, however, give us clearer light not only on his aims, but on the woven texture of tradition and innovation which is formed by the life of classical Athens.

* Originally published in *Historia* xii 1963, 22–40; this version, with updated references, published in David M. Lewis, *Selected Papers on Greek and Near Eastern History* (Cambridge University Press, 1997), 77–98, © Cambridge University Press. Reprinted with the permission of Franz Steiner Verlag, Stuttgart, and Cambridge University Press.
Important work on Cleisthenes' organisation since the original publication of this article includes the following: J. S. Traill, *The Political Organization of Attica: A Study of the Demes, Trittyes and Phylai, and their Representation in the Athenian Council* (Hesperia Supp. xiv 1975: reviewed by Lewis, *AJA* lxxx 1976, 311–12 = his *Selected Papers*, 99–101, ch. xi); P. Siewert, *Die Trittyen Attikas und Die Heeresreform des Kleisthenes* (Vestigia xxxiii; Munich: Beck, 1982: reviewed by Lewis, *Gnomon* lv 1983, 431–6 = his *Selected Papers*, 102–9, ch. xii); G. R. Stanton, 'The Tribal Reform of Kleisthenes the Alkmeonid', *Chiron* xiv 1984, 1–41; J. S. Traill, *Demos and Trittys: Epigraphical and Topographical Studies in the Organization of Attica* (Toronto: Athenians, 1986); G. R. Stanton, 'The Trittyes of Kleisthenes', *Chiron* xxiv 1994, 161–207.
[1] The two important items of the last fifteen years which do not appear in my notes are J. A. O. Larsen, *Representative Government in Greek and Roman History* (Berkeley and Los Angeles, CA: University of California Press, 1955) ch. 1, and D. W. Bradeen, *TAPA* 86 (1955), 22–30. The second starts from presuppositions which are here rejected, the first I cannot accept, largely because I believe that the bouleutic oath [council's oath] is more likely to have formalised than to have altered the situation which existed before it. This paper has been read by A. Andrewes, W. G. Forrest and A. E. Raubitschek, and much improved by them. They are not responsible for the blemishes which remain, and would, I think, differ from me on several points. (See also R. J. Hopper, *BSA* 56 (1961), 189–219.)

I REGIONAL PARTIES IN SIXTH-CENTURY ATHENS

Let us begin by sketching our evidence for regional divisions in Athenian politics before Cleisthenes' reforms. The parties of the 560s have regional names, acquired, we are told,[2] from the places where they farmed. We should emphasise that parties may include members from outside the original area of the nucleus. When Peisistratus waited at Marathon in 546, supporters came to him from Athens itself as well as from the country-villages.[3] This should also act as a warning against any easy assignment of single economic or even constitutional motives to a party. The party may be a complex of driving-forces held together by its leader; such a complex is in fact sketched for Peisistratus' party by Aristotle.[4] However, even with these qualifications in mind, it is legitimate to look for the nuclei.

The *pedieis* [men of the plain] are relatively straightforward. None will doubt that their nucleus is in the plain of Athens itself, not indeed the whole of it, for we shall see reason to exclude the area south and south-east of the city, but at least the more substantial portion to the north and west. Support for this comes from the name of their leader, Lycurgus.[5] The chances are high that he, like the later prominent men of the name, came from Boutadai, a little to the west of the city.[6] No other family can be confidently associated with this party, but one may be tempted to go back to Myron of Phlya, prosecutor of the Alcmeonids for their action against the Cylonian conspiracy.[7] He will have come from the north-east of the *pedion* [plain].

The *paralioi* [men of the coast] may best be located by looking for Alcmeonid land. Alcmeonids are found in three demes, Alopeke,[8] Agryle,[9] and Xypete,[10] all to the south and south-east of the city.[11]

---

[2] *Ath. Pol.* 13.5.

[3] Her. 1. 62.1.

[4] *Ath. Pol.* 13.4-5. My idea of the 'Parties' does not differ substantially from that formulated by R. Sealey, *Historia* 9 (1960), 163-5.

[5] Her. 1.59.3.

[6] *P.A.* 9249-9251.

[7] Plut. *Sol.* 12.4.

[8] Μεγακλῆς Ἱπποκράτους [Megakles son of Hippokrates] (*Ath. Pol.* 22.5 and numerous ostraka [potsherds used for voting in ostracisms]) and others.

[9] Λεωβώτης Ἀλκμέωνος [Leobotes son of Alkmeon] (Plut. *Them.* 23.1); cf. also Ἀλκμεωνίδης Ἐρεχθηίδος [Alkleonides of Erechtheis] (Tod 26 [= Meiggs and Lewis 33 = *IG* i³ 1147], 135).

[10] Καλλίξενος Ἀριστωνύμου [Kallixenos son of Aristonymos] (*Hesperia* 19 (1950), 376ff.).

[11] Sealey, *Historia* 9 (1960), 163 n. 41, adds Leukonoe from *IG* i² 368 [= i³ 468], 3-4. This must remain uncertain, since no certain Alcmeonid is called Megakleides. If he were accepted, we would have Alcmeonid land north of the city.

They farm the land which goes down towards the coast, and will thus have got their name. Two other families are to be associated. The principal family of the Kerykes, headed in this period by Kallias son of Phainippos, is attested as notably anti-tyrant by Herodotus.[12] After many wanderings in modern scholarship, it is now firmly settled in Alopeke.[13] Another Alopeke family, later allied with this one by marriage,[14] is the house which produced Aristides,[15] who, we are told,[16] was in early life a *hetairos* [comrade] of Cleisthenes. Alopeke is reasonably to be identified as the headquarters of the party, and this finds an echo in a partisan drinking-song which will go back to this period[17] οὐκ ἔστιν ἀλωπεκίζειν, οὐδ' ἀμφοτέροισι γίγνεσθαι φίλον*, where ἀλωπεκίζειν refers as much to the political shifts of the men of Alopeke and their leader Megakles as to the cunning of the fox.

Both of these parties will have had their supporters in the city. Alcibiades of Skambonidai and Leogoras of Kydathenaion, head of the other main branch of the Kerykes, could claim opposition to Peisistratus later.[18]

The *Hyperakrioi* [men beyond the hills] are, on the face of it, the men beyond the hills, outside the Parnes-Pentelikon-Hymettos ring.[19] *Diakrioi*, the main alternative form of their name, will come from the Diakria, which is said, on the most plausible emendation of Hesychius,[20] to run from Parnes to Brauron. It is at Brauron itself that we can safely place their leader Peisistratus.[21] Marathon, further north, is well within their area, and it is tempting to think that the

---

[12] VI.121.

[13] *Hesperia* 5 (1936), 410, *BSA* 50 (1955), 13–14, *JHS* 81 (1961), 120.

[14] Plut. *Arist.* 25.4. If Aristides had been himself a Keryx, we would have been told.

[15] *Ibid.* 1.1.

[16] *Ibid.* 2.1. His father Lysimachos may be the *tamias* [treasurer] of *IG* i² 393 = i³ 510 which presumably dates from a period of Peisistratid exile, since it has an Andocides (see n. 18). But J. K. Davies points out to me that this Lysimachos could also be a Boutad, ancestor of the family analysed in *BSA* 50 (1955), 7, which would make as good political sense.

[17] Ar. *Wasps* 1240–1.

* 'You can't be a fox, or be a friend of both.'

[18] Isoc. xvi.26; And. i.106, ii.26.

[19] So H. T. Wade-Gery, *Essays in Greek History* (Oxford: Blackwell, 1958) 167 n.2.

[20] *s.v.* Διακρεῖς ... καὶ ἡ χώρα Διακρία, ἡ ἀπὸ Πάρνηθος εἰς βαλυλῶνος [*s.v.* Diakreis ... 'and the land called Diakria, from Parnes to *valylon's*']. P. N. Ure, *The Origin of Tyranny* (Cambridge: Cambridge University Press, 1922), 312, suggested ἕως Αὔλωνος ['as far as Aulon'] which has reached Latte's *apparatus*, but Aulon is of no importance and forms no kind of landmark to define a boundary. Clear evidence for Brauron in this context comes from Bekker, *Anecdota* i. 242 Διάκρια· τόπος Ἀττικῆς ὑπὸ Βραυρῶνα Ἐλευσίνιον Δήμητρος καὶ Φερεφάττης ἱερόν ['Diakria: a place in Attica below Brauron the Eleusinian a sanctuary of Demeter and Pherephatte']. I would put a full stop after Βραυρῶνα, and regard the last five words as a totally different gloss, wrongly incorporated.

[21] Plato, *Hipp.* 228B, Plut. *Sol.* 10.3.

tyrant's party landed there in 546 and 490 because they could be sure of local support. The direct arguments for Peisistratid supporters in this area are not however very strong. Wilamowitz[22] thought that the Aristion who moved the decree for Peisistratus' bodyguard[23] was the Aristion commemorated in the well-known relief from Velanideza, who would thus have come from half-way between Brauron and Marathon, but the date of the relief is too late[24] and the name not uncommon. More hopeful supporters might be found in the two Marathonians found on ostraka of the 480s. Of these, Boutalion is a serious possibility for the missing name of the pro-tyrant ostracised in 485.[25] The other, Habron son of Patrokles,[26] I was once inclined to think identical with a Habron, archon under Hippias in 518/17,[27] possibly son of the Patrokles who dedicated the mid-sixth-century altar of Athena Nike,[28] but Lobel[29] has now made it highly unlikely that there was such an archon. The case for Peisistratid supporters in Marathon must remain largely one of probability.

Hyperakrioi is, I take it, a wider term than *Diakrioi*, and will accommodate, besides these north-eastern hills, the East Attic plain which we now call the Mesogeia. The population of this plain must already have been substantial in the time of Cleisthenes, for the descendants of the demesmen of 507 provided over an eighth of the fourth-century *boule* [council]. It is, however, extremely short of early families of importance. The one sixth-century figure is Socrates of Paiania, father of the Phye who played a part in Peisistratus' first return and married his son Hipparchus.[30] Paiania lies directly on the only route from Brauron to Athens. The Mesogeia has been described as 'the plain dominated by Brauron and Marathon.'[31] This is slightly misleading. Marathon is very much tucked away behind Pentelikon, and a sharp uphill walk is needed to take one out of the marshy valley of Brauron itself to the 120-metre level of the main Mesogeia. Nevertheless it is true that, in the absence of powerful

[22] *Aristoteles und Athen* (Berlin: Weidmann, 1893) i.261; cf. A. R. Burn, *The Lyric Age of Greece* (London: Arnold, 1960) 305.

[23] *Ath. Pol.* 14.1.

[24] See most recently G. M. A. Richter, *The Archaic Gravestones of Attica* (London: Phaidon, 1961) 47. She puts it *c.*510.

[25] *Ath. Pol.* 22.6. *Hesperia* 21 (1952), 8 with n. 15.

[26] *Hesperia* 6 (1937), 155–6, Supp. 8 (1949), 409.

[27] T. J. Cadoux, *JHS* 68 (1948), 112.

[28] A. E. Raubitschek, *Dedications from the Athenian Akropolis* (Cambridge, MA: Archaeological Institute of America, 1949) no. 329.

[29] On *P. Oxy.* xxvi.2438.

[30] Kleidemos *FGrH* 323F15.

[31] Sealey, *Historia* 9 (1960), 165.

families in the plain itself, Marathon and Brauron, both with important cults to serve as a focus, could exercise influence on the plain, which would tend to look east to them before it looked west to Athens.

Two more families of importance remain for consideration. Since Wilamowitz[32] it has been normal to associate the Philaids with Brauron and the *Hyperakrioi*.[33] The case for this has been substantially political, and the only topographical argument is that Philaios is said to have settled at Brauron, which was called Philaidai in the Cleisthenic deme-system.[34] However, it can hardly be true that Philaios bound his descendants to the site forever. On this argument, it would be surprising that Themistocles came from Phrearrhioi and not from the Lykomid centre at Phlya, and in fact the ancestors of Epicurus, the only man described as a Philaid by an ancient source, lived at Gargettos, well away from Brauron, in 507.[35] There has never been any doubt that the Kimonids, who succeeded to the position of Miltiades son of Kypselos, lived elsewhere. Their family estates were at Lakiadai,[36] west of Athens on the Sacred Way, and Kimon and doubtless his father bore that demotic.[37] Their family tombs were at Koile, just outside the city to the south-west.[38] They may indeed have been a different family, although it has recently been observed[39] that it would make better sense of Miltiades' adoption of Stesagoras II if Stesagoras I had also been a Philaid. A neglected Pindaric scholion even positively asserts the descent of Kimon from Aias.[40] A stronger positive reason for detaching the Philaids from Brauron may be found in the story of Miltiades' meeting with the Dolonkoi.[41] The Dolonkoi leave Delphi, go through Phokis and Boeotia, receiving no invitations, καὶ ἐκτρέπονται ἐπ' Ἀθηνέων ['and they turn aside towards Athens'], that is, they turn along the Sacred Way through Eleutherai and Eleusis. Miltiades, sitting by his

[32] *Aristoteles und Athen* ii. 73–4.
[33] Wade-Gery, Hignett, Hammond, Sealey, Burn, to name only a few.
[34] Plut. *Sol.* 10.3.
[35] Diogenes Laertius, x.1.
[36] *Ath. Pol.* 27.3.
[37] Plut. *Cim.* 10.2; cf. *IG* i² 295.8 = i³ 364.8.
[38] Her. vi.103.3, Marcellinus, *Vit. Thuc.* 55.
[39] Burn, *The Lyric Age of Greece* 311.
[40] On *Nemean* ii. 19, from Didymus, but I have an uneasy feeling that Didymus may have got muddled and thought that the Pherecydes genealogy quoted from him by Marcellinus, *Vit. Thuc.* 3 proved the Aiantic descent of the younger branch, which it does not. Doxopater *ad* Aphthonius p. 439. 3 Walz also goes back to this (cf. M. Schmidt, *Didymi Fragmenta* (Leipzig: Teubner, 1854) 324ff., who misses the point about the relationship of the two branches).
[41] Her. vi.34–5.

front door, sees them passing and shouts his invitation, certainly not from Brauron, but rather, we may confidently assert, from Lakiadai. Territorially, at any rate, the case for supposing the Philaids *pedieis* seems strongest.

Cleisthenes' opponent, Isagoras, presents a more difficult problem. Two recent scholars[42] have made him a Philaid, largely on the strength of his father's name, Teisandros. The name appears in other families too, and the case is hardly strengthened by a mysterious brother of Miltiades II, with a name ending in -agoras, who appears in 489.[43] Herodotus[44] says firmly that he does not know Isagoras' family, but that his συγγενέες [kinsmen] sacrifice to Ζεὺς Κάριος [Zeus Karios]. It is hard to believe that he discovered the family cults and not the Philaid blood, and even harder to believe him a deliberate liar. The best approach is probably through the family cult. Ζεὺς Κάριος has been thought to be a sneer at oriental origins [taking 'Karios' to refer to Caria, in Asia Minor] by many from Plutarch[45] onwards. But he seems to be at home in Ikaria in the Pentelikon area, where as simple Karios he seems to be the basic deity, beside whom Dionysos is an importation.[46] Here too we may place the headquarters of Isagoras' *genos* ['clan'], though he himself may have moved elsewhere.

II CLEISTHENES' REFORMS

A *The deme-names*

Obviously, there were centres of population before Cleisthenes. Cleisthenes gave them corporate existence by making *demotai* and *demarchoi* [demesmen and deme officers].[47] Aristotle[48] notes that not all places had names and Cleisthenes gave them names. The interesting names are those ἀπὸ τῶν κτισάντων [from the founders], the patronymic deme-names. Some of these, for example, Boutadai and Paionidai, are certainly also the names of *gene*. It is not stated and

---

[42] Sealey, *Historia* 9 (1960); 172; N. G. L. Hammond, *CQ* n.s. 6 (1956), 127–8.
[43] Nepos, *Milt.* 7.5.
[44] v.66.1.
[45] *Her. Mal.* 860E.
[46] *IG* i² 186 = i³ 253. This is at least the present state of our evidence, but Forrest rightly warns me that it is only in line 6 that the deity is unequivocally Κάριος and not Ἰκάριος, and that there may be an error in the reading here. If there is such an error, all reason to connect Isagoras with Pentelikon of course vanishes, and I would withdraw what is said below about the political motive for Cleisthenic reorganisation on Pentelikon, but not the reorganisation itself. [In *IG* i³ Lewis reads Ἰκάριος even in line 6. Rhodes wonders if we should read Διὶ ⟨Ἰ⟩καρίῳ in Her. v.66.1.]
[47] *Ath. Pol.* 21.4–5.
[48] *Ibid.*

there is no probability that membership of such demes was confined to members of these *gene*. It is obvious that it would be distinctly weakening to a kinship-organisation if the same name were given to a state unit of more open composition. One clear instance shows that this blow was felt. By the fourth century[49] the *genos* of the Boutadai, which held two of the most important Athenian priesthoods, has renamed itself the Eteoboutadai, the real descendants of Boutes.[50] If the blow was felt, it may well have been intended; the assumption that it was is strengthened when we recall the case for supposing that the Boutadai had headed the *Pedieis*. This may not be the only case, and observation seems to show that there is a concentration of patronymic names in the likely area of the *Pedieis*.

The game could perhaps be played both ways. That Brauron was a place of importance is clear, but its name was a word of power, the epithet of Artemis, Brauronia, and power to the wrong party. Brauron is not the name of a Cleisthenic deme. Instead the deme is called Philaidai, an annoyance to the Philaids in itself and perhaps an attempt to foster such cult of Philaios as there was away from the Philaid centre at Lakiadai.

Territorially the country-demes would have been easy to arrange. If there was gerrymandering at this level, we cannot recover its details. The real problem will have come in the city, and here we are still almost without evidence to determine the principles on which the deme-system was arranged.[51]

B The trittyes ['thirds']

It will be helpful at this point to consider the present state of our evidence on the names of the trittyes and their distribution on the map of Attica. To save space and to avoid *parti-pris* [taking a pre-conceived view], I shall almost always follow the views of Kirsten,[52] with the single qualification that I cannot follow his belief that it

[49] Dem. XXI.182 is perhaps the earliest reference.

[50] Cf. *IG* ii² 3474.3 Βουταδέων ἐτύμων ἐξ αἵ[ματος] ['of the true Boutadai from the blood'] and J. Toepffer, *Attische Genealogie* (Berlin: Weidmann, 1889) 117. There is an interesting parallel in the *genos* of the Salaminioi, which renamed itself Archaiosalaminioi [Ancient Salaminioi] *c.*300 B.C. (G. Daux, *REG* 54 (1941), 220–2).

[51] R. S. Young (*Hesperia* 20 (1951), 140–3) produces some evidence to show that main roads acted as boundaries.

[52] The best map is that in *Westermanns Atlas zur Weltgeschichte* (Braunschweig: Westermann, 1956), p. 13, the best survey of the position by E. Kirsten in *Atti del terzo congresso internazionale di epigrafia greca e latina* (Rome: L' Erma di Bretschneider, 1959) 151–71, with Tav. XXVI. The evidence is scattered through A. Philippson, *Die griechischen Landschaften* (Frankfurt a.M.: Klostermann, 1952) 1.3, and must be traced through the index of sites there, pp. 1065–8. [See now the works by Traill cited in p. 287, n. *.]

is nearly always possible to draw a neat line on the map round the territory of any individual trittys.

Erechtheis (I). The names of the trittyes are unknown. The city-trittys included no true city-deme, and was mostly taken from the territory of the old Paralia, without going down to the coast. Its principal demes were Euonymon and Agryle, the latter having Alcmeonid land. The coast-trittys was in South Attica, south-east of Hymettos, formed mainly of the demes of Lamptra and Anagyrous. The inland-trittys was in the far north-east of the Attic plain, with Kephisia its most important element. Whether by accident or design, the Boutadai, who held the hereditary priesthood of Erechtheus, were not included in this tribe, which had a priest of Erechtheus appointed by lot.[53]

Aigeis (II).We have the name of one trittys, that of the inland, Epakreis.[54] The word has some history. Strabo[55] gives Epakria as one of the twelve cities founded by Kekrops. Plutarch[56] once uses Epakreis as the name of Peisistratus' party, probably by simple confusion. An Epakria distinct from the Cleisthenic trittys is also attested by Philochorus.[57] The city-trittys included Kollytos, which is actually in the city, south-west of the Agora, but it also ran far enough to the north-west to take in Kolonos Hippios and to the north-east to take in Ankyle. It seems unlikely that it was fully contiguous.[58] The coast-trittys was on the east coast, from Brauron north to Myrrhinoutte. The inland-trittys was oddly shaped, lying mostly on Pentelikon, with a long tongue south into the Mesogeia plain to include Erchia. These two trittyes touch, and it is perhaps even doubtful to which trittys Ionidai and Teithras should be assigned.

Pandionis (III). Here we have three trittys-names, known and straightforward. The city was Kydathenaion,[59] the coast Myrrhinous,[60] the inland Paiania.[61] The city-trittys included the

---

[53] *IG* ii[2] 1146.4.

[54] *IG* ii[2] 2490.8, 1172.30.

[55] IX.1.20, p. 397.

[56] *Amat.* 763D.

[57] *FGrH* 328F206. This passage which puts the deme Semachidai, which belongs to the tribe Antiochis, in the Epakria raises an unsolved problem. The only direct evidence bearing on the site of Semachidai is the mention of a Semacheion near Laureion in a mining-lease (*IG* ii[2] 1582.54). If this is a shrine and not a mine, does it place the deme in South Attica? Trittyes of Antiochis lie both near Laureion and on Pentelikon, and are no help. This is the only piece of evidence for the Southern Diakria envisaged by Ure, *Origin of Tyranny*, and I would doubt whether it was ever really legitimate to argue from Epakria to Diakria.

[58] See *BSA* 50 (1955), 16–17.

[59] *IG* ii[2] 1748.14.

[60] *IG* i[2] 898 = i[3] 1127.

[61] *IG* i[2] 898, ii[2] 1748.

Akropolis and therefore the shrine of Pandion, and was formed only of the deme Kydathenaion. The coast-trittys was a powerful block south of Brauron, taking in part of the south-east of the Mesogeia plain. It seems to have touched the inland-trittys at an angle. This trittys was composed of the north of the Mesogeia, with the exception of Erchia. The strange feature of this tribe, to which we shall return, is its inclusion of Probalinthos, which seems likely to have been at Xylokerisa, on the coast immediately south of Marathon and separated from the rest of the coast-trittys by the whole length of the coast-trittys of Aigeis.

Leontis (IV). We have the names of the city-trittys Skambonidai and the coast-trittys Phrearrhioi; the inland-trittys, six letters in the genitive, evades identification.[62] The city-trittys has Skambonidai in the city itself and some of the plain to the north. Part of the northern section of the city-trittys of Aigeis seems to intervene. More oddly still, Halimous, well down the coast to the south-east, is completely separate from it. The coast-trittys has the southern end of the east coast down to Sounion, but the territory of Thorikos is a bite taken out of it, which effectively divided it into two. The inland-trittys has the eastern slopes of Parnes and a portion of the north-west Attic plain. As will be seen, it is difficult to make Hekale, on Pentelikon, join it.

Akamantis (V). Here we begin to run into difficulties, for we have four trittys-names. Cholargos was the name of the city-trittys c.450,[63] but it is difficult to see how *IG* i² 883 = i³ 1118 (c.420) can be restored as anything but [Κερ]αμέων.[64] The coast-trittys was Thorikos,[65] the inland-trittys Sphettos.[66] On the face of it, the city-trittys was renamed between 450 and 420.[67] These two names reflect its mixed composition. Kerameis was certainly at least partly in the city; the rest of the trittys was a part of the plain including Cholargos. Unless one draws one's lines in a very arbitrary manner, the trittys was certainly split. The coast-trittys only contained the deme of Thorikos. The inland-trittys had the whole of the south Mesogeia, except Myrrhinous.

Oineis (VI). Here we have two certain trittys-names, Lakiadai[68]

---

[62] *Hesperia* 9 (1940), 54, 30 (1961), 265.

[63] *IG* i² 900 = i³ 1131.

[64] See B. D. Meritt, *Hesperia* 9 (1940), 53–4.

[65] *SEG* x 371 = *IG* i³ 1122.

[66] *SEG* x 370 = *IG* i³ 1119.

[67] So A. E. Raubitschek, *AJA* 60 (1956), 281.

[68] *IG* i² 884 = i³ 1120.

and Thriasioi,[69] presumably the city and coast trittyes. A third appears on two stones which appear to confirm each other in the restorations Πε[δ]ιέον and [Πε]διέ[ον] [*Pedieon*].[70] This was held by Wade-Gery to be the inland-trittys, but he felt the difficulty of this view, since the inland-trittys was composed entirely of the deme of Acharnai and Thucydides[71] seems to draw a distinction between Acharnai and the *pedion*. One cannot exclude the possibility suggested to me by Mr Forrest, that this is a case analogous to Philaidai, a stroke of malice on Cleisthenes' part, putting the trittys Pedieis where there were manifestly no *pedieis* in the party-sense. However, the discovery of a name-change in Akamantis opens another possibility here, for of the two stones which give the evidence for Pedieis, one is certainly,[72] the other possibly, earlier than the stone which gives Lakiadai. A solution which makes Pedieis an earlier name for Lakiadai seems more attractive. For this city-trittys will be the heart of *pedieis* country, the plain west of Athens towards Korydallos, reaching Athens along the Sacred Way through Lakiadai and Boutadai. The coast-trittys is only partly coast. It includes the eastern part of the Thriasian plain, but reaches right up on to Parnes to include Phyle. The inland-trittys, as we have seen, is only composed of the deme of Acharnai.

Kekropis (VII). The trittys-names are unknown. The city-trittys was composed of Xypete and Melite, which cannot be made to join.[73] The coast-trittys was south of Hymettos, and mostly the territory of Aixone. The inland-trittys is geographically uneven, with parts of the north-east Attic plain and south-west Pentelikon.

Hippothontis (VIII). One inscription[74] gives us two trittys-names, Piraeus for the city, Eleusis for the coast. Another,[75] much earlier, gives us a third name, a long one, beginning with Τε or Ζε. Wade-Gery, to whom we owe the restoration,[76] assigned this automatically to the inland-trittys. But no suitable restoration is available, and the possibility of a change of name allows the chance that this may be another name for the city or coast trittys. A new suggestion is

---

[69] *IG* i[2] 899 = i[3] 1128.

[70] H. T. Wade-Gery, *Mélanges Glotz* (Paris: Presses Universitaires de France, 1932), ii. 884–6; Meritt, *Hesperia* 9 (1940), 55, 30 (1961), 265.

[71] II.20.1.

[72] *IG* i[2] 899 = i[3] 1128 has three-bar sigma.

[73] *BSA* 50 (1955), 17. My observations on the location of Melite are, I am told, confirmed by an unpublished inscription from the shrine of Artemis Aristoboule. [Published as *AΔ* 19 (1964), μελ. 31–3 no. 1 = *SEG* xxii 116.]

[74] *IG* i[2] 897 = i[3] 1129.

[75] *IG* i[2] 901 = i[3] 1130.

[76] *Mélanges Glotz* ii. 886–7.

possible, and the argument may lead us to one. The city-trittys was Piraeus with the land west along the coast and Koile in the city itself. It may be possible to join these elements, but it hardly seems necessary. The coast-trittys is Eleusis and the west of the Thriasian plain, but it goes up on to Parnes to include Oinoe. The inland-trittys is the extreme east of Parnes, Decelea, Sphendale and Oion, very widely spread in an area of thin population. The tribal centre, the Hippothontion, was, abnormally, not in Athens, but in Eleusis.[77]

Aiantis (IX). Here we have one name, for the coast-trittys, Tetrapoleis.[78] The city-trittys was composed of Phaleron alone. The coast-trittys will be discussed later. The inland-trittys was in the hills east of Parnes, mostly the territory of Aphidna. The tribal centre was not in the tribe at all, but at the Eurysakeion in Melite of Kekropis.[79]

Antiochis (X). Here we have two trittys-names, Alopeke for the city,[80] Pallene for the inland;[81] Anaphlystos has been plausibly suggested for the coast. The city-trittys was composed of Alopeke alone. The coast-trittys lay in south Attica, running inland from the west coast of Cape Sounion. The oddly-shaped inland-trittys covers the Pentelikon-Hymettos gap; its centre was Pallene, which blocks that gap.

In this survey we have on the whole assumed that our evidence, which is mainly fourth-century, is valid for Cleisthenes' reform. We should note that not much of our evidence for the tribal affiliation of demes is earlier than 450, although some of our evidence for the affiliation of trittyes is earlier. We have seen some reason to believe that some trittyes were renamed between 450 and 420, but I do not think that this should deter us from employing the only available working hypothesis, that there was no major reorganisation. Such a reorganisation should not in any case be inferred from the manuscript reading of Her. v.69.2, which seems to assert that there were only one hundred demes in the time of Cleisthenes. It is indeed theoretically possible that splitting will have increased the number of demes, but the reverse process will have had to apply to Aiantis, which never had more than six demes.[82]

[77] *IG* ii² 1149, 1153.
[78] *IG* i² 900 = i³ 1131.
[79] *Hesperia* 7 (1938), 18.
[80] *Hesperia* 30 (1961), 264.
[81] *SEG* x 374 = *IG* i³ 1125.
[82] I should however draw attention to Raubitschek's arguments (*AJA* 60 (1956), 281) for a change in or regularisation of the official order of the tribes in the middle of the fifth century (I believe *IG* i² 943 = i³ 1162 to be *c.*447 rather than *c.*440).

C *The anomalies*

It should now be clear that Cleisthenes did not just draw lines on the map. Such lines are difficult to draw, and break down notably in the city. Why the city is organised as it is, we cannot tell, and our questions will produce few profitable answers. Our best line of approach is through the anomalies outside the city, demes which appear to be enclaves, detached from their trittyes. If we can gain some insight into the reasons for these anomalies, we may find that we have some light on the reform as a whole. There seem to be three notable enclaves worth discussion, Probalinthos, Hekale, and Halimous.

For Probalinthos the explanation seems clear, and Kirsten[83] has already in part given it. One of the cities of Kekrops[84] was the Tetrapolis, which continued to exist as a separate territorial cult-organisation, sending independent embassies to Delphi and Delos, down to the first century B.C.[85] It was composed of the four units, Marathon, Oinoe, Trikorynthos and Probalinthos. These demes will have been fairly close together, and a suitable site for Probalinthos has been found at Xylokerisa, confirmed by two gravestones[86] and a dedication.[87] The antiquity and deep roots of this organisation are confirmed by the list of its sacrifices.[88] A body which sacrifices to Ἀθηναία Ἑλλωτίς, Ζεὺς Ἀνθαλής, Χλόη παρὰ τὰ Μειδύλου, Γάλιος, the Νεανίας [Athenaia Hellotis, Zeus Anthales, Chloe para ta Meidylou, Galios, the Neanias] and a succession of nameless heroes and heroines is not an artificial construction. But the unit formed by these four demes will not only have been territorially compact, but also Peisistratid territory. Efficiency will demand that it has to be some kind of administrative unit. It can even be called the trittys of the Tetrapoleis. What could be done, however, and was done, was to detach from it the prosperous deme of Probalinthos (providing five *bouleutai* [councillors] in the fourth century)[89] and to attach Rhamnous, which had totally different cults and doubtless different traditions. Probalinthos is detached, but it is attached, not to the contiguous coast-trittys of Aigeis, but to the more distant coast-trittys of Pandionis. The only explanation can be that there is little point in detaching it from Marathon in order to attach it to

[83] *Atti* (see n. 52), 162.
[84] Strabo IX.1.20, p. 397.
[85] A. Boëthius, *Die Pythais* (Uppsala: Almquist and Wiksell, 1918) 38, 107.
[86] *IG* ii² 7292, 7304.
[87] *IG* ii² 7296.
[88] *IG* ii² 1358 (some revisions in *AM* 67 (1942), 12–13).
[89] e.g. *IG* ii² 1700, 1751.

the trittys which contains Brauron. In its detachment from both, it becomes an enclave, separating the two centres of Peisistratid influence.

Here, on a larger scale, we see the same mind at work as we saw with the Boutadai. The traditional unit remains and keeps its name, but by its side we have a new unit, imposed from outside, with the same name, but of different composition. Even this may not have been felt to be enough, and there is an indication that steps may have been taken to improve the political situation. For, by shortly after 490, it is possible to appoint at Marathon to supervise a festival thirty men ἐκ τῶν ἐπιδήμων ['from the men in the deme'], representing each of the ten tribes.[90] The ambiguity of the word allows the possibilities either that these are visitors for the festival or that they are new settlers, perhaps on confiscated property, who have come to Marathon since the Cleisthenic reforms.

The second case is Hekale. Its site is a problem. It is somewhere near the Tetrapolis on the road from Athens to Marathon,[91] which probably puts it somewhere on Pentelikon, and certainly well away from any part of Leontis. It has been proposed[92] to put it at Kukunari on the north side of Pentelikon, where in fact the sacrificial calendar of the Tetrapolis was found. There was a Hekalesia at Hekale, celebrated by οἱ περὶξ δῆμοι [the surrounding demes],[93] and since the Tetrapoleis are in any case so far inland, scholars have wished to equate the groups. But Hekale is not part of the Tetrapolis, and although Theseus stayed there on his way to fight the Marathonian bull, it is not stated that the Tetrapoleis took part in the Hekalesia. Nor do Hekale or Zeus Hekalesios appear on the Tetrapolis-calendar, which is admittedly incomplete. It is probably better to see in Kukunari merely a cult-spot on a hill, and I see no real reason to deny that Hekale is at or near the present village of the name, south-west of Kukunari, but still in the north-north-west of Pentelikon. This is still far from Leontis, and the reason for detaching it from the nearby inland-trittyes of Aigeis, Kekropis and Antiochis must be its importance as a cult centre. If we knew which οἱ περὶξ δῆμοι were who celebrated the Hekalesia, we would find them in these trittyes. The suspicion that deliberate interference has been at work in drawing the trittys-boundaries in this part of the world is strengthened

[90] *SEG* x 2. 19–22 = *IG* i³ 3. 2–5.
[91] Plut. *Thes.* 14, Callimachus fr. 230.
[92] A. Milchhoefer, *Untersuchungen über die Demenordnung des Kleisthenes* (Abh. Berlin, 1982) 21–2, R. B. Richardson, *AJA* 10 (1895), 219.
[93] Plut. *Thes.* 14.2.

by a consideration of the shapes of these trittyes, all distinctly malformed. The political motive may well lie in the position of Isagoras. We have already seen grounds for placing him in Ikaria. There, as at Boutadai, a non-Cleisthenic organisation survived side by side with the deme.[94] The Cleisthenic trittys to which it belonged retained the name Epakreis. We do not know the home or domain of Zeus Epakrios,[95] but here again we may suspect that territory is removed from it[96] and that non-Epakria territory, Erchia, is brought in from the plain below.

The third anomaly, Halimous, has been explained by Kirsten[97] as belonging not to the city-trittys of Leontis, but to the inland-trittys. The deme, it is said, is composed of Alcmeonid supporters from near Leipsydrion,[98] who moved after 507 to Alcmeonid land, retaining their old trittys-affiliation.

However, the arrangement of a prytany-list [list of *prytaneis*, tribal contingents in the council of five hundred] suggests fairly strongly that the deme belongs to the city-trittys,[99] and there is no evidence that Alcmeonid land came down to the coast, for the territory of Euonymon is in the way. No clear answer can be given. This is an area of old settlement,[100] with a very primitive Demeter cult on Cape Kolias.[101] Perhaps here too there is a desire to detach a cult-site from its neighbourhood.

D *Other religious organisations*

The anomalies have indeed provided us with a clue, which suggests that it may be profitable to investigate the effect of the reforms on other religious organisations of a territorial character.

Let us begin with the Tetrakomoi. It is possible that they, like the Tetrapoleis, figured in Strabo's list of the twelve cities of Kekrops,[102]

---

[94] *IG* i² 187.3 = i³ 254.3, ii² 1178.4–5. If I had to make a firm guess, I would say that the Ikarieis were a phratry [actual or imagined kinship group], standing to ὁ δῆμος τῶν Ἰκαριέων [the deme of the Ikarians] as the Dekeleeis stood in relation to the Cleisthenic deme of that name (Wade-Gery, *Essays in Greek History* 133–4). But there are perhaps other possibilities.

[95] *Etym. Magn.* 352.49; perhaps *IG* ii² 1294.

[96] If Semachidai is in this area, this would be a certain case. See n. 57.

[97] In Philippson, i. 984 and *Atti* (see n. 52), 161.

[98] The case for supposing that Leipsydrion was in Alcmeonid land is in itself not cogent. It rests on Herodotus' statement (v.62.2) that Leipsydrion was ὑπὲρ Παιονίης ['above Paionia'] and the story in Pausanias II.18.8 that the Alcmeonidai and Paionidai came from Pylos together.

[99] *IG* ii² 1742, as analysed by R. Loeper, *AM* 17 (1892), 388.

[100] G. E. Mylonas, *Aghios Kosmas* (Princeton, NJ: Princeton University Press, 1959).

[101] Plut *Sol.* 8.4, Paus. 1.31.1; M. P. Nilsson, *Griechische Feste religioser Bedeutung* (Leipzig: Teubner, 1906) 317.

[102] IX.i.20, p. 397.

a list which certainly reflects some truth about early Attica. One name is missing, and the conjecture that their name has dropped out after that of the Tetrapoleis[103] is a plausible one. However this may be, the antiquity of their cult of Herakles is not in doubt. The four components are given by Pollux[104] as Piraeus, Phaleron, Xypete and Thymaitadai. The most likely interpretation of a fourth-century inscription shows Phaleron still possessing a *kome*-organisation,[105] and in 330/29 they still joined in a festival.[106] They are therefore a real unit with something in common. It is therefore interesting to find that Cleisthenes' reforms leave them in three different trittyes, Xypete going to Kekropis, Phaleron to Aiantis, Peiraeus and Thymaitadai to Hippothontis. It is reasonable to suppose that the splitting was intentional. We may go a stage further, and recall that Hippothontis has a trittys with an unrestored long name beginning with Τε or Ζε. It seems not unlikely that this should be Τε[τρακόμον], an earlier name for the Peiraeus trittys, which contains two of the old Tetrakomoi. The parallel with the Tetrapolis would not be exact, since the Cleisthenic Tetrapolis really contained four demes and the Cleisthenic Tetrakomon should have at least five, Peiraeus, Thymaitadai, Koile, Keiriadai and Korydallos. Either the word Tetrakomoi would not be felt to have numerical significance, or perhaps we should regard Keiriadai or Korydallos as a splinter-deme of later origin.

Pallene is the other main candidate for the missing city of Kekrops,[107] but the League of Athena Pallenis presents greater problems since its composition cannot be precisely determined. The dedication quoted by Athenaeus[108] gives us three member-demes with relative certainty, Pallene itself, Gargettos and Pithos, and the quotation from Themison which follows[109] assures us that there were a number of member-demes. Schlaifer[110] adds Acharnai to these from

---

[103] See, e.g., S. Solders, *Die ausserstädtischen Kulte und die Einigung Attikas* (Lund: Lindstedt, 1931) 107–8, following Loeper.
[104] IV.105.
[105] *IG* ii² 1598. 9ff. See P. Roussel, *Revue Archéologique* 18 (1941), 226–31, though he thinks that the two *komai* [villages] which both have komarchs from Phaleron are sub-divisions of Phaleron, and I incline to think that one is Phaleron and one one of the other three components of the old Tetrakomon, which happens to be headed by a man or men on the Phaleron deme-register.
[106] *IG* ii² 3103.
[107] It will have dropped out at the end before πάλιν in the next sentence. See Solders, *Die ausserstädtischen Kulte* 111.
[108] VI.234F.
[109] VI.235A.
[110] R. Schlaifer, *HSCP* 54 (1943), 35–67, a thorough discussion of the evidence for the League. (But see Additional Note, pp. 308–9.)

the quotation from the βασιλέως νόμοι [laws of the *basileus*] which lies between these passages, but this seems an unnecessary addition, of no great topographical probability. It seems more likely that Athenaeus is simply quoting from Polemon a number of passages bearing on parasites.[111] Some of these certainly have nothing to do with Athena Pallenis, and I would add the passage on Acharnai to their number. Even so, we are left with a cult-league centred at Pallene, with the names of at least three demes which belonged to it. Under the Cleisthenic system there was a trittys named Pallene of elongated shape, from which Gargettos and Pithos were excluded. This seems to conform well to the pattern which we have established.

The Trikomoi,[112] on the other hand, present a different picture. Their three members, Eupyridai, Kropidai and Pelekes, are all in the same trittys. We know virtually nothing of the unit, but may surmise from its situation and the lack of references that it was of little importance. Nothing of importance emerges from an examination of the Mesogeioi[113] or the Paraloi,[114] attractive though their names are in this context.

Some minor points may be briefly noted. Kirsten[115] may be right to see significance in the isolation of the ancient city of Thorikos. There is some tendency to detach old cults of the tribal *eponymoi* [heroes after whom they were named] from those tribes. The case of Erechtheus is clear. An ancient cult of Leos is attested at Hagnous,[116] which is nevertheless excluded from Leontis.[117] Similarly Erechtheis, Kekropis and Aiantis have to go outside their tribes to worship their tribal hero,[118] although Pandionis, centred on the Acropolis, and Hippothontis do not.[119]

E The purpose of the trittyes

Our entire argument so far has tended to show that demes were allotted to trittyes with some care, and that the trittyes were constructed in a deliberate attempt to create units which would be

---

[111] See Jacoby's analysis of the passage, *FGrH* IIIb, i. 147–50.

[112] Steph. Byz. *s.v.* Εὐπυρίδαι; perhaps *IG* ii² 1213.

[113] Schlaifer, *CP* 39 (1944), 22–7, has all the evidence and establishes a *prima facie* [first-sight] case for considering them a *genos*. I am not very happy about this view. The likely demes represented are Bate, Diomeia, Kydathenaion, and Kerameis, all city demes, falling into three trittyes.

[114] A very puzzling organisation. *IG* ii² 1254 shows them with *epimeletai* [curators] sacrificing to Paralos in the Paralion, but it is tied to the state-trireme by the *tamias*.

[115] *Atti* (see n. 52), 162.

[116] ἄξονες [(recorded in the) *axones*] in Steph. Byz. *s.v.* Ἅγνους.

[117] Contrast the cult of Leos in the Cleisthenic deme of Skambonidai (*IG* i² 188 = i³ 244).

[118] *IG* ii² 1146, 1143; *Hesperia* 7 (1938), 18.

[119] *IG* ii² 1138, 1149.

sufficiently distinct from existing local units to compete with them
and to destroy the influence which they gained from possessing a
common cult in a common locality. Modern scholarship has tended
to neglect the trittyes, seeing in them mere devices to ensure mixed
composition of the tribes. This is an understandable tendency, since
in the event the tribes won a success which can only be described as
surprising, while the trittyes totally failed to compete with the older
local organisations. There was a parallel failure in Cleisthenes'
attempt to redefine the qualifications for citizenship. He put the
deme beside the phratry, but could not persuade the Athenians that
phratry-membership was of no importance. Pericles had to recognise
this basic unwillingness to accept the substitute.[120] However, the fact
that the trittyes failed to establish themselves as local units does not
mean that they were not intended to have importance. The mass of
fifth-century *horoi* [markers] from the Agora and from the Peiraeus
indicates that they were intended to serve real purposes. The purposes are indeed mysterious. Raubitschek[121] has recently suggested
uses for the Agora markers. The Peiraeus *horoi* presumably served as
muster-stations on the lines that Demosthenes was trying to revive
as late as 354.[122] The division of the *prytaneis* into trittyes survived
into the time of the *Ath. Pol.*,[123] and the *epimeletai* of the tribes
were selected by trittyes in the fourth century.[124] The trittyes retained
property[125] and cults.[126]

Another substantial reason for modern depreciation of the trittyes
has been their apparent random distribution on the map of Attica.
Little attention has been paid to the enclaves, but a great deal of
attention has been given to the contrary situation, where blocks
appear to have been left untouched by the redistribution. The importance of these blocks can be overstressed. As Ehrenberg has said,
Cleisthenes was interested in people, not territory.[127] But even the
territorial arguments lose some of their force, when examined on a
contoured map. Let us work through a recent list of these blocks.[128]

[120] This has been demonstrated by A. Andrewes, *JHS* 81 (1961), 13–14.
[121] *AJA* 60 (1956), 279–82.
[122] XIV.22–3.
[123] *Ath. Pol.* 44.1; cf. *IG* ii² 1748.
[124] So in *IG* ii² 1151, 1152, 2818. I retain a suspicion, however, that [ἐπιμελητ]αί is the
correct restoration in *IG* ii² 2824, where all three come from the same deme. No-one has ever
produced an alternative which is plausible.
[125] *IG* ii² 2490.
[126] *IG* i² 190 = i³ 255, ii² 1172.
[127] V. Ehrenberg, *Neugründer des Staates* (Munich: Beck, 1925) 90.
[128] C. Hignett, *History of the Athenian Constitution* (Oxford: Oxford University Press,
1952) 134.

It is not true that the inland and coast trittyes of Akamantis join. Thorikos is an enclave in Leontis, and the territory of Phrearrhioi lies between it and Kephale, the nearest point of the inland-trittys. In Pandionis, the coast and inland trittys touch at a point, not at a line, and the centre of population of the inland trittys is at Paiania, far to the west. In Aigeis, the trittyes are contiguous, but they are quite different in character. The coast-trittys is composed of coast-towns and plain; the inland-trittys is mostly hill, and has been deliberately deformed. The case which is invariably quoted is that of Aiantis, where a flat map shows a solid north-eastern block. This of course was the case which made Beloch suspect Peisistratid influence, and a solid Peisistratid block in the north-east would contradict the general drift of our enquiry. But the case does not hold, either territorially or politically. The centre of population for the inland-trittys is at Aphidna, well up in the hills, a long and tedious climb from Marathon, while the evidence for interference with the composition of the coast-trittys is clear. Politically, it may indeed be true that Marathon remains a centre of Peisistratid influence. Can this really be the case with Aphidna, where we know of two leading families, the Gephyraioi, the family of Harmodios,[129] and Kallimachos the polemarch [the archon with military responsibilities] who led the Athenians at Marathon?[130] If Aiantis was a Peisistratid-packed tribe, they had forgotten it by the time they led the right wing in 490.[131]

There is indeed a certain contiguity of trittyes, but this is to be expected if the trittyes were, as we are told,[132] assigned to the tribes by lot. Provided that the trittyes were properly constructed in themselves, any random allocation would do. The only necessary qualification was that each tribe should have, a city, a coast and an inland trittys, ὅπως ἑκάστη μετέχη πάντων τῶν τόπων.* The trittyes cut across the most obvious local loyalties. It could be left to Apollo to create the tribes, to produce the wider loyalties to be implanted when men served together on the *boule* and, more importantly, in the army. In the event, the men of Phaleron fought side by side with those of Marathon and Aphidna, and Leontis united Sounion, Skambonidai, and eastern Parnes. Eleusis, Kerameis, and Aphidna might have been better still, but the lot would produce adequate results, and in fact it taught the right lessons.

---

[129] Plut. *Quaest. Conv.* 1.628D.
[130] Her. VI.109.
[131] Plut. *Quaest. Conv.* 1.628E.
[132] *Ath. Pol.* 21.4.
* 'So that each should have a share in each of the places.'

III CLEISTHENES

We have left some parts of the reform in the dark for want of evidence. This lack comes partly from the paradox I began with. We know about local cults, because they survived, because Cleisthenes failed with them. Other institutions did not retain their hold, and we know so little of the old tribes, the old trittyes and the old naucraries that our picture may have been substantially distorted. The naucraries in particular may well have had territorial implications[133] and Cleisthenes does not seem to have abolished them.[134] But there are other patches of darkness. Some have recently seen in Cleisthenes' moves a desire to end the old threefold distinction of caste.[135] Many have found the evidence that Cleisthenes desired to bring in new citizens unconvincing.[136] Perhaps most important of all, we have next to no evidence on the confiscation and redistribution of land in sixth-century Athens.[137] The two things which emerge most clearly are an attack on organisations which held a locality by religious ties, some of them in areas attached to political opponents of Cleisthenes, and an attempt to unify Attica by making men from different areas work and fight together.

How far was Cleisthenes a politician, how far a statesman? The Alcmeonids in the sixth century had been caught between the fires of the autochthonous landed population of the plain, secure in the possession of the most important state cults, and their fellow-Pylian Peisistratus, who in the east had built himself a remarkable coalition of varied interests and had secured himself in the tyranny by promoting economic prosperity and by giving Athena wider appeal without the aid of her traditional guardians. The Alcmeonids possessed no important local cult of their own that we know of. Their power rested solely on land and wealth, which they buttressed by looking

[133] The one name we possess, Kolias, suggests as much (Bekker, *Anecdota* i. 275).

[134] Kleidemos, *FGrH* 323F8.

[135] F. R. Wüst, *Historia* 3 (1954–5), 137–9, 6 (1957), 176–91, 8 (1959), 1-11, accepted by J. A. Oliver, *Historia* 9 (1960), 503.

[136] Wade-Gery, *Essays in Greek History* 148–9, but more firmly and less convincingly Oliver, *Historia* 9 (1960), 503, who, in order to maintain not only that there was no admission of new citizens, but that no-one ever said that there was, has to offer an impossible meaning of ἐφυλέτευσε ['enrolled in tribes'] and an extremely unlikely one of νεοπολῖται [*neopolitai*, 'new citizens'].

[137] The only pieces of evidence worth considering are these: (1) redistribution is said to have been in the air at the time of Solon's reforms (Plut. *Sol.* 16.1); (2) Peisistratus' enemies confiscated his property and auctioned it while he was in exile (Her. vi.121.2); (3) Peisistratus made money-grants to farmers (*Ath. Pol.* 16.2); (4) when he recalled Kimon Koalemos from exile, Kimon κατῆλθε ἐπὶ τὰ ἑωυτοῦ [returned to his own property] (Her. vi.103.3); (5) Peisistratus' friend Lygdamis of Naxos did indulge in confiscation (Arist. *Oec.* ii.1346B7). It is clear that Peisistratus had the power to confiscate and it would have seen surprising if he had not used it, but the positive evidence for saying so does not exist.

outside Athens to Delphi, Sicyon and Lydia.[138] In the struggle for power before Peisistratus, they had been squeezed out and forced to rely on their position outside Athens. Cleisthenes had watched this process under his father Megakles and Megakles' successor, his uncle Alkmeonides.[139] The veering of tyrannical favour which brought him home and to the archonship in 525 made no essential difference to the lesson. He had learnt the power of local cults and the value of a wider Athens.

When he came home finally in 510, the position had been transformed by Peisistratus and his sons. New classes had been given economic hope, and men had learnt to look to Athens as the undisputed centre. There were features here which he may well have disliked and which were certainly disliked by other men of power. A διαψηφισμός [*diapsephismos*, vote on men claiming citizenship] cut into the tyrants' enfranchisements.[140] Other moves may have cut into their land-distributions. Cleisthenes' main opponent came from Pentelikon, deriving strength from the close-knit religious unions of that area, perhaps from the prestige of the new dramatic festivals of Ikaria.[141] Cleisthenes had Delphi behind him, but so far Delphi had only been of use as a lever to bring in Sparta, and Cleomenes of Sparta backed Isagoras. Isagoras, with Spartan backing and using the methods of the 560s, won the upper hand.

If there was to be a place for the Alcmeonids in Athens, new methods had to be used. One lesson could be learnt from the tyrants, and Cleisthenes turned to the *demos* which the tyrants had created and favoured, which he and other dynasts had previously rejected. It is hard to see how the complexities of the reforms could have been used in themselves as a bargaining-counter to win the *demos*, even at the lowest level, the prospect of local self-government in the deme. Something more concrete will have been in the air – citizenship, probably also land. Land-hunger remains strong in Athens for the next fifteen years or so. Salamis,[142] Chalkis[143] and Lemnos,[144] all are

---

[138] I do not wish to be understood to say that they had mercantile interests. I know of no evidence for that proposition, widely held though it is.

[139] I see no good reason to disturb the manuscript reading at Her. 1.64.3. For Alkmeonides, see Raubitschek, *Dedications from the Athenian Akropolis* 338–40, where the evidence is collected. I cannot follow him in supposing that there is any strong case for supposing Anaxileos a member of the family.

[140] *Ath. Pol.* 13.5.

[141] A. W. Pickard-Cambridge, *Dithyramb, Tragedy, and Comedy* (Oxford: Oxford University Press, 1927) 97–104 (2nd edn, 1962, 69–76).

[142] Tod 11 = Meiggs and Lewis 14 = *IG* i³ 1.

[143] Her. v.77.2.

[144] Her. vi.140.2; *BCH* 36 (1912), 329–38.

attempts to meet a need which Cleisthenes could only partly satisfy in Attica, since land to satisfy it could only come from his opponents, not from his supporters.

At this point constitutional problems have been multiplied. How could the reforms have been put through while Isagoras was archon, able, as presiding officer, to block a vote? Was Cleisthenes an archon? Did he hold a special commission? How could he have obtained a majority, if his supporters had been disfranchised? These problems seem irrelevant to a revolutionary situation. Whether Isagoras was in the chair or not, whether the *neopolitai* were legally entitled to vote or not, there was nothing to prevent them carrying clubs and standing round or even on the Pnyx to shout 'All power to the ten tribes.'

Cleisthenes needed a new system. The *diapsephismos* had shown the difficulty of providing a legal basis in the phratry-system for doubtful citizenship, and to intervene directly in the phratries might alienate as many voices as it won. The creation of the deme met this difficulty, but there still remained the problem of local vested interests. This could be met by establishing the trittyes, which might curtail the powers of local organisations. The real problem came in deciding how to crown the pyramid, how to ensure that the new local units served interests wider than local ones and looked to Athens in the way Peisistratus had shown. The four Ionian tribes seem now to have represented very little.[145] Changing tribal organisation was not unparalleled in the sixth century. Cleisthenes' own grandfather, Cleisthenes of Sicyon, had changed tribe-names, and may have created a new tribe from the under-privileged.[146] At any rate, he had a tribe for the previously under-privileged, and asserted the principle that it was better than the others. At Cyrene, Demonax of Mantinea had acted rather differently.[147] Finding the original settlers organised in the three Dorian tribes and the newcomers not organised at all, he created a new three-tribe system on ethnic lines. These systems had given new citizens or settlers rights, but retained the seeds of difference and dissension. Cleisthenes realised that there was no

[145] I deduce this only from their lack of success in surviving Cleisthenes. One sacrifice (*Hesperia* 4 (1935), 5ff.) and the *phylobasileis* ['tribal kings'] (*Ath. Pol.* 57.4) exhaust the evidence.

[146] Her. v.68. That the Archelaoi were a new tribe seems to follow from the fact that a new name has to be found for them when the other tribes reverted to their Dorian names. Aigialeis [referring to Adrastus' son] is explicitly pro-Adrastus and therefore anti-Cleisthenes.

[147] Her. IV.161.3; cf. F. Chamoux, *Cyrène sous la monarchie des Battiades* (Paris: De Boccard, 1953), 138–42, L. H. Jeffery, *Historia* 10 (1961), 142–4. Miss Jeffery's preferred explanation, that Demonax, like Cleisthenes, included a cross-section *inside* each of his three tribes, does not seem to me a possible interpretation of the text.

possibility of peace and concord without mixing his disparate elements. The novelty of his solution lies in its determination to make a fresh start. All citizens, old and new, would start equal in his new demes and new tribes.

This is his most important service to Athens. Traditionally, and perhaps temperamentally, averse to tyranny, he found a way to create a pyramid of power which would have at its head, at least in theory, the people and not one person, and which would maintain the unifying force generated by the tyranny without a tyranny's disadvantages. The way he chose had distinct advantages for himself and his family. The details of his settlement could be and were manipulated to the disadvantage of traditional opponents, but the nature of the Alcmeonid position was such that it could not be affected by this settlement. The trittys-lines were drawn to leave Alcmeonids in at least three different tribes, a result which might well prove fatal to a family which depended for influence on the control of a local cult, but which could be positively welcomed by a family of land and wealth which acquired the opportunity to have a hand in the affairs of three of the new tribes. But it cannot be denied that, politician though he was, Cleisthenes was capable of seeing the advantages of Attic unity. ἀνάμιξις ['mixing up'] would have been the key word in his thought, as it was in the language of his most sympathetic commentator.[148]

> ἔτι δὲ καὶ τὰ τοιαῦτα κατασκευάσματα χρήσιμα πρός τὴν δημοκρατίαν τὴν τοιαύτην, οἷς Κλεισθένης τε Ἀθήνησιν ἐχρήσατο βουλόμενος αὐξῆσαι τὴν δημοκρατίαν, καὶ περὶ Κυρήνην οἱ τὸν δῆμον καθιστάντες. φυλαί τε γὰρ ἕτεραι ποιητέαι πλείους καὶ φρατρίαι, καὶ τά τῶν ἰδίων ἱερῶν συνακτέον εἰς ὀλίγα καὶ κοινά, καὶ πάντα σοφιστέον ὅπως ἂν ὅτι μάλιστα ἀναμειχθῶσι πάντες ἀλλήλοις, αἱ δὲ συνήθειαι διαζευχθῶσιν αἱ πρότερον.*

Every increase in our knowledge shows that Cleisthenes worked towards this aim.

Additional note. In discussing the League of Athena Pallenis, I forgot the fourth-century inscription *AM* 67 (1942), no. 26, pp. 24–9. This

---

[148] Twice in *Ath. Pol.* 21, apart from the passage which follows, which is *Politics*, VI.1319B19.

* 'Moreover, such devices are useful for such a kind of democracy as Cleisthenes used at Athens when he wanted to increase the democracy, and those who established the democracy at Cyrene. Other, additional tribes and phratries should be created, and the rites of private cults should be brought together into a few common ones, and everything should be contrived so that as far as possible all the people are mixed up with one another and the previous associations are broken up.'

complicates the matter, since it shows that *parasitoi* [those given a meal] then came from a very wide area and makes the *parasitoi* previously known unsafe guides to the composition of the League, which may or may not have been narrower originally. The four *archontes* [officials] of the inscription *may* be a safer guide; they come from Gargettos, Acharnai, Pallene, and Paiania, all four from different trittyes and tribes.

13 *Ephialtes*, Eisangelia, *and the Council**

RAPHAEL SEALEY

*Omne ignotum pro magnifico.*** The earliest extant author to talk about the attack of Ephialtes on the Areopagite Council is Aristotle. Although the work of Ephialtes aroused controversy in his lifetime, there is no indication that it continued to be discussed later in the fifth century. It seems to have become a subject of argument and reconstruction about 356 when Isokrates composed his speech *Areopagitikos.*[1] Aristotle has transmitted the wisdom of his contemporaries, and his account of the reforms of Ephialtes (*Ath. Pol.* 25.2) is in one way precise and in another unhelpful. He says that Ephialtes took some powers away from the Areopagite Council and gave some of them to the Five Hundred and the others to the Assembly and the *dikasteria* [jury-courts]. He fails to specify what these powers were, beyond calling the "additional" and saying that in virtue of them the Areopagos had exercised guardianship of the constitution, but such language sounds like a cover for ignorance.

Hence, in modern times a question: What were the powers transferred by Ephialtes to the other organs? Current hypotheses may be divided into two classes. On the one hand some scholars suppose that Ephialtes carried out extensive reforms in a conscious and somewhat doctrinaire attempt to transform Athenian public life.[2] Others, however, have tried to discover a precise and limited change which may be attributed to Ephialtes, a change which may have had wider effects than its author anticipated but did not amount to a general overhaul of the constitution. Thus H. T. Wade-Gery has argued that

---

* Originally published in G. S. Shrimpton and D. J. McCargar (eds), *Classical Contributions: Studies in Honour of Malcolm Francis McGregor* (Locust Valley, NY: Augustin, 1981), 125–34; reprinted with the permission of the author and J. J. Augustin, Inc.
** "Everything unknown is regarded as magnificent" (Tacitus, *Agricola*, 30).
[1] E. Ruschenbusch, "Ephialtes," *Historia* 15 (1966) 369–376.
[2] For an outstandingly clear statement of this view, see F. Schachermeyr, *Perikles* (Stuttgart, Berlin, Köln, Mainz 1969) 25–33. C. Hignett entitled a chapter of his *History of the Athenian Constitution* (Oxford 1952) "The Revolution of 462."

Ephialtes transformed the popular court from a court of appeal to a court of first instance.[3] I have urged that the reforms of Ephialtes were solely concerned with *euthynai,* the procedure for calling officials to account when they laid down office.[4] Recently, however, P. J. Rhodes has offered a detailed defense of the larger conception of the reformer's work.[5] While he accepts the hypothesis, derived from W. S. Ferguson, about *euthynai,* he also holds that Ephialtes transferred extensive judicial functions from the Areopagos to the Council of Five Hundred. Until 462, he supposes, the latter body was merely probouleutic [preparing business for the assembly]; its judicial competence was limited to internal discipline and *dokimasia* [vetting] of next year's councillors. Until that date, on this hypothesis, the Council of the Areopagos had judicial competence for *eisangeliai** and for *dokimasia* of archons and it judged a group of cases which Rhodes has classified together as "official jurisdiction." But, he holds, Ephialtes transferred jurisdiction of these three kinds (*eisangelia, dokimasia* of archons, "official jurisdiction") to the Council of Five Hundred.

The thesis is impressively argued and the present paper sets out to test it. It is a pleasure to offer such an inquiry to a scholar who has welcomed constantly the expression of divergent views and who has concentrated attention on large issues and on the large implications of apparently small issues. Reconstruction of the work of Ephialtes has implications for understanding the whole political scene in fifth-century Athens. The clue to the matters of jurisdiction studied by Rhodes is to be found, I believe, in a revised understanding of *eisangelia.*

EISANGELIA

Study of the procedure called *eisangelia* must start from some remarks of Hypereides in the speech *For Euxenippos.* The orator alludes to the *nomos eisangeltikos* [law of *eisangelia*] and cites clauses from it (7–8); these provided for *eisangelia* "if anyone overthrows the *demos* of the Athenians, or conspires for overthrow of the *demos,* or gathers together a *hetairikon* [group of comrades], or if

---

[3] *Essays in Greek History* (Oxford 1958) 180–200.
[4] "Ephialtes," *CP* 59 (1964) 11–22 = Sealey, *Essays in Greek Politics* (New York 1967) 42–58.
[5] *The Athenian Boule* (Oxford 1972) 144–207; a summary of the changes attributed to Ephialtes is given on pages 203–205.
* The procedure for trying charges of major offences against the state, sometimes translated "impeachment" (but see p. 320, below).

anyone betrays a city, or ships, or a force of infantry or sailors, or being an orator fails in return for bribes to give the best advice to the *demos* of the Athenians." Starting from this observation, and encouraged by some remarks in the Byzantine lexica, many scholars have tried to draw up a finite list of offences which could be prosecuted by *eisangelia*;[6] they have assumed, that is, that this procedure was available for a limited number of offences specified in the *nomos eisangeltikos*. This assumption leads to difficulties.

In the first place the statements of Hypereides in the same speech demand closer scrutiny. Evidently the clauses which he quotes stood in the law, but he does not say that his list is complete. Indeed his argument is tendentious. In the opening sections of the speech he says that in the past *eisangelia* was used for major crimes but recently it has been used improperly for petty offences. He gives examples of petty offences prosecuted of late by this procedure: Diognides and Antidoros were charged with hiring flute-girls above the legal rate of pay, Agasikles was accused of having himself enrolled in the wrong deme, and now Euxenippos is prosecuted for his report to the *demos* of a dream which he had in the temple of Amphiaraos. It appears from the speech that in fact the prosecution charged Euxenippos under the clause about failing to give the best advice to the *demos*. Even so Hypereides' reference to petty offences may suggest that the Athenians were not so eager to restrict *eisangelia* to the major offences which he specifies as he might have wished.

A more serious difficulty arises from studying the views of Hellenistic scholars as reported in the Byzantine lexica. A learned note distinguishes between the opinions of Kaikilios and Theophrastos.[7] The former said that *eisangelia* was available against "new and unwritten offences." Theophrastos, however, gave a list of offences for which *eisangelia* was available as summarized in the note, and his list overlaps that of Hypereides. The same note mentions the prosecution of Themistokles by Leobotes as according with the opinion of Theophrastos, and, after discussing other questions, it concludes: "The subject is treated in the discourses of

---

[6] For example, Th. Thalheim, "Zur Eisangelie in Athen," *Hermes* (1902) 339–352; J. H. Lipsius, *Das attische Recht und Rechtsverfahren* (Leipzig 1905–15) 176–211; A. R. W. Harrison, *The Law of Athens: Procedure* (Oxford 1971) 50–59; M. H. Hansen, "Eisangelia: The Sovereignty of the People's Court in the Fourth Century B.C. and the Impeachment of Generals and Politicians," *Odense University Classical Studies* 6 (1975) 12–20.

[7] *Lex. Rhet. Cant.*, s.v. *eisangelia*; quoted by Harrison (above, note 6) 51, note 1. This note is clearer, more discursive, and more informative than the notes offered by Pollux (8.51 f.; also quoted by Harrison) and Harpokration (s.v. *eisangelia*), but they too preserve some echo of the tradition that *eisangelia* was available for offences not defined by law.

the sophists." Evidently Hellenistic scholars inherited no uniform tradition about *eisangelia*; it was a question for research. This could not have come about if a law had been extant giving an exhaustive list of the offences which could be prosecuted by *eisangelia.*

The third reason for challenging the assumption that *eisangelia* was available for a limited number of specified offences is that scholars making this assumption have had to add repeatedly to the list of offences. Thus Thalheim (above, note 6), who treated the question with exemplary rigor, started from Harpokration's note, which distinguishes three kinds of *eisangelia,*[8] and added several more. A fourth kind, he supposed, was actions before the Council against officials for illegal conduct; a fifth was available against offences concerning things which stood under the special supervision of the Council, for example, naval equipment in the dockyards. Thalheim argued that additional laws created three further kinds of *eisangelia*: the procedure was available against anyone who deceived that *demos* by false promises, who harmed the allies in the Second Athenian League, and who committed offences on embassies.[9] More recently Hansen (above, note 6, 16) has made Hypereides' citation of the *nomos eisangeltikos* his starting point and asserted thence that *eisangelia* was available for precisely three offences, namely, treason, attempts to overthrow the democracy, and acceptance of bribes by orators to make proposals to Assembly; but Hansen has had to admit that the procedure of *eisangelia* before the Council embraced not only these three offences but any offence committed by a magistrate or by a citizen performing a public charge.[10]

There is adequate evidence that all of these miscellaneous charges could be the occasion for *eisangelia.* Surely the list would be still longer if there were more evidence. Accordingly some scholars have

---

[8] Harpokration's first type of *eisangelia,* "where the first hearing is before the Council or the *demos,*" is the type studied here. His second kind was a procedure before the archon for injury to an orphan; Aristotle (*Ath. Pol.* 56.6) calls the procedure in such cases a *graphe* ["writing": the normal term for a public prosecution], Isaios, 11, calls it indifferently *graphe* (31, 32, 35, cf. 28) and *eisangelia* (6, 15). Harpokration's third kind of *eisangelia* was available against an arbitrator (*Ath. Pol.* 53.6).

[9] Against officials: *Ath. Pol.* 45.2; cf. Ant. 6.12 and 35. Concerning naval equipment: *IG* 2.² 1631, lines 398–401; cf. Dem., 51.4. Deceiving the *demos* with false promises: [Dem.] 49.67, cf. Dem., 20.135. Thalheim inferred *eisangelia* for actions harming the allies in the Second League from *IG* 2.² 43 (= Tod, 123) lines 51–63; 111 (= Tod, 142) lines 37–40; and 125 (= Tod, 154) lines 51–63; but the word does not occur in these passages. *Parapresbeia* [misconduct on an embassy]: *eisangelia* was the procedure employed against Philokrates (Dem., 19.116; Aischin., 3.79); it is also mentioned in general terms as appropriate for charges against ambassadors (Aischin., 2.139; Dem., 19.103). Harrison (above, note 6, 53–54) follows Thalheim in trying to list the offences for which *eisangelia* was available.

[10] Above, note 6, 28; *Ath. Pol.* 45.2; [Dem.], 47.41–44.

proposed a view like that of Kaikilios, that there was no statutory limit to the types of offences for which *eisangelia* was available. Thus Bonner and Smith wrote: "... the law was intended only to insure the use of the process in certain political cases. ... The law never forbade that offenses other than those mentioned in the law should be tried by *eisangelia*, but merely made certain that these specified offenses should be so tried"; they also noted that *eisangelia* came to be used for trivial offences, as Hypereides complained.[11] Following them, Rhodes has urged accepting "the non-specific strand" in the tradition on the law of *eisangelia*; he holds that this procedure could be employed against "any major public offence."[12] Indeed even the words "major" and "public" may be too restrictive; the speaker of [Demosthenes] 47 had recourse to *eisangelia* before the Council in seeking redress for a fistfight in the doorway of a private house (41–44), although it must be admitted that the fight arose from a dispute about the public charge of the trierarchy.[13]

If indeed the law on *eisangelia* had a "non-specific strand," it was in harmony with other Athenian laws on criminal procedure. One may call to mind the *graphe hybreos*.* This charge is attested as admissible "if anyone commits *hybris* against anyone, whether against a child or a woman or a man, from among free persons or slaves, or does anything unlawful (*paranomon*) against any of these."[14] It has been plausibly suggested that the law on *hybris* was passed in the time of Perikles when the value of money had decreased since the age of Solon and the old laws providing for compensation in fixed amounts of valuables no longer sufficed. Essentially the new

---

[11] R. J. Bonner and G. Smith, *The Administration of Justice from Homer to Aristotle* 1 (Chicago 1930) 294–309; the quotation is from page 307 and the comment from 309.

[12] Above, note 5, 162–164.

[13] Hansen (above, note 6, 19–20) argues against Bonner and Smith and Rhodes; he insists that all known cases of *eisangelia* fall under the headings of treason, attempt to overthrow the democracy, and corruption among orators, as defined in the laws of *eisangelia*. He notes that putative exceptions dissolve on closer scrutiny; thus the act committed by Leokrates may not have been an offence defined in the laws, but the prosecution tried to call it treason, and in the trial of Lykophron the prosecution misrepresented adultery as an attempt to overthrow the democracy. But Hansen has subsumed an excessively large variety of offences under the term "treason"; and it appears from Thalheim's study that the lists of offences given by Hypereides and Theophrastos are far from complete. In 415 Pythonikos was said to *eisangellein* ["make an *eisangelia*"] when he told the Assembly that Alkibiades had performed the Eleusinian mysteries in a private house (Andok., 1.14, 27, cf. 11); surely the Athenians called this offence neither treason nor an attempt to overthrow the democracy nor corruption among orators, but *asebeia* [impiety].

* The public prosecution for *hybris*, "outrage."

[14] Dem., 21.47; Aischin, 1.15. My understanding of the law on *hybris* is drawn from Ruschenbusch, "Hybreos Graphe. Ein Fremdkörper im athenischen Recht des 4. Jahrhunderts v. Chr.," *Zeitschrift der Savigny-Stiftung für Rechtsgeschichte* 82 (1965) Romanistische Abteilung 302–309. Cf. Lipsius (above, note 6), 420–429.

law empowered the court to assess the penalty, and, because of its second clause, "if anyone does anything unlawful against any of these," this law was so general as to embrace all offences against the person. The law on *eisangelia* may have completed its list of offences with a clause of comparable generality.

This conclusion has a bearing on the origin of *eisangelia* (and hence on Ephialtes). Some scholars (Thalheim, Bonner and Smith, Hansen) have supposed that the law in almost its final form was passed in or about 411/10, later changes being small. It must be admitted that the clause against gathering together a *hetairikon* seems appropriate among the reforms following the overthrow of the Four Hundred. Doubtless the provisions about *eisangelia* were re-enacted, perhaps modified, when the laws were codified in 403–399. For the earliest stage in the development of *eisangelia*, historians have often relied on a remark of Aristotle (*Ath. Pol.* 8.4); he says that Solon passed a law of *eisangelia*, whereby the Council of the Areopagos should try persons who drew together for the purpose of overthrowing the *demos.*[15] Hansen (above, note 6, 17–19) has rightly questioned the truth of Aristotle's statement. As he points out, the wording of Aristotle's remark, in which the phrase *katalysis tou demou* is essential, is quite unlike the language of Solon's poems. One may add that the crucial phrase, *katalysis tou demou*, is quite unlike the diction of those among the allegedly Solonian laws which have the best claim to be considered authentic, for example, the law of amnesty.[16] Hansen suggests persuasively that the fiction of a Solonian law of *eisangelia*, empowering the Areopagos to try charges of subverting the constitution, was concocted in the second half of the fourth century; for in that period there was speculative and tendentious discussion of the powers of the Areopagos, the slogan *patrios politeia* [traditional constitution] was current,[17] and a new procedure, called *apophasis* ["report"] and somewhat resembling *eisangelia*, was introduced, a procedure in which the Areopagite Council took part.

---

[15] Confirmation should not be sought in *Ath. Pol.* 25.3–4 where Aristotle says that Themistokles told the Areopagite Council that some people had drawn together for the purpose of overthrowing the constitution; the anecdote of Ephialtes in shirt sleeves on the altar is not admissible as historical evidence.

[16] Plut., *Sol.* 19.4 = F 70 in Ruschenbusch, *Solonos Nomoi: Die Fragmente des solonischen Gesetzeswerkes mit einer Text- und Überlieferungsgeschichte* (*Historia*, Einzelschriften 9 [1966]). For its authenticity see Ruschenbusch, *Historia* 9 (1960) 132–134.

[17] This slogan did not arise as early as the late fifth century; see the important argument of K. R. Walters, "The 'Ancestral Constitution' and Fourth-Century Historiography in Athens," *American Journal of Ancient History* 1 (1976) 129–144.

More plausibly Aristotle (*Ath. Pol.* 4.4), describing the condition
of Athens before Solon, says: "A person suffering injury was allowed
to make a report (*eisangellein*) to the Council of the Areopagites,
declaring what law was transgressed by the injury." This statement
occurs in suspicious proximity to the spurious "constitution of
Drakon," but it is not intrinsically objectionable; even if it rests on
conjecture, the conjecture is in accord with what may be presumed
about the history of *eisangelia* (see below, p. 323). For the present all
that need be said is that Aristotle's statement does not necessarily
imply an enabling law which created *eisangelia*; Aristotle merely says
that people could bring their complaints to the Areopagite Council
(a reasonable thing to do in archaic conditions), not that a law
authorized them to do so. The procedure of *eisangelia* is first attested
with certainty in the prosecution of Themistokles by Leobotes.[18]
Some other famous trials of the first half of the fifth century may have
followed the same procedure. In particular the first trial of Miltiades
may be instructive. The charge is said to have been tyranny in the
Chersonese; this is credible if the later law of *eisangelia* had a "non-
specific strand." The trial was conducted, according to Herodotos
(6.104.2), before a *dikasterion*; this may be important for recon-
structing the procedure of *eisangelia* (see below, pp. 319–20), for
there is no need to suppose that Herodotos' term for the court is
anachronistic.

Rejecting a Solonian origin, Hansen holds "that the *eisangelia*
was a democratic institution introduced by Kleisthenes" (p. 19). This
hypothesis proves to be the answer to a false question, if one follows
a different line of thought. One may start from Hansen's important
observation (p. 10) that the Athenians were much more interested
in procedural law than in substantive law. They devoted far more
thought and ingenuity to devising procedures than to laying down
substantive rules. The generality of the law on *hybris* illustrates their
indifference to the substantive issue of defining offences. Scholars
studying the early history of *eisangelia* seem to have supposed that
the Athenians thought about actual or possible offences of treason or
subversion and consequently devised a procedure to deal with these.
But it would be more in accordance with Athenian habits to devise a
criminal procedure without having any specific charge in mind. That
is, if anyone in Athens thought that an act deserving punishment had
been committed, he could report his information to an appropriate
authority; he did not necessarily have to specify a substantive pro-

[18] Krateros, *FGrH* 342, F 11; Plut., *Them.* 23. Krateros calls the procedure *eisangelia*.

vision of criminal law against which the alleged act offended; he reported the act because he found it outrageous and deserving of punishment. There were procedures available, such as *eisangelia, graphe,* and *endeixis** so that the authority receiving the information could hear pleas on both sides, the suspect could defend himself, and a verdict could be reached. These procedures were defined and distinguished from one another, not by the nature of the alleged offence, but by the identity of the authority receiving the first information. If the information was given to the Assembly or the Council of Five Hundred, the procedure was *eisangelia*; if it was given to one of the nine archons, the procedure was *graphe*; if it was given to the Eleven, the procedure was *endeixis.*[19] If offences concerning the state were often reported to the Council or the Assembly, this was a matter of convenience.

For the purpose of the present inquiry, the crucial point is that a procedure can arise by custom without specific enactment to lay it down. Hence to suppose that Kleisthenes (or Solon) introduced *eisangelia* is to answer a false question. If someone in Athens believed that Miltiades had exercised tyranny in the Chersonese or that Alkibiades had performed the mysteries in a private house, he could report his suspicions and his grounds to the Assembly. This does not mean that a statute had specified the Assembly as the proper body to receive such allegations. The information was given to the Assembly merely because a meeting of the Assembly happened to be conveniently available. Clearly information about profanation of the mysteries did not necessarily have to be reported to the Assembly and lead to *eisangelia*; it could alternatively be the subject of a *graphe asebeias,* the information being reported to the *basileus*** (*Ath. Pol.* 57.2).

In all probability *eisangelia* did not arise from an enabling statute. As soon as the community of Athenian citizens was strong enough to punish acts threatening its welfare, it could receive information alleging that such acts had been performed. In classical Athens the peculiar feature of almost all forms of procedure (all, that is, except the procedures for homicide and related offences) is that each case was heard in two stages. At the first stage the party initiating the

---

* "Pointing out" an offender to the authorities.

[19] My thinking has been helped much by G. M. Calhoun, *The Growth of Criminal Law in Ancient Greece* (Berkeley 1927) 57–62 and Ruschenbusch, "Untersuchungen zur Geschichte des athenischen Strafrechts," *Graezistische Abhandlungen,* Band 4 (Köln und Graz 1968) 73.

** The "king," the member of the board of nine archons who dealt with charges of religious offences.

suit approached an executive or legislative organ, often one of the
nine archons, and that organ conducted a preliminary hearing called
proanakrisis.[20] Unless it became clear at the *proanakrisis* that there
was no case against the defendant,[21] the suit then passed to its second
stage, which was a hearing before a *dikasterion*. The word for the
process of transferring the case from the first organ receiving it to the
dikasterion was *ephesis*. This word can best be translated "transfer"
or "reference"; it is much wider in meaning than "appeal." *Ephesis*
could indeed come about in consequence of appeal by a disappointed
litigant, but it could occur because of other causes, and in many
circumstances it was compulsory.[22] *Ephesis* to the *dikasterion* was
the safeguard of individual liberty and security against arbitrary
behaviour by magistrates and public bodies. The modern doctrine of
the separation of the powers was unknown. Instead it was taken for
granted that any public authority, which we might call legislative
or executive, should have some power, of the kind which we would
call judicial, to enforce its will and to remedy wrongs; the citizen's
guarantee against abuse of that judicial power was *ephesis* to the
dikasterion.

Eisangelia may be defined as the criminal procedure in which the
first of the two stages is a hearing before the Council of Five Hundred
or the Assembly. Hansen has clarified the subject by insisting on
the procedural distinction between *eisangelia* to the Council and
eisangelia to the Assembly.[23] In *eisangelia* to the Council, the Council
voted at the first stage to decide whether there was a *prima facie*
[first-sight] case against the accused; such a decision was called a
katagnosis, and, after it had been taken, the case was sent to the
dikasterion for the second stage of the trial.[24] In *eisangelia* to the

---

[20] *Ath. Pol.* 3.5; Wade-Gery (above, note 3), 173, 175.

[21] Even the nine archons had a modest power to dismiss a case on these grounds: Harp.,
s.v. *anakrisis*.

[22] Ruschenbusch, "Ephesis. Ein Beitrag zur griechischen Rechtsterminologie," *Zeitschrift
der Savigny-Stiftung* 78 (1961) Romanistische Abteilung 386–390, and "Heliaia. Die Tradition
über das solonische Volksgericht," *Historia* 14 (1965) 381–384.

[23] Above, note 6, 21–28. He draws on *Ath. Pol.* 45.2; 59.2–4; Dem., 24.63; [Dem.],
47.42–43; Xen., *Hell.* 1.7; *IG* 1.² 110 [=1.³ 102] = Meiggs and Lewis, 85, lines 39–47; *IG* 2.²
125 = Tod 154 lines 6–10.

[24] But the Council could impose a fine up to 500 drachmas without allowing *ephesis* to the
dikasterion. This rule is known from [Dem.], 47.43; cf. *IG* 1.² 76 [= 1.³ 78] = Meiggs and Lewis
73, lines 57–59. I follow Rhodes (above, note 5, 147, 164, 171) in understanding the rule about
500 drachmas thus. Hansen (above, note 6, 24) interprets the rule differently, saying "the
Council was empowered to pass the final verdict in the second type of *eisangelia* if the accused
was sentenced to a fine of 500 dr. maximum and if he did not appeal against the Council's
verdict." I cannot follow Hansen on this, since I am not persuaded that *ephesis* in *Ath. Pol.*
45.2 means "appeal" rather than "compulsory transfer." But the question is immaterial for the
present argument.

Assembly, a preliminary vote was taken by the Council, whether on its own initiative or on instructions from the Assembly, but the measure passed by this preliminary vote was a *probouleuma*,* not a *katagnosis*; the action taken by the Assembly on this *probouleuma* was the first stage of the hearing, and afterwards the case usually went to a *dikasterion* for the second stage.

It is important to observe that both in *eisangelia* to the Council and in *eisangelia* to the Assembly the second and final stage of the trial was a hearing before a *dikasterion*. On this point there is substantial agreement as concerns *eisangelia* to the Council; the case was referred to a *dikasterion*, unless the penalty voted by the Council was less than 500 drachmas (see note 24). Concerning *eisangelia* to the Assembly, it is admitted that cases were most often referred to a *dikasterion* for final decision, but many people believe that the Assembly itself could and occasionally did sit as a court and issue a final verdict. Attempting a comprehensive survey, Hansen (p. 51) finds that in eighty-six cases of *eisangelia* to the Assembly the final decision was taken by a *dikasterion*, and in eleven such cases the final decision was taken by the Assembly. But concerning these eleven cases one must be on one's guard against a possible gap in the evidence. Extant sources hardly ever give a full report of the whole course of a trial. It may be that in some of the eleven cases the issue was heard by a *dikasterion*, after the Assembly had voted, but the guilt of the accused had become so evident in the hearing before the Assembly that the decision of the *dikasterion* was a foregone conclusion, and so the extant sources only mention the more memorable stage of the trial. This may be true of the trial of Timotheos in 373/2; the meeting of the Assembly was memorable, not least because Jason and Alketas were present; the accused withdrew into the service of the Persian King soon afterwards, and the extant source of information is a speech ([Demosthenes] 49) delivered eleven years later. It may also be true of others among Hansen's eleven cases, for example, for the second trial of Miltiades; Herodotos (6.136) says that he was accused before the *demos* and that the *demos* voted to inflict a fine of fifty talents; evidently the hearing before the Assembly was politically decisive, but that does not exclude the possibility that a formal hearing before a *dikasterion* followed. In only one case is it certain that the final verdict was issued by the Assembly without even the formality of a hearing before a *dikasterion*; that case was the trial of the generals after the battle of Arginousai. This occurrence

---

* "Preliminary resolution," the word used of resolutions of the Council sent forward to the Assembly.

was not a model of correct procedure; indeed it was the only occasion (as far as known to me) when the Assembly accepted the doctrine that the *demos* may do as it pleases.[25]

Since *eisangelia* was a proper trial and the accused enjoyed the safeguard of *ephesis* to the *dikasterion*, one may regret the habit, common among writers of English, of translating *eisangelia* with "impeachment." They only similarity arises because the legislature played a part in both procedures. But *eisangelia* conformed to the two-stage pattern of criminal (and civil) proceedings in Athens, so that the accused had some chance of a fair hearing. Impeachment is a procedural monstrosity, more political than judicial, the misshapen offspring of the mother of parliaments, now happily obsolete in the land of its birth, but preserved as a fossilized relic in the Constitution of the United States and revived irresponsibly from time to time for strictly partisan reasons.[26]

To sum up. In classical Athens someone who believed that a crime or outrageous act had been committed could report his information to the Council of Five Hundred or to the Assembly. He might think one of these bodies particularly appropriate to receive the report if the alleged act affected the public interest. To make such a report was *eisangellein*. In the archaic period such reports may often have been made to the Council of the Areopagos, but this practice ceased when that body became impaired in personnel in consequence of the unforeseen effects of the change of 488/7 in the mode of selecting the nine archons.[27] Instead the reports were habitually made to the Assembly or the Council of Five Hundred, once meetings of those bodies became conveniently frequent. A *nomos eisangeltikos* [law of *eisangelia*], listing specific offences but including a general clause, may have been passed ca. 411/0; doubtless such a law was enacted or reenacted in the codification of 403–399. There is no need to suppose that a statute of Solon or of Kleisthenes or of any other legis-lator created *eisangelia* and specified the organ to receive the reports. Likewise there is no good reason to suppose that a statute of

---

[25] I have avoided deliberately the obscure question of the origin of the *dikasteria*. For diver-gent views see Wade-Gery (above, note 3) 173–179, 182–197; Ruschenbusch (above, note 19), 78–82; Hansen (above, note 6), 51–52. The *heliaia* was the parent of the *dikasteria* and bore some relationship to the assembled *demos*; but the nature of the relationship between 6,000 sworn jurors aged at least thirty years and the whole body of adult male citizens is not yet clear.

[26] I think Thomas G. Barnes for discussing this point with me; he is not to blame for the inadequacy of my presentation. I admit to being one of those who have translated *eisangelia* with "impeachment."

[27] Wade-Gery (above, note 3, 105–106) argued that the reform of 488/7 led to a decline in the quality of the personnel of the Areopagos. But a different view can be defended; see E. Badian, "Archons and *Strategoi*," *Antichthon* 5 (1971) 1–34.

Ephialtes transferred the function of hearing *eisangeliai* from one organ to others; judicial procedure can develop by practice and custom without statutory change.

"OFFICIAL JURISDICTION"

Rhodes has collected together a group of cases, heard by the Council of Five Hundred, under the heading "official jurisdiction" and has sought to distinguish them from *eisangelia*. But the group is highly miscellaneous. Under this heading Rhodes notes that the Council could try officials on its own initiative or in response to a report made to it by a private person (above, note 9). It had jurisdiction over offences concerning the tribute of the Delian League.[28] It judged offences concerning naval equipment in the dockyards (above, note 9). It supervised public works and reported offences concerning them to the Assembly, so that the case would be referred to a *dikasterion* if the *demos* condemned the accused.[29] It had jurisdiction over some religious offences concerning the Eleusinian mysteries.[30] Sometimes the Assembly instructed the Council to investigate unusual offences and refer them to a court.[31] As indicated above (note 24), the Council's power to penalize was limited to a fine of 500 drachmas; if any greater penalty was at stake, the case was referred to a *dikasterion*. No account need be taken here of the Council's power to imprison people who failed to pay debts due to the state on time;[32] that should be regarded, not as a judicial power to issue a verdict, but as a mode of administrative coercion intended to compel payment.

Rhodes believes that "official jurisdiction," originally less extensive than in the fully developed constitution, was exercised until 462 by the Council of the Areopagos but was transferred by Ephialtes to the Council of Five Hundred. Moreover he thinks that the "official jurisdiction" of the Five Hundred, increasing with the growth of public business, influenced the development of *eisangelia*. That is, he thinks that Ephialtes may have intended *eisangeliai* to be heard by the Council of Five Hundred with reference to the *demos* sitting as a court; but the Assembly, being short of time, may have ordered

---

[28] Meiggs and Lewis 46 [= *IG* 1.³ 34], lines 31–43, 69, lines 38–40 and 48–50.
[29] *Ath. Pol.* 46.2.
[30] *IG* 1.² 76 [= 1.³ 78] = Meiggs and Lewis 73, lines 57–59; Andok., 1.110–116.
[31] *SEG.* 12.32 = A. G. Woodhead, *Hesperia* 18 (1949) 78–83 [= *IG* 1.³ 85], *IG* 1.² 110 [= 1.³ 102] = Meiggs and Lewis, 85, lines 39–44.
[32] *Ath. Pol.* 48.1.

the Council to send such cases on to a *dikasterion*, and the Council itself may have referred the cases to a *dikasterion* by assimilating *eisangelia* to its "official jurisdiction."

Enough has been said above against the last part of this thesis. The practice of referring *eisangeliai* to a *dikasterion* is to be explained by the privilege of *ephesis* to the *dikasterion*; this privilege was un-restricted (except in homicide and related cases) and according to Athenian tradition it was created by Solon.[33] If the procedure of *eisangelia* arose in the archaic period, as seems likely (cf. Calhoun, above, note 19), it is more likely to have provided the pattern for the growth in "official jurisdiction" of the Council than vice versa.

The word *eisangelia* is used in extant sources for some types of case which Rhodes classifies as "official jurisdiction." It is used, for example, for trials of offences concerning naval equipment. A some-what crucial question arises in relation to the Council's authority to try officials. Aristotle (*Ath. Pol.* 45.2) says: "The Council judges most officials and especially those who have charge of money. Its verdict is not final but subject to *ephesis* to the *dikasterion*. Private citizens too may make a report (*eisangellein*) against any of the officials whom they wish, alleging that he does not observe the laws; officials in these cases too enjoy *ephesis* to the *dikasterion*, if the Council votes for their condemnation." Here Aristotle indicates two kinds of charges that were made against officials and that came before the Council. The one kind was charges initiated by the Council. The other was charges initiated by private citizens, who brought their complaints to the Council. Charges of this latter kind could be called *eisangeliai*, since Aristotle uses the verb *eisangellein* of them. Were charges of the first kind, those initiated by the Council itself, also *eisangeliai*? Criticizing Rhodes, Hansen has argued convincingly that they were.[34]

Thus some at least of the cases now classified as "official juris-diction" of the Council could properly be called *eisangeliai*. It is possible that all cases so classified belong to the procedure of *eisangelia*. Indeed this conclusion can scarcely be avoided if it is true that the *nomos eisangeltikos* did not restrict *eisangelia* to a limited list of specified offences. Even if that hypothesis is mistaken, the difference (for example) between *eisangelia* to the Council on a charge of treason and trial before the Council and a *dikasterion* of

---

[33] *Ath. Pol.* 9.1. The tradition may be right, but I refrain from asking what "Solon" means in this context and await an inquiry into the authenticity of the extant laws attributed to him.

[34] Above, note 6, 49–50. The argument depends on the law of Timokrates quoted in Dem., 24.63.

an offence concerning the tribute of the Delian League is merely verbal; the procedure was the same. The true historical question concerns the hypothesis that Ephialtes transferred "official juris-diction" from the Areopagos to the Five Hundred. Here the miscel-laneous character of "official jurisdiction" should give pause. Clearly cases of these different types first came within the purview of the Council of Five Hundred at different times. In some cases enactments were passed ordering the Council to take cognizance of offences of a specified kind; this possibility is illustrated by decrees concerning the tribute of the Delian League (above, note 28); the Assembly considered the Council a convenient body to deal with such matters. In other instances it may have become customary for the Council to receive cases of a specifiable kind, simply because individual com-plainants on their own initiative reported their information to the Council; the informer, like the Assembly, considered the Council a convenient body to deal with such matters. This may account for the Council's share in dealing with offences concerning public works. In the archaic period it is not unlikely that "official jurisdiction" of a less extensive character was exercised by the Council of the Areopagos, although doubtless its verdicts were subject to *ephesis* to the *dikasterion* (*heliaia*?), once that Solonian privilege had been asserted. Later the Council of the Areopagos ceased to exercise "official jurisdiction"; the reason is that, when the personnel of that body deteriorated, the Assembly and individual informers no longer considered it a convenient body to deal with their complaints; they did not need Ephialtes to tell them that.

EPHIALTES

So far it has been maintained in this paper that the development of *eisangelia* and of "official jurisdiction" (whether they are same or different) can best be explained by considerations of practice, custom and convenience, not by the specific enactments of a legislator such as Ephialtes. Possibly a general hypothesis could be enunciated: in constitutional history custom precedes statute. That is, a practice arises by custom and, if it is not challenged, it remains customary and subject to changes of custom; but if it is challenged, it is regulated, modified or reaffirmed by statute.

Of the changes attributed by Rhodes to Ephialtes there remains, apart from the matter of *euthynai*, the transfer of the *dokimasia* of the nine archons from the Areopagos to the Five Hundred. In the time of Aristotle (*Ath. Pol.* 45.3; 55.2–4) the *dokimasia* of the nine archons was conducted by the Council of Five Hundred in the first instance and then passed by *ephesis* to the *dikasterion*. Since the nine archonships were a much older institution than the Five Hundred, and since the Council of the Areopagos consisted of former archons, it is reasonable to suppose that originally the Areopagite Council conducted the *dokimasia* of the archons. The change must have required specific enactment and it may well have been proposed by Ephialtes, for by 462 the Council of the Areopagos had had twenty-five years to deteriorate and to become unfit for scrutinizing the incoming archons.

If Ephialtes changed the procedure for hearing *euthynai* and for *dokimasia* of archons, his goal becomes clear. He was concerned about the way officials performed their tasks; the two procedures bearing on the performance of officials were *dokimasia*, which tested their formal qualifications, and *euthynai*, where they were called to account for their shortcomings. To classify him among "radical democratic leaders" does not explain his work;[35] he was a man seeking to remedy abuses of a perhaps extensive but certainly limited and specifiable kind.[36]

[35] R. W. Wallace, "Ephialtes and the Areopagos," *GRBS* 15 (1974) 259–269; the offending phrase occurs on page 266. One may deplore such language as "ambitious *strategoi* of the left" (263). It has become popular of late; one is told that the career of Kallias, husband of Elpinike, showed a "shift to the Left" (J. K. Davies, *Athenian Propertied Families* [Oxford 1971] 259) and one reads of "a political *diabole* [slander] of Right Wing origin" (506). Even in present-day political contexts the terms "right" and "left" belong to propaganda, not analysis.

[36] P. J. Rhodes, "ΕΙΣΑΓΓΕΛΙΑ in Athens," *JHS* 99 (1979) 103–114 appeared while this article was in press.

PART IV

A View of Democracy

Introduction to Part IV

This book concludes with a general study. C. Meier has taught in various German universities, finally as Professor of Ancient History at Munich. His earliest work was on Roman history, but he has increasingly devoted his attention to the development of politics (or, as he would prefer to say, 'the political') and political thinking in Greece. Chapter 14, his contribution to a series of lectures at Freiburg in Breisach in 1981/2 on the theory of history as universal history, is a short exposition of the view to be found in several of his publications. In asking why these developments occurred in Greece between the eighth and the fifth centuries, and not in other societies at the same or other times, he starts from the explosion of activity in Greece in the eighth century, and takes account of the rise and fall of tyrants, and (to a greater extent than other scholars) of the influence of wise men and lawgivers, and of Delphi as a centre for the exchange of information and ideas. In Athens he focuses on Solon, who had a vision for the whole citizen body but expected the people to follow their leaders, and on Cleisthenes, who created a new structure which enabled the citizens to become conscious of themselves as citizens; and he places the achievement of 'more genuine democracy' after the Persian Wars and shortly before the middle of the fifth century, i.e. when Ephialtes reformed the council of the Areopagus.

14 *The Greeks: The Political Revolution in World History**

CHRISTIAN MEIER

The question to be discussed here is mostly posed in retrospect. One then asks: What have the Greeks given us? The title of a book first published in 1921 and rewritten by new authors in 1981, *The Legacy of Greece*,** is particularly indicative of this dominant interest. The Greeks did, in innumerable fields, pave the way for the Occident; the Occident has returned to them, again and again, and is still doing so. In a general sense, this is a commonplace, but the details are problematic. It is not at all easy to determine in a more precise way the direct and indirect contribution of the Greeks to Roman, medieval and modern history.

But this is not my theme. Here the question relates to the beginning of Greek history: How did Greek culture emerge? And this question should not be taken lightly. We cannot assume that the Greeks were a particularly gifted people. As far as we know, the notion of gift belongs to individual psychology. If whole peoples seem to be gifted, this can only mean that they had particular possibilities to develop the gifts present among them as among others. And these possibilities cannot, in turn, be derived from specific collective characteristics: they must be explained together with those characteristics. However

---

* Originally published in German, as 'Die Griechen: Die politische Revolution der Weltgeschichte', in *Saeculum* xxxiii 1982, 133–47. This English version first published in J. P. Arnason and P. Murphy (eds), *Agon, Logos, Polis: The Greek Achievement and its Aftermath* (Stuttgart: Steiner, 2001), 56–71; reprinted with the permission of the author and Franz Steiner Verlag, Stuttgart.

In an introductory note in the German version Prof. Meier referred for further discussion and annotation to his book *Die Entstehung des Politischen bei den Griechen* (Frankfurt: Suhrkamp, 1980; 2nd ed. 1983) [translated by D. McLintock as *The Greek Discovery of Politics* (Cambridge, MA: Harvard University Press, 1990)].

** R. W. Livingstone (ed.), *The Legacy of Greece: Essays by G. Murray* [et al.] (Oxford: Oxford University Press, 1921); M. I. Finley (ed.), *The Legacy of Greece: A New Appraisal* (Oxford: Oxford University Press, 1981).

ready we may be to credit the Greeks with all manners of excellence, we must admit that the reasons for doing so need explanation and do not explain anything by themselves. We are still far from having satisfactory answers to the question about the origins of Greek culture. Historical research on classical antiquity has not done much to help us, and modern theories of evolution are of no use.

Above all, such theories miss two decisive points: The totally exceptional character of the Greeks in relation to all other cultures, including the so-called axial civilizations, and consequently, the fact that democracy and the political in a specific sense developed only among the Greeks. In my opinion, the fashionable underestimation of the political and of democracy is dangerous (it is also, in a disquieting sense, distinctively German). But it is particularly misguided when it comes to the interpretation of universal history. With all due respect for social history, relations of production and property rights: The decisive moment of world history between the early civilizations and the Christian West was a political one, namely the emergence of the political among the Greeks. Perhaps we should, by analogy with the neolithic revolution, speak of a world-historical political revolution, brought about by the Greeks. And with all due respect for structural history: This very moment belongs to the history of events from the viewpoint of universal history, it was highly contingent.

A first tentative observation can be made without detailed study or scholarly knowledge: Civilizations interdependent or, in the most crucial cases, independent of each other took shape in various parts of Asia, Africa and America. With the exception of Greek civilization, they were all characterized by the central role of monarchy in the sociogenetic process. There is much to be said about the challenges which the monarch faced and which enabled him to innovate. We should also remember the role of priesthoods, temples and mythologies; and it may be possible to identify common features of mutually independent civilizations, which would suggest some lawlike patterns of development. Here we must leave all these things aside, as well as many others. The decisive point is, in my opinion, that a monarch stood at the center of all these cultures, and that he together with his apparatuses and other (especially priestly) authorities constructed a system whose functioning and preservation continued to be bound to the monarchy. It could be usurped or destroyed, but there was no positive alternative to monarchy. Everything was dependent on and oriented towards it, not least in many cases the maintenance and protection of numerous technical preconditions of these cultures. There was, in other words, a very far-reaching and stable concentration of power, wealth, knowledge, and capacity to act in one single place. In such cases, we can to a much greater extent than in regard to the Greeks observe a process of "state" formation, however different the result may still be from the modern state.

The civilizational achievements of these cultures were often of a very high order, and in many respects significantly superior to the Greeks. Important "learning processes" could take place. But inasmuch as all learning is also unlearning (to learn is to perceive, or to take seriously. certain possibilities within a broader range, and to neglect the others), all acts of learning in these cultures were adapted to or confined within the basic monarchic structure. And alternatives to it were unlearned.

By contrast, monarchs played only a marginal role in Greek history. The sociogenetic processes unfolded from within society. Before the Hellenistic phase, there was no stable and dominant concentration of power, wealth, knowledge and capacity to act in the hands of single individuals. The example of the tyrants, who at a later stage and only in some cities temporarily monopolized power and the capacity to act, also shows how difficult it was to extend the monopoly to knowledge, and to create the legitimacy needed to stabilize a new monarchy.

There is no point in asking whether or to what extent this was a cause or consequence of the process that led to the emergence of democracy. As with the question of the chicken and the egg, a closer examination must focus on the process that gave rise to both things. In any case, this "shortcoming" of the Greeks was, from a certain point in time onwards, decisive for the whole sociogenetic context not as a cause, but as a precondition. This aspect – the different distribution of power and knowledge, as well as of wealth and of individual capacity to act – was essential to the development of political forms, the specific Greek modes of thought and creation, and the position of the Greeks in the world. The results affected the whole subsequent course of history.

With regard to both starting-point and outcomes, the Greeks are thus the great exception among major civilizations. And if we can reasonably assume that their influence on Rome and Christianity, on medieval and modern Europe, and on the whole modern world was decisive, we may see the Greeks as a needle's eye through which world history had to pass in order to reach the stage of European and worldwide modernity. Obviously, this presupposes that Rome and Christianity as well as the medieval and modern worlds could only become what they were on the basis of Greek inputs. The crucial contributions may be due to the level of rationality reached by the Greeks, or the impact of Aristotelian concepts revived in the medieval West by Thomas Aquinas; to the idea of humanity, developed by the Romans but inconceivable without the Greeks; or to the notions of democracy, freedom, equality and citizenship, which had to be invented before they could be implemented on the enlarged scale of the West. Greek myth and Greek plastic arts (or the Roman art strongly influenced by the Greeks) must also be considered. And it seems likely that the foundation of the modern state, together with its demarcation from the church and thus also the momentous separation of state and society, was only made possible by the use of philosophical concepts and perspectives inherited from the Greeks.

But one can only speculate about these things. I do not see how we could arrive at more precise conclusions: for we cannot isolate the Greek elements that were involved in successive turns of history, and then analyze the remaining factors. And we don't know enough about the possibilities of evolution.

In short, we must rest content with a historian's observation: whatever might otherwise have happened, the actual course of events was in any case strongly affected by Greek culture and can only be understood in relation to it.

But what led to the rise of this culture and the creation of the legacy that it left to all later generations? To use a problematic term: What was the pattern of Greek evolution? Here, too, we seem to be faced with uncertain facts and insoluble problems. The sources are extremely unsatisfactory, and there will be no major change for the better; archaeological findings, the only ones that can be expected to increase, are on the whole of limited significance.

Even so, there are deficits of research that can be made good. It seems likely that even the meager available sources could directly or indirectly be used to back up insights that have yet to be formulated. On the one hand, the question of the origins of Greek culture has been neglected, because an exceptional capacity to create culture was taken for granted. On the other hand, the possibilities and necessities of interdisciplinary research in this field were not even properly perceived, let alone exhausted. Comparative research is underdeveloped. On closer examination, many features that have been seen as defining characteristics of the Greeks or invoked to explain their history can be found elsewhere. Early popular assemblies, often taken to mark the beginning of the road to democracy, are more or less known (i.e. can be concluded) to have existed in Mesopotamia as well as in India and Iran, although subsequent developments did not follow the same path. Apparent peculiarities of the Homeric poems are characteristic of early heroic epics in general. There are, of course, other features that remain distinctively Homeric or Greek. But only comparative research can tell us exactly what they are and what they mean. As for the numerous parallels between Chinese and Greek or Jewish and Greek history, we can only note them in passing.

But comparative research is not only an antidote to misconceptions about the particular characteristics of peoples studied by specialized historians. It can also generate new insights of its own. However, it is not enough for results in one field to be appropriated by scholars in another, or by theorists of evolution (although that would already be of some use). It is often the case that these results reflect very specific questions, which in turn presuppose the horizon of a particular discipline. They are therefore often unable to provide answers to questions coming from elsewhere, even if the sources themselves are conducive to such answers. What we need is a co-operative, mutually participatory effort to confront problems, develop questions, and to acquire knowledge of possible connections, factors and constellations. That might make the sources more amenable to further interpretations. Such a framework for more systematic questioning would both allow us to link the sources more effectively to available knowledge and tell us more precisely what we do not know.

If we can give a clearer account of contrasts and convergences in the results of different lines of development, it should be possible to draw conclusions about the specific preconditions and motive powers at work in each case. But then we also have to search for counter-examples and see realities within the horizon of possibilities. The question is not only why something happened as it did, but also why it did not happen in another way. Every analysis of connections seemingly conducive to development must be accompanied by a survey of other cases where similar connections may have prevailed without causing any comparable changes. In the case of certain cultures that flourished during the last millennium BC (Karl Jaspers's "axial period"), a marginal position with regard to older cultures and stronger powers seems to have been of some importance. That applies, in particular, to the Greeks and to Ancient Israel. But before drawing any general conclusions about the significance of such marginality, we should consider counter-examples; this might show that only a particular kind of marginality, or a combination with (or absence of) other factors made this situation so favorable. Marginality may only be a particular case of a more general constellation: if the early development of autonomous intellectuals in Greece was linked to the marginal position and the multi-central character of a culture confined within narrow spatial bounds, the same development in China might be due to the size of the country and the plurality of strong centers. The debates on the origin and diversity of axial civilizations, organized by S. N. Eisenstadt, have shown how geopolitical hypotheses can be modified and refined by specialists working on Greece, Israel, India and China.* Similar issues and hypotheses will emerge as the relevant disciplines draw closer to each other and begin to share not only results, but also ways of questioning, and to pose questions to each other.

But as long as no such interdisciplinary research gets off the ground, one can only formulate one's own questions, as precisely as possible, and try to communicate the results. As we move from the preconditions and beginnings of the historical process, mere questions may give way to conjectures or even to conclusive findings. The overall picture will nevertheless remain unclear.

Archaeological sources suggest that the Greeks were from the beginning of the eighth century involved in significant and rapidly expanding trade in the Aegean area as well as in Syria and Italy. Colonization, which began a little later (around 750), then quickly led to the foundation of new cities on the various coasts of the Mediterranean. Until the end of the ninth century, the Greeks seem to have led a rather isolated life. In any case, the eighth century saw a relatively abrupt and many-sided outbreak of activity, including a significant increase in seafaring and shipbuilding (for the purposes of piracy as well as trade), and a much higher level of mobility. Many skills of different kinds must have been developed; new patterns of cooperation and rivalry emerged; new relationships took shape between individuals within small groups, between communities, and between the various groups and cities. Social differentiation went hand in hand with political change, new possibilities of gain and loss, and new occupations.

We do not know much more about the details. But it is on record

---

* See K. Jaspers, *Die Achsenzeit der Weltgeschichte* (special issue of *Der Monat* i 1949); S. N. Eisenstadt (ed.), *The Origins and Diversity of Axial Age Civilizations* (State University of New York Press, 1986).

or can be assumed that monarchic rule in the Greek communities was abolished or at least seriously weakened during the eighth and early seventh centuries; sometimes the kings were confined to priestly roles. New forms of rule and new ways of balancing power were developed, and they were bound to affect the relationship between the nobility and the rest of the population.

Furthermore, the Greeks borrowed writing from the Phoenicians probably during the eighth century and adapted it to their language by introducing signs for the vowels that the Phoenicians had left unmarked.

Then, towards the end of the century, the *Iliad* and the *Odyssey* were composed. Old epic songs, transmitted and enriched through generations, were combined with new parts in a systematic fashion, and probably written down at the same time. Greek written tradition thus begins with one of the masterpieces of world literature. And since so much of what counts as distinctively Greek can be found in Homer, we must ask ourselves whether the defining character of Greek culture had not taken shape at this very early stage before any marked increase in activity and mobility. But much may also be due to further elaboration at the beginning of the period of colonization. As Wolfgang Schadewaldt puts it: "The memories of a past age, together with a self-confident will to shape the future, created a situation exceptionally favorable to poetry." He adds that "the spirit of the Delphic oracle was already at work."[1]

On the other hand, many features commonly seen as Homeric are as noted above less characteristic of the Greeks in particular than of early epic poetry as such. There are stories about the heroes of an earlier and greater age. The heroes are endowed with exceptional strength and courage; they take pleasure in fighting, hunting and feasting; and they are committed to knightly ideals of honour. The stories claim to be true and contain realistic description of various details. Homer's distinctive language, liveliness and charm are another matter; so are his gods and many other things. But in view of the parallels with other cases, historians have to face the task of finding out what is specifically Homeric or specifically Greek about the Homeric poems. And even if many of the things involved seem distinctively Greek, it might be the case that the Greeks had then and later simply retained much of the freedom which epic poetry tends to ascribe to the remote past. For example, we might think that kings are portrayed in a way which suggests an easy path to democracy:

[1] Cf. W. Schadewaldt, *Der Aufbau der Ilias* (Frankfurt a.M. 1975) 91ff.

their world, the world of public action, resembles that of uncon-strained village life, and the concepts used to describe power show how weak its institutional foundations were. But if such an image of kingly authority is widespread in early epics, the characteristic trait of the Greeks would consist in the fact that their evolution preserved things which were elsewhere abolished for the sake of evolution, i.e. for the purpose of building strong monarchies. In that case, it would be misleading to see the Homeric world as marked by a particular "evolutionary openness"; rather, it would be a result of later devel-opments that Homeric features remained present in Greek life. I do not think we are in a position to give a clear answer to this question.

It is also an open question whether Greek peculiarities as they had developed until the eighth century were in some way particularly favorable to changes in a democratic direction. This might be a matter of specific characteristics of the Dorian immigrants (although they may not have been very different from other Indo-Europeans), their relationship to the pre-existing population, particular forms of landed property, or particular forms of primitive popular assemblies as well as many other things.

Comparative study is the only way to arrive at any plausible conclusions about the beginnings of Greek development. If we can for example assume that the formation and consolidation of mon-archy in other cultures led to the elimination of many "primitive" or "original" features, the real Greek enigma has less to do with the starting point than with the course of later history. In short, it is at least for the time being unclear how far the Greek road was deter-mined by older precognitions or by the particular character of the "take-off."

The abrupt and enormous increase in Greek activity during the eighth century is probably due to population growth or, more precisely, to the fact that a growing population could no longer live on the land available at home. If increased demand for imported foods or iron plays a role, this was probably for the same reason. In this situation there were roughly speaking two possibilities. Individual rulers or leaders could use the opportunities to accumulate power and embark on conquest or the surplus population could somehow be moved elsewhere. Whatever may have been attempted or in part achieved in some places, it was on the whole the second solution that prevailed. This may have something to do with structural conditions, such as the traditional weakness of monarchy in the area and the geographical obstacles to concentration of power. Seafaring was, in any case, an obvious outlet for the Greeks, and the interests of long-distance traders who wanted to establish outposts could easily combine with those of landless peasants' sons who wanted to acquire their own farms; in addition, it was easy to found new cities in various parts of the Mediterranean. But it is not clear whether this was enough to divert surplus energies away from Greece, or whether more contingent combinations of motives, successes and expectations were needed to unleash the dynamic of colonization.

In any case, several factors combined to give an untypical direction to Greek development.

I.   The immigrants who destroyed Mycenaean society were not highly organized; they could not or would not appropriate the Mycenaean administrative apparatus, and in whatever shape they may have arrived, they dispersed into a multitude of small communities after the conquest.

II. In the first centuries of the last millennium BC, a power vacuum in the Aegean area enabled the Greek communities to survive in isolation.

III. When a more active society turned to expansion in the eighth century, the monarchic centers were on the whole so weak that they could not utilize the results to strengthen their own power basis.

IV. An unusually large space for expansion, as well as a specific combination of motives, led the Greeks to export problems which might otherwise have led to the formation of stronger power centers and larger political units.

V.   It was obviously of some importance that the Greeks were not too close to and not too distant from the more advanced Oriental civilizations. They could thus avoid political dependence and at the same time appropriate goods, knowledge and most importantly new needs which inspired new activities; this complex of borrowings accelerated the historical process, and that made it even more difficult for individuals – monarchs or usurpers – to harness the whole dynamic to their particular purposes.

Under these circumstances, the results of increased activity and more rapid change were widely shared by many cities, as well as many individuals and families within them. All participated in the process and benefited from growing wealth, influence, fame and experience. The momentous developments of these few decades, which led to growing differentiation and expanding possibilities of action, were thus at the same time conducive to further stabilization of the original constellation: a relatively broad distribution of power and resources within the *poleis* and in the whole "poly-political" world of the Greeks.

The impact of particular characteristics of the Greek environment can only be understood within this context. It is true that the rugged landscape separated many small areas from each other; but this geographical factor does not seem to have prevented the political unification of relatively large areas during the Mycenaean epoch. And there can be no geographical explanation for the fact that many independent communities continued to coexist in small areas and on individual islands, whereas Athens was capable of unifying Attica and Sparta conquered the whole area of Messenia across the Taygetos. There were obviously more factors at work: the absence of a powerful neighbour like Minoan Crete, which seems to have been an external stimulus to the formation of large power blocs in the second millennium, the relative simplicity of Greek needs after the destruction of Mycenaean culture, the weakness of political centers, and the outward direction of activity after the turning point of the eighth century. But there was also a positive factor, clearly strong but difficult to evaluate: the Greeks were very attached to the idea of living in very small, independent and transparent cities.

There were exceptions such as Attica and parts of the Argolis; there were the various synoecisms [amalgamations of communities]. The segregating trend was not absolute, but it was strong. Its logic is not easy to understand. Was it a result of the strong consciousness of belonging, characteristic of the Greek communities of cult and sacrifice? Or was this factor a product of later developments? If it was a survival from earlier times, the question is, how was it preserved? Survival could not be taken for granted. How important was a general human preference for managing one's own affairs, if there are no particular obstacles to that and no particular reasons for doing otherwise? Was this inclination at least strong enough to motivate resistance to the building of stronger power structures, and at the same time for the most part to preserve the unity and independence of those who lived together in one place? Was it of some significance that large political units were never needed, because the climatic and geographical conditions made it possible to do without them? And that colonization then channeled much of Greek activity outwards? Could it be the case that the condition of living together in small units was only later transformed into a strong will, and only because it had not been disrupted by any higher authorities, so that broader social strata could adopt it as a value of their own?

However that may be, the self-contained character and the relative independence of small communities, together with the versatility of the aristocracy and later on of broader social strata, were essential preconditions for the emergence of institutions compatible with freedom.

All these factors and many others mobilized the Greek world and broadened the scope of its activities, without imposing new constraints or giving rise to new powers capable of destroying the roots out of which freedom could revive. New possibilities, varying in kind and degree, were opened up not only for the aristocracy, but also especially through colonization to members of middle and lower strata.

It remains an open question whether we can with some justification single out individual factors as primary causes for the whole process; and it seems more likely that their contingent conjunction in successive situations was decisive for the early phase of Greek evolution.

Nor is it clear how easy the road to democracy was after these beginnings. The only obvious point to make is that the Greek world in general and its economic as well as political centers in particular drifted towards a major and probably inevitable crisis. Rising expectations seem to have gone beyond expanding possibilities, and this led to indebtedness, exploitation, debt slavery, misery and revolt. At the same time, the upward and downward mobility of many families caused unrest: major enterprises were risky and could lead to life-threatening losses as well as to massive gains. Other factors intensified the crisis. There seems to have been a general loosening of bonds and a transformation of mentalities. Problems of foreign policy added to the difficulties. Innovations in weaponry and military tactics, as well as the growing involvement of middle strata in warfare, were of major importance. Colonization was no longer an effective outlet.

The crisis, which cannot be discussed in further detail here, began as an economic and social one, but it affected political and moral order. The result was a general loss of orientation, and a search for new foundations of individual and social life. The main issue was now: who would be able to find a way out of the crisis?

Tyranny prevailed in many places. Ambitious individuals of aristocratic origin managed to rally large numbers of discontented people. At the same time, they developed new methods of acting, accumulated capital, and invested in projects, especially public building, which created employment. In some cases they attracted foreign artisans, or improved the legal situation of lower strata. In short, they played a significant part in overcoming the economic crisis. Their rule was nevertheless short-lived; in most cases, they lacked the resources to extend their power beyond their own city. And they could not prevent the mainstream of Greek opinion from turning against tyranny and branding it as incompatible with just and good order. To sum up, the power of tyranny was in the context of the Greek world as a whole of limited importance and of a particularistic kind. This form of domination was, despite its achievements, a failure (even if it lasted longer in some places, for example in the Sicilian cities, where it fulfilled more important functions).

The failure of tyranny was partly due to the fact that a wholly new kind of power had emerged in Greece and this new power, early Greek political thought, drew further strength from the defeat of tyranny. It became central to the process that now unfolded towards the positive goal of more participation by broader strata.

To speak of political thought is not to suggest the kind of political theory developed later by the sophists or by Plato. Rather, the term refers to early reflections on the political life of the *polis*, its presuppositions and its context; such intellectual efforts were closely linked to practice and to existing realities without visible alternatives. This thought became more political as it learnt and taught others to respond more adequately to the problems of the *polis*. A learning process was, in other words, needed for people to become citizens and thereby members of the *polis* as a political community. In the long run, the politicization of the citizen and the democratization of the *polis* went hand in hand. The development of political thought was a specific and central but often underestimated part of the social-historical process that shaped the Greek world.

Our sources refer to seven wise men; this is probably a symbolic term for a larger group of people who lived in various parts of Greece during the archaic age and became known for giving advice on various matters. We are also told and it seems likely that they exchanged ideas, directed questions to each other and shared their experiences. They may have engaged in a kind of intellectual competition that reinforced the dynamic of a broader cultural process.

Further assumptions can be made on the basis of our knowledge of the power structures of the time. In contrast to other cultures, such as ancient Egypt, where intellectuals were subordinated to kings and priests and had to adjust their thought to that condition, no power capable of such control on a large scale emerged in Greece. Individual sages may have advised tyrants, and one of them became a tyrant.

But since their advice was valued everywhere and on every side, they must have retained a certain independence. On the whole, they were less bound by ties to any power than by the obligations of an intellectual task.

If we take other sources into account, a more detailed picture can be reconstructed. Since the wise men were needed and proved competent, they acquired authority. In the cities, meanwhile, cases of political stalemate became more frequent; no powerful leaders could provide a solution (power was too difficult to concentrate, or there was no trust to build on), and it was therefore tempting to seek advice from a sage. He could be asked questions, or he could be commissioned to carry out tasks of a specific or general kind. Cities confronted with major crises empowered one of their own citizens or an outsider to implement reforms and restore order. This is known to have happened in several cases and must have happened more often. In this connection, we should also think of "law-finders", often appointed to record in writing the laws that had hitherto been transmitted orally and therefore open to arbitrary interpretation.

A very clear consciousness of problems must have developed; solutions were invented, remembered, compared and improved; various institutions were designed, and people learnt to think in institutional terms. Expectations rose in regard to intellectual crisis management, and they seem to have survived all failures.

These conclusions can be drawn from a wide range of references to the seven wise men, as well as to the Delphic oracle with which they were closely connected. Delphi appears to have been a kind of intellectual emporium, a center urgently needed by this world of many cities and therefore almost bound to emerge. In particular, its role during the colonization period enabled it to gather not only information on economic and geographical issues, but also knowledge about political techniques and problems, as well as ideas about the ultimate norms and needs of political life. Only a part of this knowledge was transmitted through oracles; much more must have found its way into conversations. Delphi may have made partisan decisions, and individual wise men may have sought direct political influence, popularity or remuneration. But it remains true that they could not have acquired their authority or at least not retained it for so long if they had not by and large been neutral towards the major powers of the time. They gave advice, not instruction. And they gave it to many sides; that was what earned them respect. They must on the whole have taken care to ensure that their advice was sound and useful, rather than adapting it to particular interests. At least, this attitude must have prevailed in the long run. Their gain – sometimes of a material kind – and their fame depended on intellectual performance. In that sense, they became a kind of third force, an autonomous intelligentsia operating in the space between the *poleis*. This position was reflected in the ideas that they developed.

It seems to me that this intelligentsia with its specific position was the driving force behind the trend towards *isonomia* ["legal equality"], the constitutional form that enabled active participation of broad strata and thus paved the way for democracy.

The meagre sources available to us, together with our knowledge of the conditions of the times, cannot prove this, but they allow us at least to make plausible conjectures. Such conclusions are, of course, always risky. But the risk is less serious when we are talking about processes rather than events. And it seems in any case very improbable that a phenomenon as significant as the emergence of *isonomia* could have been due to short-term accidents.

To say that political thinking played a decisive role in that process is not to suggest that various other well-known factors were of little or no importance. They include military changes, such as the rise of the hoplite phalanx; economic developments which led to exploitation and resistance, but also to new ways of earning one's living; more intensive communication, the need for legal security, as well as religious factors and many others. And nobody would deny that the archaic Greeks were as strongly motivated by concrete interests as human beings in general. But the way people define and understand their interests depends on opinions, those of particular individuals as well as those of society in general. And these opinions are in turn related to knowledge and expectations, to relations between individuals, and to real or possible bonds of community. They can lead individuals to understand their interests in relatively concrete or relatively abstract terms; more specifically, the abstract and remote interests may appear as urgent alongside the concrete and pressing ones. Opinions may guide people towards a more self-centered or more communal pursuit of their goals, or more precisely inspire them to translate their own interests into collective efforts to change the general state of things. When indebted peasants, forced to mortgage their farms, resist the threat of slavery, they are responding to a perceived common condition and trying to avert a common danger. They may or may not succeed in improving their economic or legal situation, but those who lead them in attempting to do so can usually increase their share of power.

But how do members of broader strata arrive at the idea of a new political order that would give them more say in public affairs? Economic and legal issues may touch on relatively concrete interests, but the wish for more political participation, let alone a new political order, is more abstract. Moreover, this wish is not simply a reaction to temporary nuisances; rather, it represents a conclusion drawn from a whole range of troubling experiences. The lesson is difficult to learn and even more difficult to implement; all the more so because the institutionalization of participation must, if anything is to change in the long run, be more lasting than the problems which gave rise to the demand for it. It is not easy to reach agreement on such matters.

But that is precisely what the Greeks achieved at least in a significant number of cities. The secondary interest of many individuals in more participation became a dominant, common and unifying interest. As such, it gained extraordinary strength. Since the Greek regimes of *isonomia* and democracy demanded direct involvement of the citizens, the interest had to be accompanied by a lasting readiness of a large number of people to take an active and regular part in politics, without becoming specialists in that field (such specialization only became possible in the later exceptional conditions of Periclean democracy).

This readiness cannot have arisen all of a sudden. And the same applies to other preconditions of *isonomia*: the mental preparation for new institutions, the acquisition of necessary knowledge, and the development of necessary expectations. Because the Greeks had no Greeks to learn from, they did not know anything about the possibility of *isonomia* (not to mention democracy) before they translated it into reality. There is, admittedly, no need to assume that the *goal* of *isonomia* was consciously formulated long before it was achieved. Rather, the movement in that direction may for most of the time have been articulated in terms of legal security, abolition of arbitrary power and other such concerns. There were, as noted above, many complaints that could motivate action.

But then there must have been a force capable of transforming diffuse discontent into political demands, of making it clear that people should not rest content with bearable or even relatively good economic conditions, and would not be well advised to adapt to the existing situation and put their trust in individual politicians; rather the thing most worth striving for and the only way to lead a satisfactory life was effective political participation by a wide public. People had to become citizens in the full political sense. For the Greeks, civic equality was (as Jacob Burckhardt noted) incompatible with political inequality: "To protect himself against injury, the poor citizen had to be able to vote, and to become judge as well as magistrate."[2]

Such insights, however, take time to be won, diffused and consolidated. For at least two centuries, the Greek cities were on the whole ruled by aristocracies, apart from the cases where individual aristocrats monopolized the power of their social groups and became tyrants. During this time, the idea of a genuine sharing of power by lower strata can only have matured slowly.

But how could that happen? How did political thinking come to identify with the community beyond the nobility, with the weak and the needy? What brings an intelligentsia to do that? This was, moreover, an intelligentsia living in a world without a philosophy of history, and therefore in search of a static and unchanging model of good order; and as far as we can judge, it had no need for the refined combination of luxury and a good conscience based on commitment to the underprivileged. We need, of course, not assume that the whole history of political thought took place within the ranks of this intelligentsia. It also and importantly involved the reception, diffusion and elaboration of the new ideas throughout society. But the decisive impulses must have come from a relatively narrow circle, which possessed the necessary knowledge and experience and had the necessary time and ability to produce ideas of a new kind. The interests of this group went beyond the immediate demands of the times, and they were reinforced by permanent communication.

In this way, an intellectual public sphere emerged; its activities took many different directions, but on the whole, the practical proposals of the intelligentsia responded to widespread expectations; aspirations, ideas and successful projects reinforced each other. In this sphere, arguments (or at least insights) counted for more than political interests. Certain standards of debate were established, and in the long run, they came albeit very slowly into general use. Our sources speak of proposals and programs submitted to public scrutiny and debate.

Most importantly, criteria and conceptions of proper order seem to have taken hold and acquired prescriptive authority. In this way, the specific third position of the intelligentsia was institutionalized. And as particular tendencies took shape and prevailed, they came to play the decisive role in developments. This trend was no less peculiar than the final outcome: The course of events was determined by

---

[2] J. Burckhardt, *Griechische Kulturgeschichte* vol. 1 (Munich 1977) 206.

a group of people who had power only in so far as it was entrusted to them by others, and whose primarily intellectual interests had to do with general order.

The beginnings of archaic Greek thought are in many ways reminiscent of the "wisdom" of the Near East, especially Egypt and Israel. Eastern influences must have been important, all the more so because the economic and social problems to be tackled were similar. And the tyrants, who in many ways embodied new and promising possibilities of action, may even for some time have inspired the sages. The course chosen by the Greek intelligentsia cannot have been certain from the outset.

But in the long run, other tendencies got the upper hand. Around 600 BC, Solon's conception of order as *eunomia* [a good legal state] already represents a determined rejection of one-man rule. We do not know how new this idea was then, nor whether it was in line with the dominant current of political thought. There are, however, good reasons to believe that Solon's ideas soon came to be seen as authoritative.

These ideas were based on the observation of law-like patterns inherent in the *polis*. There was an obvious causal connection between the exploitation of the peasantry by the nobility, the discontent of the peasants and the outbreak of civil war. For Solon, this confirmed the old maxim that unjust action would be followed by punishment. Nomological knowledge and concrete observation reinforced each other. Such conclusions and other similar ones led Solon to construct a model of proper order that he believed to be predetermined by the gods. It could not include things that would have damaging consequences. By eliminating such things, one would arrive at *eunomia*, the order willed by the gods. Given the problems of the times, this order had to be defined in a comprehensive way. It had political, economic and social aspects, as well as ethical and religious ones. It was, on the whole, interpreted in a conservative sense. When in doubt, Solon tended to assume that inherited arrangements were good; he only sought to remedy abuses. For him, it was therefore self-evident that the nobility should rule and the people should follow. But the people should not be without rights. Free ownership of land by the peasants was a part of *eunomia*, and so was among other things the observance of certain norms by the nobility.

But however conservative this conception of order may have been (it could, under the circumstances, hardly have been otherwise, and a return to earlier conditions may even have been the best thing for those in need of help), it also opened up the possibility of distinguishing between proper order and the status quo. It provided criteria for judgment on political order, liberated criticism and stimulated activity in order to achieve *eunomia*. The most essential characteristic of Solon's model was that it instituted a whole that was, in its capacity of order, beyond the reach of any single power. The ruling nobility had to operate within this framework. Order itself and as such was not negotiable. If it was defective in some way, it was the task of wise men to restore what was missing, or to give the appropriate advice. Order itself had a transcendent status and could not be identified with a particular power standing above others.

Soon afterwards, a similar view of the cosmos as an order going beyond all particular divine powers was formulated; it was obviously based on an analogy with the political model. Anaximander followed Solon in seeing order as a matter of balance between forces, rather than domination. But Solon only sought a synchronic balance within the properly ordered *polis*, whereas Anaximander sought a balance also in diachronic terms; one that allowed for the rise and decline of powers (this was clearly modeled on the destinies of families, dynasties and perhaps empires, rather than on the constitution of the *polis* as such).

From now on, political thought was committed to this idea of order, and therefore to the *polis* as a whole. If it wanted to take part in creating such an order, it had to oppose all excess and take the side of the underdog, if only in the interest of civil peace.

In the long run, however, it was bound to become clear that the profound political and ethical crisis of the Greek world called for more radical remedies: public order in the cities could only be improved if the population was provided with institutional means to protect itself. This could mean different things: councils to express the will of the community, popular courts, or more regular and powerful popular assemblies.

Solon had already appealed to all citizens and sought to convince them that they were responsible for order in the city. Even before that, the main body of the citizenry had at least been mobilized to the extent of demanding legislation by wise men. In the course of time, it became apparent that the public had to be motivated to more active and regular involvement; institutions appropriate to this purpose had to be created. In some of the most conflict-ridden cities, this meant nothing less than the construction of a new civic identity.

That is what Cleisthenes's reforms achieved in Athens at the end of the sixth century. But it was made possible by the growing prosperity of the general population under the tyranny of Peisistratos: economic stabilization had focused public attention on remaining political problems.

It was, in short, the institutionalized interest of the intelligentsia in general order that led to identification with the general public after a phase of struggle on behalf of the *polis* as a whole, in the absence of social forces that had yet to take shape and become capable of representing the whole. This involved a variety of factors that cannot be covered in this brief outline; for example, the transvaluation of values, expressed in lyric poetry, or the weakening of ties to the aristocracy. To cut a long story short, a general erosion of previously self-evident foundations sensitized the Greeks to new insights, modes of thought, and intellectual orientations, but also to new forms of friendship, citizenship and collective life.

As the political thought of the wise men (and then of broader circles) became more critical of the existing state of affairs and more responsive to new aspirations and sensibilities, it tended towards political empowerment of the people; and in this connection, the small size of the communities acquired a new significance. It was one of the preconditions for effective participation, just as the large number of separate cities was a precondition for the independence of the intelligentsia. Both factors were reinforced by others: the easily legible alphabet, the short distances between the communities, and the common language which they all used. The new military organization, a century older than *isonomia*, became politically significant when the peasant-hoplites knew that they could and should strive for regular participation in public decision-making. Hesiod's belief in justice could now be translated into desire, will, action and success. A broad spectrum of conditions and forces converged in one direction.

The availability of appropriate institutions that could secure the principles of participation against the nobility and against the inertia of the general population is perhaps less surprising than other aspects of early Greek history. Other cases (for example, the very different history of the early Roman republic) show that ways and means can be found to institutionalize a political will. The real difficulties had to do with giving this will political mass and momentum. The Roman plebeians had aristocratic leaders whom they trusted and who did fight for their cause. The structure of plebeian organization reflected that of Roman society as a whole. By contrast, the middle and lower strata of Greek society had to become much more directly involved in politics; in this they could be helped and had to be helped by individual aristocrats, but they had to insist on equal political rights. As a result, an artificial political order had to be created in opposition to the social one. And the population had to be politically active on a regular basis, not just in exceptional situations.

In short, the aristocrats who introduced *isonomia* in Greece were forced to provide the people with an organization which allowed for activity independent of particular leaders, and were capable of functioning on their own. These institutions were designed to generate a new kind of power that did not belong to leaders. The individuals who initiated change could only indirectly pursue their own interests. By giving political rights to the people, they destroyed the power basis of their opponents; for themselves, they gained prestige and influence. They did not profit from the institutions as such, only from the act of creating them. Greek institutions were, in other words, conceived in a more objective and abstract way than the Roman ones. For that reason too, a relatively long preparatory phase of thinking about institutions was needed.

This short discussion cannot deal with all aspects of the situation. We can only outline the constellation and the process that gave rise to *isonomia*, as well as the questions that arise on closer examination. To conclude, we should once more underline the thoroughly surprising character of this prehistory of the first political order based on effective popular participation. And let us note the importance of political thought, independent of the powers of the time. For it seems to me that the intellectual preparation of democracy had to begin with an effort to think about the *polis* as a whole, and a search for balance and compromise in the interest of this whole. Exploitation and resistance to it, military mobilization of broad social strata and the specific conditions of small communities and various other factors may have been important. But only political thought defined in the sense of the social-historical process that I have tried to sketch could channel these forces in the direction of democracy. And that, in turn, was only possible because of a peculiar distribution of power, which for a long time prevented single rulers from imposing their solution to the crisis and then, in the absence of predominant powers, made it possible to invent orders which were neither centered on power nor initiated by a single overpowering actor.

The transition to more genuine democracy towards the middle of the fifth century was a matter of historical contingency: the prime cause was the victory over the Persians. Only then did the core question of the political order, whether one, few or many should rule, become a matter of human choice and decision. Established and more or less modifiable orders were replaced by constructed ones (even if they were constructed step by step). This opened up enormous possibilities, and gave rise to a unique consciousness of the ability to know and shape the accessible world. This new attitude reached far beyond politics and found expression in art, architecture, literature and philosophy. But the decisive role was played by politics. Because politics was central to the *polis*, the transformation of all political structures affected the whole human condition and posed a radical challenge to art and thought. The responses to this challenge, the ways of elaborating them and opening up new possibilities, became the "legacy of Greece." Inasmuch as the whole culture was particularly strongly influenced by politics, the Greek revolution in world history was pre-eminently political; more precisely, it consisted in the creation and/or discovery of the political, which then became directly or indirectly the dominant presence in Greek life.

Intellectual Chronology

B.C.

594/3   Reforms of Solon in Athens
508/7   Reforms of Cleisthenes in Athens
462/1   Reforms of Ephialtes in Athens
c.431–424?   [Xenophon], *Athenian Constitution* (the 'Old Oligarch')
1st half C4   Plato, *Republic*
335–322   Aristotle, *Politics* completed
330s–320s   [Aristotle], *Athenian Constitution* written and revised

A.D.

1817   A. Boeckh, *Die Staatshaushaltung der Athener*
1819   G. F. Schoemann, *De Comitiis Atheniensium Libri Tres*
1891   First modern edition of [Aristotle], *Athenian Constitution*
1908   A. F. Bentley, *The Process of Government*
1920/6   G. Busolt, ed. H. Swoboda, *Griechische Staatskunde*, 3rd
               edition
1967   R. Sealey, *Essays in Greek Politics*
1971   W. R. Connor, *The New Politicians of Fifth-Century Athens*
1987   M. H. Hansen, *The Athenian Assembly in the Age of
               Demosthenes*
1989   J. Ober, *Mass and Elite in Democratic Athens*
1993/4   Celebrations of 2,500th anniversary of reforms of Cleisthenes

Guide to Further Reading

A full collection of Greek texts with facing English translations is available in the Loeb Classical Library (Cambridge, MA: Harvard University Press); there is a good range of translations in the Penguin Classics series (Harmondsworth: Penguin); and for popular authors such as Herodotus and Thucydides there are many other translations. I mention some other translations below.

The single most important text for the study of the Athenian democracy is the *Athenaion Politeia* = *Athenian Constitution*, which was one of a collection of 158 constitutions made in the school of Aristotle (but I am among those who do not believe that it was written by Aristotle himself). None of these survived in the western manuscript tradition, but a copy of the *Athenaion Politeia* on papyrus (lacking a few pages at the beginning) has been found, and was first published in 1891. The first two thirds give a history of the Athenian Constitution to the democratic restoration of 403; the last third gives an account of the working of the constitution in the 330s, with a few revisions made in the 320s. I have written a large commentary, and a translation with short notes for Penguin Classics.

Herodotus dealt with Cylon's bid for tyranny, the rise and fall of the Pisistratid tyranny and the reforms of Cleisthenes. Thucydides dealt with Cylon, the fall of the Pisistratids and the oligarchic revolution of 411, and his narrative gives a picture of the Athenian democracy under Pericles and under his successors. Xenophon in his *Hellenica* dealt with the oligarchy of the Thirty in 404–403. The 'Old Oligarch' (the unknown author of the *Athenaion Politeia* preserved with the works of Xenophon), probably in the 420s, reluctantly praised the democracy from an oligarchic point of view. The other sources available to the author of the Aristotelian *Athenaion Politeia* have not survived: important among them were the *Atthides*, histories of Athens; the fragments (quotations by later writers) of the *Atthis* by Androtion, written not long before the *Athenaion Politeia*, are translated and discussed by P. Harding, *Androtion and the Atthis*. Of later writers the most important is Plutarch (1st–2nd centuries A.D.), whose *Lives* include *Solon* and many fifth- and fourth-century Athenians.

A high proportion of the Greek literature that survives from the fifth and fourth centuries was written in Athens, and much of it sheds light on the formal and informal working of the democracy and on the thinking of the democrats and their opponents: in particular, the comedies of Aristophanes from the late fifth and early fourth centuries (there are editions of all his plays, with translations and commentaries, by A. H. Sommerstein), and the speeches of several orators, mostly for trials in the law-courts, written between about 420 and 320 (a complete series of translations is in progress in the Oratory of Classical Greece series). The fourth-century philosophers Plato (*Republic* and other works) and Aristotle (especially *Politics*: he was not an Athenian but spent much of his career in Athens) discussed different forms of constitution and were not lovers of democracy. More can be learned about the working of the democracy from the decrees of the assembly and other documents inscribed on stone from the mid fifth century onwards: selections are translated by C. W. Fornara (to the end of the fifth century) and P. Harding (fourth century), *Translated Documents of Greece and Rome*, i–ii; and P. J. Rhodes and R. Osborne, *Greek Historical Inscriptions*, 404–323 B.C., give a selection of fourth-century texts with translations and commentaries.

The particular episodes in Athens' development are treated in the various histories of Greece, including the 2nd edition of the *Cambridge Ancient History*, vols iii. 3–vi. Of works in English on the mechanics of the democratic constitution, G. Gilbert's *The Constitutional Antiquities of Sparta and Athens* is still useful as a repository of facts, and M. H. Hansen has followed a large number of specialised studies with *The Athenian Democracy in the Age of Demosthenes* (the 2nd edition contains 'one hundred and sixty theses' added to make it clear which of his assertions are controversial). In the 1950s A. H. M. Jones assembled a collection of essays in his *Athenian Democracy*; recent books include C. Carey. *Democracy in Classical Athens*; R. K. Sinclair, *Democracy and Participation in Athens*; D. Stockton, *The Classical Athenian Democracy* (this last book to the end of the fifth century only).

Some of the most important books approaching the Athenian democracy in other ways have been mentioned in the General Introduction (pp. 5–8). M. Ostwald in *From Popular Sovereignty to the Sovereignty of Law* and R. Sealey in *The Athenian Republic* have argued that what Athens achieved in the fourth century was not so much democracy as the rule of law. J. Ober's *Mass and Elite in Democratic Athens* has been followed by *Political Dissent in Democratic Athens* and a collection of essays, *The Athenian Revolution*. He was prominent in the celebration in 1993/4 of the 2,500th anniversary of Cleisthenes' reforms and in exploring the significance of Athenian democracy for our own world, and one product of that has been J. Ober and C. W. Hedrick (eds), *Demokratia*.

Bibliography

of works cited in the editorial sections of this book

The Athenian Agora: A Guide to the Excavation and Museum (Athens: American School of Classical Studies at Athens, ⁴1990)

Bentley, A. F., *The Process of Government* (Chicago: University of Chicago Press, 1908)

Bicknell, P. J., *Studies in Athenian Politics and Genealogy* (*Historia* Einzelschriften xix 1972)

Boeckh, A., *Die Staatshaushaltung der Athener* (Berlin: Realschulbuchhandlung, 1817; ³rev. Fränkel, M., Berlin: Reimer, 1886); trans. Lewis, G. C., as *The Public Economy of Athens* (London: Murray, 1828; ²Parker, 1842)

Busolt, G., *Griechische Staats-, Kriegs- und Privataltertümer* (Handbuch der Altertumswissenschaft, IV. i. 1. 1st edition Nördlingen: Beck, 1887); 3rd edition entitled *Griechische Staatskunde* and partly ed. by Swoboda, H. (Munich: Beck, 1920–6)

*Cambridge Ancient History*², vols iii. 3, iv, v, vi (Cambridge: Cambridge University Press, 1982–94)

Carey, C., *Democracy in Classical Athens* (London: Duckworth [Bristol Classical Press], 2000)

Connor, W. R., *The New Politicians of Fifth-Century Athens* (Princeton, NJ: Princeton University Press, 1971)

—— *et al.*, *Aspects of Athenian Democracy* (Copenhagen: Museum Tusculanum Press, 1990)

Croiset, M., *Aristophane et les partis à Athènes* (Paris: Fontemoing, 1906); trans. Loeb, J., as *Aristophanes and the Political Parties at Athens* (London: Macmillan, 1909)

Davies, J. K., *Athenian Propertied Families, 600–300 B.C.* (Oxford University Press, 1971)

—— 'Democracy Without Theory', in Derow, P., and Parker, R. (eds), *Herodotus and his World: Essays from a Conference in Memory of George Forrest* (Oxford: Oxford University Press, 2003), 319–35

—— *Wealth and the Power of Wealth in Classical Athens* (New York: Arno, 1981)

de Ste Croix, G. E. M., *The Class Struggle in the Ancient Greek World* (London: Duckworth, 1981)

Dow, S., *Prytaneis: A Study of the Inscriptions Honoring the Athenian Councillors* (*Hesperia* Supplement i 1937)

Euben, J. P., Wallach, J. R., and Ober, J. (eds), *Athenian Political Thought and the Reconstruction of American Democracy* (Ithaca, NY: Cornell University Press, 1994)

Evans, R. J., *In Defence of History* (London: Granta, 1997; revised edition, with Afterword responding to critics, n.d. [2001]) (a US edition, *In Defense of History* [New York: Norton, 1999], was revised from the 1st edition and is differently paginated)

Fornara, C. W., *Translated Documents of Greece and Rome,* i. *Archaic Times to the End of the Peloponnesian War* (Baltimore, MD: Johns Hopkins University Press, 1977; ²Cambridge: Cambridge University Press, 1983)

Gelzer, M., 'Die Nobilität der Kaiserzeit', *Hermes* l 1915, 395–415

—— *Die Nobilität der römischen Republik* (Leipzig: Teubner, 1912)

—— the two works above trans. Seager, R., as *The Roman Nobility* (Oxford: Blackwell, 1969)

Gilbert, G., trans. Brooks, E. J., and Nicklin, T., *The Constitutional Antiquities of Sparta and Athens* (London: Sonnenschein, 1895)

Grote, G., *History of Greece* (1st edition London: Murray, 1846–56)

—— 'Institutions of Ancient Greece', a review of Clinton, H. F., *Fasti Hellenici*, ii (Oxford: Oxford University Press, 1824), *Westminster Review* v (January–April 1826), 269–331

Hansen, M. H., 'On the Importance of Institutions in an Analysis of Athenian Democracy', *Classica et Mediaevalia* xl 1989, 107–13

—— 'Solonian Democracy in Fourth-Century Athens', *Classica et Mediaevalia* xl 1989 [publ. 1993], 71–99

—— *The Athenian Assembly in the Age of Demosthenes* (Oxford: Blackwell, 1987)

—— *The Athenian Democracy in the Age of Demosthenes* (Oxford: Blackwell, 1991; ²London: Duckworth [Bristol Classical Paperbacks], 1999)

—— *The Athenian Ecclesia* (Opuscula Graecolatina xxvi. Copenhagen: Museum Tusculanum Press, 1983)

—— *The Athenian Ecclesia, II* (Opuscula Graecolatina xxxi. Copenhagen: Museum Tusculanum Press, 1989)

Harding P., *Androtion and the Atthis* (Oxford: Oxford University Press, 1994)

—— *Translated Documents of Greece and Rome,* ii. *From the End of the Peloponnesian War to the Battle of Ipsus* (Cambridge: Cambridge University Press, 1985)

Humphreys, S. C., *Anthropology and the Greeks* (London: Routledge, 1978)

—— *The Family, Women and Death* (London: Routledge, 1983; ²Ann Arbor: University of Michigan Press, 1993)

—— 'The Work of Louis Gernet', *History and Theory* x 1971, 172–96

Jones, A. H. M., *Athenian Democracy* (Oxford: Blackwell, 1957)

Morris, I., 'The Strong Principle of Equality and the Archaic Origins of Greek Democracy', in Ober and Hedrick (eds), *Demokratia* (see below), 19–48

Münzer, F., *Römische Adelsparteien und Adelsfamilien* (Stuttgart: Metzler, 1920); trans. Ridley, T., as *Roman Aristocratic Parties and Families* (Baltimore, MD: Johns Hopkins University Press, 1999)

Ober, J., *Mass and Elite in Democratic Athens: Rhetoric, Ideology and the Power of the People* (Princeton, NJ: Princeton University Press, 1989)

—— *Political Dissent in Democratic Athens: Intellectual Critics of Popular Rule* (Princeton, NJ: Princeton University Press, 1998)

—— *The Athenian Revolution: Essays on Ancient Greek Democracy and Political Theory* (Princeton, NJ: Princeton University Press, 1996)

—— 'The Nature of Athenian Democracy', *Classical Philology* lxxxiv 1989, 322–34

—— and Hedrick, C. W. (eds), *Demokratia: A Conversation on Democracies, Ancient and Modern* (Princeton, NJ: Princeton University Press, nominally 1996 but in fact 1997)

Oratory of Classical Greece, series published Austin, TX: University of Texas Press, 1988–

Osborne, R., 'Changing Visions of Democracy', forthcoming

Ostwald, M., *From Popular Sovereignty to the Sovereignty of Law: Law, Society and Politics in Fifth-Century Athens* (Berkeley and Los Angeles: University of California Press, 1986)

Paine, T., *The Rights of Man* (London: Jordan, 1791–2); I quote from the World's Classics edition (Oxford: Oxford University Press, 1995)

Raaflaub, K. A., 'Contemporary Perceptions of Democracy in Fifth-Century Athens', *Classica et Mediaevalia* xl 1989 [publ. 1993], 33–70

Rhodes, P. J., *A Commentary on the Aristotelian Athenaion Politeia* (Oxford: Oxford University Press, 1981; reissued with addenda 1993)

—— *Ancient Democracy and Modern Ideology* (London: Duckworth, 2003)

—— *Aristotle: The Athenian Constitution* (Penguin Classics. Harmondsworth: Penguin, 1984; reissued with revisions 2002)

—— 'Democracy and its Opponents in Fourth-Century Athens', forthcoming

—— 'Nothing to Do with Democracy: Athenian Drama and the *Polis*', *Journal of Hellenic Studies* cxxiii 203, 104–19

—— *The Athenian Boule* (Oxford: Oxford University Press, 1972; reissued with addenda 1985)

—— 'The Athenian Revolution', in *CAH*, v² (1992), 62–95

—— 'The Reforms and Laws of Solon: An Optimistic View', forthcoming

—— and Osborne, R., *Greek Historical Inscriptons, 404–323 B.C.* (Oxford: Oxford University Press, 2003)

Robinson, E. W., *The First Democracies: Early Popular Government Outside Athens* (*Historia* Einzelschriften cvii 1997)

Schoemann, G. F., *De Comitiis Atheniensium Libri Tres* (Greifswald: Mauritz, 1819); trans. P[aley], F. A., as *A Dissertation on the Assemblies of the Athenians in Three Books* (Cambridge: Grant, 1838)

Sealey, R., *Essays in Greek Politics* (New York: Manyland, 1967)

—— *The Athenian Republic: Democracy or the Rule of Law?* (University Park: Pennsylvania State University Press, 1987)

Sinclair, R. K., *Democracy and Participation in Athens* (Cambridge: Cambridge University Press, 1988)

Sommerstein, A. H., editions of plays by Aristophanes (Warminster: Aris & Phillips, 1980–2001)

Stockton, D., *The Classical Athenian Democracy* (Oxford: Oxford University Press, 1990)

Sullivan, J. P., 'Editorial', *Arethusa* viii. 1 1975, 5–6

Syme, R., *The Roman Revolution* (Oxford: Oxford University Press, 1939)

White, H. V., *The Content of the Form: Narrative Discourse and Historical Representation* (Baltimore, MD: Johns Hopkins University Press, 1987)

Whittaker, C. R., 'Moses Finley, 1912–1986', *Proceedings of the British Academy* xciv '1996 Lectures and Memoirs', 459–72

Index

The spelling of Greek words and names is not uniform between different chapters of this book, but it is hoped that readers will not be seriously inconvenienced. Under some headings, principal references are given first, followed by a semi-colon; ancient writers are indexed for major discussions of a text only.